P9-CDB-850

Culture Shock

Culture Shock

A READER IN MODERN CULTURAL ANTHROPOLOGY

PHILIP K. BOCK, ed.
University of New Mexico

ALFRED A. KNOPF

NEW YORK

THIS IS A BORZOI BOOK PUBLISHED BY ALFRED A. KNOPF, INC.

 Published in the United States by Alfred A. Knopf, Inc., New York, and simultaneously in Canada by Random House of Canada Limited, Toronto. Distributed by Random House, Inc., New York.

Library of Congress Catalog Card Number: 76-82519

Manufactured in the United States of America

9 8 7 6 5 4 3

What is man?

Surely, man is a wonderful, vain, diverse and wandering subject.
MONTAIGNE

Man is the measure of all things. PROTAGORAS

Man is the only animal that laughs and weeps; for he is the only animal that is struck with the difference between what things are, and what they ought to be. HAZLITT

Man is by nature a political animal. ARISTOTLE

What a chimera, then, is man! What a novelty! What a monster, what a chaos, what a subject of contradiction, what a prodigy! A judge of all things, feeble worm of the earth, depositary of the truth, *cloaca* of uncertainty and error, the glory and shame of the universe. PASCAL

Reason is a very inadequate term with which to comprehend the forms of man's cultural life in all their richness and variety. But all these forms are symbolic forms. Hence, instead of defining man as an animal rationale, *we should define him as an* animal symbolicum. *By so doing we can designate his specific difference, and we can understand the new way open to man—the way to civilization.*
CASSIRER

We drink without being thirsty and make love at any time; that is all that distinguishes us from other animals. BEAUMARCHAIS

MAN, n. An animal so lost in rapturous contemplation of what he thinks he is as to overlook what he indubitably ought to be. His chief occupation is extermination of other animals and his own species, which, however, multiplies with such insistent rapidity as to infest the whole habitable earth and Canada. AMBROSE BIERCE

Man is a maker of tools, rules, and moral judgments.

PHILIP BOCK

Man is the ape that wants to be a god. WALTER KAUFFMAN

Man is a rational animal who always loses his temper when he is called upon to act in accordance with the dictates of reason.

OSCAR WILDE

What a piece of work is man! how noble in reason! how infinite in faculty! in form and moving how express and admirable! in action how like an angel! in apprehension how like a god! the beauty of the world! the paragon of animals! SHAKESPEARE

Chaos of thought and passion, all confused;
Still by himself abused and disabused;
Created half to rise, and half to fall;
Great lord of all things, yet a prey to all;
Sole judge of truth, in endless error hurled;
The glory, jest and riddle of the world! ALEXANDER POPE

Class: Mammalia
Order: Primates
Family: Hominidae
Genus: Homo
Species: sapiens LINNAEUS

Man is something that shall be surpassed. What have you done to surpass him? NIETZSCHE

Contents

Foreword: On "culture shock"

"What should they know of England who only England know?" asked Kipling; and few would disagree with his sentiment. But in this age of jet planes and air-conditioned tourist hotels in every major city, it is not necessarily true that travel is broadening. It is quite possible to go around the world without ever once directly experiencing anything different from one's normal routine, no matter how many quaint scenes are captured on color slides. Careful planning (and enough money) can insulate the traveler from the inconveniences of an unfamiliar environment. The same effect can be produced by a state of mind that automatically views anything foreign as inferior and/or disgusting. Such an "ethnocentric" viewpoint—which judges all peoples and practices according to standards learned in childhood—is an effective defense against upsetting experiences; unfortunately, it also blocks any chance of learning about other ways of life or of gaining perspective on one's own culture.

Culture, in its broadest sense, is what makes you a stranger when you are away from home. It includes all those beliefs and expectations about how people should speak and act which have become a kind of second nature to you as a result of social learning. When you are with members of a group who share your culture, you do not have to think about it, for you are all viewing the world in pretty much the same way and you all know, in general terms, what to expect of one another. However, direct exposure to an alien society usually produces a disturbing feeling of disorientation and helplessness that is called "culture shock." There are varying degrees of culture shock. As Philip L. Newman noted in *Knowing the Gururumba*:

> A man brought up in Los Angeles who moves to New York City will find most of his expectations about people's behavior fulfilled. With only minor adjustments he will be able to operate in the new situation and interact with the people there. If, however, he moves into a community of forest-dwelling people in the Amazon basin, he will find his habitual systems of expectations so unreliable that unless the host community has special techniques designed to care for strangers, he may not survive.

In general, the more "exotic" the alien society and the deeper one's immersion in its social life, the greater the shock. The outstanding features of culture shock include inability to make any sense out of the behavior of others or to predict what they will say or do. One's customary categories of experience are no longer useful, and habitual actions elicit seemingly bizarre responses. A friendly gesture may be treated as a threat, whereas a serious and sensible question provokes laughter or uncomprehending silence. For a brief time, the novelty of the situation may be pleasant or amusing. But the person subject to extreme culture shock is often unsure whether he has gone mad or whether all the people around him are crazy—perhaps both! Even the experience of not understanding the language that is being spoken at a social gathering can be extremely disturbing, and the fact that others are communicating with evident ease does not help one's own situation. Add to this the need to satisfy some pressing biological need or social imperative, and you begin to comprehend the meaning of culture shock.

Culture shock should not be confused with the "life shock" that results from direct exposure to certain experiences from which many members of our society have been carefully shielded. Birth, death, and disease are particularly disturbing when they are first encountered in an unfamiliar setting; but there is nothing inherently exotic about these phenomena. The life shock that many soldiers, Peace Corps volunteers, and social workers frequently experience dramatizes the effectiveness of the social arrangements that protect middle- and upper-class Americans from unpleasant realities. But no one who has spent time behind the scenes at a slaughter house, a mortuary, or a hospital emergency room will be particularly shocked at the "cruelty" of men who hunt for a living or the "callousness" of people who must cope daily with situations that we delegate to specialists. (Nevertheless, there are culturally patterned ways of dealing with the various life crises; and it does take some time to adjust to, say, the custom of a widow wearing her dead husband's jawbone about her neck as a *memento mori*.)

Genuine culture shock is largely an emotional matter; but it also implies the attempt to *understand* an alien way of life, by choice or out of necessity. Since human society began, immigrants, refugees, and all kinds of travelers have been subject to varying degrees of culture shock. Some, by holding themselves aloof from the alien society or by living in enclaves of fellow migrants, have managed to survive and to perpetuate themselves for many generations with a minimum of concessions to the host culture. This type of cultural pluralism has been a characteristic of urban life for thousands of years. And there are always other migrants who attempt to merge into the host society, turning away, sometimes violently, from the traditions of their ancestors. For them the shock may be greater, but so are the opportunities resulting from assimilation to the dominant group.

Given the fact that culture shock is always disconcerting and often unpleasant, why in the world should anyone seek out this type of experience? The answer to this question was suggested in the first paragraph: direct confrontation with another society is the best way to learn about alien modes of life or to gain perspective on one's own culture. This is why one or more years of "fieldwork" is expected to be part of the training of every cultural anthropologist. For someone who plans to spend his working life studying, writing, and teaching about other cultures, the direct experience of (and participation in) another culture is essential. Culture shock is not valued for its own sake. Its value lies in the liberation and understanding that can come from such an experience: the full realization that strange customs are not quaint or meaningless to those who practice them; that other languages are not gibberish or merely awkward substitutes for English; and that other perceptions of reality are just as valid to those who live according to them as our own belief and value systems are to us. Just as the student of psychiatry must himself be analyzed, the anthropologist goes into the field in part to increase his self-knowledge by discovering the roots of his own ethnocentrism.

Anthropological fieldwork can be a stimulating, challenging, and fruitful experience; but it is not the kind of enterprise that should be undertaken lightly. It requires years of preparation, a great deal of money, and lots of plain hard work (see Part IV, "The Anthropologist at Work"). Field trips often end in failure; and the life and health of anthropologists may be endangered in a number of ways. Fortunately, there are ways of experiencing some types of culture shock without incurring dysentery, frostbite, or expense at the same time. Great works of literature, aided by the reader's imagination, can often communicate more about other ways of life than the average person could learn from months of direct experience. If you read *Alice in Wonderland* at the right age, and identified to some extent with Alice's curiosity and frustrations, then you have already had one vicarious experience of culture shock. Certain anthropologists, such as Margaret Mead, Oscar Lewis, and Elizabeth Thomas, are also famous for their ability to capture and communicate the essence of other societies. And there are few more revealing views of American society than those we glimpse through the astonished eyes of Humbert Humbert or Timofey Pnin in Vladimir Nabokov's novels *Lolita* and *Pnin*. Great film makers, too, from Robert Flaherty to Richard Lester, present us with their condensed visions of human social life. Indeed, the sensitive contemplation of any work of art—from the Homeric poems to a Picasso painting—can broaden our conception of humanity as well as deepen our understanding of ourselves. These are worthwhile goals for a humanistic anthropology.

The aim of this anthology is to provide a vivid (though necessarily second-hand) experience of what life has been like for men and women living in other times and other places. The selections range from ethnographic descriptions to fictionalized history; they include linguistic texts, literary excerpts, and autobiography. Some deal with our contemporaries, others with our ancestors. Some selections will shock the reader by their strangeness, others by their familiarity.

In choosing the readings I applied three criteria: vividness, veracity, and variety. If even a few of the selections succeed in giving the reader a genuine experience of another person's way of life, I shall be satisfied. My assumption, of course, is that such an experience can be liberating as well as exciting. Beyond this, I have no particular theoretical axe to grind. The organization of the selections parallels that of the topics in my *Modern Cultural Anthropology: An Introduction* (New York: Knopf, 1969). The two books can be profitably read in conjunction; but all of the selections in this reader speak very well for themselves.

PHILIP K. BOCK
Albuquerque, New Mexico

PART ONE

The human capacity for culture

Were it possible to rear a human being of normal genetic constitution under circumstances depriving it of all cultural tradition—which is impossible not only for ethical but also for biological reasons—the subject of the cruel experiment would be very far from representing a reconstruction of a prehuman ancestor, as yet devoid of culture. It would be a poor cripple, deficient in higher functions in a way comparable to that in which idiots who have suffered encephalitis during infantile or fetal life lack the higher functions of the cerebral cortex. . . . Man's whole system of innate activities and reactions is phylogenetically so constructed, so "calculated" by evolution, as to need *to be complemented by cultural tradition. For instance, all the tremendous neuro-sensory apparatus of human speech is phylogenetically evolved, but so constructed that its function presupposes the existence of a culturally developed language which the infant has to learn. . . . No man, not even the greatest genius, could invent, all by himself, a system of social norms and rites forming a substitute for cultural tradition.*

KONRAD LORENZ

INTRODUCTION

In addition to the physical environment that he shares with all earthly creatures, man inhabits a world of ideas and ideals created by his fellow men. Every normal human being acquires a particular cultural world as a consequence of growing up in some particular society. It is man's *capacity for culture* that enables him to enter into a world of space and time, filled with entities which can be named, manipulated, and valued. Culture enables us to communicate complex messages to our fellows, for it includes the conventions of language. Culture also teaches us what we can expect of others, and they of us. It allows us to act upon our physical environment with tools and sources of energy that lie outside our own bodies. And it provides us with a more or less coherent view of the world, including notions of our proper place in nature and in human society.

How does it happen that our species is able to create such cultural worlds? And what are the processes by which culture is transmitted from one generation to the next? These are the questions dealt with by the first few selections in this book. Weston LaBarre puts the human capacity for culture into biological perspective by discussing the anatomical preconditions for a cultural way of life. He also describes the advantages of cultural development as a mode of adaptation in contrast to the slow and uncertain results of organic evolution. Craig MacAndrew and Robert Edgerton underline the significance of the normal human brain in the acquisition of culture by vividly sketching the behavior of a group of institutionalized idiots—individuals who appear to lack the capacity for culture.

Any child with a normal brain, hearing, and vocal apparatus can learn to speak and understand any human language. The capacity for language is, then, a universal; but exactly what language will be learned depends upon where an individual is born, that is, his environment during the early years of life. The Navaho Indians who live in the American Southwest speak a subtle and complex tongue which differs in nearly every respect from English. Clyde Kluckhohn and Dorothea Leighton, after providing an outline of the sound system and the grammar of the Navaho language, show how the grammatical patterns of the language channel the expression of ideas by Navaho speakers and, perhaps, affect the thought processes themselves.

Margaret Mead's account of a Samoan childhood is notable for its vivid description of the impact of culture upon the growing child. From birth through adolescence, cultural notions of proper behavior increasingly mold the actions of every youth, turning a child who was born with a very general capacity to learn into a living exponent of the Samoan way of life. The village, the household, and the systems of kinship and rank define the life chances of each person. But even in this brief narrative we can see how unpredictable factors of individual preference and endowment affect the actualization of Samoan cultural ideals.

Other selections which emphasize *enculturation*—the process of learning a culture—include those by Oscar Lewis and Theodora Kroeber in Part II and, particularly, the article by Harold Conklin in Part IV.

WESTON LABARRE

The human animal in biological perspective

Weston LaBarre is a professor of anthropology at Duke University. He is particularly known for his work in culture and personality and for his study of the peyote cult.

Early man was an earth-bound ape, with empty hands. But it was these same empty hands that changed completely the whole manner of evolution in man and made him unique beyond all comparison with any other living creature. Seen in its separate aspects, the human hand is nothing special. Five-toed paws were part of the original pattern of lungs and legs of even the early amphibians, and they are thoroughly commonplace in later land animals descended from the amphibians. For man to have five fingers would be the usual thing to expect: it is the pterodactyl's little-finger flying, the bat's long-fingered wing-hand, the bird's arm-wing, and the whale's hand-flippers that are the anatomically clever, the functionally spectacular, variations on the basic pentadactyl theme. Human hands are not unusual, either, as the freed limbs of bipedal animals: there are plenty of instances of this, from reptilian dinosaurs to marsupial kangaroos and mammalian jerboas. Nor is the hand unique as a grasping organ in man: many of the tree-living primates were even four-handed, and thus two up on man—whose specialized foot has lost just about all its one-time prehensile skill.

The uniqueness of man's hand is functional, not physical. Of course his primate ancestors' sojourn in the trees did greatly improve the grasping ability of the old amphibian-reptilian-mammalian paw. It is also true that the fully opposable thumb in man is a further improvement on the primate hand. But in purely physical terms, monkey hands could probably do nearly everything a man's hands could. The main significance of the human hand lies in its being one member of a functional complex of hands, brains, and eyes.

When man, heir of four limbs, uses only two of them for walking, his clever primate hands are then finally freed from use in any kind of locomotion whatever. They can now be used for purely exploratory grasping. The advantages of this are not to be underestimated. Some New World monkeys, it is true, have prehensile tails, but these are still largely locomotor in function; besides, the tail has the grave disadvantage of not being ordinarily in the monkey's field of vision. A better case of exploratory prehensility is the elephant's trunk—perhaps significantly combined, as is man's hand, with great intelligence. But the elephant's trunk is mainly used for feeding; and, besides, there is only one of them. Nor do elephants have stereoscopic vision, to put together a muscular with a visual space-sense. Still, a sensitive grasping trunk is not to be sneezed at as a biological advantage. At least in the past, the elephant family had the adaptive radiation that often shows up in a successful animal type; for elephant-like creatures once made themselves at home in a variety of environments from Siberia to Sumatra, from England to Africa, and from Saskatchewan to South America. But judgment must respect the fact that all of these are extinct, some of them with man's assistance, except for the elephants of Africa and of Southeast Asia—and these too are dying out.

Emancipated hands are not enough: many dinosaurs had them, but they lacked sufficient brains. Intelligence is not enough: elephants have a great deal of intelligence behind their trunks, but they do not have stereoscopic sight; the prehensile-tailed monkeys are intelligent too, and they have stereoscopic vision as well, but they do not ordinarily see their tails. Stereoscopic eyes are not enough either: for the intelligent, tree-living apes have them, with color vision and the yellow spot in the retina to boot. It is the combination that counts. Man has paired grasping organs, fully in his field of vision and wholly freed from locomotor duties, in a stereoscopic-sighted, big-brained mammal—and these add up to the answer.

Anaxagoras claimed that man had brains because he had hands, but Aristotle argued that man had hands because he had brains. When the implications of these statements are better understood and the dust of battle has settled a bit, modern anthropologists are inclined to give the decision to Anaxagoras rather than to Aristotle. But hands, brains, and eyes are a case, really, of hens-and-eggs causality; nor did it all begin, strictly speaking, with man. For in all primate evolution they influence each other mutually and develop progressively together; and the ability to "monkey with things" that man got from his primate ancestors is still one of the keystones of human nature. Certainly such hands and eyes and brains put an animal into closer object-relationship with reality and enlarge the animal ego in the technical sense of increasing awareness and testing of reality. Very literally, such an animal as man has more *contacts* with reality.

But when we remember the conflict of brains and snout for possession of the skull (the total size of which is limited by pelvic birth), it is probable that the mouth is also part of the hand-brain-eye complex. Eating is just as much a function of the primate hand as are tree-acrobatics. Food, as much as safety, both available in the trees, probably took the primates originally into the trees. And at least some students believe that food available on the ground brought them down again—after a refashioning of locomotion itself in the service of nutrition. When primary grasping with the snout is given up, the sense of smell is less important as a guide. But if snout-smelling gives pleasure in feeding, hands will now share in the pleasurable accomplishment of the basic organic satisfaction, eating. While smell still plays a large role in eating enjoyment, the relative insignificance of the snout anatomically and of smell functionally indicates that they are overshadowed in man.

The matter is probably more complex than this. It should be remembered that grasping the mother's fur is part of the association of food and security in primate babies. It is significant too that in human babies the two major reflexes fully prepared at birth are the "sucking reflex" and the "grasping reflex" (such that a baby can actually support its weight and hang from a bar tightly grasped in its hands). Also, one gets the decided impression in watching older babies that half the fun of eating lies in playing with the food. All in all, it seems quite probable that human hands have an "erotized" interest in handling things, which is borrowed from their pleasurable association with feeding. Anatomically, man has obviously moved beyond a mere nutritional "oral" interest in his environment. His hands show a controlling, manipulative concern with non-nutritional *objects*, with a desire and an ability to coerce reality beyond his own body and body-contents, or potential body-contents like food; just as, similarly, the permanent human breast and heightened sexuality evidence a persistent and organically rooted inter-individual interest in other *persons*.

In this hand-brain-mouth-eye complex, the close brain-eye tie-up is quite clear: we have only to look at the large optic lobe in the brain of later animals to see this. The brain-hand nexus is very evident neurologically, for the nerve-supply of the hand is almost fantastically rich—even in so archaic a sense as touch, the hand (as compared, say, with the thigh, the leg, or the back) is developed in discrimination and sensitivity to an extravagant degree. The hand-eye connection is easily appreciated on study of muscle-sense, stereoscopic seeing, and space-awareness in man. The hand-mouth relationship is shown in several ways. The new-born human baby is very undeveloped neurologically, that is, many of its nerves do not grow to make final connections with muscles until a couple of years after birth; and, in this context, the neurological maturity of the sucking and that of the grasping reflexes is particularly striking. Furthermore, the representation of the lips in the cerebral cortex is quite enormous in comparison with other parts of the body. Also, in a baby old enough to sit up, anything that the eye can see and the hand can grasp is immediately sent to the mouth for consultation and confirmation.

The price in irreversible specialization in his foot, which man has paid for this new significance of the hand, seems a small one indeed when its advantages are noted. For it must be admitted that the human foot is now as hopelessly specialized as the limbs and appendages of most other warm-blooded creatures, and it is difficult to imagine its ever being useful for anything but bipedal walking. The accidents of evolution rarely give an animal a chance for more than one or perhaps two adaptive specializations of any organ: the more exactly and efficiently an organ is adapted anatomically to some special aspect of the environment, the more fatally dependent it is on the accidents of environmental change. The large-scale extinction of animal species in the past fully illustrates this fact. It is as if that species goes farthest which holds off its physical specializations as long as possible; it can then build its own minor specialization on as large a collection of prior major animal accomplishments as possible.

But this suggests a greater planning and self-consciousness in organisms than is really visible in evolution. The value to organisms of getting a hold on things must be a general one, for it is found in many kinds of animals. The general idea of hands has been stumbled on again and again in evolution, from crabs and scorpions and their claws to the various backboned animals (the two-legged dinosaurs, and "three-legged" wallabies and kangaroo rats) that sit or stand up to use their front paws in holding things. In this light, the hand in man is a venture backed by the biological capital of all the long line of body patents to which he is the heir, in the main line of amphibians, reptiles, mammals, and primates. But the double arch of the human foot—that came from changing from the land to the trees and then back again from the trees to the ground—shows that man's line has already taken all his probable chances at adaptive specialization of the hind limbs. As far as the foot is concerned, man is now in the same evolutionary boat as every other specialized animal: an adaptation, once made, is a hostage to fortune and a commitment to future evolutionary fate. The human foot has "had it."

The great bargain that this specialization represents in man, however, removes him from any comparison with any other animal. The human hand is the adaptation to end all adaptations: *the emancipated hand has emancipated man from any other organic evolution whatsoever*. With man, genetic evolution and organic experiments have come to an end. Without involving the animal body and its slow, blind genetic mechanisms, man's hands make the tools and the machines which render his own further physical evolution unnecessary; they replace the slow, cumbrous, expensive, uncertain, and painful mechanism of organic evolution with the swift, conscious, biologically free, and painless making of machines.

Nothing like this has ever happened before in evolution. Machines not only can do man's flying, diving, and superhuman seeing and hearing for him, but also *they do his evolving for him.* (Indeed, in a cybernetic "feed-back" machine like a thermostat—in which the results of its action are automatically scanned by the machine to correct and modify its future action according to man's preconceived, built-in intentions—man is already creating a quasi-organism, with one sense and a part-brain, after his own image. Nor does it invite disrespect to realize that with his brain man can build mathematical thinking machines better than his own for their particular purpose.) The critical fact is that the making of machines is done with no narrow and irreversible commitment whatever of man's body. With human hands, the old-style evolution by body adaptation is obsolete. All previous animals had been subject to the *autoplastic* evolution of their self-substance, committing their bodies to experimental adaptations in a blind genetic gamble for survival. The stakes in this game were high: life or death. Man's evolution, on the other hand, is through *alloplastic* experiments with objects outside his own body and is concerned only with the products of his hands, brains, and eyes—and not with his body itself. True, a flaw in the design of an experimental jet plane may kill a pilot, but that does not make the human race extinct or even wipe out aeronautical engineers as a species.

It is an error to suppose that a spider's web is in this sense a "tool." For, besides being instinctive (a genetically given function), the spider web is merely an autoplastic extension into space of its own non-living substance or metaplasm. No more is a bird's nest a "tool," since neither insight nor tuition and neither memory nor experience plays any part in this instinctual activity. Even the most generous interpretation would allow temporary or accidental nonce "tools" only to anthropoids. But then these tools are not socially hereditary, for the best that apes have is insight or imitation-by-contiguity, and not human culture.

It is not only the genetic freedom of man's new kind of evolution that is significant; one has to consider also the fantastic speed of it as well. It took millions and millions of years from fish to whale to evolve a warm-blooded marine mammal: but man evolved submarines from dream to actuality in a mere few centuries and at no genetic price in physical specialization. It took innumerable genera of birds uncountable eons since *Archaeopteryx* for their autoplastic experimentation with flying: but man, in only some fifty years since Kitty Hawk, flies not only as well as birds but actually far better. In objective physical terms of speed, altitude, and range, man already flies faster than sound (something no bird will ever do with moving wings), higher than any bird (since birds must breathe the open air), and farther than even the most miraculous migratory bird (with its settled complex of methods, materials, and metabolism). Even by the admittedly crude evolutionary criterion of gross size, man's airplanes are even now far larger and far heavier than any eagle or condor, whereas a bird as large as an ostrich is already permanently grounded. Man makes a new model of plane and tinkers with its mechanical "bugs" much more cheaply biologically and more efficiently and quickly than any bird can modify its form by evolution.

Since man's machines evolve now, not anatomical man, he has long since gone outside his own individual skin in his functional relatedness to the world. The real evolutionary unit now is not man's mere body; it is "all-mankind's-brains-together-with-all-the-extrabodily-materials-that-come-under-the-manipulation-of-their-hands." Man's very physical ego is expanded to encompass everything within reach of his manipulating hands, within sight of his searching eyes, and within the scope of his restless brain. An airplane is part of a larger kinaesthetic and functional self; it is a larger ownership of reality by the questing ego of life. And airplanes are biologically cheap. For, as unconcernedly as a man changes an auger for a reamer in an electric drill, he exchanges the joy-stick of a plane for the driving wheel of a car. Without being, through specialization, a biological amputee, he attaches all sorts of prosthetic devices to his limbs. This *evolution-by-prosthesis* is uniquely human and uniquely freed from the slowness of reproduction and of evolutionary variation into blind alleys from which there is no retreat. Man, with tools as his projected body and machines the prosthetic creatures of his hands, is not merely a promising animal biologically: he makes every other animal wholly obsolete, except as they serve *his* purposes of prosthetic metabolism, locomotion, manufacture of materials and of biological medicines.

This new kind of human evolution is fully proved in the positive sense by man's conquest of reality. All the standard biological criteria, save one, can be applied in his case. As monkeys go, man is a large animal. In number of individuals, man is certainly now the most common large mammal on earth, and his numbers are increasing. In range and in variety of environmental adjustments, no other animal remotely rivals him. But this new kind of evolution is further proved negatively in terms of the striking inapplicability of another biological criterion—that of adaptive radiation. Man himself has stopped evolving physically in any massive or significant way. The basic type of man, the human species generously conceived, has been much the same since 500,000 to 1,000,000 years ago. This is an astounding thing in an animal as spectacularly successful biologically as man is. *Man is the only successful animal never to undergo adaptive radiation.*

We have seen that adaptive radiation is the commonplace of evolution: with each new and successful animal discovery or invention comes a variety of divergent additional adaptations built upon the basic patent. Thus when the arthropods added the achievement of land existence to chitin and exoskeleton, the insect group taken alone proliferated into some 600,000 or more separate and distinct species. The verticality of *Homo sapiens* is a change of at least the magnitude of the arthropod change of habitat—indeed it is actually far greater—and yet *Homo sapiens* exists in only one species! Now it is true that in the races of man we find objective and measurable differences, some of which (though fewer than one imagines) are genetic in nature. But the extraordinary thing is that racial differences in man are neither *racial* adaptations in the exact sense, nor are they even racial *adaptations*.

The first point is quite plain. Whatever changes of whatever scale have occurred all the way from proto-hominids to the type we choose to designate *Homo sapiens*, it is quite obvious that one race is not evolving its hands into hammers, another into pincers, and still others into screw-drivers or chisels. This kind of process is entirely absent in man. The reason for this is that man's genetic promiscuity and geographical getting around have always prevented the genetic and geographic isolation necessary for the rise of divergent animal species. True, this mixing of races and of stocks is a very slow process in time—one that waits upon such large-scale events as the great invasions out of central Asia, the almost explosive medieval migrations of peoples outward from Arabia and Scandinavia, the discovery of the New World, and European imperialism in Asia and in Africa. But slow also is the tempo of generations in man.

Some students have reasonably pointed out that these conditions may not always have been exactly the same throughout the history of *Homo sapiens*. Washburn estimates that in the hunting and gathering stage of culture, there were probably only about 7,000,000 human beings in the entire world. This poverty in absolute numbers and the dispersal of people owing to the way of life would favor the conditions of relative geographical (continent-wise) isolation, the accidents of "genetic sampling," and the genetic drift which are evidenced in the fact of races today. But this relative inbreeding of early man can never have been absolute; for, as Washburn conservatively points out, "Each living race has had at least one hundred times as much of its human ancestry in common with all the other races as it has had alone." Furthermore, Hooton considers that the primary race-making stage in man's biology ended about 15,000 to 20,000 years ago, at the close of the Pleistocene.

It is an old and still respectable opinion that modern races represent local climatic types. It is argued, for example, that the non-projecting nose and fat-padded slit eyes of the Mongoloids are adaptations to a cold, dry climate. This seems plausible; but one might well ask such reasonable questions as "Why then the projecting cheekbones?" and "Why then their hairless bodies?" It is easy to see that one could quickly become lost in a tangle of *ad hoc* arguments, depending on which climate one wished to rationalize, for men do move about. In this case, however, the argument is a good one, for we have every reason to believe that this same general human type has lived in central East Asia since the remotest human times. The immediate next question would be, "Why has this alleged climatic type not been modified as it moved southward?" Certainly Singapore is not cold, or Siam dry, and yet Mongoloid and Chinese types have retained their racial identity in these new climates.

The answer to this would be easy. Even if the southward drift of Mongoloids in Asia began long before the slow pressure of Chinese culture from north China (beginning in the Shang Dynasty Bronze Age), Mongoloids remain Mongoloids wherever found in Asia, because in slow-breeding man they have not had enough time yet to change genetically. The trouble with this argument, however, is that it is inconsistent with the case of the American Indian, an ancient offshoot of Asiatic Mongoloids. The American Indian has certainly been in the New World since the end of the last Ice Age, and probably before—a rather longer time ago than the Chinese Bronze Age. In the New World the Indian has certainly been placed in a great variety of environments, from the Barren Grounds of northwestern Canada to the rich woodlands of the southeastern United States, and from the cool, dry highlands of Peru and Mexico to the dank, hot lowlands of Amazonia and the Caribbean islands. And yet, with all this greater time depth and with all this variety of climate, the American Indian is essentially the same unspecialized Mongoloid from Alaska to Patagonia!

Surely the genetic and geographic isolation possible with two whole empty continents open before them was much greater for the American Indians than when hunting tribes were, relatively speaking, crowding one another out of eastern Siberia across the Bering Straits. The great difficulty is that if the race-climatologists demand a still longer time for genetic change than the period since the end of the Ice Age, they do so at their peril. For with the Ice Age comes a great change in just that climatic stability on which such adaptation depends, and the whole argument falls to the ground.

We are therefore prepared to agree that genetic drift in early man has made for large-scale, continent-wise differences in race. But we cannot see how the observed genetically stable types could have threaded their way so successfully through immense ranges of time and into such climatically diverse areas, if racial traits are simply adaptations to climate. For if once adaptive, why not always adaptive? The fact is, slow-breeding man gets around too fast—indeed, climates themselves change too rapidly—to account for the observed anthropological facts.

Once again, if races are adaptive types of man, we have to enlarge the scope of the term *Homo sapiens*, so that we may call upon the larger reaches of time that seem to be needed to explain the observed genetic facts. The definition of man in niggling taxonomic or minor anatomical terms misses the genetic boat. And so far as the major races of man are concerned, there must be other factors operating than simple climatic adaptation.

In any case, with the enormous rise in absolute numbers, the increased migrations of man in at least historic times, and still greater mobility in modern times (with consequently increased geographic and genetic impingement of one group upon another), the relative outbreeding of historic man is increasingly dominant over the relative inbreeding of early mankind. Therefore, in this absence of genetic and geographic isolation, whatever imaginable variations arise in physical man of the future, these will never assume the scale of differences of species. Thus, even if these physically differing varieties of man happen to be adaptations (and not something else), the adaptations would remain the genetic property of mankind at large. In other words, because of the constant and indeed increasing inter-breeding of groups in *Homo sapiens*, any "adaptive" variations that should arise in one race of man would remain genetically available to the whole species.

Perhaps this can best be explained in terms of genes, those units of heredity, each of which has a definite position on one of the rod-shaped chromosomes in the nucleus of a germ cell. In joining together at fertilization, germ cells add to the total gene potential of an organism by the fusion of two heredities. But fission in the production of specialized body cells means a subtraction of possibilities. That is, a fertilized germ cell can give rise in the new individual to more different kinds of cells than can any already specialized kind of body cell. For example, a nerve cell—by virtue of its high specialization at the end of many body-cell divisions—is poorer in genes than is a fertilized germ cell. In becoming a nerve cell, it has lost a germ cell's potentialities for becoming any kind of body cell whatsoever; more than that, a nerve cell has lost much of its ability to reproduce, by fission, even another nerve cell, with the result that only very limited repair and regeneration are possible when a nerve is injured. Meanwhile, the germ cell, by not specializing, has retained its "totipotentiality," i.e., the power, on fusing with another germ cell, of giving rise to a whole new individual made up of all kinds of cells. In human beings these germ cells are segregated from the body cells in the earliest divisions of the fertilized ovum. Thus these germ cells retain their ability to be ancestral to any kind of body cell (in an individual of the next generation). But the body cells, in giving rise to a new individual (in this generation), gradually lose more and more of their genes as they are specialized more and more into the various parts of the individual's body.*

Something of the same kind is true of animal species. The more specialized an animal species is, the more genetic possibility has become somatic actuality. A species with selective adaptation to an environment *and with genetic or geographic isolation from closely related species* (which is one of the basic criteria of what constitutes separate species) is poorer in genes than the total mother-stock. That is, any one species of animal is poorer in total variety of genes than is a whole group of related species. For example, there is greater variety of genes in the sum total of South African antelopes (springbok, steenbok, hartebeest, duiker, eland, nylghau, gnu, etc.) than there is in any one of the species alone. But a springbok's adaptations are not a bit of good to the gnu, or the gnu's to the springbok, so long as they are genetically isolated from one another as separate species. As a result, the non-inter-breeding of these species makes the great total variety of antelope genes mutually unavailable in the separate species.

Contrast this perfectly normal situation in animals with the atypical case of man. For all its spectacular variety, mankind is obviously a morphological and genetic unity. (Indeed, the fossil evidence, e.g., the Mount Carmel finds, suggests that this has been true since the most ancient past.) Mankind appears to have arisen, with different local gene concentrations, from a large and miscellaneous mass of closely related proto-hominids inhabiting much of the Old World. But, instead of further differentiating into gene-impoverished separate species (like the South African antelopes), these local varieties of *Homo sapiens* maintained at least enough genetic contact with one another for all modern races to be able to inter-breed—with the result that the species *Homo sapiens* is fantastically rich genetically.

In this remarkable fact, man is obviously once again a different *kind* of species from any wild-animal species. The total number of germ cells contained within even one pair of a wild-animal species could probably reproduce all the limited traits and variabilities (hair color, etc.) of that

---

* Recent genetic experiments (with frogs) have cast doubt upon the generalizations in this paragraph. Cf. *Scientific American*, December, 1967. [Ed.]

entire species; but man is genetically far too complex for this. Spuhler has ingeniously calculated human gene-loci (the actual locations on the chromosomes of the controllers of identifiable hereditary traits) as being of the order of 20,000–42,000. But even ignoring the fact that each gene-locus is not necessarily limited to controlling only one genetic trait, the treasure trove of alternative human genes is too enormous for traits of even one major race to be contained within the germ cells of a single pair of human parents.

Suppose, for the sake of argument, that man scrapes along with a bare 30,000 gene-loci. Suppose, also, that there were only two alternative possibilities for each gene (e.g., yellow versus black skin) in human beings. This is, of course, a great over-simplification of the facts; but, conservatively, we would then have genetic possibilities of the order of $2^{30,000}$. In other words, all the human beings who have ever lived throughout the Pleistocene period have not scratched the surface of possible gene combinations in *Homo sapiens*. Actually the human kind of animal may not especially need such an extravagant adaptive potential. But in survival terms this biological booty of genes in man is fabulous. Very probably, descendants of *Homo sapiens* will still be around when the last of all the antelope species will have become extinct, even in zoos. The representative from Buncombe County may get gasping fits at this disclosure and the Senator from Mississippi blow a gasket, but the fact is that man's best biological future lies precisely in his present out-breeding behavior: it is not his sin, but his salvation.

CRAIG MACANDREW *and* ROBERT EDGERTON

Man without culture

Craig MacAndrew is a member of the Department of Psychiatry of the University of California, Los Angeles. Robert Edgerton is an anthropologist with the Neuropsychiatric Institute of the University of California, Los Angeles. They have worked together on other aspects of mental retardation, and Edgerton has studied native cures for mental illness in Africa.

It has been variously estimated that there are 100,000 idiots in the United States today. Because approximately half of these, including almost all of the adults, are in public institutions, common sense knowledge of idiots is typically both sketchy and ridden with clichés. Unfortunately, our scientific knowledge concerning idiots is not a great deal better. While there is a substantial, but spotty, body of medical information at hand, detailed understanding of the psychological functioning of idiots is notably deficient and knowledge of their social behavior is virtually non-existent.

There is a sense, of course, in which we know what idiots are: operationally, they are those who score less than 20 on a standard IQ test and who are judged to be organically incapable of scoring higher. They are, then, the most profound of mental incompetents, as is indicated by the following typical professional definition:

> The idiot is ... a person so deeply defective in mind from birth, or from an early age, as to be unable to guard himself against common physical danger.

Specifically, we are instructed that:

> They have eyes but they see not; ears, but they hear not; they have no intelligence and no consciousness of pleasure or pain; in fact, their mental state is one entire negation.

From Craig MacAndrew and Robert Edgerton, "The Everyday Life of Institutionalized 'Idiots,'" *Human Organization*, 23, 4 (1964), 312–318. Reprinted by permission of the authors and publisher.

We are also advised that they are typically incapable of speech:

Their utterances mostly consist of inarticulate grunts, screeches and discordant yells.*

Finally, we are informed that they are characteristically physically handicapped and frequently disfigured; references to their appearance often use words such as "stunted, misshapen, hideous, bestial," and the like. In a word, what we know—or at least what we think we know—about idiots is little more than a slightly elaborated set of first impressions.

Most importantly, we know practically nothing about their everyday *conduct*—about what they actually *do* in the course of living their lives in the institutions which are their typical abodes. In this article we attempt to provide a description of the everyday lives of institutionalized idiots as they are actually lived in one such institution. To our knowledge, the literature contains no such systematic description. In the discussion section we recommend the uniquely informing character of a detailed understanding of such profoundly retarded beings to certain of the perennial problems which are peculiar to a proper study of mankind—not the least of which is the elucidation of the very notion of "man" itself.

The physical setting

Pacific State Hospital is a large state institution for the mentally retarded. Its 494-acre grounds are occupied by over 3,000 patients and 1,500 staff members who respectively live and work in an elaborate, self-contained complex of lawns, parks, roads, and some 70 major buildings. Located outside the city of Pomona, California, the hospital was founded in its present location in 1927 as Pacific Colony. While this location was characterized by rural seclusion at the time of its founding, it has since become increasingly surrounded by the expanding residential and commercial areas of the Southern California megalopolis and is now less than a mile from one of the major links in the greater Los Angeles freeway system. This agglutination process is pithily evidenced in the population statistics of the area: while the population of Pomona stood at 20,000 in 1927, it will soon top 100,000 and its rate of growth shows little sign of leveling off.

Accompanying this change in environs, at least equally dramatic changes have taken place in administrative philosophy. While the inmates of Pacific Colony once cultivated acres of farm land under a policy

---

* A. F. Tredgold, *Mental Deficiency,* William Wood and Co., New York, 1956, pp. 199, 205, 202.

of primarily custodial care, the custodial tradition was radically revised some ten years ago when the administrative orientation shifted to one of treatment and rehabilitation. In the process, the "colony" became a "hospital," the "cottages" became "wards," and the "inmates" became "patients."

Included in the hospital's 3,000 resident mentally defective patients are approximately 900 idiots who are domiciled in various wards throughout the institution. The present paper is concerned with one such ward, a ward reserved for the most severely retarded ambulatory adult male patients in the hospital. Built in 1954, at a cost in excess of $210,000, Ward Y is a low, tile-roofed building separated from several other wards of similar design by stretches of lawns and shrubbery. While the ward is large and well constructed, both its design and detailing reflect the characteristic institutional stamp of unimaginative drabness and of a grossly inadequate provision for the entrance of natural light.

Patients and staff

The 82 patients who reside in Ward Y range in age from 15 to 52; their average age is 27.1 (S.D. = 8.45). As for their measured intelligence, if we remove eight patients—about whom more in a moment—who comprise a clearly demarcated minor second mode in their IQ distribution, the mean IQ of the remaining 74 patients is 15.4 (S.D. = 9.05). In terms of the contemporary nomenclature, these remaining 74 patients are, without exception, either severely or profoundly retarded. The eight relatively high IQ patients have been assigned to Ward Y for diverse reasons—as helpers, because they cannot get along on the higher grade wards, etc. Most of them have come to perform a number of assigned duties on the ward. In addition to these eight "in residence" helpers, six additional mildly retarded patients are detailed to Ward Y to assist the staff during morning and afternoon hours.

The staff consists of from 11 to 13 male attendants and three female attendants all of whom bear the title of psychiatric technicians. Their work hours are set up on a standard three-shift basis with 7 on the day shift (6:30 a.m.–3:00 p.m.), 5 to 6 on the afternoon shift (2:45 p.m.–11:15 p.m.), and 2 to 3 on the night shift (11:00 p.m.–7:00 a.m.).

First impressions of Ward Y

Words, however well chosen, cannot begin adequately to convey the combined sights, sounds, and smells which initially confront and affront the outsider on his first visit. What follows is at best an approximation.

Despite the size of Ward Y, the simultaneous presence of its 82 patients evokes an immediate impression of overcrowding. Additionally, most of the patients are marked by such obvious malformations that their abnormal status appears evident at a glance. One sees heads that are too large or too small, asymmetrical faces, distorted eyes, noses and mouths, ears that are torn or cauliflowered, and bodies that present every conceivable sign of malproportion and malfunction. Most patients are barefooted, many are without shirts and an occasional patient is—at least momentarily—naked. What clothing is worn is often grossly ill-fitting. In a word, the first impression is that of a mass—a mass of undifferentiated, disabled, frequently grotesque caricatures of human beings.

Within moments, however, the mass begins to differentiate itself and individuals take form. A blond teen-ager flits about rapidly flapping his arms in a bird-like manner, emitting bird-like peeping sounds all the while. A large Buddha-like man sits motionless in a corner, staring straight ahead. A middle-aged man limps slowly in a circle grunting, mumbling, and occasionally shaking his head violently. A shirtless patient lies quietly on a bench while a small patient circles about him furiously twirling a cloth with his left hand. A blind youngster sits quietly digging his index fingers into his eyes, twitching massively and finally resolving himself into motionless rigidity. A red-haired patient kneels and peers intently down a water drain. A portly patient sits off in a corner rocking. Another patient rocks from a position on all fours. Still another patient, lying supine, rolls first to one side then to the other. Several patients walk slowly and aimlessly around, as if in a trance, showing no recognition of anyone or anything. A microcephalic darts quickly about, grinning, drooling and making unintelligible sounds. An early twentyish mongol wearing an oversized cowboy hat strides about with his hands firmly grasping the toy guns in his waistband holsters. Others smile emptily, many lie quietly, still others from time to time erupt into brief frenzies of motion or sound.

A few patients approach the newcomer to say, "Daddy," or "Wanna go home," or to give their name or to offer some paradoxical phrase such as "tapioca too, ooga, ooga." One or another patient may attempt to touch, pull, or grasp the stranger, but such attempts at interaction are usually of the most fleeting duration. Others may approach and observe from a distance before moving away. Most pay no attention to a new face.

In the background, strange and wondrous sounds originate from all sides. Few words can be distinguished (although many utterances, in their inflection, resemble English speech); rather, screams, howls, grunts, and cries predominate and reverberate in a cacophony of only sometimes human noise. At the same time, loud and rhythmic music is coming out of the loudspeaker system.

There are, finally, the odors. Although many patients are not toilet trained, there is no strong fecal odor. Neither is there a distinct smell of sweat. Yet there is a peculiar smell of something indefinable. Perhaps it is a combination of institutional food and kitchen smells, soap, disinfectant, feces, urine, and the close confinement of many human bodies.

In sum, Ward Y and its inhabitants constitute a staggering visual, auditory and olfactory assault on the presupposedly invariant character of the natural normal world of everyday life. Here, to a monumental degree, things are different.

The daily routine

The day on Ward Y begins at 6:00 a.m. when the lights go on and the relatively high IQ helpers begin to get out of bed. By 6:15 these helpers are dressed and together with the employees they begin to rouse the more defective patients from their sleep. These patients are awakened in groups of 12, the number being determined by the number of toilets on the ward. With few exceptions, they sleep without clothing, and thus they are led, nude, into the bathroom where each is toileted. After they eliminate, helpers apply toilet paper appropriately, wash their hands, and lead them out of the washrooms. Each is then dressed in denim trousers with an elastic waistband and a shirt. This completed, they are permitted to go into the day hall where they mill about while the next group of 12 is awakened, toileted, washed, and dressed. As this is going on, one or two employees strip those beds which have been soiled during the night and helpers follow them making up all the beds.

By 7:15 a.m. most of the toileting, washing, and dressing has been completed and the most capable helpers are given their breakfasts in the dining room. No food is prepared on the ward; it all comes from a central kitchen and is delivered to the several wards by food truck. By 7:30, the helpers have finished and the 23 least capable patients—referred to by the staff as "the babies"—are led into the dining room. Since the babies are capable neither of carrying a tray nor of feeding themselves, they are individually led to a table, seated, and literally spoon-fed by an employee or a "detail." Feeding the 23 babies consumes about thirty minutes. Thus at about 8:00, the babies have finished their breakfast and are led out of the dining room and back to the bathroom where they are again toileted and washed before being led to the play yard where their incontinence is both less disturbing to, and more easily handled by, the staff. As the babies leave, the remaining 50-odd patients, most of whom have been standing in line in the corridor just outside the dining room, are allowed to enter. Just before the door is opened, those who have not been waiting outside are herded into this corridor by an employee whose job it is to check the entire ward for strays. Upon entering, they are led single file to a cafeteria-like serving line where they pick up a tray and proceed along the counter. Both food and utensils are placed on the tray by employees or "details" as they move along. Some of these relatively more competent patients seem only dimly aware of what is happening and must be led by an employee both along the serving line and to a table. Others, however, exhibit great interest in the food, chatter excitedly, and once through the serving line walk off toward a table unaided and undirected.

As soon as all the patients have filed into the dining room, the door is locked. This measure is taken to prevent the premature exit of patients who might get into trouble if they were allowed to wander about the ward without supervision. In a very few minutes, all have been served and are seated, usually four to a table. Each has a spoon but no knife or fork. Their deportment at the table varies greatly. At some tables, the eating may proceed in a reasonably—indeed, remarkably—decorous fashion, but at other tables such is not at all the case. Whole hard-boiled eggs are eaten at a gulp, oatmeal with milk is eaten with the fingers, prunes drop to the floor, trays are over-turned, neighbors have cups of milk poured or sloshed on them, and so on. While in the course of breakfast two or three arguments typically arise which on occasion lead to fights or tantrums, and while there are always some wanderers who leave their tables and stroll about, breakfast progresses, for the most part, with a significant semblance of order and propriety. Once breakfast is completed, about thirty minutes after commencement, these patients are led out of the dining room, leaving behind them an ample residue of spilled food and drink on tables, chairs and floor. As they file out, helpers, details and employees clean up behind them.

Leaving the dining room, these patients, like the babies, are led once more to the bathroom, where each is again undressed and toileted. Again, toilet paper is handled only by helpers and employees, for when left to their own devices, some have been known to flush entire rolls down the toilet—a sport which occasions major dislocations in the plumbing. After being toileted, each patient's hands are once again washed. Next comes tooth brushing; each patient has his own toothbrush identified by name, but only a few are capable of brushing their teeth unaided. Consequently, most patients, still undressed, wander about the bathroom waiting to have their teeth brushed by a helper or an employee. When a patient is finished, he files out of the bathroom where he is met at the door by another helper who wipes the excess toothpaste and saliva from his mouth with a cloth. This completed, he is once again dressed.

About 9:00 am.—some three hours after arising—all the patients are at last ready to meet the day. It is at this point that play activity, which for most patients is a euphemism for free time, begins. Just as in the case of the early activities—toileting, dressing and feeding—the patients are again separated into competence groupings but now there is a territorial dimension to their division. The least competent patients, approximately 55 in number, go to the outside play yard (or in bad weather to the porch), while the more competent patients remain within the ward proper.

The play yard is a large asphalt-paved rectangle enclosed on two sides by the ward itself and on the other two sides by an 8½-ft.-high wire fence. Within the enclosure are several wooden benches, a tether ball and two roofed structures which provide shade. Aside from the tether ball, which is typically not in use, the only objects provided for patients' amusement are balls of various sizes which an employee occasionally makes available. Employees and helpers sometimes attempt to induce organized activity by engaging a few of the relatively more able patients in throwing a ball back and forth. Such activity is never sustained for any length of time however; few of the patients are interested in such activities and those who are interested can neither catch nor throw in any effective manner. Besides these natural handicaps, a few of the patients delight in capturing the ball and throwing or kicking it over the fence, whence the employee must retrieve it.

Thus, while the patients in the play yard are under constant supervision they are in fact left almost entirely to their own singularly limited devices. At least 20 patients do nothing but sit, rock, or lie quietly. The activity of the remaining 30 or so consists of running, pacing, crying, or shouting, and this typically in a manner oblivious of their surroundings. Aside from an occasional ephemeral outburst when, for instance, two patients bump into each other or when one pushes or strikes another, there is little interaction between them. What interaction does occur is almost entirely limited to the tactual: there is occasional cuddling, stroking, huddling together and amorphous, exploratory probing. These interactions have the quality of "pure happenings"; they are characteristically without relation either to past or future: in a word, they have the appearance of occurring outside of history. Occasionally one patient may approach another and launch into an outpouring of gibberish, gesturing frantically all the while, only to be met by a vacant stare or, contrariwise, he may stop in mid-passage as inexplicably as he began. Here truly, one sees the *in vivo* prototype of a "billiard-ball" theory of personality.

To the consternation of the staff, one activity which does occur with inexplicable frequency is spontaneous disrobing. A major task for the supervising employee and his two details consists in maintaining the minimal proprieties of everyday dress. While most patients are barefooted and while shirts are more often off than on, nothing whatsoever is done about the former and, except in case of sunburn, little, if anything, is done about the latter. Trousers, however, are intimately involved with considerations of decency and their absence is quite another matter indeed. Trousers must be put back onto patients who simply remove them and they must be removed from patients who have soiled themselves. Approximately 25 patients on Ward Y are totally incontinent and another 25 are sometimes so. As has already been noted, virtually all of these are in the group sent to the play yard. There are two clothes hampers in the yard, one containing clean clothes and the other soiled clothes. As trousers are soiled, they are thrown into the one hamper and clean ones are taken from the other. Because trouser sizes are not marked, and because both patients and garments come in many sizes, one often sees some patients enshrouded by enormous pants and others constricted by tiny ones.

Inextricably combined with these matters of moral appropriateness is an imperative concern for the physical health of the patients. Enteric disease—especially bacillary dysentery and its complications—is an ever-present danger. Fecal matter is not always ignored by the incontinent idiot: it is sometimes smeared, played with, thrown, and even eaten. It is for these reasons, too, that incontinence is counted as a matter requiring urgent staff attention. Nor is every patient aware that all water is not fit to drink; some patients have been known to drink water out of the toilet bowls and from the shower room floors. There is, too, the constant danger that despite the plentiful administration of tranquilizers, certain of the patients might at any moment do grave physical damage to themselves or others. Such outbursts are as a rule without apparent cause; a patient may bite, scratch or gouge either himself or another patient. These occurrences are sufficiently frequent that periods of calm may correctly be seen as preceding the storms that will inevitably follow. There is, finally, the danger of accidental injury. Seizures occur unpredictably and handicapped patients such as these not infrequently slip and fall. The possibility of accidental injury is so great for some patients that the staff seldom permits them to enter the play yard because they feel a fall on its rough asphalt surface would be more likely to cause injury than would a similar fall on the polished cement floors of the ward.

Among the 25 or 30 patients who remain inside, the problems of incontinence and nudity are much less pressing. The demands for supervision are lessened by confining all patients to the day room and TV room, access between which is open at all times. Such confinement is accomplished by the simple policy of locking all other doors. Within the confines of these two rooms, then, the patients typically sit, sleep, watch TV or pace about aimlessly; only rarely do they interact with one another. Their interaction with staff, too, is limited to brief encounters which more frequently than not consist of staff directives to refrain from doing one thing or another—to stay out of the office, to leave so-and-so alone, to stop masturbating, to stop hitting one's head against the wall, etc. Much time is spent in staring intently at one or another staff member as he goes about his duties. In general the scene one confronts in the day room is not greatly different from that of the play yard.

From a pool of 20 select patients, rotating groups of six or seven are daily given special training in the occupational therapy room. This training consists of such activities as coloring in coloring books, playing with plastic toys, listening to music, and practicing some elementary manipulative skills. Aside from this, those who remain inside the ward are, like their counterparts in the play yard, left for the most part to their own devices.

Throughout this period of play activity most of the staff is engaged in a variety of routine tasks. One employee, as we noted, supervises the play yard; another spends all or most of the day in the ward clinic dispensing medication and treating minor injuries or illnesses; another must supervise details and helpers in cleaning the dining room, bathroom, and the ward in general; one employee is required to be responsible for the patients who are in the occupational therapy room; another must each day take those patients who are scheduled for clinic appointments to the hospital. Finally, the ward charge must be on hand to meet the ward physician when he calls, must make out a number of written reports and must oversee all activity on the ward.

At 11:00 a.m. play activity stops, and preparations for lunch begin. All patients are again toileted and washed, with the babies being undressed in order both to make toileting proceed more effectively and to insure against the stuffing of clothing into the toilets. The daily luncheon preparation occupies both patients and staff for the better part of an hour. Lunch itself begins around noon and follows the same pattern as breakfast: helpers first, babies next, then the rest of the patients. Following the meal, each patient is again toileted and washed. The entire luncheon operation lasts from 11:00 a.m. to about 1:30 p.m.

At 1:30, play activity is resumed. It follows the morning pattern in all major details and lasts until 4:00 p.m. On a nice day, 50 or more patients are usually taken to an open grassy area ("the park") about a quarter of a mile distant from the ward where they are allowed to roam about. Little advantage is taken of this opportunity, however; the patients generally remain clustered together around the supervising staff members. Aside from this trip away from the ward, the afternoon activities parallel those of the morning.

At 4:00 p.m. toileting and washing begins again in preparation for the evening meal which lasts from 5:00 to 6:00, once more along the same pattern. The evening meal too is followed by a brief toileting and washing which is generally concluded by 6:30. This, in turn, is followed by the third play activity period of the day which lasts until about 7:30. This time the porch replaces the play yard and the TV room tends to draw a larger audience than during the day. During this period, patients are frequently assembled and marched around the day hall for several minutes (ostensibly in order to work off unspent energy in preparation for bedtime).

The hour between 7:30 p.m. and 8:30 p.m. is devoted to bedtime preparation. After being toileted, each patient is directed under the shower where employees apply soap here and there, supervise the rinsing, and then towel the patients dry. They are next inspected for cuts, bruises, rashes and the like and following this they are at last sent off to bed. As noted earlier, almost all patients sleep without clothing. While the beds are labelled with the patient's names, none of the patients, of course, can read. Although some know their own bed, many do not and must be led there by staff. The beds of patients who characteristically get up during the night, of those given to nocturnal noise making, and of those subject to frequent convulsive seizures, are placed close to the office in order that night shift employees can observe them more closely and respond to them when necessary with minimal disturbance to the remaining patients.

While an occasional patient is simply unable to sleep, in which case he is typically dressed and brought into the day room where he sits silently, until morning, the most striking feature of the night is the ease with which it passes.

Periodically recurring events

There are other events in the lives of the idiots which, while they are no less constitutive of the routine of their institutional life, do not recur daily. In this category we include: the weekly bath, the fortnightly pinworm inspection, the monthly weighing, the monthly haircut, and the aperiodic visits of relatives.

One night a week all patients are given baths. The procedure is as follows: the drain in the large shower room is plugged, the room is flooded and soap is liberally added to the water. Small groups of patients enter, sit on the floor and soak themselves. Two male employees then strip to their shorts, wade into the now pond-like shower room and scrub the patients. This completed, the patients are led under the showers to be rinsed and then are taken out of the shower room where they are dried. Following this, they are given their daily cut, bruise, and rash inspection and their fingernails and toenails are clipped as needed, while the next group of patients is being led in to soak.

Once every two weeks, all patients are inspected for pinworms. About midnight, after all have settled down, two employees enter the dormitory and turn the patients one by one onto their stomachs. The buttocks are then spread and with the aid of a flashlight the presence or absence of pinworms is determined. This seemingly bizarre practice is so routinized that little disturbance is created; in fact, many of the patients do not even awaken.

Once each month all patients are weighed. A large scale is set up in the day room and the patients are disrobed and lined up for weighing. If a patient cannot or will not stand quietly on the scale, an employee must hold him still until a reading is obtained. Not only is this weighing a part of standard records-keeping, but the discovery of any marked changes in weight causes serious staff concern and typically leads to requests that patients evidencing these weight changes be examined medically.

A hospital barber spends one day a month on Ward Y and cuts as many patients' hair as he has time for. Those whom the barber misses—at least 20 and often many more than this—must be given haircuts by one or another employee. For reasons of efficiency, ease of care and prevention of disease, patients are given crew-cuts (the only patients exempted are those whose parents object to this kind of haircut). Patients are also shaved at least once a week. Shaving takes place in the ward barber shop, and is ordinarily performed by a helper who uses an electric razor. Some patients, however, are frightened by the buzzing noise of the electric razor and must be shaved with a safety razor; in these cases, an employee does the shaving.

Patients on Ward Y received a total of 812 visits during the last year—an average of 15.6 visits per week. Although there is an occasional open house or family party, visits usually consist of one or both parents of a patient spending a part of the day with their son in the ward's reception room, on the hospital grounds, or off the grounds entirely. When patients are scheduled to receive visitors—and administrative efforts are made to schedule these visits in advance—they are bathed, shaved, and dressed in company clothes immediately prior to the appointed visit.

The round of life here described is notably bleak and impersonal in its objective characteristics. However, the attitude of the staff does much to balance this. Ward employees do, in fact, evince an entirely sincere interest in the patients and regularly display both kindness and sympathy toward them. Nor is either staff or administration content with merely guiding their charge through an endless succession of similar appearing days. For example on Saturday nights one staff member often shows travelogues, cartoons, and home movies on the ward. These films are projected onto the wall of the day hall and are viewed by all patients. Also, on most Saturday afternoons there is a party. Girls for these occasions are provided by Ward Q, which houses equally retarded ambulatory female patients. One week the party is on Ward Y, the next week it is held on the female ward. Only the toilet trained and better behaved patients participate; the others remain on the porch or in the play yard, indifferent to the festivities. Party-going patients are dressed in their best clothing, the ward is decorated, refreshments are served, phonograph records are played and dancing is attempted with at least an occasional semblance of partial success. It should also be noted that the hospital provides a variety of recreational activities in which varying numbers of patients from Ward Y sometimes participate. Thus, the more competent patients are frequently taken to the hospital canteen, and sometimes to the swimming pool or to listen to music. Once every month or so, some are taken off the hospital grounds to public parks, the beaches, restaurants, amusement parks, zoos, fairs, sport events and the like. Needless to say, however, the participation of the least competent patients in these off-ward activities is of necessity strictly limited.

This said, it remains that these special events, while instantial of the good intentions of both staff and administration, stand in stark contrast to the mundane ward routine which *is* the patients' everyday life.

Discussion

At least one child out of every 1,000 born in the United States will be an idiot—a person totally incapable throughout life of caring for his own needs. Many of these will be completely infirm and will live a vegetative existence, confined either to a hospital crib or to a wheelchair. Even those who are ambulatory, like the patients on Ward Y, will require institutional care of a most comprehensive nature. The preceding account of the institutional lives of the patients on Ward Y should have given some indication of the nature of the problems an institution faces in providing such care.

The cost of this care—roughly $300,000 per year for the 82 patients on Ward Y—is considerable. Not only is institutional care for the profoundly retarded costly, it is both practically and morally problematic for it is subject to the vicissitudes of parental pressures, of state budgets, of administrative and legislative dicta and of conflicting professional interests and circumstances. While students of social organization have directed much attention to institutions for the mentally ill, interest in institutions for the mentally retarded has been virtually non-existent.

This singular neglect is the more curious when one considers the paradigmatic relevance of the mentally retarded to so many of social sciences' perennial issues. We invite, for instance, the consideration of the profoundly retarded as instructive examples of human beings whose capacity for culture is dramatically impaired. So construed, they stand on the threshold between man and not-man, and thus permit simultaneous inquiry into both the nature of man and the nature of culture-bearing animals.

Idiots' capacity for language is minimal (although it is greater than that of any of the non-human primates). This lack of language skills is, of course, related to their impoverished cultural and social behavior, but even the most rudimentary explication of the nature of this relationship awaits consideration. While they respond to some symbols, they create symbols only rarely if at all, they sustain little culture, develop few rules of their own, evidence relatively little exploratory curiosity, and their interaction with one another is both minimal and peculiarly ahistorical. In at least certain respects, then, they are *less* human than some infra-human species. In short, the relationship between language, social interaction and rule-oriented behavior is available here *in vivo* in a manner different from that found either among normal humans or normal non-humans.

We recommend, too, that in the interaction between patients and staff it is possible to obtain a unique perspective on such concerns as responsibility, trust, competence, reciprocity, and the like—all of which have been from the beginning and remain quintessential to a proper study of mankind. Here such matters find a natural laboratory, for staff is necessarily concerned both with creating and sustaining the human character of its charge against a background of continually recurring evidence to the contrary.

In summary, the whole area of mental retardation is, for the social scientist, a research backwater; and profound mental retardation is totally ignored. The foregoing description of the everyday lives of institutionalized idiots is intended to provide an introduction to these profoundly incompetent beings. Our own research has already taken us into analyses of both the practical and theoretical problems posed by such as these. By describing what has previously not been recorded and by recommending its theoretical relevance, we would hope to interest others in similar inquiry.

CLYDE KLUCKHOHN *and*
DOROTHEA LEIGHTON

The language of the Navaho Indians

Clyde Kluckhohn was a professor of anthropology at Harvard and a lifelong student of the Navaho. A collection of his essays has been published under the title *Culture and Behavior*. His other major works include *Mirror for Man* and *Navaho Witchcraft*. Dorothea Leighton, a medical doctor with interests and training in both anthropology and psychiatry, is presently a professor of mental health at the University of North Carolina School of Public Health. She and Clyde Kluckhohn collaborated on two books dealing with the Navaho: *Children of the People* (Navaho refer to themselves as *diné*, "the people") and *The Navaho*, from which the following selection is taken.

Since the Navahos, like all other peoples, necessarily think with words, at least a superficial conception of the main peculiarities of the Navaho language must be gained before endeavoring to see the world as it appears to The People. The forms of each language impose upon its speakers certain positive predispositions and certain negative restrictions as to the meanings they find in their experience.

From characteristic types of expressions even an outsider may safely infer some of the assumptions which The People make about the nature of things. For example, the Navahos do not say, "I am hungry" or "I have hunger." They always put it as "hunger is killing me" and "thirst is killing me." Similarly, they prefer the active, personalized "water is killing me" to the English description of the impersonal process of natural forces, "I am drowning." From such examples an immediate insight is gained into the Navaho manner of conceiving such events. To The People, hunger is not something which comes from within but something to which the individual is subjected by an outside force. Indeed if an articulate Navaho is pressed for an explanation of this linguistic idiom he is likely to say, "The spirit of hunger sits here beside me."

From the psychological point of view, there are as many different worlds upon the earth as there are languages. Each language is an instrument which guides people in observing, in reacting, in expressing themselves in a special way. The pie of experience can be sliced in all sorts of ways, and language is the principal directive force in the background. It is a great pity that most Americans have so strong an emotional block against the formal analysis of linguistic structures. They have been made to suffer so much from having to memorize rules and from approaching language in a mechanical, unimaginative way that they tend to think of "grammar" as the most inhuman of studies. Looked at in another way, nothing is more human than the speech of an individual or of a folk. No clues are so helpful as those of language in leading to ultimate, unconscious psychological attitudes. Moreover, much of the friction between groups and between nations arises because in both the literal and the slangy senses they don't speak the same language.

For the Navaho case, Robert Young and William Morgan have well put the basic problems:

> The pattern of Navaho thought and linguistic expression is totally unlike that of the European languages with which we are most commonly familiar. We learn such foreign languages as Spanish, French, Italian, and German with a minimum of difficulty because there exist so many analogies, both with respect to grammar and to words, with our own native English. Moreover, the pattern according to which we conceive and express our thoughts in English and in these common European languages is basically the same throughout. We translate readily from one to the other, often almost word for word. And lastly, similar or very closely related sound systems prevailing throughout make the words easy to pronounce and to remember.
>
> On the other hand, the Navaho language presents a number of strange sounds which are difficult to imitate, and which make the words very hard to remember at first. Secondly, the pattern of thought varies so greatly from our English pattern that we have no small difficulty in learning to think like, and subsequently to express ourselves like the Navaho. An understanding of the morphology and structure of the language, and an insight into the nature of the thought patterns involved can go far in aiding to solve the puzzle.

The tacit premises that are habitually present in the thinking of Navahos elude the outsider until he actually studies somewhat minutely some native utterances recorded in text and compares them with translations given by several different English-speaking Navahos. Better still, if he learns a little Navaho and tries to express himself—even on very simple matters—he is speedily compelled to realize that the categories in which one classifies experience and tries to communicate it to others are not altogether "given" by the events of the external world. Every language is a different system of categorizing and interpreting experience. This system is the more insidious and pervasive because native speakers are so unconscious of it as a system, because to them it is part of the very nature of things, remaining always in the class of background phenomena. That is, the very fact that Navahos do not stop every time they talk about hunger and say to themselves, "When I talk this way I am personalizing hunger as a force outside myself," makes for difficulty of understanding between whites and The People. They take such ways of thought as much for granted as the air they breathe, and unconsciously assume that all human beings in their right minds think the same way.

It is primarily for this reason that administrators, teachers, missionaries, and others who have to do with the Navahos—or any foreign people—would do well to learn something of the salient features of the linguistic structure. It is also for this reason that anyone who wants to understand the Navahos at all must know something about their language and the way in which it molds thought, interests, and attitudes.

There is no doubt that Navaho is a difficult language, but this is not sufficient cause for throwing up one's hands and avoiding the whole subject like the plague. There is a difference between learning a language and using a language. Few whites have the time or the skill to learn to speak Navaho so well that they can dispense with an interpreter. But mastering the tongue or remaining completely ignorant of it are not the only alternatives. The white person who will make the effort necessary to gain a general orientation to the language will not only find the information intensely interesting but will also discover that he can use even this limited knowledge very effectively. If he will then take the further step of talking a bit, in spite of the mistakes he is certain to make, he will be rewarded for this venture considerably beyond his expectations.

The purpose of this [selection] can clearly be neither to give a scientific description of the language nor to provide a manual for learning Navaho. The aim is to sketch some structural features to show the reader how the climate of feeling, reacting, and thinking created by the Navaho language is different from that created by English and other European languages.

Navaho sounds

White people despair at learning Navaho not only because of its unfamiliar and difficult sounds but also because Navahos are accustomed to respond to small variations which in English are either ignored or used merely for expressive emphasis. For example, a small clutch of the breath ("glottal closure"), which the speaker of European languages scarcely notices, often differentiates Navaho words. *Tsin* means "log," "stick," or "tree," whereas *tsʔin* (the ʔ representing glottal closure) means "bone." Similarly, *bitaʔ* means "between," but *bitʔaʔ* means "its wing."

The Navahos also distinguish quite separate meanings on the basis of pronouncing their vowels in long, intermediate, or short fashion. For example, the words *bitoʔ* (his water) and *bitooʔ* (its juice) are absolutely identical save for the fact that the second vowel in the latter is lingered over.

Finally, the Navahos, like the Chinese, pay very careful attention to the tones of vowels (and of the sound "n" which is sometimes used in Navaho with vowel quantity). Four separate tones (low, high, rising, falling) are differentiated. The only difference between *ʔazeeʔ* (medicine) and *ʔazééʔ* (mouth) is that the final long vowel of the latter has a high pitch, as indicated by the accent mark. The same thing is true for the difference between *ʔanaaʔ* (war) and *ʔanááʔ* (eye). The phonetic variations in the following five words are almost imperceptible to the untrained white ear.

bíniʔ,	his mind	*biniiʔ*,	his face
bíníʔ,	his nostrils	*bini*,	in it
biníʔ,	his waist		

Perhaps in the case of most nouns, as in the examples just given, meanings would ordinarily become clear from context. But when we come to verbs, differences in pronunciation so slight as to pass unnoticed by those habituated to tongues of Indo-European pattern make for a bewildering set of variations, many of which would be equally suitable to an identical context. For example:

naashʔá, I go around with the round object.
naashʔaah, I am in the act of lowering the round object.
náshʔááh, I am in the act of turning the round object upside down (or over).
naashʔáah, I am accustomed to lowering the round object.

Any of these expressions might easily be confused with *náshʔa*, which means "I am skinning it."

The importance of these minute variations in Navaho cuts both ways in complicating the problems of communication between whites and Navahos. These variations make it difficult for whites to speak Navaho, and they also make it difficult for Navahos to learn English sounds accurately. The very fact that the Navahos themselves are sensitized from childhood to these (and not to other) types of sound patterns and alternations makes the phonetics of English or Spanish hard for them to master.

So far as pronunciation alone is concerned, there are languages whose systems of sounds present more problems to the speaker of European background than does Navaho. There are a number of sounds in Navaho that are not found in English, but there are parallels to almost all (except glottalization) in German, Welsh, Polish, and other European languages. The real difficulty with Navaho rests in the fact that the small phonetic differences of the sort that have been illustrated above cannot be by-passed. There is no leeway. In the language of the Sioux Indians there are also long vowels; one can, however, communicate quite effectively without rendering them very accurately. But there is nothing slouchy about Navaho. Sounds must be reproduced with pedantic neatness. Tones can be ignored in Chinese for the sake of stress. Not so in Navaho. The language of The People is the most delicate known for phonetic dynamics.

A few white persons (children of traders or missionaries) who have learned Navaho as small children, speak "without an accent." A very few other whites have learned as adults to speak fluent and correct Navaho but have failed to acquire certain nuances in the sheer style of speaking. Learners may take comfort against their mistakes and embarrassment from the realization that the only recipe for pronouncing Navaho perfectly is to take the precaution of being born of or among Navahos. The talk of those who have learned Navaho as adults always has a flabby quality to the Navaho ear. They neglect a slight hesitation a fraction of a second before uttering the stem of the word. They move their lips and mouths too vigorously. Native Navaho has a nonchalant, mechanical flavor in ordinary discourse—almost as if a robot were talking.

Navaho words

It is often said that the word range of all "primitive" peoples is small and that vocabularies of more than a few thousand words are rare. This is pure mythology. It is impossible to say how many "words" there are in Navaho without the statement's being susceptible of misunderstanding, for everything depends upon the standard adopted as to what constitutes a separate word, a peculiarly acute problem in Navaho. But it may be asserted without qualification that Navaho has a very rich vocabulary. Some suggestion of extent may be given by noting that there are more than a thousand *recorded* names for plants, that the technical terms used in ceremonialism total at least five hundred, that every cultural specialization or occupation has its own special terminology.

The language has shown itself flexible in its capacity for dealing with new objects (the parts of an automobile, for example) and new experiences. But this has been done, for the most part, by making up new words in accord with old patterns rather than by taking over Spanish and English words and pronouncing them in Navaho fashion. "Tomato" is "red plant." An elephant is "one that lassoes with his nose." Many American Indian languages have enlarged their vocabularies by incorporating European words, but Navaho has admitted very few. An automobile is called by one of two terms (*chidí* or *chuggi*) which imitate the sound of a car. "Gasoline" then becomes *chidí bi tó*, "car's water."

Words are very important to The People. They are things of power. Some words attract good; others drive away evil. Certain words are dangerous—they may be uttered only by special persons under specially defined conditions. Hence there are specialized vocabularies known only to those who are trained in a craft or ceremonial skill. Young Navahos who have spent much time away at a boarding school or among whites will often complain of an uncle or grandfather, "He uses hard words. I can't understand him."

Not only are many words differentiated from each other by small sound changes, but there are many actual homonyms, words which have very similar or identical sounds but quite different meanings. The presence of these homonymous words and syllables gives rise to the many puns in which the Navahos delight. For instance, *haˀátˀíishąˀ nílį́* means either "what is flowing?" or "what clan are you?" and The People tell stories with many embellishments about this question's being asked of a man who was standing beside a river. Another favorite pun hangs on the fact that the same verb means either "to decide on the matter" or "to put the round object down." This is often employed to satirize the ponderous dealings of important people or, less kindly, to jibe at the hunched back (round object) of a cripple. Still another worn joke arises from the fact that *hodeeshtał* means equally "I will sing" or "I will kick him." And so there are many anecdotes of this pattern:

"So-and-so has gone over yonder."
"What for?"
"He is going to give one a kick." (i.e., The man [a Singer] will perform a chant.)

Many puns are more subtle than they appear on the surface. To enter fully into their humor requires sensitiveness to no less than three or four changes of linguistic front.

A quick glance at Navaho grammar

Navaho grammar is primarily a matter of the verb. The other parts of speech can, however, be used by the beginner to make himself fairly well understood.

There are few true Navaho nouns, though the list does include some of the commonest and most basic words in the language. Most words which English speakers are apt to term nouns are really nominalized verbs. Some nouns, in fact, can be conjugated after the fashion of neutral verbs. Adjectives are almost entirely the third-person forms of neuter verbs that denote quality, state, or condition. In the formal sense Navaho has no adjectives. Other parts of speech are: pronouns, postpositions, and particles.

Many pronouns are absorbed in verbs, but they are also used independently or prefixed to nouns and postpositions. Navaho pronouns present features of usage and nuances of meaning which it is hard indeed for the European to grasp. For example, "it" as the object of a verb has several different forms, depending upon whether "it" is thought of as definite or indefinite or as a place. The speaker must also choose between a number of possible alternatives for a third-person subject of a verb. One of these, which has been called "the person of preferred interest," makes a nice discrimination that is typically Navaho. This form of "he" designates the hero of the story as opposed to others, a Navaho as opposed to a member of another tribe, and so on.

Independent possessive pronouns have two forms, distinguished only by the length of the final vowel. One form signifies merely the state of possession; the other indicates that the owner just came into possession of the object. In the case of body parts, the Navahos make use of another subtle distinction. Thus, *shibeˀ* means "my milk" in the sense of milk which actually came from my breasts, whereas *sheˀabeˀ* means "my milk" in the sense of milk owned by me.

Postpositions are roughly the Navaho equivalent of our prepositions, except that they follow rather than precede their objects. There are a great variety of these, and their usage is relatively simple. They are a godsend to the foreigner, for by combining nouns and postpositions one may communicate many meanings without venturing into the intricacies of the Navaho verb. For instance, one may dodge the very difficult verb "go" by saying, "Your father, how about him?" and the child will state where the father has gone.

Navaho nouns have no gender and, with a few exceptions, have the same forms for singular and plural. Save for a few subtleties in the use of pronominal possessives, nouns are quite easy to handle. Thus, a white man can say a good deal in Navaho if he learns a few hundred nouns and ten or twenty postpositions.

. . .

Navaho has a peculiarly intricate construction of verbs which derive quite definite meanings from the assembling of elements that are generalized and colorless in themselves. Indeed, it might be called a chemical language. That is, the basic process is that of utilizing the varying effects of small elements in different combinations. Syntax, to the Navaho consciousness, is locked up, confined within the verb.

In a sense, the conjugation of the verb is primarily a matter of making the proper alterations in the prefixes. The verb stem conveys an image which remains constant. However, this nuclear notion is much more minutely specific than is that of the vast majority of English verbs. Verbs of going, for example, are a great nuisance in all Athabascan languages.* The first difficulty is that there are usually entirely different stems when one, two, or three or more persons are involved in the action. Thus one stem for the simplest kind of "going" is *-ghááh* in the singular, *-ʔaash* in the dual, and *-kááh* in the plural.

deesháál, I shall go.
diitʔash, We (two) will go.
diikah, We (more than two) will go.

The complications are bewildering to a white person:

nił deeshʔash, I'll go with you. (The verb has a singular subject but the dual stem is used because two persons are involved in the action.)
nihił deeshkah, I'll go with the two of you. (The subject is still singular but the plural stem must be used because more than two people are involved.)

On the other hand:

deʔnohháah, One of you come here. (*-noh-* refers to plural "you" but, since only one person is expected to act, the stem is singular.)
deʔnínááh, Come here (you, singular).
deʔnohkááh, Come here (you, plural, in a group).
deʔhohkááh, Come here (you, plural, one after another).

In short, where English is loose, Navaho is fussy about the finest shades of meaning, which it expresses by small permutations of verbal elements.

Navaho is compact as well as precise. The last example above shows

* Navaho is classified together with Apache as the southern branch of the Athabascan language family; this family also includes a large number of languages spoken by scattered migratory tribes in northwestern Canada and the interior of Alaska and a few tongues formerly spoken in isolated spots along the Pacific coast of the U.S. [Ed.]

how with great economy the Navaho language by the simple substitution of a monosyllable conveys ideas which take many words in English. Take two more examples along the same line.

dadiikah, We will each go separately.
hidiikah, We will go one after another, in succession.

Some of these prefixes are difficult to distinguish in English translation. For instance, *ná-* and *náá-* are ordinarily both rendered by "again," but actually there is a significant shade of difference.

deeskʔaaz hazlį́į́, It (the weather) got cold.
deeskʔaaz náhásdlį́į́, It got cold again.
deeskʔaaz nááhásdlį́į́, It got cold again.

But really the third form means "it got cold *back*"; that is, a return to a previous state is specified.

Navaho is likewise very finicky in expressing agency. *Tsinaaʔeeł shił níʔéél*, *tsinaaʔeel shił ʔaníłʔéél*, and *tsinaaʔeeł níłʔéél* may all be rendered: "I came by boat." But the first form implies that the boat floats off of its own accord, the second that the movement is caused by an indefinite or unstated subject, the third that the movement of the boat was caused by the speaker.

. . .

The inflections of the verb in most European languages perform as one of their principal functions those distinctions between past, present, and future which we call "tense." It is an arguable question whether there are tenses in the European sense in Navaho. The language of The People is interested primarily in the category the grammarians call "aspect."

Aspect defines the geometrical character of an event, stating its definability with regard to line and point rather than its position in an absolute time scale or in time as broken up by the moving present of the speaker. Traces of aspect inflection may be found in modern Greek, German, and Spanish, but only in Slavic languages such as Russian and Polish does it have any systematic importance among contemporary European tongues. Aspect indicates different types of activity. Thus, the momentaneous aspect in Navaho means that action is thought of as beginning and ending within an instant, while the continuative suggests that action lasts. . . .

Grammarians also consider modes as one of the principal verbal categories in Navaho. Some modes are similar to, but not identical with, the tenses of English. Others indicate the way an act is performed—repeatedly or customarily, etc. For example, *biih náshdááh* (iterative mode) means "time and again I put it on," whereas *biih yíshááh* (usitative mode) means "habitually I put it on." The usitative mode implies the speaker's interest is general, not in a specific event. Often it should be translated "our custom is so and so." It may indeed refer to events that are hypothetical so far as the speaker is concerned. Hence sometimes it must be rendered "if I were to" or "whenever." The iterative, in contrast, refers to actual repetition of acts.

Future, present, and past time may be left unspecified or may be indicated by suffixes, but sometimes they are made clear by the combination of aspect and mode. For instance, *ʔáásh ʔliił* (imperfective aspect, progressive mode) may be rendered "I am (progressively) making it." The imperfective aspect most often conveys a sense analogous to that of English indefinite present. But the primary idea which The People express through this aspect is that of uncompleted action. So far as time is concerned, the act may take place in the past, provided that the act is uncompleted. Or it may refer to the future when one is about to do or in the act of doing something. Depending upon context and upon the mode with which it is combined, therefore, the imperfective must be rendered "I am in the act of" or "I was in the act of" or "I am about to be in the act of," and in a great variety of other ways.

. . .

By their speech shall ye know them

Any language is more than an instrument for the conveying of ideas, more even than an instrument for working upon the feelings of others and for self-expression. Every language is also a means of categorizing experience. What people think and feel, and how they report what they think and feel, is determined, to be sure, by their individual physiological state, by their personal history, and by what actually happens in the outside world. But it is also determined by a factor which is often overlooked; namely, the pattern of linguistic habits which people have acquired as members of a particular society. The events of the "real" world are never felt or reported as a machine would do it. There is a selection process and an interpretation in the very act of response. Some features of the external situation are highlighted; others are ignored or not fully discriminated.

Every people has its own characteristic classes in which individuals pigeonhole their experiences. These classes are established primarily by the language through the types of objects, processes, or qualities which receive special emphasis in the vocabulary and equally, though more subtly, through the types of differentiation or activity which are distinguished in grammatical forms. The language says, as it were, "Notice this," "Always consider this separate from that," "Such and such things belong together." Since persons are trained from infancy to respond in these ways they take such discriminations for granted, as part of the inescapable stuff of life. But when we see two peoples with different social traditions respond in different ways to what appear to the outsider to be identical stimulus-situations, we realize that experience is much less a "given," an absolute, than we thought. Every language has an effect upon what the people who use it see, what they feel, how they think, what they can talk about.

As pointed out in the section on grammar, the language of The People delights in sharply defined categories. It likes, so to speak, to file things away in neat little packages. It favors always the concrete and particular, with little scope for abstractions. It directs attention to some features of every situation, such as the minute distinctions as to direction and type of activity. It ignores others to which English gives a place. Navaho focuses interest upon doing—upon verbs as opposed to nouns or adjectives.

Striking examples of the categories which mark the Navaho language are the variations in many of its verb stems according to the types of their subjects or objects. As has been illustrated above, the verb stem used often depends upon whether its subject (or object) is in the long-object class (such as a pencil, a stick, or a pipe), the granular-mass class (such as sugar and salt), the things-bundled-up class (such as hay and bundles of clothing), the animate-object class, and many others.

It must not be thought that such classification is a conscious process every time a Navaho opens his mouth to speak. It would, of course, paralyze speech if one had to think, when about to say a verb, "Now I must remember to specify whether the object is definite or indefinite; whether it is something round, long, fluid, or something else." Fortunately this is no more necessary in Navaho than in English. The Navaho child simply learns that if he is talking about dropping baseballs or eggs or stones he uses a word different from the word he would use if he spoke of dropping a knife or a pencil or a stick, just as the English-speaking child learns to use different words (herd, flock, crowd) in mentioning a group of cows, sheep, or people.

The important point is that striking divergences in manner of thinking are crystalized in and perpetuated by the forms of Navaho grammar. Take the example of a commonplace physical event: rain. Whites can and do report their perception of this event in a variety of ways: "It has started to rain," "It is raining," "It has stopped raining." The People can, of course, convey these same ideas—but they cannot convey them without finer specifications. To give only a few instances of the sorts of discrimination the Navaho must make before he reports his experience: he uses one verb form if he himself is aware of the actual inception of the rain storm, another if he has reason to believe that rain has been falling for some time in his locality before the occurrence struck his attention. One form must be employed if rain is general round about within the range of vision; another if, though it is raining round about, the storm is plainly on the move. Similarly, the Navaho must invariably distinguish between the ceasing of rainfall (generally) and the stopping of rain in a particular vicinity because the rain clouds have been driven off by wind. The People take the consistent noticing and reporting of such differences (which are usually irrelevant from the white point of view) as much for granted as the rising of the sun.

Navaho is an excessively literal language, little given to abstractions and to the fluidity of meaning that is so characteristic of English. The inner classification gives a concreteness, a specificity, to all expression. Most things can be expressed in Navaho with great exactness by manipulating the wide choice of stems in accord with the multitudinous alternatives offered by fusing prefixes and other separable elements in an almost unlimited number of ways. Indeed Navaho is almost overneat, overprecise. There is very little "give" in the language. It rather reminds one of a Bach fugue, in which everything is ordered in scrupulous symmetry.

The general nature of the difference between Navaho thought and English thought—both as manifested in the language and also as forced by the very nature of the linguistic forms into such patterns—is that Navaho thought is prevailingly so much more specific, so much more concrete. The ideas expressed by the English verb "to go" provide a nice example. To Germans the English language seems a little sloppy because the same word is used regardless of whether the one who goes walks or is transported by a train or other agency, whereas in German these two types of motion are always sharply distinguished in the two verbs *gehen* and *fahren*. But Navaho does much more along this line. For example, when one is talking about travel by horse, the speed of the animal may be expressed by the verb form chosen. The following all mean "I went by horseback."

łį́į́ shił níyá,	(at a walk or at unspecified speed).
łį́į́ shił yíldloozh,	(at a trot).
łį́į́ shił neeltą́ą́ʔ,	(at a gallop).
łį́į́ shił yílghod,	(at a run).

When a Navaho says that he went somewhere he never fails to specify whether it was afoot, astride, by wagon, auto, train, or airplane. This is done partly by using different verb stems which indicate whether the traveler moved under his own steam or was transported, partly by naming the actual means. Thus, "he went to town" would become:

kintahgóó ʔííyá, He went to town afoot or in a nonspecific way.
kintahgóó bił ʔiʔííbą́ą́z, He went to town by wagon.
kintahgóó bił ʔoʔootʔaʔ, He went to town by airplane.
kintahgóó bił ʔiʔííʔéél, He went to town by boat.
kintahgóó bił ʔoʔooldloozh, He went to town by horseback at a trot.
kintahgóó bił ʔoʔooldghod, He went to town by horseback at a run (or perhaps by car or train).
kintahgóó bił ʔiʔnooltą́ą́ʔ, He went to town by horseback at a gallop.

Moreover, the Navaho language insists upon another type of splitting up the generic idea of "going" to which German is as indifferent as English. The Navaho always differentiates between starting to go, going along, arriving at, returning from a point, etc., etc. For instance, he makes a choice between:

kintahgi níyá, He arrived at town.
kintahgóó ʔííyá, He went to town and is still there.
kintahgóó naayá, He went to town but is now back where he started.

Let us take a few more examples. The Navaho interpreter, even though his behavior or side comments may make it perfectly apparent that he feels there is a difference, will translate both *háájísh ʔííyá* and *háágósh ʔííyá* as "where did he go." If you say to him, "The Navaho sounds different in the two cases and there must be some difference in English meaning," the interpreter is likely to reply, "Yes, there is a difference all right, but you just can't express it in English." Now this is not literally true. Almost anything which can be said in Navaho can be said in English and vice versa, though a translation which gets everything in may take the form of a long paraphrase which sounds strained and artificial in the second language. In the case of the examples given above, the nearest equivalents are probably: "in what direction did he leave" and "for what destination did he leave."

In English one might ask, "Where did he go" and the usual answer would be something like, "He went to Gallup." But in Navaho one would have to select one of eight or ten possible forms which, if rendered exactly into English, would come out something like this: "He started off for Gallup," "He left to go as far as Gallup," "He left by way of Gallup," "He left, being bound for Gallup (for a brief visit)," "He left, being bound for Gallup (for an extended stay)," etc.

The People are likewise particular about other differentiations, similar to some of those discussed earlier in this [selection]:

kin góneʔ yah ʔiikai,	We went into the house (in a group).
kin góneʔ yah ʔahiikai,	We went into the house (one after another).

or:

chizh kin góne yahʔíínil,	I carried the wood into the house (in one trip).
chizh kin góne yah ʔakénil,	I carried the wood into the house (in several trips).

It is not, of course, that these distinctions *cannot* be made in English but that they *are not* made consistently. They seem of importance to English-speakers only under special circumstances, whereas constant precision is a regular feature of Navaho thought and expression about movement.

The nature of their language forces The People to notice and to report many other distinctions in physical events which the nature of the English language allows speakers to neglect in most cases, even though their senses are just as able as those of the Navaho to register the smaller details of what goes on in the external world. For example, suppose a Navaho range rider and a white supervisor see that the wire fence surrounding a demonstration area is broken. The supervisor will probably write in his notebook only: "The fence is broken." But if the range rider reports the occurrence to his friends he must say either *béésh ʔalcʔastʔi* or *béésh ʔalcʔaatʔi*; the first would specify that the damage has been caused by some person, the second that the agency was nonhuman. Further, he must choose between one of these statements and an alternative pair—the verb form selected depending on whether the fence was of one or several strands of wire.

Two languages may classify items of experience differently. The class corresponding to one word and one thought in Language A may be regarded by Language B as two or more classes corresponding to two or more words and thoughts. . . .

How the Navaho and English languages dissect nature differently perhaps comes out most clearly when we contrast verbal statements. Take a simple event such as a person dropping something. The different "isolates of meaning" (thoughts) used in reporting this identical experience will be quite different in Navaho and in English (see Figure 1). The only two elements which are the same are "I" and "sh," both of which specify who does the dropping. A single image "drop" in English requires two complementary images (*naa* and *ʔaah*) in Navaho. English stops with what from the Navaho point of view is a very vague statement—

"I drop it." The Navaho must specify four particulars which the English leaves either unsettled or to inference from context:

1. The form must make clear whether "it" is definite or just "something."
2. The verb stem used will vary depending upon whether the object is round, or long, or fluid, or animate, etc., etc.

ENGLISH specifies
1. Subject: *I*
2. Type of action: *drop*
3. Time of action: while speaking or just before

NAVAHO specifies
1. Subject: *sh*
2. Direction of action: downward–*Naa*
3. Definite or indefinite object: (verb form)
4. Type of object: (verb stem) here a bulky, roundish, hard object–*Naa*
5. Amount of control of subject over process:

in act of lowering

in act of letting fall

6. From area of the hand: *-lakʔ ee*

Naashʔaah lakʔee

(I am in the act of lowering the definite, bulky, roundish, hard object from my hand.)

Naashneʔ lakʔee

(I am in the act of letting the definite, bulky, roundish, hard object fall from my hand.)

FIGURE 1. "I drop it."

3. Whether the act is in progress, or just about to start, or just about to stop or habitually carried on or repeatedly carried on must be rigorously specified. In English, "I drop it" can mean once or can mean that it is customarily done (e.g., in describing the process of getting water from my well by a bucket). All the other possibilities are also left by English to the imagination.
4. The extent to which the agent controls the fall must be indicated: *naashʔaah* means "I am in the act of lowering the round object" but *naashneʔ* means "I am in the act of letting the round object fall."

To make the analysis absolutely complete, it must be pointed out that there is one respect in which the English is here a bit more exact. "I drop it" implies definitely (with the exception of the use of the "historical present") that the action occurs as the speaker talks or just an instant before, while the two Navaho verbs given above could, in certain circumstances, refer either to past or to future time. In other words, Navaho is more interested in the type of action (momentaneous, progressing, continuing, customary, etc.) than in establishing sequences in time as related to the moving present of the speaker.

Many other sorts of difference could be described. A full technical treatment would require a whole book to itself. The widest implications have been beautifully phrased by one of the great linguists of recent times, Edward Sapir:

> Language is not merely a more or less systematic inventory of the various items of experience which seem relevant to the individual, as is so often naively assumed, but is also a self-contained, creative symbolic organization, which not only refers to experience largely acquired without its help but actually defines experience for us by reason of its formal completeness and because of our unconscious projection of its implicit expectations into the field of experience. In this respect language is very much like a mathematical system which, also, records experience in the truest sense of the word, only in its crudest beginnings, but, as time goes on, becomes elaborated into a self-contained conceptual system which previsages all possible experience in accordance with certain accepted formal limitations. . . . [Meanings are] not so much discovered in experience as imposed upon it, because of the tyrannical hold that linguistic form has upon our orientation in the world. Inasmuch as languages differ very widely in their systematization of fundamental concepts, they tend to be only loosely equivalent to each other as symbolic devices and are, as a matter of fact, incommensurable in the sense in which two systems of points in a plane are, on the whole, incommensurable to each other, if they are plotted out with reference to differing systems of coordinates. . . .

In many ways the Navaho classifications come closer to a freshly objective view of the nature of events than do those of such languages as English or Latin.

MARGARET MEAD

Childhood in Samoa

Margaret Mead is Curator of Ethnology at the American Museum of Natural History and an adjunct professor of anthropology at Columbia University. Many of her books, such as *Growing Up in New Guinea* and *Sex and Temperament in Three Primitive Societies*, are ethnographic classics and have won great popularity with the American public.

The education of the Samoan child

Birthdays are of little account in Samoa. But for the birth itself of the baby of high rank, a great feast will be held, and much property given away. The first baby must always be born in the mother's village and if she has gone to live in the village of her husband, she must go home for the occasion. For several months before the birth of the child the father's relatives have brought gifts of food to the prospective mother, while the mother's female relatives have been busy making pure white bark cloth for baby clothes and weaving dozens of tiny pandanus mats which form the layette. The expectant mother goes home laden with food gifts and when she returns to her husband's family, her family provide her with the exact equivalent in mats and bark cloth as a gift to them. At the birth itself the father's mother or sister must be present to care for the newborn baby while the midwife and the relatives of the mother care for her. There is no privacy about a birth. Convention dictates that the mother should neither writhe, nor cry out, nor inveigh against the presence of twenty or thirty people in the house who sit up all night if need be, laughing, joking, and playing games. The midwife cuts the cord with a fresh bamboo knife and then all wait eagerly for the cord to fall off, the signal for a feast. If the baby is a girl, the cord is buried under a paper mulberry tree (the tree from which bark cloth is made) to ensure her growing up to be industrious at household tasks; for a boy it is thrown into the sea that he may be a skilled fisherman, or planted under a taro

---

From *Coming of Age in Samoa*, by Margaret Mead. Chapters 3 and 4 reprinted by permission of William Morrow Company, Inc. and the author.

plant to give him industry in farming. Then the visitors go home, the mother rises and goes about her daily tasks, and the new baby ceases to be of much interest to any one. The day, the month in which it was born, is forgotten. Its first steps or first word are remarked without exuberant comment, without ceremony. It has lost all ceremonial importance and will not regain it again until after puberty; in most Samoan villages a girl will be ceremonially ignored until she is married. And even the mother remembers only that Losa is older than Tupu, and that her sister's little boy, Fale, is younger than her brother's child, Vigo. Relative age is of great importance, for the elder may always command the younger—until the positions of adult life upset the arrangement—but actual age may well be forgotten.

Babies are always nursed, and in the few cases where the mother's milk fails her, a wet nurse is sought among the kinsfolk. From the first week they are also given other food, papaya, cocoanut milk, sugar-cane juice; the food is either masticated by the mother and then put into the baby's mouth on her finger, or if it is liquid, a piece of bark cloth is dipped into it and the child allowed to suck it, as shepherds feed orphaned lambs. The babies are nursed whenever they cry and there is no attempt at regularity. Unless a woman expects another child, she will nurse a baby until it is two or three years old, as the simplest device for pacifying its crying. Babies sleep with their mothers as long as they are at the breast; after weaning they are usually handed over to the care of some younger girl in the household. They are bathed frequently with the juice of a wild orange and rubbed with cocoanut oil until their skins glisten.

The chief nurse-maid is usually a child of six or seven who is not strong enough to lift a baby over six months old, but who can carry the child straddling the left hip, or on the small of the back. A child of six or seven months of age will assume this straddling position naturally when it is picked up. Their diminutive nurses do not encourage children to walk, as babies who can walk about are more complicated charges. They walk before they talk, but it is impossible to give the age of walking with any exactness, though I saw two babies walk whom I knew to be only nine months old, and my impression is that the average age is about a year. The life on the floor, for all activities within a Samoan house are conducted on the floor, encourages crawling, and children under three or four years of age optionally crawl or walk.

From birth until the age of four or five a child's education is exceedingly simple. They must be housebroken, a matter made more difficult by an habitual indifference to the activities of very small children. They must learn to sit or crawl within the house and never to stand upright unless it is absolutely necessary; never to address an adult in a standing position; to stay out of the sun; not to tangle the strands of the weaver;

not to scatter the cut-up cocoanut which is spread out to dry; to keep their scant loin cloths at least nominally fastened to their persons; to treat fire and knives with proper caution; not to touch the kava* bowl, or the kava cup; and, if their father is a chief, not to crawl on his bed-place when he is by. These are really simply a series of avoidances, enforced by occasional cuffings and a deal of exasperated shouting and ineffectual conversation.

The weight of the punishment usually falls upon the next oldest child, who learns to shout, "Come out of the sun," before she has fully appreciated the necessity of doing so herself. By the time Samoan girls and boys have reached sixteen or seventeen years of age these perpetual admonitions to the younger ones have become an inseparable part of their conversation, a monotonous, irritated undercurrent to all their comments. I have known them to intersperse their remarks every two or three minutes with, "Keep still," "Sit still," "Keep your mouths shut," "Stop that noise," uttered quite mechanically although all of the little ones present may have been behaving as quietly as a row of intimidated mice. On the whole, this last requirement of silence is continually mentioned and never enforced. The little nurses are more interested in peace than in forming the characters of their small charges and when a child begins to howl, it is simply dragged out of earshot of its elders. No mother will ever exert herself to discipline a younger child if an older one can be made responsible.

If small families of parents and children prevailed in Samoa, this system would result in making half of the population solicitous and self-sacrificing and the other half tyrannous and self-indulgent. But just as a child is getting old enough so that its wilfulness is becoming unbearable, a younger one is saddled upon it, and the whole process is repeated again, each child being disciplined and socialized through responsibility for a still younger one.

This fear of the disagreeable consequences resulting from a child's crying is so firmly fixed in the minds of the older children that long after there is any need for it, they succumb to some little tyrant's threat of making a scene, and five-year-olds bully their way into expeditions on which they will have to be carried, into weaving parties where they will tangle the strands, and cook-houses where they will tear up the cooking leaves or get thoroughly smudged with the soot and have to be washed —all because an older boy or girl has become so accustomed to yielding any point to stop an outcry.

This method of giving in, coaxing, bribing, diverting the infant

---

* Kava is an intoxicating drink made from the root of a pepper bush. It is used throughout Polynesia and has many supernatural associations. [Ed.]

disturbers is only pursued within the household or the relationship group, where there are duly constituted elders in authority to punish the older children who can't keep the babies still. Towards a neighbour's children or in a crowd the half-grown girls and boys and even the adults vent their full irritation upon the heads of troublesome children. If a crowd of children are near enough, pressing in curiously to watch some spectacle at which they are not wanted, they are soundly lashed with palm leaves, or dispersed with a shower of small stones, of which the house floor always furnishes a ready supply. This treatment does not seem actually to improve the children's behaviour, but merely to make them cling even closer to their frightened and indulgent little guardians. It may be surmised that stoning the children from next door provides a most necessary outlet for those who have spent so many weary hours placating their own young relatives. And even these bursts of anger are nine-tenths gesture. No one who throws the stones actually means to hit a child, but the children know that if they repeat their intrusions too often, by the laws of chance some of the flying bits of coral will land in their faces. Even Samoan dogs have learned to estimate the proportion of gesture that there is in a Samoan's "get out of the house." They simply stalk out between one set of posts and with equal dignity and all casualness stalk in at the next opening.

By the time a child is six or seven she has all the essential avoidances well enough by heart to be trusted with the care of a younger child. And she also develops a number of simple techniques. She learns to weave firm square balls from palm leaves, to make pin-wheels of palm leaves or frangipani blossoms, to climb a cocoanut tree by walking up the trunk on flexible little feet, to break open a cocoanut with one firm well-directed blow of a knife as long as she is tall, to play a number of group games and sing the songs which go with them, to tidy the house by picking up the litter on the stony floor, to bring water from the sea, to spread out the copra to dry and to help gather it in when rain threatens, to roll the pandanus leaves for weaving, to go to a neighbouring house and bring back a lighted fagot for the chief's pipe or the cook-house fire, and to exercise tact in begging slight favours from relatives.

But in the case of the little girls all of these tasks are merely supplementary to the main business of baby-tending. Very small boys also have some care of the younger children, but at eight or nine years of age they are usually relieved of it. Whatever rough edges have not been smoothed off by this responsibility for younger children are worn off by their contact with older boys. For little boys are admitted to interesting and important activities only so long as their behaviour is circumspect and helpful. Where small girls are brusquely pushed aside, small boys will be patiently tolerated and they become adept at making themselves useful. The four or five little boys who all wish to assist at the important business of helping a grown youth lasso reef eels organize themselves into a highly efficient working team; one boy holds the bait, another holds an extra lasso, others poke eagerly about in holes in the reef looking for prey, while still another tucks the captured eels into his *lavalava*. The small girls, burdened with heavy babies or the care of little staggerers who are too small to adventure on the reef, discouraged by the hostility of the small boys and the scorn of the older ones, have little opportunity for learning the more adventurous forms of work and play. So while the little boys first undergo the chastening effects of baby-tending and then have many opportunities to learn effective co-operation under the supervision of older boys, the girls' education is less comprehensive. They have a high standard of individual responsibility but the community provides them with no lessons in co-operation with one another. This is particularly apparent in the activities of young people; the boys organize quickly; the girls waste hours in bickering, innocent of any technique for quick and efficient co-operation.

And as the woman who goes fishing can only get away by turning the babies over to the little girls of the household, the little girls cannot accompany their aunts and mothers. So they learn even the simple processes of reef fishing much later than do the boys. They are kept at the baby-tending, errand-running stage until they are old enough and robust enough to work on the plantations and carry foodstuffs down to the village.

A girl is given these more strenuous tasks near the age of puberty, but it is purely a question of her physical size and ability to take responsibility, rather than of her physical maturity. Before this time she has occasionally accompanied the older members of the family to the plantations if they were willing to take the babies along also. But once there, while her brothers and cousins are collecting cocoanuts and roving happily about in the bush, she has again to chase and shepherd and pacify the ubiquitous babies.

As soon as the girls are strong enough to carry heavy loads, it pays the family to shift the responsibility for the little children to the younger girls and the adolescent girls are released from baby-tending. It may be said with some justice that the worst period of their lives is over. Never again will they be so incessantly at the beck and call of their elders, never again so tyrannized over by two-year-old tyrants. All the irritating, detailed routine of housekeeping, which in our civilization is accused of warping the souls and souring the tempers of grown women, is here performed by children under fourteen years of age. A fire or a pipe to be kindled, a call for a drink, a lamp to be lit, the baby's cry, the errand of the capricious adult—these haunt them from morning until night. With the introduction of several months a year of government schools these children are being taken out of their homes for most of the day. This brings about a complete disorganization of the native households which have no precedents for a manner of life where mothers have to stay at home and take care of their children and adults have to perform small routine tasks and run errands.

Before their release from baby-tending the little girls have a very limited knowledge of any of the more complicated techniques. Some of them can do the simpler work in preparing food for cooking, such as skinning bananas, grating cocoanuts, or scraping taro. A few of them can weave the simple carrying basket. But now they must learn to weave all their own baskets for carrying supplies; learn to select taro leaves of the right age for cooking, to dig only mature taro. In the cook-house they learn to make *palusami*, to grate the cocoanut meat, season it with hot stones, mix it with sea water and strain out the husks, pour this milky mixture into a properly made little container of taro leaves from which the aromatic stem has been scorched off, wrap these in a breadfruit leaf and fasten the stem tightly to make a durable cooking jacket. They must learn to lace a large fish into a palm leaf, or roll a bundle of small fish in a breadfruit leaf; to select the right kind of leaves for stuffing a pig, to judge when the food in the oven of small heated stones is thoroughly baked. Theoretically the bulk of the cooking is done by the boys and where a girl has to do the heavier work, it is a matter for comment: "Poor Losa, there are no boys in her house and always she must make the oven." But the girls always help and often do a great part of the work.

Once they are regarded as individuals who can devote a long period of time to some consecutive activity, girls are sent on long fishing expeditions. They learn to weave fish baskets, to gather and arrange the bundles of fagots used in torch-light fishing, to tickle a devil fish until it comes out of its hole and climbs obediently upon the waiting stick, appropriately dubbed a "come hither stick"; to string the great rose-coloured jellyfish, *lole*, a name which Samoan children give to candy also, on a long string of hibiscus bark, tipped with a palm leaf rib for a needle; to know good fish from bad fish, fish that are in season from fish which are dangerous at some particular time of the year; and never to take two octopuses, found paired on a rock, lest bad luck come upon the witless fisher.

Before this time their knowledge of plants and trees is mainly a play one, the pandanus provides them with seeds for necklaces, the palm tree with leaves to weave balls; the banana tree gives leaves for umbrellas and half a leaf to shred into a stringy "choker"; cocoanut shells cut in half, with cinet strings attached, make a species of stilt; the blossoms of the *Pua* tree can be sewed into beautiful necklaces. Now they must learn to recognize these trees and plants for more serious purposes; they must learn when the pandanus leaves are ready for the cutting and how to cut the long leaves with one sure quick stroke; they must distinguish between the three kinds of pandanus used for different grades of mats. The pretty orange seeds which made such attractive and also edible necklaces must now be gathered as paint brushes for ornamenting bark cloth. Banana leaves are gathered to protect the woven platters, to wrap up puddings for the oven, to bank the steaming oven full of food. Banana bark must be stripped at just the right point to yield the even, pliant, black strips needed to ornament mats and baskets. Bananas themselves must be distinguished as to those which are ripe for burying, or the golden curved banana ready for eating, or bananas ready to be sun-dried for making fruit-cake rolls. Hibiscus bark can no longer be torn off at random to give a raffia-like string for a handful of shells; long journeys must be made inland to select bark of the right quality for use in weaving.

In the house the girl's principal task is to learn to weave. She has to master several different techniques. First, she learns to weave palm branches where the central rib of the leaf serves as a rim to her basket or an edge to her mat and where the leaflets are already arranged for weaving. From palm leaves she first learns to weave a carrying basket, made of half a leaf, by plaiting the leaflets together and curving the rib into a rim. Then she learns to weave the Venetian blinds which hang between the house posts, by laying one-half leaf upon another and plaiting the leaflets together. More difficult are the floor mats, woven of four great palm leaves, and the food platters with their intricate designs. There are also fans to make, simple two-strand weaves which she learns to make quite well, more elaborate twined ones which are the prerogative of older and more skilled weavers. Usually some older woman in the household trains a girl to weave and sees to it that she makes at least one of each kind of article, but she is only called upon to produce in quantity the simpler things, like the Venetian blinds. From the pandanus she learns to weave the common floor mats, one or two types of the more elaborate bed mats, and then, when she is thirteen or fourteen, she begins her first fine mat. The fine mat represents the high point of Samoan weaving virtuosity. Woven of the finest quality of pandanus which has been soaked and baked and scraped to a golden whiteness and paper-like thinness, of strands a sixteenth of an inch in width, these mats take a year or two years to weave and are as soft and pliable as linen. They form the unit of value, and must always be included in the dowry of the bride. Girls seldom finish a fine mat until they are nineteen or twenty, but the mat has been started, and, wrapped up in a coarser one, it rests among the rafters, a testimony to the girl's industry and manual skill. She learns the rudiments of bark cloth making; she can select and cut the paper mulberry wands, peel off the bark, beat it after it has been scraped by more expert hands. The patterning of the cloth with a pattern board or by free hand drawing is left for the more experienced adult.

Throughout this more or less systematic period of education, the girls maintain a very nice balance between a reputation for the necessary minimum of knowledge and a virtuosity which would make too heavy demands. A girl's chances of marriage are badly damaged if it gets about the village that she is lazy and inept in domestic tasks. But after these first stages have been completed the girl marks time technically for three or four years. She does the routine weaving, especially of the Venetian blinds and carrying baskets. She helps with the plantation work and the cooking, she weaves a very little on her fine mat. But she thrusts virtuosity away from her as she thrusts away every other sort of responsibility with the invariable comment "Laititi a'u" (I am but young). All of her interest is expended on clandestine sex adventures, and she is content to do routine tasks as, to a certain extent, her brother is also.

But the seventeen-year-old boy is not left passively to his own devices. He has learned the rudiments of fishing, he can take a dug-out canoe over the reef safely, or manage the stern paddle in a bonito boat. He can plant taro or transplant cocoanut, husk cocoanuts on a stake and cut the meat out with one deft quick turn of the knife. Now at seventeen or eighteen he is thrust into the *Aumaga*, the society of the young men and the older men without titles, the group that is called, not in euphuism but in sober fact, "the strength of the village." Here he is badgered into efficiency by rivalry, precept and example. The older chiefs who supervise the activities of the *Aumaga* gaze equally sternly upon any backslidings and upon any undue precocity. The prestige of his group is ever being called into account by the *Aumaga* of the neighbouring villages. His fellows ridicule and persecute the boy who fails to appear when any group activity is on foot, whether work for the village on the plantations, or fishing, or cooking for the chiefs, or play in the form of a ceremonial call upon some visiting maiden. Furthermore, the youth is given much more stimulus to learn and also a greater variety of occupations are open to him. There is no specialization among women, except in medicine and mid-wifery, both the prerogatives of very old women who teach their arts to their middle-aged daughters and nieces. The only other vocation is that of the wife of an official orator, and no girl will prepare herself for this one type of marriage which demands special knowledge, for she has no guarantee that she will marry a man of this class.

For the boy it is different. He hopes that some day he will hold a *matai* name, a name which will make him a member of the *Fono*, the assembly of headmen, which will give him a right to drink kava with chiefs, to work with chiefs rather than with young men, to sit inside the house, even though his new title is only of "between the posts" rank, and not of enough importance to give him a right to a post for his back. But very seldom is he absolutely assured of getting such a name. Each family holds several of these titles which they confer upon the most promising youths in the whole family connection. He has many rivals. They also are in the *Aumaga*. He must always pit himself against them in the group activities. There are also several types of activities in one of which he must specialize. He must become a house-builder, a fisherman, an orator or a wood carver. Proficiency in some technique must set him off a little from his fellows. Fishing prowess means immediate rewards in the shape of food gifts to offer to his sweetheart; without such gifts his advances will be scorned. Skill in house-building means wealth and status, for a young man who is a skilled carpenter must be treated as courteously as a chief and addressed with the chief's language, the elaborate set of honorific words used to people of rank. And with this goes the continual demand that he should not be too efficient, too outstanding, too precocious. He must never excel his fellows by more than a little. He must neither arouse their hatred nor the disapproval of his elders who are far readier to encourage and excuse the laggard than to condone precocity. And at the same time he shares his sister's reluctance to accept responsibility, and if he should excel gently, not too obviously, he has good chances of being made a chief. If he is sufficiently talented, the *Fono* itself may deliberate, search out a vacant title to confer upon him and call him in that he may sit with the old men and learn wisdom. And yet so well recognized is the unwillingness of the young men to respond to this honour, that the provision is always made, "And if the young man runs away, then never shall he be made a chief, but always he must sit outside the house with the young men, preparing and serving the food of the *matais* with whom he may not sit in the *Fono*." Still more pertinent are the chances of his relationship group bestowing a *matai* name upon the gifted young man. And a *matai* he wishes to be, some day, some far-off day when his limbs have lost a little of their suppleness and his heart the love of fun and of dancing. As one chief of twenty-seven told me: "I have been a chief only four years and look, my hair is grey, although in Samoa grey hair comes very slowly, not in youth, as it comes to the white man. But always, I must act as if I were old. I must walk gravely and with a measured step. I may not dance except upon most solemn occasions, neither may I play games with the young men. Old men of sixty are my companions and watch my every word, lest I make a mistake. Thirty-one people live in my household. For them I must plan, I must find them food and clothing, settle their disputes, arrange their marriages. There is no one in my whole family who dares to scold me or even to address me familiarly by my first name. It is hard to be so young and yet to be a chief." And the old men shake their heads and agree that it is unseemly for one to be a chief so young.

The operation of natural ambition is further vitiated by the fact that the young man who is made a *matai* will not be the greatest among his former associates, but the youngest and greenest member of the *Fono*. And no longer may he associate familiarly with his old companions; a *matai* must associate only with *matais*, must work beside them in the bush and sit and talk quietly with them in the evening.

And so the boy is faced by a far more difficult dilemma than the girl. He dislikes responsibility, but he wishes to excel in his group; skill will hasten the day when he is made a chief, yet he receives censure and ridicule if he slackens his efforts; but he will be scolded if he proceeds too rapidly; yet if he would win a sweetheart, he must have prestige among his fellows. And conversely, his social prestige is increased by his amorous exploits.

So while the girl rests upon her "pass" proficiency, the boy is spurred to greater efforts. A boy is shy of a girl who does not have these proofs of efficiency and is known to be stupid and unskilled; he is afraid he may come to want to marry her. Marrying a girl without proficiency would be a most imprudent step and involve an endless amount of wrangling with his family. So the girl who is notoriously inept must take her lovers from among the casual, the jaded, and the married who are no longer afraid that their senses will betray them into an imprudent marriage.

But the seventeen-year-old girl does not wish to marry—not yet. It is better to live as a girl with no responsibility, and a rich variety of emotional experience. This is the best period of her life. There are as many beneath her whom she may bully as there are others above her to tyrannize over her. What she loses in prestige, she gains in freedom. She has very little baby-tending to do. Her eyes do not ache from weaving nor does her back break from bending all day over the tapa board. The long expeditions after fish and food and weaving materials give ample opportunities for rendezvous. Proficiency would mean more work, more confining work, and earlier marriage, and marriage is the inevitable to be deferred as long as possible.

The Samoan household

A Samoan village is made up of some thirty to forty households, each of which is presided over by a headman called a *matai*. These headmen hold either chiefly titles or the titles of talking chiefs, who are the official orators, spokesmen and ambassadors of chiefs. In a formal village assembly each *matai* has his place, and represents and is responsible for a the members of his household. These households include all the individuals who live for any length of time under the authority and protection of a common *matai*. Their composition varies from the biological family consisting of parents and children only, to households of fifteen and twenty people who are all related to the *matai* or to his wife by blood, marriage or adoption, but who often have no close relationship to each other. The adopted members of a household are usually but not necessarily distant relatives.

Widows and widowers, especially when they are childless, usually return to their blood relatives, but a married couple may live with the relatives of either one. Such a household is not necessarily a close residential unit, but may be scattered over the village in three or four houses. No one living permanently in another village is counted as a member of the household, which is strictly a local unit. Economically, the household is also a unit, for all work upon the plantations is under the supervision of the *matai* who in turn parcels out to them food and other necessities.

Within the household, age rather than relationship gives disciplinary authority. The *matai* exercises nominal and usually real authority over every individual under his protection, even over his father and mother. This control is, of course, modified by personality differences, always carefully tempered, however, by a ceremonious acknowledgment of his position. The newest baby born into such a household is subject to every individual in it, and his position improves no whit with age until a younger child appears upon the scene. But in most households the position of youngest is a highly temporary one. Nieces and nephews or destitute young cousins come to swell the ranks of the household and at adolescence a girl stands virtually in the middle with as many individuals who must obey her as there are persons to whom she owes obedience. Where increased efficiency and increased self-consciousness would perhaps have made her obstreperous and restless in a differently organized family, here she has ample outlet for a growing sense of authority.

This development is perfectly regular. A girl's marriage makes a minimum of difference in this respect, except in so far as her own children increase most pertinently the supply of agreeably docile subordinates. But the girls who remain unmarried even beyond their early twenties are in nowise less highly regarded or less responsible than their married sisters. This tendency to make the classifying principle age, rather than married state, is reinforced outside the home by the fact that the wives of untitled men and all unmarried girls past puberty are classed together in the ceremonial organization of the village.

Relatives in other households also play a role in the children's lives. Any older relative has a right to demand personal service from younger relatives, a right to criticize their conduct and to interfere in their affairs. Thus a little girl may escape alone down to the beach to bathe only to be met by an older cousin who sets her washing or caring for a baby or to fetch some cocoanut to scrub the clothes. So closely is the daily life bound up with this universal servitude and so numerous are the acknowledged relationships in the name of which service can be exacted, that for the children an hour's escape from surveillance is almost impossible.

This loose but demanding relationship group has its compensation, also. Within it a child of three can wander safely and come to no harm, can be sure of finding food and drink, a sheet to wrap herself up in for a nap, a kind hand to dry casual tears and bind up her wounds. Any small children who are missing when night falls are simply "sought among their kinsfolk," and a baby whose mother has gone inland to work on the plantation is passed from hand to hand for the length of the village.

The ranking by age is disturbed in only a few cases. In each village one or two high chiefs have the hereditary right to name some girl of their household as its *taupo*, the ceremonial princess of the house. The girl who at fifteen or sixteen is made a *taupo* is snatched from her age group and sometimes from her immediate family also and surrounded by a glare of prestige. The older women of the village accord her courtesy titles, her immediate family often exploits her position for their personal ends and in return show great consideration for her wishes. But as there are only two or three *taupos* in a village, their unique position serves to emphasize rather than to disprove the general status of young girls.

Coupled with this enormous diffusion of authority goes a fear of overstraining the relationship bond, which expresses itself in an added respect for personality. The very number of her captors is the girl's protection, for does one press her too far, she has but to change her residence to the home of some more complacent relative. It is possible to classify the different households open to her as those with hardest work, least chaperonage, least scolding, largest or least number of contemporaries, fewest babies, best food, etc. Few children live continuously in one household, but are always testing out other possible residences. And this can be done under the guise of visits and with no suggestion of truancy. But the minute that the mildest annoyance grows up at home, the possibility of flight moderates the discipline and alleviates the child's sense of dependency. No Samoan child, except the *taupo*, or the thoroughly delinquent, ever has to deal with a feeling of being trapped. There are always relatives to whom one can flee. This is the invariable answer which a Samoan gives when some familial impasse is laid before him. "But she will go to some *other* relative." And theoretically the supply of relatives is inexhaustible. Unless the vagrant has committed some very serious offence like incest, it is only necessary formally to depart from the bosom of one's household. A girl whose father has beaten her over-severely in the morning will be found living in haughty sanctuary, two hundred feet away, in a different household. So cherished is this system of consanguineous refuge, that an untitled man or a man of lesser rank will beard the nobler relative who comes to demand a runaway child. With great politeness and endless expressions of conciliation, he will beg his noble chief to return to his noble home and remain there quietly until his noble anger is healed against his noble child.

The most important relationships within a Samoan household which influence the lives of the young people are the relationships between the boys and girls who call each other "brother" and "sister," whether by blood, marriage or adoption, and the relationship between younger and older relatives. The stress upon the sex difference between contemporaries and the emphasis on relative age are amply explained by the conditions of family life. Relatives of opposite sex have a most rigid code of etiquette prescribed for all their contacts with each other. After they have reached years of discretion, nine or ten years of age in this case, they may not touch each other, sit close together, eat together, address each other familiarly, or mention any salacious matter in each other's presence. They may not remain in any house, except their own, together, unless half the village is gathered there. They may not walk together, use each other's possessions, dance on the same floor, or take part in any of the same small group activities. This strict avoidance applies to all individuals of the opposite sex within five years above or below one's own age with whom one was reared or to whom one acknowledges relationship by blood or marriage. The conformance to this brother and sister taboo begins when the younger of the two children feels "ashamed" at the elder's touch and continues until old age when the decrepit, toothless pair of old siblings may again sit on the same mat and not feel ashamed.

Tei, the word for younger relative, stresses the other most emotionally charged relationship. The first maternal enthusiasm of a girl is never expended upon her own children but upon some younger relative. And it is the girls and women who use this term most, continuing to cherish it after they and the younger ones to whom it is applied are full grown. The younger child in turn expends its enthusiasm upon a still younger one without manifesting any excessive affection for the fostering elders.

The word *aiga* is used roughly to cover all relationships by blood, marriage and adoption, and the emotional tone seems to be the same in each case. Relationship by marriage is counted only as long as an actual marriage connects two kinship groups. If the marriage is broken in any way, by desertion, divorce, or death, the relationship is dissolved and members of the two families are free to marry each other. If the marriage left any children, a reciprocal relationship exists between the two households as long as the child lives, for the mother's family will always have to contribute one kind of property, the father's family another, for occasions when property must be given away in the name of the child.

A relative is regarded as someone upon whom one has a multitude of claims and to whom one owes a multitude of obligations. From a relative one may demand food, clothing, and shelter, or assistance in a feud. Refusal of such a demand brands one as stingy and lacking in human kindness, the virtue most esteemed among the Samoans. No definite repayment is made at the time such services are given, except in the case of the distribution of food to all those who share in a family enterprise. But careful count of the value of the property given and of the service rendered is kept and a return gift demanded at the earliest opportunity. Nevertheless, in native theory the two acts are separate, each one in turn becoming a "beggar," a pensioner upon another's bounty. In olden times, the beggar sometimes wore a special girdle which delicately hinted at the cause of his visit. One old chief gave me a graphic description of the behaviour of someone who had come to ask a favour of a relative. "He will come early in the morning and enter quietly, sitting down in the very back of the house, in the place of least honour. You will say to him, 'So you have come, be welcome!' and he will answer, 'I have come indeed, saving your noble presence.' Then you will say, 'Are you thirsty? Alas for your coming, there is little that is good within the house.' And he will answer, 'Let it rest, thank you, for indeed I am not hungry nor would I drink.' And he will sit and you will sit all day long and no mention is made of the purpose of his coming. All day he will sit and brush the ashes out of the hearth, performing this menial and dirty task with very great care and attention. If someone must go inland to the plantation to fetch food, he is the first to offer to go. If someone must go fishing to fill out the crew of a canoe, surely he is delighted to go, even though the sun is hot and his journey hither has been long. And all day you sit and wonder, 'What can it be that he has come for? Is it that largest pig that he wants, or has he heard perhaps that my daughter has just finished a large and beautiful piece of tapa? Would it perhaps be well to send that tapa, as I had perhaps planned, as a present to my talking chief, to send it now, so that I may refuse him with all good faith?' And he sits and studies your countenance and wonders if you will be favourable to his request. He plays with the children but refuses the necklace of flowers which they have woven for him and gives it instead to your daughter. Finally night comes. It is time to sleep and still he has not spoken. So finally you say to him, 'Lo, I would sleep. Will you sleep also or will you be returning whence you have come?' And only then will he speak and tell you the desire in his heart."

So the intrigue, the needs, the obligations of the larger relationship group which threads its carefully remembered way in and out of many houses and many villages, cuts across the life of the household. One day it is the wife's relatives who come to spend a month or borrow a fine mat; the next day it is the husband's; the third, a niece who is a valued worker in the household may be called home by the illness of her father. Very seldom do all of even the small children of a biological family live in one household and while the claims of the household are paramount, in the routine of everyday life, illness or need on the part of the closer relative in another household will call the wanderers home again.

Obligations either to give general assistance or to give specific traditionally required service, as in a marriage or at a birth, follow relationship lines, not household lines. But a marriage of many years' duration binds the relationship groups of husband and wife so closely together that to all appearances it is the household unit which gives aid and accedes to a request brought by the relative of either one. Only in families of high rank where the distaff side has priority in decisions and in furnishing the *taupo*, the princess of the house, and the male line priority in holding the title, does the actual blood relationship continue to be a matter of great practical importance; and this importance is lost in the looser household group constituted as it is by the three principles of blood, marriage and adoption, and bound together by common ties of everyday living and mutual economic dependence.

The *matai* of a household is theoretically exempt from the performance of small domestic tasks, but he is seldom actually so except in the case of a chief of high rank. However, the leading role is always accorded to him in any industrial pursuit; he dresses the pig for the feasts and cuts up the cocoanuts which the boys and women have gathered. The family cooking is done by the men and women both, but the bulk of the work falls upon the boys and young men. The old men spin the cocoanut fibre, and braid it into the native cord which is used for fish lines, fish nets, to sew canoe parts together and to bind all the different parts of a house in place. With the old women who do the bulk of the weaving and making of bark cloth, they supervise the younger children who remain at home. The heavy routine agricultural work falls upon the women who are responsible for the weeding, transplanting, gathering and transportation of the food, and the gathering of the paper mulberry wands from which bark will be peeled for making tapa, of the hibiscus bark and pandanus leaves for weaving mats. The older girls and women also do the routine reef fishing for octopuses, sea eggs, jelly fish, crabs, and other small fry. The younger girls carry the water, care for the lamps (today, except in times of great scarcity when the candle nut and cocoanut oil are resorted to, the natives use kerosene lamps and lanterns), and sweep and arrange the houses. Tasks are all graduated with a fair recognition of abilities which differ with age, and, except in the case of individuals of very high rank, a task is rejected because a younger person has skill enough to perform it, rather than because it is beneath an adult's dignity.

Rank in the village and rank in the household reflect each other, but village rank hardly affects the young children. If a girl's father is a *matai*, the *matai* of the household in which she lives, she has no appeal from his authority. But if some other member of the family is the *matai*, he and his wife may protect her from her father's exactions. In the first case, disagreement with her father means leaving the household and going to live with other relatives; in the second case it may mean only a little internal friction. Also in the family of a high chief or a high talking chief there is more emphasis upon ceremonial, more emphasis upon hospitality. The children are better bred and also much harder worked. But aside from the general quality of a household which is dependent upon the rank of its head, households of very different rank may seem very similar to young children. They are usually more concerned with the temperament of those in authority than with their rank. An uncle in another village who is a very high chief is of much less significance in a child's life than some old woman in her own household who has a frightful temper.

Nevertheless, rank not of birth but of title is very important in Samoa. The status of a village depends upon the rank of its high chief, the prestige of a household depends upon the title of its *matai*. Titles are of two grades, chiefs and talking chiefs; each title carries many other duties and prerogatives besides the headship of a household. And the Samoans find rank a never-failing source of interest. They have invented an elaborate courtesy language which must be used to people of rank; complicated etiquette surrounds each rank in society. Something which concerns their elders so nearly cannot help being indirectly reflected in the lives of some of the children. This is particularly true of the relationship of children to each other in households which hold titles to which some of them will one day attain. How these far-away issues of adult life affect the lives of children and young people can best be understood by following their influence in the lives of particular children.

In the household of a high chief named Malae lived two little girls, Meta, twelve, and Timu, eleven. Meta was a self-possessed, efficient little girl. Malae had taken her from her mother's house—her mother was his cousin—because she showed unusual intelligence and precocity. Timu, on the other hand, was an abnormally shy, backward child, below her age group in intelligence. But Meta's mother was only a distant cousin of Malae. Had she not married into a strange village where Malae was living temporarily, Meta might never have come actively to the notice of her noble relative. And Timu was the only daughter of Malae's dead sister. Her father had been a quarter caste which served to mark her off and increase her self-consciousness. Dancing was an agony to her. She fled precipitately from an elder's admonitory voice. But Timu would be Malae's next *taupo*, princess. She was pretty, the principal recognized qualification, and she came from the distaff side of the house, the preferred descent for a *taupo*. So Meta, the more able in every way, was pushed to the wall, and Timu, miserable over the amount of attention she received, was dragged forward. The mere presence of another more able and enterprising child would probably have emphasized Timu's feeling of inferiority, but this publicity stressed it painfully. Commanded to dance on every occasion, she would pause whenever she caught an onlooker's eye and stand a moment wringing her hands before going on with the dance.

In another household, this same title of Malae's *taupo* played a different role. This was in the household of Malae's paternal aunt who lived with her husband in Malae's guest house in his native village. Her eldest daughter, Pana, held the title of *taupo* of the house of Malae. But Pana was twenty-six, though still unmarried. She must be wedded soon and then another girl must be found to hold the title. Timu would still be too young. Pana had three younger sisters who by birth were supremely eligible to the title. But Mele, the eldest of twenty, was lame, and Pepe of fourteen was blind in one eye and an incorrigible tomboy. The youngest was even younger than Timu. So all three were effectually barred from succession. This fact reacted favourably upon the position of Filita. She was a seventeen-year-old niece of the father of the other children with no possible claims on a title in the house of Malae, but she had lived with her cousins since childhood. Filita was pretty, efficient, adequate, neither lame like Mele nor blind and hoydenish like Pepe. True she could never hope to be *taupo* but neither could they, despite their superior birth, so peace and amity reigned because of her cousins' deficiencies. Still another little girl came within the circle of influence of the title. This was Pula, another little cousin in a third village. But her more distant relationship and possible claims were completely obscured by the fact that she was the only granddaughter of the highest chief in her own village and her becoming the *taupo* of that title was inevitable so that her life was untouched by any other possibility. Thus six girls in addition to the present *taupo* were influenced for good or evil by the possibility of succession to the title. But as there are seldom more than one or two *taupos* in a village, these influences are still fairly circumscribed when compared with the part which rank plays in the lives of boys, for there are usually one or more *matai* names in every relationship group.

Rivalry plays a much stronger part here. In the choice of the *taupo* and the *manaia* (the titular heir-apparent) there is a strong prejudice in favour of blood relationship and also for the choice of the *taupo* from the female and the *manaia* from the male line. But in the interests of efficiency this scheme had been modified, so that most titles were filled by the most able youth from the whole relationship and affinity group. So it was in Alofi. Tui, a chief of importance in the village, had one son, an able intelligent boy. Tui's brothers were dull and inept, no fit successors to the title. One of them had an ill-favoured young son, a stupid, unattractive youngster. There were no other males in the near relationship group. It was assumed that the exceedingly eligible son would succeed his father. And then at twenty he died. The little nephew hardly gave promise of a satisfactory development, and so Tui had his choice of looking outside his village or outside of his near relationship group. Village feeling runs high in Tui's village. Tui's blood relatives lived many villages away. They were strangers. If he did not go to them and search for a promising youth whom he could train as his successor, he must either find an eligible young husband for his daughter or look among his wife's people. Provisionally he took this last course, and his wife's brother's son came to live in his household. In a year, his new father promised the boy, he might assume his dead cousin's name if he showed himself worthy.

In the family of high chief Fua a very different problem presented itself. His was the highest title in the village. He was over sixty and the question of succession was a moot one. The boys in his household consisted of Tata, his eldest son who was illegitimate, Molo and Nua, the sons of his widowed sister, Sisi, his son by his first legal wife (since divorced and remarried on another island), and Tuai, the husband of his niece, the sister of Molo and Nua. And in the house of Fua's eldest brother lived his brother's daughter's son, Alo, a youth of great promise. Here then were enough claimants to produce a lively rivalry. Tuai was the oldest, calm, able, but not sufficiently hopeful to be influenced in his conduct except as it made him more ready to assert the claims of superior age over his wife's younger brothers whose claims were better than his. Next in age came Tata, the sour, beetle-browed bastard, whose chances were negligible as long as there were those of legitimate birth to dispute his left-handed claims. But Tata did not lose hope. Cautious, tortuous-minded, he watched and waited. He was in love with Lotu, the daughter of a talking chief of only medium rank. For one of Fua's sons, Lotu would have been a good match. But as Fua's bastard who wished to be chief, he must marry high or not at all. The two nephews, Molo and Nua, played different hands. Nua, the younger, went away to seek his fortune as a native marine at the Naval Station. This meant a regular income, some knowledge of English, prestige of a sort. Molo, the elder brother, stayed at home and made himself indispensable. He was the *tamafafine*, the child of the distaff side, and it was his role to take his position for granted, the *tamafafine* of the house of Fua, what more could any one ask in the way of immediate prestige. As for the future—his manner was perfect. All of these young men, and likewise Alo, the great-nephew, were members of the *Aumaga*, grown up and ready to assume adult responsibilities. Sisi, the sixteen-year-old legitimate son, was still a boy, slender, diffident, presuming far less upon his position as son and heir-apparent than did his cousin. He was an attractive, intelligent boy. If his father lived until Sisi was twenty-five or thirty, his succession seemed inevitable. Even should his father die sooner, the title might have been held for him. But in this latter possibility there was one danger. Samala, his father's older brother, would have a strong voice in the choice of a successor to the title. And Alo was Samala's adored grandson, the son of his favourite daughter. Alo was the model of all that a young man should be. He eschewed the company of women, stayed much at home and rigorously trained his younger brother and sister. While the other young men played cricket, he sat at Samala's feet and memorized genealogies. He never forgot that he was the son of Sāfuá, the house of Fua. More able than Molo, his claim to the title was practically as good, although within the family group Molo as the child of the distaff side would always outvote him. So Alo was Sisi's most dangerous rival, provided his father died soon. And should Fua live twenty years longer, another complication threatened his succession. Fua had but recently re-married, a woman of very high rank and great wealth who had a five-year-old illegitimate son, Nifo. Thinking always of this child, for she and Fua had no children, she did all that she could to undermine Sisi's position as heir-apparent and there was every chance that as her ascendency over Fua increased with his advancing age, she might have Nifo named as his successor. His illegitimacy and lack of blood tie would be offset by the fact that he was child of the distaff side in the noblest family in the island and would inherit great wealth from his mother.

Of a different character was the problem which confronted Sila, the stepdaughter of Ono, a *matai* of low rank. She was the eldest in a family of seven children. Ono was an old man, decrepit and ineffective. Lefu, Sila's mother and his second wife, was worn out, weary from bearing eleven children. The only adult males in the household were Laisa, Ono's brother, an old man like himself, and Laisa's idle shiftless son, a man of thirty, whose only interest in life was love affairs. He was unmarried and shied away from this responsibility as from all others. The sister next younger than Sila was sixteen. She had left home and lived, now here, now there, among her relatives. Sila was twenty-two. She had been married at sixteen and against her will to a man much older than herself who had beaten her for her childish ways. After two years of married life, she had run away from her husband and gone home to live with her parents, bringing her little two-year-old boy, who was now five years old, with her. At twenty she had had a love affair with a boy of her own village, and borne a daughter who had lived only a few months. After her baby died her lover had deserted her. Sila disliked matrimony. She was conscientious, sharp-tonuged, industrious. She worked tirelessly for her child and her small brothers and sisters. She did not want to marry again. But there were three old people and six children in her household with only herself and her idle cousin to provide for them. And so she said despondently: "I think I will get married to that boy." "Which boy, Sila?" I asked. "The father of my baby who is dead." "But I thought you said you did not want him for a husband?" "No more do I. But I must find someone to care for my family." And indeed there was no other way. Her stepfather's title was a very low one. There were no young men within the family to succeed to it. Her lover was industrious and of even lower degree. The bait of the title would secure a worker for the family.

And so within many households the shadow of nobility falls upon the children, sometimes lightly, sometimes heavily, often long before they are old enough to understand the meaning of these intrusions from the adult world.

PART TWO

Social systems

In any long-standing community the people who make it up are, of course, sorted out into kinds, and the connections each has with each of many other people are kinds too; fathers are a kind, a class, and paternal attitudes toward sons, or specifically toward elder sons, may be a class persistent in that society and susceptible of description. Further, we may find that these kinds of people and their kinds of relationships to others have orderly and coherent connections with one another. Now we are conceiving a system that may at points connect with the ecological system but that is different from it.

ROBERT REDFIELD

INTRODUCTION

Every part of a culture is ultimately related to every other part. For example, in the selection in Part I describing the enculturation of Samoan children, we necessarily dealt with several aspects of the social system such as kinship, the household, and the rank system. Nevertheless, it is often useful to separate out certain aspects of culture for description and study. A *social system* is that part of a culture that governs the interaction among members of a society. It does this by defining various kinds of persons (social roles) and kinds of groups and by specifying rules for how these parts of the social system should behave toward one another. That is, the social system divides a population into a limited number of *categories* (roles and groups), and it associates with each of these categories an expected *plan of action* in relation to other categories. Members of a society can (and often do) violate the rules of their social system; but it is their shared knowledge of these rules that helps them to anticipate the behavior of others.

Social systems vary in both the kinds of categories they employ and the plans they associate with each category. For example, the specialized role of neurosurgeon is limited to certain modern, industrial societies, whereas the universal role of "brother" is associated with very different social expectations in, say, Samoan, Navaho, and American middle-class society. This is why, in a situation of culture shock, the outsider is unable to make sense out of what is going on around him: he is probably trying to understand interaction in terms of his own social system, and his expectations are (therefore) constantly upset. If he wishes to predict what members of the host society will do, and what they expect him to do, he must somehow learn what categories they are using and the plans that go with each category.

The social systems described in the selections in this part represent a tiny sample of the social systems known to anthropologists. The Book of Ruth dates back to the fifth century B.C., and the society portrayed is clearly very different from our own; yet the motives of the actors are familiar, and we can understand how the expectations associated with kinship roles affect the behavior of Naomi, Ruth, and Boaz.

Iceland was settled by Vikings who came there from Norway in the ninth century A.D. *Njal's Saga* is a great prose epic composed during the twelfth century but telling of actual events that took place several generations earlier. Kinship relations were very important in Icelandic society; yet men also had considerable choice of how to act, and they attached themselves to leaders whose personal qualities attracted them. Violations of social rules can, by the consequences that follow from them, often be quite revealing of the ways a social system works. In this brief excerpt we learn about some of the ways disputes started, sides were taken, and arguments settled.

H. S. Bennett's imaginative re-creation of peasant life in medieval England presents manor life as a miniature social system, but one upon which the prestige and authority of church and aristocracy constantly impinge. The peasants were continually drawn out of their household- and field-centered existence by representatives of institutions that extended far beyond the peasants' limited social horizon. Oliver Statler's semifictional account of events at a Japanese inn late in the seventeenth century also depicts a social system in which differences of rank pervaded nearly all interactions, and it gives a revealing account of two-way culture shock.

On the other hand, the selection by Oscar Lewis gives us a picture of rural Mexican life that is based on his own first-hand observations. No one family is "typical" of an entire culture, but careful study of the daily life of the Martínez family certainly gives a feeling for the quality of existence in this setting. (A longer account of this same family is found in Lewis' book *Pedro Martínez.*)

Finally, in *The Inland Whale*, Theodora Kroeber relates a tale of the Yurok Indians which is as revealing in its social details as it is touching in its emotional contents. Many students have commented on the similarity of Yurok culture to American culture, at least in certain respects. Certainly, this story of the poor boy who makes good as a consequence of thrift and industry should strike a familiar chord with many readers, even though the general circumstances of Yurok life were very different from anything most of us have experienced.

The trials of a young widow

(THE BOOK OF RUTH)

The Book of Ruth was written down several centuries after the events its narrates. Though the characters are probably fictional, the customs and social relations described are most likely historically accurate. Archaeologists in particular have increasingly found the Bible to be an accurate guide to the location of ancient cities and peoples.

Chapter 1

Now it came to pass in the days when the judges ruled, that there was a famine in the land. And a certain man of Beth-lehem-judah went to sojourn in the country of Moab, he, and his wife, and his two sons. And the name of the man was Elimelech, and the name of his wife Naomi, and the name of his two sons Mahlon and Chilion, Ephrathites of Beth-lehem-judah. And they came into the country of Moab, and continued there. And Elimelech Naomi's husband died; and she was left, and her two sons. And they took them wives of the women of Moab; the name of the one was Orpah, and the name of the other Ruth: and they dwelled there about ten years. And Mahlon and Chilion died also both of them; and the woman was left of her two sons and her husband. Then she arose with her daughters-in-law, that she might return from the country of Moab: for she had heard in the country of Moab how that the LORD had visited his people in giving them bread. Wherefore she went forth out of the place where she was, and her two daughters-in-law with her; and they went on the way to return unto the land of Judah. And Naomi said unto her two daughters-in-law, "Go, return each to her mother's house: the LORD deal kindly with you, as ye have dealt with the dead, and with me. The LORD grant you that ye may find rest, each of you in the house of her husband." Then she kissed them; and they lifted up their voice, and wept. And they said unto her, "Surely we will return with thee unto thy people." And Naomi said, "Turn again, my daughters: why will ye go with me? are there yet any more sons in my womb, that they may be

---

"The Book of Ruth," *The Reader's Bible* (New York: Oxford University Press, 1951).

your husbands? Turn again, my daughters, go your way; for I am too old to have an husband. If I should say, I have hope, if I should have an husband also tonight, and should also bear sons; would ye tarry for them till they were grown? would ye stay for them from having husbands? nay, my daughters; for it grieveth me much for your sakes that the hand of the LORD is gone out against me." And they lifted up their voice, and wept again: and Orpah kissed her mother-in-law; but Ruth clave unto her. And she said, "Behold, thy sister-in-law is gone back unto her people, and unto her gods: return thou after thy sister-in-law." And Ruth said, "Intreat me not to leave thee, or to return from following after thee: for whither thou goest, I will go; and where thou lodgest, I will lodge: thy people shall be my people, and thy God my God: where thou diest, will I die, and there will I be buried: the LORD do so to me, and more also, if aught but death part thee and me." When she saw that she was steadfastly minded to go with her, then she left speaking unto her. So they two went until they came to Beth-lehem. And it came to pass, when they were come to Beth-lehem, that all the city was moved about them, and they said, "Is this Naomi?" And she said unto them, "Call me not Naomi, call me Mara: for the Almighty hath dealt very bitterly with me.* I went out full, and the LORD hath brought me home again empty: why then call ye me Naomi, seeing the LORD hath testified against me, and the Almighty hath afflicted me?" So Naomi returned, and Ruth the Moabitess, her daughter-in-law, with her, which returned out of the country of Moab: and they came to Beth-lehem in the beginning of barley harvest.

Chapter 2

And Naomi had a kinsman of her husband's, a mighty man of wealth, of the family of Elimelech; and his name was Boaz. And Ruth the Moabitess said unto Naomi, "Let me now go to the field, and glean ears of corn after him in whose sight I shall find grace." And she said unto her, "Go, my daughter." And she went, and came, and gleaned in the field after the reapers: and her hap was to light on a part of the field belonging unto Boaz, who was of the kindred of Elimelech. And, behold, Boaz came from Beth-lehem, and said unto the reapers, "The LORD be with you." And they answered him, "The LORD bless thee." Then said Boaz unto his servant that was set over the reapers, "Whose damsel is this?" And the servant that was set over the reapers answered and said, "It is the

---

*Naomi means "sweetness," but the name Mara signifies "bitterness." [Ed.]

Moabitish damsel that came back with Naomi out of the country of Moab: and she said, 'I pray you, let me glean and gather after the reapers among the sheaves': so she came, and hath continued even from the morning until now, that she tarried a little in the house." Then said Boaz unto Ruth, "Hearest thou not, my daughter? Go not to glean in another field, neither go from hence, but abide here fast by my maidens: let thine eyes be on the field that they do reap, and go thou after them: have I not charged the young men that they shall not touch thee? and when thou art athirst, go unto the vessels, and drink of that which the young men have drawn." Then she fell on her face, and bowed herself to the ground, and said unto him, "Why have I found grace in thine eyes, that thou shouldest take knowledge of me, seeing I am a stranger?" And Boaz answered and said unto her, "It hath fully been shewed me, all that thou hast done unto thy mother-in-law since the death of thine husband: and how thou hast left thy father and thy mother, and the land of thy nativity, and art come unto a people which thou knewest not heretofore. The LORD recompense thy work, and a full reward be given thee of the LORD God of Israel, under whose wings thou art come to trust." Then she said, "Let me find favour in thy sight, my lord; for that thou hast comforted me, and for that thou hast spoken friendly unto thine handmaid, though I be not like unto one of thine handmaidens." And Boaz said unto her, "At mealtime come thou hither, and eat of the bread, and dip thy morsel in the vinegar." And she sat beside the reapers: and he reached her parched corn, and she did eat, and was sufficed, and left. And when she was risen up to glean, Boaz commanded his young men, saying, "Let her glean even among the sheaves, and reproach her not: and let fall also some of the handfuls of purpose for her, and leave them, that she may glean them, and rebuke her not." So she gleaned in the field until even, and beat out that she had gleaned: and it was about an ephah of barley. And she took it up, and went into the city: and her mother-in-law saw what she had gleaned: and she brought forth, and gave to her that she had reserved after she was sufficed. And her mother-in-law said unto her, "Where hast thou gleaned today? and where wroughtest thou? blessed be he that did take knowledge of thee." And she shewed her mother-in-law with whom she had wrought, and said, "The man's name with whom I wrought today is Boaz." And Naomi said unto her daughter-in-law, "Blessed be he of the LORD, who hath not left off his kindness to the living and to the dead." And Naomi said unto her, "The man is near of kin unto us, one of our next kinsmen." And Ruth the Moabitess said, "He said unto me also, 'Thou shalt keep fast by my young men, until they have ended all my harvest.'" And Naomi said unto Ruth her daughter-in-law, "It is good, my daughter, that thou go out with his maidens, that they meet thee not in any other field." So she kept fast by the maidens of Boaz to glean unto the end of barley harvest and of wheat harvest; and dwelt with her mother-in-law.

Chapter 3

Then Naomi her mother-in-law said unto her, "My daughter, shall I not seek rest for thee, that it may be well with thee? And now is not Boaz of our kindred, with whose maidens thou wast? Behold, he winnoweth barley tonight in the threshingfloor. Wash thyself therefore, and anoint thee, and put thy raiment upon thee, and get thee down to the floor: but make not thyself known unto the man, until he shall have done eating and drinking. And it shall be, when he lieth down, that thou shalt mark the place where he shall lie, and thou shalt go in, and uncover his feet, and lay thee down; and he will tell thee what thou shalt do." And she said unto her, "All that thou sayest unto me I will do." And she went down unto the floor, and did according to all that her mother-in-law bade her. And when Boaz had eaten and drunk, and his heart was merry, he went to lie down at the end of the heap of corn: and she came softly, and uncovered his feet, and laid her down. And it came to pass at midnight, that the man was afraid, and turned himself: and, behold, a woman lay at his feet. And he said, "Who art thou?" And she answered, "I am Ruth thine handmaid: spread therefore thy skirt over thine handmaid; for thou art a near kinsman." And he said, "Blessed be thou of the LORD, my daughter: for thou hast shewed more kindness in the latter end than at the beginning, inasmuch as thou followedst not young men, whether poor or rich. And now, my daughter, fear not; I will do to thee all that thou requirest: for all the city of my people doth know that thou art a virtuous woman. And now it is true that I am thy near kinsman: howbeit there is a kinsman nearer than I. Tarry this night, and it shall be in the morning, that if he will perform unto thee the part of a kinsman, well; let him do the kinsman's part: but if he will not do the part of kinsman to thee, then will I do the part of a kinsman to thee, as the LORD liveth: lie down until the morning." And she lay at his feet until the morning: and she rose up before one could know another. And he said, "Let it not be known that a woman came into the floor." Also he said, "Bring the veil that thou hast upon thee, and hold it." And when she held it, he measured six measures of barley, and laid it on her: and she went into the city. And when she came to her mother-in-law, she said, "Who art thou, my daughter?" And she told her all that the man had done to her. And she said, "These six measures of barley gave he me; for he said to me, 'Go not empty unto thy mother-in-law.'" Then said she, "Sit still, my daughter, until thou know how the matter will fall: for the man will not be in rest, until he have finished the thing this day."

Chapter 4

Then went Boaz up to the gate, and sat him down there: and, behold, the kinsman of whom Boaz spake came by; unto whom he said, "Ho, such a one! turn aside, sit down here." And he turned aside, and sat down. And he took ten men of the elders of the city, and said, "Sit ye down here." And they sat down. And he said unto the kinsman, "Naomi, that is come again out of the country of Moab, selleth a parcel of land, which was our brother Elimelech's: and I thought to advertise thee, saying, Buy it before the inhabitants, and before the elders of my people. If thou wilt redeem it, redeem it: but if thou wilt not redeem it, then tell me, that I may know: for there is none to redeem it beside thee; and I am after thee." And he said, "I will redeem it." Then said Boaz, "What day thou buyest the field of the hand of Naomi, thou must buy it also of Ruth the Moabitess, the wife of the dead, to raise up the name of the dead* upon his inheritance." And the kinsman said, "I cannot redeem it for myself, lest I mar mine own inheritance: redeem thou my right to thyself; for I cannot redeem it." Now this was the manner in former time in Israel concerning redeeming and concerning changing, for to confirm all things; a man plucked off his shoe, and gave it to his neighbour: and this was a testimony in Israel. Therefore the kinsman said unto Boaz, "Buy it for thee." So he drew off his shoe. And Boaz said unto the elders, and unto all the people, "Ye are witnesses this day, that I have bought all that was Elimelech's, and all that was Chilion's and Mahlon's, of the hand of Naomi. Moreover Ruth the Moabitess, the wife of Mahlon, have I purchased to be my wife, to raise up the name of the dead upon his inheritance, that the name of the dead be not cut off from among his brethren, and from the gate of his place: ye are witnesses this day." And all the people that were in the gate, and the elders, said, "We are witnesses. The LORD make the woman that is come into thine house like Rachel and like Leah, which two did build the house of Israel: and do thou worthily in Ephratah, and be famous in Beth-lehem: and let thy house be like the house of Pharez, whom Tamar bare unto Judah, of the seed which the LORD shall give thee of this young woman." So Boaz took Ruth, and she was his wife: and when he went in unto her, the LORD gave her conception, and she bare a son. And the women said unto Naomi, "Blessed be the LORD, which hath not left thee this day without a kinsman, that his name may be famous in Israel. And he shall be unto thee a restorer of thy life, and a nourisher of thine old age: for thy daughter-in-law, which loveth thee, which is better to thee than seven sons, hath borne him." And Naomi took the child, and laid it in her bosom, and became

---

* i.e., to father children in behalf of Ruth's dead husband. [Ed.]

nurse unto it. And the women her neighbours gave it a name, saying, "There is a son born to Naomi"; and they called his name Obed: he is the father of Jesse, the father of David.

Now these are the generations of Pharez: Pharez begat Hezron, and Hezron begat Ram, and Ram begat Amminadab, and Amminadab begat Nahshon, and Nahshon begat Salmon, and Salmon begat Boaz, and Boaz begat Obed, and Obed begat Jesse, and Jesse begat David.*

---

* King of Israel, 1010–974 B.C. [Ed.]

The Viking temper

(NJAL'S SAGA)

This excerpt from one of the great Icelandic sagas presents a vivid picture of social relations among the proud and combative Vikings. The main characters are Njal Thorgeirsson, his family, and his friend Gunnar of Hlidarend, the great warrior. Although the outcome of the story is tragic for both Gunnar and Njal, the present episode ends on a note of temporary peace. (The Althing, to which several references are made, is the Icelandic parliament.)

A man called Gizur Teitsson, known as Gizur the White, lived at Mosfell. He was a powerful chieftain.

He had a cousin called Geir the Priest, who lived at Hlid. He and Gizur acted together in everything.

At this time, Mord Valgardsson was living at Hof, in the Rang River Plains. He had a vicious, cunning nature. His father, Valgard the Grey, was abroad, and his mother, Unn, was dead by now. Mord bitterly envied Gunnar of Hlidarend. He was a wealthy man.

A man called Otkel Skarfsson lived at Kirkby. He was a kinsman of Gizur the White. He was prosperous, and had a son called Thorgeir, who was a promising young man.

Otkel had a friend called Skamkel, who lived at Lesser-Hof. He, too, was prosperous, but he was a malicious man, a liar, and a very unpleasant person to have any dealings with.

Otkel had a brother called Hallkel living with him, a tall, strong man. There was another brother called Hallbjorn the White, who had once brought to Iceland an Irish slave called Melkolf, who was not much liked. Hallbjorn came to stay with Otkel, bringing Melkolf with him.

Melkolf kept saying how happy he would be if Otkel were his master. Otkel liked him, and gave him a knife and belt and a set of clothing; and the slave did anything that Otkel wished. So Otkel asked Hallbjorn to sell him the slave; Hallbjorn said that he could have him for nothing, but

---

Njal's Saga, trans. by Magnus Magnusson and Herman Pálsson (Baltimore: Penguin Books, 1960), pp. 119–130 (sections 46–51). Reprinted by permission of the publisher.

added that he was not quite the treasure that Otkel imagined. As soon as Melkolf came into Otkel's service, his work grew worse and worse. Otkel frequently complained to Hallbjorn the White that he thought the slave lazy; Hallbjorn replied that Melkolf had worse faults than that.

This was a time of great famine in Iceland, and all over the country people were going short of hay and food. Gunnar shared out his own stocks with many people, and turned no one away empty-handed while they lasted, until he himself ran short of both hay and food. Then he asked Kolskegg to accompany him on a journey; together with Thrain Sigfusson and Lambi Sigurdarson they went to Kirkby and asked Otkel to come out. Otkel greeted them; Gunnar responded well to the greeting and said, "The fact is that I have come to buy hay and food, if you have any."

"I have both," said Otkel, "but I will sell you neither."

"Will you then give me some?" asked Gunnar. "And trust me to be generous in repayment?"

"No," said Otkel. He was being encouraged by Skamkel's malicious promptings.

Thrain Sigfusson said, "It would serve him right if we took it by force and paid him what it was worth."

"The men of Mosfell would have to be dead and buried," said Skamkel, "before you Sigfussons managed to rob them."

"I won't have anything to do with robbery," said Gunnar.

"Would you like to buy a slave from me?" asked Otkel.

"I have no objection to that," said Gunnar. He bought Melkolf from Otkel, and went back home.

Njal heard about all this, and said, "It was a bad deed to refuse to sell to Gunnar. There is little hope for others there, when men like Gunnar cannot buy."

"Why do you have to talk so much about it?" said Bergthora. "It would be more generous just to give Gunnar the hay and food he needs, since you are short of neither."

"That is perfectly true," said Njal. "I shall certainly let him have something."

He went up to Thorolfsfell with his sons, and they loaded fifteen horses with hay and five others with food. Then they went to Hlidarend and asked Gunnar to come out. Gunnar welcomed them warmly.

Njal said, "Here is some hay and food I want to give you. And I want you to turn to me and never to anyone else if ever you find yourself in need."

"Your gifts are good," said Gunnar, "but I value even more highly your true friendship and that of your sons."

With that Njal returned home. The spring wore on.

In the summer, Gunnar rode to the Althing. A large number of men from Sida, in the east, had stayed with him overnight, and he invited them to be his guests again on the way back from the Althing; they accepted the invitation, and they all rode off to the Althing. Njal and his sons were also there. It was an uneventful gathering that year.

Meanwhile, at Hlidarend, Hallgerd had a word with the slave Melkolf.*

"I have an errand for you," she said. "You are to ride to Kirkby."

"What am I to go there for?" he asked.

"You are to steal from there enough food to load two horses, particularly butter and cheese, and then set fire to the storehouse. Everyone will think it happened through carelessness, and no one will suspect that there has been a theft."

"I may have done bad things," said Melkolf, "but I have never been a thief."

"Listen to it!" said Hallgerd. "You pretend to be innocent when you're not only a thief but a murderer as well. Don't you dare refuse, or I'll have you killed."

He felt sure that she would do so if he did not go. That night he took two horses, put on their pack-harness, and went off to Kirkby. The dog there, recognizing him, did not bark, but ran out to welcome him. Melkolf went to the storehouse, opened it up, and loaded the two horses with food from it; then he burned the shed and killed the dog.

On his return journey along Rang River, his shoe-thong broke. He took his knife to repair it, but left the knife and belt lying there. When he reached Hlidarend he noticed that his knife was missing, but did not dare to go back to fetch it. He brought the food to Hallgerd; she was pleased.

Next morning the people of Kirkby came out of doors and saw the great damage that had been done. A messenger was sent to the Althing to tell Otkel, who took the loss calmly and said that it must have been due to the fact that the storehouse adjoined the kitchen. And that was what everyone else thought must have caused it.

When the Althing ended, a large number of people rode to Hlidarend. Hallgerd set food on the table, and brought in cheese and butter. Gunnar knew that no such provisions had been in stock, and asked Hallgerd where they had come from.

"From a source that should not spoil your appetite," said Hallgerd. "And besides, it's not a man's business to bother about kitchen matters."

Gunnar grew angry. "It will be an evil day when I become a thief's accomplice," he said, and slapped her on the face.

Hallgerd said that she would remember that slap and pay him back if

---

Hallgerd was Gunnar's strong-willed wife. She often made trouble for him. [Ed.]

she could. They both left the room. The tables were cleared and mea
was brought in instead. Everyone thought that this was because the mea
was considered to have been more honestly obtained. After that, th
people who had been at the Althing went on their way.

Skamkel happened to be looking for sheep up by Rang River. H
noticed something glinting on the path, and dismounted to pick it up. I
was a knife and belt, both of which he thought he recognized. He too
them to Kirkby. Otkel was outside and welcomed him warmly.

"Do you recognize these things at all?" asked Skamkel.

"Certainly I know them," said Otkel.

"Whose are they?" asked Skamkel.

"They belong to Melkolf the slave," replied Otkel.

"We must get others to identify them too," said Skamkel, "for I an
now going to give you some really good advice."

They showed the articles to many people, all of whom recognize
them.

"What do you plan to do now?" asked Skamkel.

Otkel replied, "We shall go over to see Mord Valgardsson and ask hi
opinion."

They went to Hof and showed Mord the articles, and asked if h
recognized them.

"Yes," said Mord, "but what about them? Do you think that there i
anything of yours to be found at Hlidarend?"

"This is a delicate matter to handle," said Skamkel, "when we are u
against such powerful opponents."

"That's true," said Mord. "But I know a thing or two about Gunnar'
household that neither of you know."

"We will pay you for it," they said, "if you will look into the matter.

"The money would be dearly earned," said Mord. "But perhap
I shall look into it after all."

They gave him three marks of silver for his promise of help. Mor
then advised them to send women round the district offering small ware
to housewives, and see with what they were paid—"because," he ex
plained, "people are inclined to rid themselves first of any stolen good
that may be in their possession; and that's what will happen now if
crime is involved. The women are to show me what they were given i
each place, and then, if the evidence is established, I want nothing mo
to do with the matter."

They agreed on this, and then Skamkel and Otkel went back hom
Mord sent some women out round the district. They were away for
fortnight, and came back with bulging packs. Mord asked them whe
they had been given the most; they replied that it had been at Hlidaren

and that Hallgerd had been particularly generous. Mord asked what they had been given there. "Cheese," they replied. Mord asked to see it, and they showed it to him; there were a number of slices.

Mord took charge of the cheese, and a little later he went to see Otkel. He asked Otkel to fetch his wife's cheese-mould, and when it was brought he laid the slices into it. They fitted perfectly. They discovered that the women had been given a whole cheese.

Mord said, "You can now see that Hallgerd must have stolen it." They assembled all the evidence, and with that Mord said that he had fulfilled his part of the bargain, and took his leave.

Kolskegg had a talk with Gunnar, and said, "I have bad news. Everyone is saying that Hallgerd has committed theft and was responsible for all the damage that was done at Kirkby."

Gunnar said that he thought it all too likely. "What should we do now?" he asked.

Kolskegg said, "Obviously you are the one who has to make amends for your wife, and I think the best plan is to go and see Otkel and make him a good offer."

"That is a good suggestion," replied Gunnar. "So be it."

Soon afterwards, Gunnar sent for Thrain Sigfusson and Lambi Sigurdarson, and they came at once. Gunnar told them where he was planning to go; they approved. They rode off in a group of twelve, and when they reached Kirkby they asked for Otkel.

Skamkel was there too, and he said to Otkel, "I shall go out with you; we shall need to have all our wits about us. I want to be closest to you when your need is greatest, as it is at this very moment. I would advise you to stand on your dignity."

Then they went outside—Otkel, Skamkel, Hallkel, and Hallbjorn the White. They greeted Gunnar, who returned the greeting. Otkel asked him where he was going.

"No farther than here," said Gunnar. "The purpose of my visit is to tell you that the disastrous loss you suffered here was caused by my wife and that slave I bought from you."

"I'm not surprised," said Hallbjorn.

Gunnar said, "Now I want to make you a fair offer. I suggest that the best men in the district should assess the compensation."

"That sounds well," said Skamkel, "but it certainly is not a fair offer. You are popular with the farmers round here, but Otkel is not."

Gunnar said, "Then I offer to assess your compensation myself, here and now. With it I will pledge my friendship, and I will pay the entire sum at once. I offer to pay you double the amount of your losses."

Skamkel said to Otkel, "Don't accept. It would be beneath you to allow him self-judgement when you are entitled to it yourself."

Otkel announced, "I am not going to give you self-judgement, Gunnar."

Gunnar said, "I recognize the influence of others here, who will some day get the reward they deserve. But come, assess the compensation yourself, then."

Otkel leaned over towards Skamkel and said, "What do I answer now?"

"Say that it is a handsome offer," said Skamkel, "but refer your decision to Gizur the White and Geir the Priest; then many people will say that you are just like your grandfather Hallkel, who was a great champion."

Otkel announced, "This is a handsome offer, Gunnar, but nevertheless I want you to give me time to consult Gizur the White and Geir the Priest."

"Do what you like," said Gunnar. "But some would say that you cannot recognize honour when you are being shown it, if you refuse the terms I have offered you."

With that, Gunnar rode back home. As soon as he was gone, Hallbjorn said, "What a sorry contrast in men. Gunnar made you good offers, and you refused to accept any of them. What do you expect to gain by fighting against Gunnar, a man without equal? Still, he is the sort of man who would let these offers stand if you decided to accept them after all; my advice to you is to go to see Gizur the White and Geir the Priest without delay."

Otkel had his horse fetched, and prepared himself for the journey. His eye-sight was poor. Skamkel walked with him a short way and then said, "I was amazed that your brother did not offer to do this task for you. I want to offer to go in your place, for I know that you find travelling difficult."

"I accept your offer," said Otkel. "But be sure to keep strictly to the truth."

"I will indeed," said Skamkel.

He took Otkel's horse and travelling-cloak, and Otkel walked back home.

Hallbjorn was outside, and said to Otkel, "It is bad to have a slave for your bosom-friend. We are always going to regret that you turned back. It is stupidity itself to send such a liar on a mission which you might well call a matter of life and death."

"You would be terrified if Gunnar raised his halberd," said Otkel, "if you are like this already."

"I don't know who would be the more frightened then," said Hallbjorn, "but one day you will learn that Gunnar wastes no time over taking aim with his halberd, once his anger is aroused."

"You are all cowering, except Skamkel," said Otkel.

By this time they were both furious.

Skamkel arrived at Mosfell and repeated to Gizur the White all the offers that had been made.

"It seems to me," said Gizur, "that these were generous offers. Why did Otkel not accept them?"

"It was chiefly because everyone wished to pay you a compliment," replied Skamkel. "That's why Otkel delayed his own decision, for yours will undoubtedly be the best for all concerned."

Skamkel stayed at Mosfell overnight. Gizur sent a messenger for Geir the Priest, who came over early in the morning. Gizur told him what had happened. "What do you think should be done now?" he asked.

"What you yourself must already have decided—to settle as best we can," replied Geir. "And now we shall make Skamkel repeat the whole story once more and see how he tells it this time."

After this was done, Gizur said, "Your version must be correct after all, although to me you look thoroughly dishonest. Appearances must be deceptive indeed if you prove to be a man of integrity."

Skamkel rode off home. He went first to Kirkby and called Otkel out. Otkel welcomed him warmly. Skamkel said that he brought greetings from Gizur and Geir; and he added, "There is no need to be secretive about our case. It is their wish that no settlement be accepted. Gizur's advice was that we go and serve a summons* on Gunnar for receiving stolen goods, and on Hallgerd for theft."

"We shall do exactly what they advise," said Otkel.

Skamkel added, "What impressed them most of all was the decisive way you behaved. I made you out to be a very great man."

Otkel told his brothers all about this. Hallbjorn said, "This is all an enormous lie."

Time passed, until the last day for serving an Althing summons arrived. Otkel called on his brothers and Skamkel to ride with him to Hlidarend to deliver the summonses. Hallbjorn agreed to go, but said that they would have cause to regret the journey in the course of time. In a group of twelve they rode to Hlidarend; Gunnar was out of doors when they reached the home-meadow, but did not notice them until they had come right up to the house. He did not go inside, and Otkel at once shouted out the summons.

---

* The last day for serving an Althing summons was four weeks before the first day of the Althing. The Althing met on the eleventh Thursday of summer, i.e. late in June; the Icelandic summer was reckoned from the middle of April to the middle of October. *Translators' note.*

When it was finished, Skamkel asked, "Was that correct, farmer?"

"You should know best," said Gunnar. "But one day I shall remind you of this visit, Skamkel, and of the part you have played."

"That won't hurt us much," said Skamkel, "if your halberd isn't up."

Gunnar was furious. He walked inside and told Kolskegg what had happened. Kolskegg said, "It's a pity we were not outside with you. Their journey would have turned very sour on them if we had been at hand."

"All in good time," said Gunnar. "But this journey will never be to their credit."

A little later he went and told Njal. Njal said, "Do not let this worry you, for it will turn out greatly to your credit before the Althing is over. We shall all support you to the full with advice and help."

Gunnar thanked him and rode back home.

Otkel rode to the Althing with his brothers and Skamkel.

Gunnar rode to the Althing accompanied by all the Sigfussons and by Njal and his sons; they all went about together, and it was said that no other group there looked as formidable. One day Gunnar went to the Dales booth. Hrut and Hoskuld were standing beside the booth, and they welcomed Gunnar warmly. Gunnar told them all about the case.

"What does Njal advise?" asked Hrut.

"He told me to see you two brothers," replied Gunnar, "and tell you that he would agree to whatever you suggest."

"I gather, then," said Hrut, "that he wants me, as your kinsman by marriage, to give my advice. Very well. You must challenge Gizur the White to single combat, if they don't offer you self-judgement, and Kolskegg must challenge Geir the Priest. We can get others to deal with Otkel and his men; our combined force is now so strong that you can accomplish whatever you want to do."

Gunnar walked back to his own booth and told Njal.

Ulf Aur-Priest got wind of these plans and told Gizur. Gizur then asked Otkel, "Who advised you to take Gunnar to court?"

"Skamkel told me that it was the advice given by you and Geir the Priest," said Otkel.

"Where is that lying wretch now?" asked Gizur.

"He is ill in bed, in his booth," replied Otkel.

"And may he never rise from it," said Gizur. "We must all go, at once, to see Gunnar and offer him self-judgement; but I'm not so sure that he will accept it now."

There were many harsh things said to Skamkel, who remained in his sick-bed throughout the Althing. Gizur and his companions set off for Gunnar's booth. They were seen approaching and someone went in to tell

Gunnar; Gunnar and all his men came outside and formed up. Gizur, who was in the lead, said, "We have come to offer you self-judgement in this case, Gunnar."

"Then it cannot have been your idea to serve summons on me," said Gunnar.

"No, it was not my idea," said Gizur, "nor Geir's either."

"Then you will want to give me proof to clear yourself," said Gunnar.

"What proof do you want?" asked Gizur.

"I want you to swear an oath."

"Certainly," said Gizur, "if you agree to accept self-judgement."

"That was my original offer," said Gunnar, "but I feel that the issue has become much graver now."

Njal said, "You should not refuse the offer of self-judgement. The graver the issue, the greater is the honour involved."

Gunnar said, "I shall accept self-judgement, then, to please my friends. But I advise Otkel not to give me any more trouble."

Hoskuld and Hrut were sent for, and they came. Then Gizur and Geir the Priest swore their oaths, and Gunnar made his assessment of the compensation without consulting anyone.

Announcing his decision, he said, "This is my finding: there is liability for the cost of the storehouse and the food it contained; but for the slave's crime I will pay you nothing, because you concealed his faults. Instead, I am going to hand him back to you, on the principle that the ears fit best where they grew. In addition, I find that you served summons on me with intent to disgrace me, and for that I award myself damages to the exact value of the house and its contents destroyed in the fire.

"But if you would prefer not to accept a settlement at all, I shall offer no objections; for I have another plan to meet just such a contingency, and I shall not hesitate to carry it out."

"We agree that you should make no payment," said Gizur, "but we ask that you become Otkel's friend."

"Never, as long as I live," said Gunnar. "He can have Skamkel's friendship; that is what he has always relied on."

"Anyway," said Gizur, "we agree to conclude a settlement, even though you alone dictate the conditions."

They shook hands on all the terms of the settlement. Gunnar said to Otkel, "It would be more advisable for you to go and live with your kinsmen. But if you insist on staying on at Kirkby, take care not to interfere with me again."

Gizur said, "That is sensible advice; let him follow it."

Gunnar won great credit from the outcome of this case, and afterwards people went home from the Althing. Gunnar went back to his farming at Hlidarend; and everything was quiet for a while.

H. S. BENNETT

English peasants of the fourteenth century

H. S. Bennett is emeritus university reader in English at Cambridge and a life fellow of Emmanuel College. He is an outstanding expert on English social history during the Middle Ages. Among his major works are *The Pastons and Their England*, *England from Chaucer to Caxton*, and *Six Medieval Men and Women*. The following account of events on an English manor is fictionalized but based on fact.

The sun rose early, for it was late June, but not much earlier than the peasants of the little village of Belcome, in the year 1320. As the light strengthened, bit by bit the village became visible, and the confused medley, in which here a roof and there a bit of wall stood out, began to arrange itself as a narrow street with flimsy houses dotted about in little groups. In the centre of it all the stone-built church loomed up high and very new-looking above everything about it, and made the peasants' houses appear small and insignificant. On closer view, the village was seen to radiate from the church and down each of the winding ways that led up to it the peasants had built their homes. There they stood, some neat and trim, with their thatched roofs and roughly finished walls in good repair, while others were dilapidated and showed evident signs of neglect and decay. The larger houses stood a little back from the lane, so that the ground in front of each of them was roughly enclosed and set with young cabbage, onions and parsley, and here and there a few herbs were growing along the sides of the pathway to the house. Most of them had a rudely constructed shed or lean-to at the back of the house, and running away from this stretched another enclosed piece of ground. This was mainly broken up and planted with vegetables, and both here and in the rough grass beyond there were a few apple and cherry trees. At the bottom of the garden where it ran down to the stream the pigs had their styes, and any villager fortunate enough to own a cow tethered it there in among the rankly growing grass. Smaller houses had meagre plots about

---

H. S. Bennett, *Life on the English Manor* (New York: Macmillan, 1938), pp. 4–25.

them, with sparse room for cabbage or onion, and only rarely a pig or a few fowls.

Within most of these houses men were stirring, and before long began to appear at their cottage doors, taking a look at the sky before they ate a brief meal (if such it might be called) of a lump of bread and a draught of ale. Then they came out again, fetched their scythes and rakes from the sheds, and started off down the street, so that for a few minutes the noisy chatter and greetings of neighbours broke the silence. They soon passed by the church and came out into open country, for no hedges or fences were to be seen. One large tract, however, had clearly been cultivated recently, for as they passed they saw how it was divided into narrow plots, each with grassy raised strips dividing it from its neighbours. Now, however, this field was fallow, and, early as it was, one of their fellows was there before them, and was guarding the sheep which were quietly feeding on such sparse vegetation as was to be found, for the first ploughing had already taken place, and next month any weeds the sheep might leave would all be ploughed in.

A little farther on they passed a stone cross. Almost unconsciously (some even in perfunctory fashion) they crossed themselves, and a moment later turned from the main path to follow a track which led to a piece of meadow land. This, unlike the fallow, was enclosed on three sides with a hedge, whilst a little stream formed its other boundary. On entering the field the peasants broke up in little groups, some going to one and some to another part of the meadow, for amongst the long grass there were little pegs and twigs marking off one portion of the field from another. By this time the sun was well up and the dew was drying rapidly as they prepared for work. The wide blade of the scythe was sharpened with the whetstone, and then they turned, and with rhythmic movement began to mow the grass in wide sweeping swathes.

In one corner of the field John Wilde and his two sons, Richard and Roger, kept to their task for some time without pause. The younger son moved steadily across the strip, turning the hay which had been cut on the previous morning, while his brother Richard worked on side by side with his father at the mowing. Save for a pause when the scythes were re-sharpened they worked without resting and with but little to say, for there was much to do and time was short, since this was Sunday, and ere long they would have to leave their work for Mass. Indeed, they were fortunate to be on the field at all on such a day, but Sir William, their vicar, had always been lenient in times of harvest; and, although he looked with concern at such work, he did not absolutely forbid it, so long as the Mass itself were not neglected. So all three continued until the sun was getting well up in the heavens, when they stopped their work and left the field together with many others. As they passed the church John glanced at the Mass clock on its wall near the door, and saw by the shadow of its style that they had good time before the service, as it was not yet eight.

During their absence the house had not been untended, and after a while the good wife Agnes and her daughter Alice appeared from a room which led out of the main living room. Alice ran out in the garden close, and soon the clucking of the hens was heard, and a little later she returned and set down on the wooden bench inside the door a rough earthenware jar of milk which she had just taken from the cow. Meanwhile, her mother had brushed up the embers and had piled together the kindling and a few logs, and already a fire was burning cleanly, and over it hung a large metal pot of water. Then she and her daughter went into the small inner room, which was cleaner and less sooty than its neighbour, and pulled back the thick coverlets and remade the only two beds that stood there. Once this was done, the rough earthen floors of both rooms were swept out with a brush of large twigs, and then the trestle-table was put in its place near the side of the room. Some bread and a little ale satisfied Agnes' hunger, while Alice took a drink of the milk she had just brought in. All being done, they turned to prepare for Mass. A large wooden tub on the trestle-table served for a washbowl, and after a little washing they occupied themselves for some time in plaiting and arranging their hair, before they drew out of a wooden chest, that stood at the foot of the bed, the bright coloured dresses which they wore only on Sundays and festivals. There were other childish garments in the chest, but they had not been worn these many days, for they were those of the two little girls, both dead now for ten years and more, one of the plague, and one lost by what the coroner called "misadventure." What this was exactly her mother never knew; for, while she was at play, she had fallen from the bridge over the big river, but no one could be found to say what had taken her so far from home, or how the end had come. Other children there had been, but like so many others they had died at birth or very soon after, and were no more than distant memories.

The return of the men-folk threw the cottage into confusion, for there was little room, and they all tried to wash and dress themselves for Mass at the same time. It did not take them long, however—the old "tabard" or sleeveless smock with all its traces of weekday work ("baudy tabard" Chaucer called it) was discarded for that kept for Sundays and special occasions, and they were ready. The bell was already ringing, and they moved off and were soon joined by friends and neighbours as they made their short journey to the church. John noticed that the low wall which enclosed the church and the graveyard was rapidly breaking down in several places: for many months now it had been cracking and stones falling away from it here and there, but nothing had been done to repair it, in spite of the archdeacon's periodical warnings. On two or three occasions John had noticed that pigs and sheep had wandered into the graveyard itself and had started to graze among the tombs. But he had little time to reflect on this, for his neighbours were pressing into the church since the time for service had come, and even the men-folk, who habitually lingered outside in little groups till the last moment, had turned to go in.

So he entered with his wife through that selfsame door at which they had stood when the priest had married them over twenty-five years ago. They touched the holy water, and crossed themselves as they moved into the nave, and there they parted to take up their places on either side of the aisle. They remained standing, as there were not yet even rudimentary seats or pews for them, for this was not one of the richest village churches. Only behind the chancel-screen were there any seats, but these were reserved for the clergy, although the lord of Hemings Manor and his family, when they were at the manor house, were also privileged to seat themselves there. Hubert Longfellow, the parish clerk, was the only other parishioner who had his seat within the chancel, and that because he was a bachelor. His predecessor had been a married man, and therefore, although he was in Minor Orders, he was kept out and had to stand with the ordinary congregation in the nave.

While they were waiting an animated conversation was going on, but at last Sir William, the vicar, entered followed by the parish clerk, and for a moment the congregation was still. As the service began, however, many resumed their whisperings and mutterings, while some lounged by pillars and seemed to be taking but small notice of the service. The priest's voice droned on: here and there it was raised for a moment while he intoned a prayer, or while he and the clerk sang their versicles and brief responses. But, for the most part, even the keenest ear could catch little more than an unintelligible murmur, interspersed with a *Dominus vobiscum*, or *Oremus*, or *Amen*, which, by countless repetitions, had familiarized itself to the ear. Even in those churches where traditionally the priest read the service aloud, it was not audible even to a Latinist, and the village congregation rarely had any such lettered person among its number. So the service went on its way, and John meditated awhile. It was all very familiar to him, for ever since he was a child he had faithfully attended the Sunday Mass—now these fifty years and more—and, when his lord's service did not forbid it, he frequently came on holy-days as well. He understood little, but yet there was something about it all that was dear to him. He knew that in some mysterious way Christ's body was made anew at this service: the bell would ring while the priest prayed, and then, after a pause, Sir William would turn and hold up before them all the blessed bread and wine now made God. But that great moment had not yet come, and his thoughts wandered as he looked about him in the high-roofed church. For a moment his eyes fell on the painting of the Last Judgment which had recently been renewed on the wall over the chancel arch. It fascinated him to contemplate the calm and severe majesty of Christ, as He sat enthroned in glory and meting out doom. The ecstasy of the saved as they were caught up in the arms of the angels, or the three naked souls cosily nestling in Abraham's bosom, were so vividly portrayed that his eyes lingered on them, and only with reluctance turned to gaze on those damned souls, who stood on the left hand of the throne of grace, and in varying attitudes of pleading, fear and bewilderment expressed their horrible condition. Others, even more fearful to behold, were already enduring the tortures destined for them, as the devils savagely seized them with flesh-hooks and pitched them into the cauldron and the everlasting fire.

Other pictures painted on the walls also told their story, and recalled to him fragments of sermons and tales, especially some of those told in the vivid and understandable language of a passing friar. Their own priest had no such gift. Indeed, how should he have such powers? The marvel was that now, at this very minute, the Latin phrases were flowing from his lips and he was God's minister to them all. Yet he had been born in this selfsame village, and was the youngest brother of John's own wife Agnes. He had always been about the church as a boy, and was taught how to read and to sing the service by their old priest Sir John Walters. Then, he had become the holy-water carrier, and, little by little, had learnt all Sir John could teach him, and had been sent away to school. And now, here he was, back in the parish, and living in the vicar's house with its garden and stone wall round it, hard by the church, and standing at the head of them all. As John looked at him he recalled some of his kindly actions: no parishioner was too distant for him to visit if need arose, and no one led a more model life than he. "If gold rust, what shall iron do?," was his watchword, and he taught his flock more by what he was than by anything he was able to say. All men knew him to be their friend, and yet there was something about him which forbade men to be too familiar. Even his sister regarded him with the awe born of more than one snibbing he had administered to her, and which her conscience admitted to be just.

By this time, however, the Creed had been said, and Sir William had come from the altar steps to the door of the rood-screen. He looked grave, for it was but seldom that he attempted to teach his flock in a set discourse, rather than by short explanations of the main points of the Faith. But the bishop was constantly urging upon the clergy the need for more sermons, and he must obey. As he waited, his people settled themselves down, most of them squatting in the rushes which covered the floor, while a few lounged against the pillars and seemed to care little for what was to come. When all were settled, he reminded them of earlier sermons he had preached at intervals on the seven deadly sins, and then turned to speak of the fourth of these, namely sloth. Slothfulness kept men from church, and encouraged them to be inattentive at Mass, and to put off the day of repentance till it was too late. All this, as he said, would inevitably have to be paid for in purgatory, unless they were truly penitent and shriven. Not only in church, but in ordinary worldly affairs, idleness was to be shunned, and young men and women should be made to work and serve their masters with love and cheerfulness. Therefore, parents must chastise naughty children, or they would grow up idle and disobedient as were the sons of Eli. The tale of the death of the prophet and his two sons followed, and Sir William concluded his short sermon by bidding his hearers to think on Eli and his sons, and to chastise their children, and to see they learnt to labour well and truly while there was yet time, and further to think how best to labour for their souls as well as their bodies.

All this was listened to in comparative quiet, although a few took but little notice of the discourse, and kept up a desultory conversation among themselves; and throughout the nave there was more whispering and occasional chatter than Sir William liked to hear, but he was powerless to stop it, for no one could remember when a little talking or even joking in church had been forbidden. When the sermon was ended he went back to the altar, and the service continued. Ere long the ringing of the bell called even the most inattentive to their devotions, since the great moment of the Mass had now come. *Paternoster*, *Ave* and Creed were all that John could say, but these he repeated again and again; and later, when he heard the priest intoning the *Paternoster*, he joined in heartily. Then, while Sir William was rinsing his holy vessels, he prayed silently again until the service came to an end with its *Ite, missa est*, and after the priest had retired, he too rose to leave. Many "sons of Belial" had not waited so long, and had hurried off, as soon as the consecration had been finished, as if they had seen not God but the Devil, for some wanted to get to their work again, while others were only concerned to cross the green to the ale-house where they might refresh themselves and gossip at their ease.

Once out in the churchyard again John stopped to talk with his neighbours. One group was looking with interest at the platform, which was as yet but half-erected, at the one end of the churchyard. Here, in a week's time, they would see the actors from the neighbouring town, as well as some of their own folk performing in the Miracle Plays. Hubert, the parish clerk, was particularly skilful, and all remembered his performance as Herod, "that moody King," two years before, and also how masterful it had been. Besides this, however, there had been much to amuse them in the rough boisterous performances of many of the actors. They hoped to see Cain bullying his boy at the plough and ranting at his brother Abel, or Pilate shouting and raging as he had done the last time the plays had come. On the other hand, John recalled the affecting scenes in which the players had presented to them many of the poignant moments of the Gospel story, and he and his mates discussed with zest the scenes they would like to see again.

When he left this group he was stopped by two neighbours who wanted him to join with them in some work waiting to be done on their strips which lay side by side in the great east field. This he promised to do towards the end of the week when he had carried his hay; and, with a parting look at the sundial, he moved from the churchyard, and caught up his wife and daughter near their home. Agnes was full of news she had gleaned from her gossips: Cicely Wode was to marry John Freman of the neighbouring town, and she and her old mother were to leave the manor as soon as the marriage could take place. Matilda, the reeve's daughter, was in trouble, and would be accused at the next Manor Court of incontinency. Agnes Atwater had scalded her legs badly by overturning a vat of boiling water in her brew-house—and so on.

They soon reached their cottage; and, while the women-folk went indoors to prepare the midday meal John went behind the house and down to the bottom of the close where the pig was kept. He emptied into the trough the remainder of a bucket containing some sour milk and scraps of household waste, and pulled up a few rank-growing weeds and threw them into the trough. Then he turned to his garden and worked at this and that, for he had a good conscience, and his brother-in-law, Sir William, took a reasonable view of the Fourth Commandment. At last Roger came to call him in to dinner. Meanwhile, Agnes and her daughter had been busy in the house. The fire had been made up, and the large pot, in which the soup of peas and beans had been prepared on the previous day, was hung over it and heated. The trestle-table was now standing in the middle of the room, and the beechen bowls and spoons arranged on it. A few mugs and an earthen jug filled with good ale stood ready, for John was not one of those landless labourers in whom it was presumptuous to drink anything more than penny ale. They all sat down, and soon were supping noisily the thick pottage and eating with it large hunks of a dark coloured bread. A good lump of home-made green* cheese followed, and with this and mugs of the good ale they made their simple meal.

There was much to be done in the garden at this time of year, and

* Green = fresh, new.

John and his sons spent part of the afternoon in weeding and thinning out their cabbages. Some of their neighbours returned to the meadows and continued their haymaking, but John knew how much Sir William disliked this, and how often he had spoken against Sunday work, unless it were absolutely necessary to avoid spoiling the crop. Hence he stayed at home, and did a little here and there to clear things up in his garden. In this way the afternoon wore on, and when John went into the house he found that his wife and daughter had gone off to Vespers at the church. Sir William liked to see a good congregation at this service, especially on Sundays, and most of the women, and a considerable number of men, attended this short simple service as the day began to close. John's sons, however, had but little thought for this, for they were more interested in the pleasure they hoped for a little later in the evening, and after a while both left the house to forgather with their companions. When Agnes returned, the evening meal was soon on the table, for as it was Sunday they had already eaten the most substantial meal of the day. Now they fared on a few eggs, a bit of oatcake and some cheese. Both the women drank milk, but John refused this, and said he preferred a mug of ale since some still remained of his wife's last brewing.

As the shadows lengthened they left the house, and a short walk brought them on to the green, which looked at its best in the evening light, and already many of the villagers were there. Soon, to the sound of a rebeck and pipe the dancing began, for here again Sir William's moderate and friendly rule did not prohibit the dance, although he had a sharp word for any whose behaviour on these occasions seemed to call for correction. The measures were simple, and were trodden with an unaffected grace which seemed to recall a happier and more innocent age—far removed from the toil and difficulties of everyday life. Young men and maidens with linked hands went through the evolutions of the dance and smiled one at the other, and "dallied with the innocence of love." Yet, even so, there were some matrons who looked on with but half-approving eye, as if underneath the seeming innocence there lurked who knew what dangers? Agnes, partly from native prudery and partly as Sir William's sister, would not let Alice join in the dances, although her friends called to her from time to time, and she darted envious eyes on Joan and Cicely as they moved in concert to the music. Even while they stood there the airs seemed to grow a little less restrained, and very soon Alice and her mother moved away towards home. The dances, however, went on, and as dusk fell and journeys to the ale-house on the edge of the green became more common, the shrill cries of the rebeck were answered by the shrill cries and laughter of the girls, and by the lower laughter and snatches of song of some of the men. John watched all this with an indulgent eye, and sat for a while with some of his cronies on the ale-house bench, and listened to the shouts and sounds of revelry coming from within the devil's chapel, as a friar had once called it, in a sermon which told of how three men, after drinking and dicing there, had set off to find Death so that they might slay him, and of what had befallen them. The noise within grew louder: "there was laughing and lowering, and 'let the cup go,'" and at last Clement Cooke, notorious in the village for his inability to carry his liquor, got up to go

> . . . like a gleeman's bitch,
> Sometimes aside and sometimes backwards,
> Like one who lays lures to lime wild-fowl.
> As he drew to the door all dimmed before him,
> He stumbled on the threshold and was thrown forwards.

John thought it was time for him also to get home, for there was a good day's work to do with the hay on the morrow, and with a "Good-night" to his friends set off quickly. He soon came to the church, which seemed very tall and new in the fast fading light, and then, in a few minutes, he was once again at his door. The house was dark, since for some time now their scanty stock of rush-lights had been spent, though this was of small moment for they were seldom to be found out of bed long after dusk. He turned to go in, when a glance down the street showed him Walter, the beadle, going from door to door. He knew well what that meant, and had half feared his coming, so that he waited only for a moment while Walter called out to him that the lord had asked for a "love-boon" on the morrow. His own hay, he reflected, would have to wait, and with a last look at the sky and a hope for a few fine days, he went in and closed the door.

The next morning saw another early start, for John knew well the Lord Prior's officers would be on the look-out for latecomers; and indeed, it was only a few years since they had tried to insist on everyone appearing at dawn. Though that had been declared contrary to the custom of the manor when it had been discussed at the Manor Court, and therefore had been quietly dropped, nevertheless, it was still unwise to appear much later than the neighbours. So John roused up the two boys, and Alice as well, for on these days everyone, save the housewife, had to appear, and help with the lord's hay. As they started they soon met many neighbours: it was a far larger party than that of yesterday, all making their way to the lord's great meadow (for on this manor all the Prior's pasture was in one immense field) which lay in the little valley to the west of the village, and through the midst of which the streamlet flowed so sweetly. Soon after they arrived they had been divided up into groups, and placed in different parts of the field by the reeve and the hayward, who bustled about from place to place to see that all was well and that work was beginning in good earnest.

So to the music of whetstone striking on scythe the work began, and the mowers bent to their task, sweeping down the grass in wide swathes, as they slowly moved from side to side of the piece allotted to them. John was glad to see old William Honiset already in the field. He could no longer use a scythe, but he was very crafty in the straightening and sharpening of obstinate blades, and the whole day long sat under a great beech tree in one corner of the field with hammer and stone and put a new edge on many a scythe before nightfall. As the sun rose higher and higher the blades swung to and fro, while up and down the field moved a man, with a stave in his hand, whose duty it was to oversee the workers. John looked at him as he passed, recalling his own early days, and how often he and the father of this man who now stood over him had worked together in this very meadow, for they had been partners, or "marrows," as the country people termed it, and so did whatever was possible to help one another. But, in his old age, his friend had bought his freedom at a great price, for he had paid to the Lord Prior six marks of silver, the savings of a lifetime, and as much as the yearly income of Sir William, the vicar, himself. Now, therefore, his son was free of everything except a few small services from time to time, of which this was one.

The workers paused to sharpen their scythes, or for a momentary rest, or better still to listen while some belated arrival poured his tale into the ear of an incredulous reeve, or while some careless fellow, who was working in lazy or incompetent fashion, was soundly berated by the hayward. At other moments, again, there was a most welcome respite, for this was fortunately a "wet boon," and old Alice atte Mere, who had only a tiny cot on the edge of the village, held it on the homely tenure of carrying ale to the workers at these boons. Hence, she was continuously going to and fro from the manor house for reinforcements of ale which the thirsty labourers seemed to consume almost as soon as it was doled out to them. Although this was only the drink rationed out to the manorial servants, and was not exactly the corny ale—the *melior cerevisia*—brewed for the brethren of the priory, yet, perhaps this *secunda cerevisia* was a more prudent drink for the labourers, and certainly it seemed doubly delicious in the heat of the day. Steadily the work went on till well-nigh noon, when at last the hayward's horn was heard. John straightened himself, and made for the shade with his companions. There they threw themselves down, and soon the manor servants appeared, some carrying great loaves and cheeses, while others brought the ever-welcome barrels of ale. John and his family were given four of the loaves for themselves, and as they cut them open they saw that these were the good wheaten loaves, which so seldom came their way. They ate ravenously of these and of the cheese after their six hours in the open air, and called again and again for ale, of which there was no stint, for this was one of the few days of the year on which the customal specified that they were to "drink at discretion."

After this meal there was a short welcome rest, and then they went back to the field once more. Steadily the work went on, and from time to time the now tiring mowers looked at the sky, and watched the slow course of the sun over the big trees which bordered the field. The girls and women busied themselves in raking and turning the first cut hay, while the officials were moving busily from place to place trying to keep the workers at their tasks. At last the long-awaited sound of the hayward's horn was heard, and in a few minutes the field was deserted, and old and young were making their way and chattering together as they went towards the manor house. The toil of the day was over, and all that remained was the good evening meal that the Lord Prior always gave them as a reward for their labours. As they reached the manor house they saw that one of the large outhouses had been made ready with trestle-tables down the centre and at the sides of the building, and platters and mugs were soon laid out ready for the repast. In the courtyard the great cauldrons were steaming, and the hungry people were busy carving into hunks the remainder of their midday loaves. Soon the manorial servants brought in the cauldrons, and a mess of thick pease pottage was served out, to which had been added a little meat for flavouring. This, and a draught of ale, took the sharp edge off their hunger, and they awaited with pleasurable anticipation the next course. The winter had been a hard one, and few of them had been able to buy flesh, or to expect more than a bit of boiled bacon from time to time. Some could afford to keep but few chickens or geese, and had to exist as best they might on their scanty produce, and on cheese and curds, with oatmeal cake or thick oatmeal pottage to satisfy their ever-hungry children. This and a sour bread of peas and beans had been the lot of many for several months, so that the entry of the servants with great dishes of roast meat caused a hum of satisfaction to go up around the room. Each group tackled the portion set down before them with eagerness, and with many a call to a friend here and a joke with a neighbour at another table, the meal wore on. Ale flowed liberally, and there was "cheese at call" for those who were still hungry. When some of the women showed signs of wishing to leave, the hayward blew his horn for silence, and the reeve announced that if the weather remained fine there would be two more boons on the Wednesday and the following Monday, and by then he hoped all the hay would be cut and carried into the great manor courtyard. Little by little the company dispersed, most of them ready enough to get home and do whatever was necessary about the house before they went to bed. John and his family walked back together, and saw as they passed their own meadow that Agnes had been at work during the day. The hay that was dry had been raked up into small cocks, and she had turned most of that which had only been cut the previous morning.

Much of their time in the next few days was spent by the peasants either on the lord's hayfield or on their own. John had but little more to cut on his allotted portion, and all was done by the Wednesday evening. The following Friday he and his boys spent the afternoon in loading it onto a wagon they borrowed from a friend, Roget the ox pulled it home, and they stored it away in the little shed behind the house.

What little time John and his sons had from the haymaking seemed to go all too rapidly in a variety of tasks. The work which he had promised to do in the east field with his neighbours took up the Thursday afternoon, and besides this they were hard at work on an "assart" or clearing they were making near the edge of the great wood. The prior had granted this to John only the previous autumn; and, although it was but three acres in extent, the work of grubbing up the furze and briars and cleaning the land so that they could sow it this coming autumn seemed endless. Richard spent all the time he could at this, for he hoped one day to make this plot the site of a home for himself, since he was now fully grown and eager to marry Johanna, the daughter of William Sutton, an old friend of his father.

The other two days of work on the lord's meadow passed much like the first, except that there was no ale provided at the second boon, for it was a "dry-reap," but they had to work only till midday. The last boon, however, surpassed all the rest, for not only was there ale again, but other pleasures as well. As the last load was carried from the field the hayward loosed a sheep in their midst. All watched this poor frightened beast with interest, for if it remained quietly grazing they could claim it for a feast of their own, but if it wandered out of the field they lost it, and it remained the lord's property. As they looked on, restraining the children from noise or sudden movement, the sheep gazed around and then began to eat what it could find. Little did it think how in lingering over this Esau's mess it had sealed its fate.

All was not yet over, however. Indeed, many thought the best was yet to come, and John and the other householders next moved off to a part of the field where the reeve stood by a very large cock of hay. Everyone knew what was to be done, and no one wished to be the first to start. At last the reeve called on Robert Day to begin, and with a sly look at some of his neighbours he gathered together a great mass of hay, and rapidly bound it into a bundle. Then, carefully placing his scythe-head under the bundle, he slowly raised it from the ground amidst the encouraging cries of the onlookers. Others were not so fortunate, and some through greed or lack of skill were unable to raise the load without letting the scythe-handle touch the ground, or still more unfortunate, without breaking the handle altogether. Accompanied by the laughter and rude criticisms of their fellows, they retired in confusion. So the ceremony went on till all had had a sporting chance. Once this was over the farm servants rapidly forked the remainder into a small cart, and accompanied by the reeve and hayward left the field. John and his friends, bearing their trophies aloft in victory, started happily for home. For them it was a moment for rejoicing: the three "boons" were over, and they knew that there were no further calls to be made on them beyond the weekly service that went on from year end till year end. Not before the Gules of August would any extra works be again demanded of them.

Their happiness, however, was a little dashed within a few minutes, for as they rounded a corner a small cavalcade rapidly drew towards them. As the riders came nearer, John and his friends recognized them, and when the party reached them all the peasants doffed their hats and louted low, for the imperious looking man who rode at their head, clothed in flowing garments of fine black cloth, was none other than the cellarer himself. Two others of the brethren rode just behind him, followed by two servants. A few moments later John overtook old Margery who had been at work at the Manor Court all day strewing the rooms with rushes, and making the beds with sheets and counterpanes—for these great ones demanded every comfort. On the morrow the Manor Court would be held, and much time would be lost, so John and his friends hurried on to do what they could overnight.

On the next morning John was up and about his close from an early hour, and this kept him busy until it was time to go to the Manor Court. He called his two sons, for it was no ordinary court, but a Leet Court, at which all over twelve years of age were bound to attend. Thus they started out, and reached the manor house a little before eight, and waited about outside chatting aimlessly with their friends. At last the beadle came out, and summoned them all into the court room. They entered, and found themselves in a long panelled room with a fine timber roof which showed up well from the light that streamed in from the large east window, as well as from the smaller mullioned windows on either side. They took up their places on the rush-strewn floor, and chattered away until the reeve and hayward entered, followed by the beadle, whose command for silence was still echoing in the hall when the cellarer entered from a side door at the west end of the room. He took his seat on a raised dais with his clerk by his side, and after the clerk had unfolded the great parchment Court Roll, and had begun to write with his quill the day and year of the Court, the cellarer nodded, and the beadle cried out an "Oyez" thrice repeated, and ordered all who had business and owed service to the Lord Prior of Honiwell to draw near.

At once several men stepped forward: one asked for a neighbour to be excused attendance since he was sick in bed; another pleaded that his friend was absent in the King's wars, while others told the cellarer that their man was unable to attend for various reasons, and pledged themselves to produce him at the next Court. All these facts were noted by the clerk on his roll, and then the reeve was told to put forward his pleas. First, he presented Roger le Bacheler to the cellarer, and said that he asked permission to take over the land of Alice Tunstall since she was a widow with no children, and could not work the twenty acres which were her holding. The cellarer allowed this, and told Roger that he might hold the land at the same rent and services as had Alice's husband, and that he would have to pay 6*s*. 8*d*. as a fine for entry. Since he willingly agreed to this, he was called forward, and the cellarer formally admitted him to the holding, handing him, in token of the exchange, a white wand. This done, Roger fell on his knees, and placing his hands between those of the cellarer, swore "so help me God and all His Saints" that from this day forth he would be true and faithful to the Lord Prior, and should owe fealty for the land which he held of him in villeinage, and that he would be justified by him in body and goods, and would not take himself off the lord's manor.

Next, the reeve told a long tale of many dilapidations that had accrued since the last Court: some houses were falling into serious disrepair; the path outside certain cottages was continuously foul; many man had taken timber from the Lord Prior's wood without leave; three men . . . So he droned on, and John paid but slight attention, for he was not conscious of having broken any of the manorial laws, and only noticed with dismay that the name of his brother Henry was constantly mentioned. All these matters took but a short time, for no one denied his guilt, and a fine of twopence or threepence was generally imposed by the cellarer. The reeve then told the cellarer of the misdemeanours of several men at the recent haymaking—of their late-coming, their laziness or their impudence. These received short shrift, and were fined twopence each, all except Richard Cook, who spoke opprobrious words to the cellarer, for which he was sternly rebuked and fined sixpence. Lastly, the reeve brought forward Thomas Attegate, who told the cellarer how his son was eager for book-learning, and how Sir William thought so well of him that he wanted to send him to the grammar school in the near-by town if this were allowed. After some questions the cellarer gave his consent, on the assurance that the boy wished to devote himself to learning in the hope of rising to the dignity of the priesthood in due course. His father thanked the cellarer in halting words, and paid the sixpence demanded of him for the permission, and then fell back among his fellows once more.

After this the beadle called for the tithing men to come forward and make their reports. Each in his turn told the steward of how matters stood in so far as he was responsible. William Sleford presented that Richard Tubbing and Johanna atte Grene were common brewers and had broken the prior's orders about the sale of ale, and they were each fined twelvepence. John Morgan presented that a stray horse had been found by one of his tithing and surrendered to the beadle and was now in the village pound. He also asked that William Bonesay might be enrolled in his tithing as he was now twelve years of age. William Cook complained that Richard Jamys had received one John Freeman into his house, and that John was not in any tithing and was suspected of being a night-walker and eavesdropper. Richard was ordered to produce John at the next Court and to be ready to answer for him. Lastly, John atte Hethe was removed from his office of tithing man, and in his place William Craft was elected and sworn.

So the proceedings came to an end; and, after the cellarer had reminded them that the next Court would be held on that day six weeks, he withdrew to his private chamber, and amid a general chattering the peasants began to disperse. John left the Court with his sons who soon joined their own friends and set off homewards. He, however, made a roundabout circuit so as to pass by the great west field, for he was anxious to see how things were coming on, for the whole week past had been so taken up with haymaking and work elsewhere that he had had no time even to do an hour's work there. As he came round by the field his eye rapidly moved from strip to strip and he saw there was much to be done. St. John's Day was already past, so they must set to work at once at the weeding, he thought, and he determined to spend the rest of the day at this. For a few minutes before turning homeward to his midday meal he sat down and looked across the great field at the village as it straggled over the neighbouring slope—a familiar sight, but dearer to him than any other place on earth. There stood the church, clean and white in the midday sun, and there a few hundred yards to the right his own little house and its narrow close which, with his land in the common fields, represented all he had in the world.

It seemed little enough, yet, he reflected, things might be worse. The last winter had been hard, and the death of his only cow had made life even harder. Now, however, his twenty-four half-acre pieces were all ploughed and planted with crops which promised well, but everyone knew that twelve acres was none too much, if more than the barest existence was hoped for. Last year the crops had been poor, and for several months food had been scarce, so that many of his neighbours had been half starved, and nearly everyone in the village was forced to live on victuals lacking in flavour or variety. The oats had been their salvation: with oatcake and porridge, and with the bread they had made from a mixed corn of barley and rye they had been able to hold off the worst pangs of hunger; but for weeks on end no meat or flesh, except an occasional chicken or something snared by night in the prior's woods, had come their way. Since then, however, the summer had come, and the hay crop had been a good one, and hope sprang up once again. At the next Court, he thought, he would ask for leave to build a little cot on the piece of new land they had been clearing near by the great wood. Then Richard and Johanna could be married and live there, and could grow something on the three acres to help them all to live. His wife would know how to make the best of everything that came into the house: no one could make a bushel of corn go farther than she. That was the root of his brother Harry's trouble. His wife had been careless and slatternly, and their home was always uncared for and the meals ill-prepared. And yet, despite it all, Harry had been heartbroken when she went off with Thomas Oxenden, a rising burgess of Thorpston near by. Since then, Harry had gone down hill fast: his holding was badly kept, his house a disgrace, while his time was mainly spent with bad friends snaring in the prior's woods, or in drinking and "Hi tooral hay" at the ale-house. John reflected sadly as to the end of all this, but what was to be done to stay it he could not tell. Life was so strange and in his fifty odd years he had seen ups and downs in the village. Some he had played with as a boy had stolen away by night, and had been heard of no more; some, like his wife's brother, had become priests, and were now important people; some, like his own brother, had lost their grip on life, and had become a byword in the village. But there it was, and each must abide his fate. As Sir William had often told them, they were in the hand of God, and He and His holy angels would protect them all their days. Then, as he rose to go, the sound of the midday bell rang out clear over the fields. He crossed himself, and after repeating an *Ave*, went quickly to his own home.

OLIVER STATLER

At the Japanese inn

Oliver Statler lived in Japan for eleven years. He became interested in Japanese art and wrote *Modern Japanese Prints: An Art Reborn.* The original edition of *Japanese Inn*, which traces the history of the Minaguchi-ya in Okitsu from its founding in 1582 up to the present, is illustrated with beautiful prints by Hiroshige and other Japanese masters.

Principal Characters

ITO, *merchant and patron of the Minaguchi-ya*
DENZAEMON, *head of the post house at Okitsu station*
ICHIKAWA, TEZUKA — *Headmen of Okitsu and owners of its* honjin
ENGLEBERT KAEMPFER, M.D., *physician to the Dutch mission*
MOCHIZUKI HANZO, *sixth master of the Minaguchi-ya*

It was a spring day to remember. The sun was warm, the breeze fluttered promises on which small boys flew kites against a newly washed sky. In fields along the highway, farmers broke the ground and released the strong, sharp smell of earth. Ito had never felt so alive. He hiked briskly, reveling in the power of his legs and the thrust of his chest, and the rapture of being twenty-five and healthy.

He had walked all day, savoring the clean, sure working of his body, not willing to trade that buoyancy for jostled torpor in a palanquin. His companion had kept pace with him. Several times Ito had urged the older man to ride for a while, but each time he had firmly refused.

The man was a good traveling companion, Ito thought. He had been a little unhappy when his father had insisted that the firm's chief clerk come along. He himself would have chosen someone nearer his own age. But now he was pleased with the arrangement. The clerk had made this trip to Edo many times with Ito's father, now two years in retirement, and frequently along the way young Ito had been grateful for his com-

---

panion's knowledge of special places to eat, or of ways to shake off undesirable fellow travelers, or of how to dismiss beggars with the least fuss and expense. And now that they were halfway to Edo, the young man was more than willing to admit that he was going to be glad to have the clerk's support when he moved among the shrewd merchants of the Shogun's capital. Since his father's retirement, young Ito had been head of Nagoya's most famous kimono and dry-goods house, but he was a little apprehensive about this first trip on his own. Their firm had no branch in Edo, but it was eying the prospects.

All along the highway, too, the chief clerk had displayed an astonishing fund of lore about each area they passed through. He could talk for hours on local legend or local history, but he could also be silent. Ito was thankful for both, and for the man's sure sense of when each was wanted.

It was now midafternoon or a little past, and they were approaching Okitsu, where they would spend the night at the Minaguchi-ya. Neither had spoken in some time, but as they topped a low hill and saw the village and the beach before them, the older man drew out of his memory a pensive quotation from a thirteenth-century travel diary: "When one passes through this village, smoke from the salt fires is faintly seen. There are small fishes drying in the fields, scattered pines, the shady color of the sea."

They passed Seikenji, looming above them on the mountainside. At the row of salve shops lining the road opposite the temple, young salespersons cried that he must try their special medicine. Glancing their way, young Ito flushed and quickened his pace. He threw a covert look at his chief clerk, found that man's face impassive.

Now they were in Okitsu station. Inns lined the road and waitresses hailed them to stop for the night. Just ahead, two girls hauled a traveler bodily into an inn. When Ito reached that open-fronted hostelry he saw the waylaid man with his feet already in a tub of water. One girl was washing travel grime from his legs while the other immobilized him in an embrace. "His howls are not convincing," said the chief clerk.

At the Minaguchi-ya they were greeted personally by Hanzo, the sixth generation of Mochizukis at Okitsu. Leading the way to the inn's finest suite, Hanzo assured Ito that the Minaguchi-ya was honored by his visit, representing as it did a new generation continuing an old association. He inquired after the elder Ito's health and complimented the younger on his vigor. After he retired, the service was most attentive.

The youngest of the maids caught Ito's eye at once. Her make-up was light and her skin glowed clear and clean. It was she who helped him out of his travel kimono and into a fresh one provided by the inn, and when she tied his sash in back he thought that her hands fluttered over his hips for one unnecessary instant. But when he turned, her face was demure.

He came back from his bath with body tingling. "There is nothing," he said to himself, "like a vigorous scrub and a hot tub after a good day's walk." As he draped his towel over a rack where the garden breeze would catch it, the young maid slid open the door to bring him tea. "Well, hardly anything," he mentally amended.

He sat on the cushion she laid for him in the place of honor, and she poured his tea. He liked her hands. She had the door open to leave when he thought of something else. "Will you please," he asked, "bring ink and a brush."

He watched her as she made his ink, pouring a few drops of clear water on the stone, rubbing the stick of ink through the pool until the liquid grew richly black. Her little frown of concentration made him smile and his eyes danced to the rhythm of her hand, her arm, her shoulder, her breast. A wisp of hair escaped from her elaborate coiffure and fell across her cheek. He reached forward to touch it. She was not startled, but with his hand still on her cheek she looked up and smiled back. She smiled a promise.

The chief clerk returned from the bath then, and after very audibly drinking his tea, fished out his diary and began meticulously to complete the day's accounts. He would not, Ito knew, be off one-tenth of a *mon* when they reached Edo.

Ito found his own diary. He did not have to bother with travel expenses but he made it a rule to set down a few notes every day. He took up his brush but sat without writing. The fresh green of the garden shimmered in the twilight, the air was kissed with the scent of pine from supper fires, and he had a long, delicious night to look forward to.

Finally he dipped his brush in the ink that the girl had made for him, set down the date, and wrote: "Stopped tonight in Okitsu at the Minaguchi-ya, where we were most warmly received..." At that moment there was a soft murmur from the corridor, and the maids brought in supper.

Next morning, for some reason, Ito was slow getting started, and it was well after dawn before he and his clerk were ready to leave the inn. Hanzo brought the bill and thanked them for their patronage. Ito assured him that they had enjoyed their stay. It had occurred to him, he remarked, that the comfort he had enjoyed at the Minaguchi-ya was a far cry from what his grandfather or great-grandfather had encountered when they had journeyed to Edo.

This was one of Hanzo's favorite topics. "Indeed things have changed," he cried. "In Ieyasu's time, your great-grandfather had to carry his food with him. The most he could have expected from the usual inn was a little hot water to soften his cooked, dried rice. And most inns were crude affairs where a fastidious traveler was thrown together with Lord knows what kind of riffraff, not to mention thieves and murderers.

"Of course, as you know, there are still thieves and murderers on the highway, but the government is doing its best to eradicate them. Why, only last week we received a circular about some vagabond who inveigled a traveler into sharing a room at an inn, and then robbed him. They caught the rogue and cut off his head and put it up on a stake near the scene of his crime, but there are many others—do be careful of over-friendly strangers."

In the inn's entry, Ito and his companion each thrust his sword into his sash. They were commoners, but even a commoner was permitted to wear a sword while on a journey. A traveler had no choice but to carry all the money required for his trip: this made him a tempting target, and no one denied him the right to be armed against the perils of the road.

As they replied to a chorus of farewells, Hanzo caught the lingering glance between Ito and the young maid. "Aha," he thought, "no wonder he was hard to rouse this morning." And he made a mental note that if Ito stopped at the Minaguchi-ya on his way home, which now seemed likely, the same maid must be assigned to him.

Hanzo had decided to walk with his guests a few minutes to speed them on their way. "I'm happy," he remarked, as they paced through the village, "that you'll be crossing Satta in broad daylight. There are still cutthroats up there, and I've heard of a brutish renegade priest who extorts money at sword's point. Of course he calls it an offering. A man is a fool to attempt the pass alone at night. Do you know the story of Heisaku?"

Ito and the clerk did not.

"It happened years ago, just how many I'm not sure. Heisaku was a young man of Okitsu. He went to Edo to work, and three years went by without his seeing his father. The thought that he was neglecting his filial duty preyed on his mind. He wanted to ease his father's last years, and so he quit his job, and taking his savings and a parting gift from his employer, he set out for home.

"He wasted no time on the highway and by sunset of the fifth day he reached Yui. He had an aunt living there and he stopped to call on her.

"The old lady was overjoyed to see him. She told him his father was hale and hearty, and prattled on about the family, as women will, until it was quite dark. She wanted him to spend the night but he insisted he could not stop so near home. She had heard of highwaymen attacking travelers on Satta and sometimes killing them, but he belittled her fears and set out on the last leg of his journey.

"His aunt spent a sleepless night, worrying about him, and early next morning she started for Okitsu to make certain that he had arrived safely.

"She found Heisaku's father, aged but stalwart, sitting alone in his house. At first he appeared not to understand her talk of Heisaku, but as she poured out her story his eyes wandered to some clothes hanging on the wall. Following his gaze, the woman saw the kimono that Heisaku had been wearing the day before. She almost wept with relief, thinking that Heisaku was safe at home after all, but his father grew pale and continued to stare distractedly at the clothes. Suddenly he began to scream, 'It was a mistake! It was a mistake!' and he dashed from the house.

"Later they found two bodies on the rocks at the foot of Satta, the bodies of Heisaku and his father. And if you look sharp along the path at the top of the mountain you'll see a monument to the memory of a traveler who was killed by his father, and a highwayman who killed his son, all unknowing."

With this cheerful tale Hanzo bid good-bye to his guests, wishing them a safe and profitable journey. Then he retraced his steps towards the Minaguchi-ya, accepting homage in the form of bows from lesser innkeepers whose establishments lined the road. When he reached the middle of town it occurred to him to stop for a chat at the post house, where his friend Denzaemon held forth.

The post house was the heart of any Tokaido station. In Okitsu it dominated the village, an imposing two-story building with white plaster walls, set back from the highway so that its clutter of men and horses would not block traffic.

In front was the square where government notices were posted. There were traffic regulations, injunctions to thrift and filial piety, and the standing ban on Christianity with its inducement of gold for a tip exposing a Christian. It had been a long time since anyone around Okitsu had been able to collect such a reward. Beside the post house was a courtyard where pack horses were stabled and loaded, and where hostlers and kago-carriers loitered until called for duty. The kago was the standard travel vehicle on the Tokaido, a light palanquin hung from a pole carried on bearers' shoulders.

Hanzo skirted the public notices, which he knew by heart, glanced into the courtyard, noisy as usual, and entered the post house. There he picked his way through a maze of clerks to the rear where Denzaemon was ensconced to oversee his empire. A boy quickly appeared with tea.

Like Mochizuki, Denzaemon was an important man in Okitsu. Otherwise he would not have been head of the post house. It and its counterparts in the other fifty-two stations were neither inns nor eating places but they were the backbone of the government's traffic system.

Their men and horses were available first, and without charge, to travelers on government business. Daimyo paid the official rate, which was set in Edo. If things were not too busy, Denzaemon could extend the same rate to samurai, to merchants who purveyed to the Shogun, and to those pampered darlings, the big-bellied *sumo* wrestlers. If things were slack, even a commoner could rest his blisters at a price set in spirited haggling, man to man.

In addition to kago-bearers and pack horses, Denzaemon had eight fleet-footed runners to relay the Shogun's letters and edicts. When runners from a neighboring village streaked in with such a message, secure in a black-lacquered box bearing the Tokugawa crest, Denzaemon's men were ready to speed it on its way. They ran in pairs, in case one should meet with an accident; and at the sound of their bell even great daimyo yielded the road. . . .

With a hundred horses and a hundred kago-bearers, the post house employed a large part of the village. But during the seasonal migration of daimyo to or from their enforced residence in Edo, this pool was not enough. Then Denzaemon had the power to levy more men and horses from the neighboring villages. It was one more tax and it hit the farmers hard because it came at their busy season. In some areas their anger flared into revolt, but Denzaemon's peasants seldom did more than complain, however bitterly. Either they trudged in with their horses or they sent him a penalty payment. He was just as happy with the latter, for then he hired roustabouts as substitutes, and pocketed the difference.

The men who lived by their labors on the highway were a special breed, rough, tough, and magnificently tatooed. In summer their tattoos and their loincloths were all they wore. In midwinter they might tolerate a kimono, but even then they would, in one observer's words, "for expedition's sake tack their gowns quite up to their belt exposing their back and privy parts naked to everybody's view, which they say, they have no reason at all to be ashamed of."

They could be instantly recognized by great calluses on their shoulders, from carrying kago, and signs of buboes in their groins, from consorting with wrong women. Their songs were ribald, and their jargon mystifying. They drank liquor from teacups, gambled with passion, and whored with vengeance.

They regulated their service by the amount of their tip, and they were not above increasing it by threats in some lonely spot. But if they made trouble for a stingy customer, they could be a great help to a generous one. If, for example, it seemed impossible to reach a checkpoint before closing hour, one of them might take a sliding door off the kago, and run ahead with it. When he came to the barrier, he would mark time and make a great show of shouting, "Go on! Go on!" as though he were carrying the whole load. The rule was that a palanquin which reached the gate before closing time could go through that night, and this act was enough to satisfy the requirement.

Even when their customer was a daimyo, the tip regulated the service. They couldn't threaten him, but they could regale him with a jolly song if they were pleased, or embarrass him with a sarcastic one if they were not.

Denzaemon's contingent of this lusty brotherhood lived in a rowdy encampment behind the post house. As boss and hands they were natural enemies, but they granted each other a kind of wary respect and managed to get along.

But Hanzo had not stopped at Denzaemon's to chat about kago-bearers. Both men were concerned over that recent directive from the travel commissioner which Hanzo had mentioned to young Ito. In addition to citing the case of the thief who had already lost his head, the circular went on to declare that there were too many such crimes, and it ordered local officials into action. All men who frequently stopped at inns, or stayed at them overlong, were to be investigated, and the suspicious ones reported without delay. Failure in this would bring down drastic punishment on station officials. Hanzo and Denzaemon considered this, and shuddered.

But they managed a grin as they read together the next portion of the directive. It cited reports that travelers were sometimes forced to pay excess charges at river crossings: coolies would go out of their way to wade through deep holes and then demand more money because they were wet "all the way up to here," or they would discover in midstream that their passenger was so heavy that only a healthy bonus would enable them to deliver him safely. These practices must cease, the commissioner thundered. River officials would see to it that charges were based strictly on the depth of water at the proper crossing, and they would insure that even minor travelers were protected from extortion.

Ichikawa and Tezuka were in charge of Okitsu's river crossings. Tezuka ran the upper crossing with seven assistants and a force of a hundred and seventy coolies. Ichikawa was in charge of the lower, with the same number of assistants and two hundred fifty laborers.

These two men were unquestionably the village's leading citizens. Hanzo and Denzaemon were obliged to defer to them, and while relations were cordial enough, there was secret pleasure in seeing superiors discomfited. And this circular was certain to do just that.

Ordinarily, a town's Headman ran the post house, but since in Okitsu that job was delegated to Denzaemon while Ichikawa and Tezuka took over the river crossings, it is evident that the river office was more important, or more profitable, which is the same thing.

The same two men also operated the town's two leading inns, which were called *honjin*. All up and down the Tokaido, *honjin* were designated for the exclusive use of daimyo and court nobility. Next in grade were *waki-honjin*, or side-*honjin*, which were ordinarily used by a daimyo's chief lieutenants but could be used by a daimyo if traffic piled up so that the *honjin* were already taken; if not busy with some daimyo, *waki-honjin* were free to take general travelers. The Minaguchi-ya was a *waki-honjin*. A *honjin* could never have accommodated a businessman like Ito, but the Minaguchi-ya could.

It was unfair, and they knew it, but Hanzo and Denzaemon shared a joke about the advantages of running both a *honjin* and the river crossing: if one were blessed with a well-paying guest, how simple to hold on to him by closing the river as being too dangerous to cross. There was not one whit of evidence that either Tezuka or Ichikawa ever succumbed to such unworthy thoughts, but it was a standing jest around Okitsu that whenever Tezuka, a close-fisted man, was blessed with a wealthy daimyo, he prayed for high water.

So Hanzo and Denzaemon sipped their tea and managed to raise each other's spirits, so recently dampened by the clear implication in the highway commissioner's circular that village elders were to be held responsible for any unfortunate incident in their town. Even with this threat hanging over their heads, it was difficult to be downhearted in the face of the burst of prosperity that was almost upon them. The very next evening not one but two daimyo would stay in Okitsu, appropriating both *honjin*, and, in addition, the Dutch from Nagasaki were scheduled to stop over on their yearly journey to Edo. The Dutch were given daimyo status for their trip and hence were entitled to *honjin* accommodations, but in every encounter with daimyo the Hollanders invariably found themselves outranked, as they were on this date in Okitsu: they would therefore be installed at the Minaguchi-ya. Hanzo was delighted, for they were the most exotic guests an innkeeper could look forward to.

The Japanese saw other foreigners from time to time. They saw Koreans and Ryukyuans and Chinese. But the only Europeans who were now tolerated in the island empire were the Dutch. They brought a breath of the strange and forbidden Western world. Their light coloring was fascinating in itself. The Japanese tagged them "Red-hairs."

The Dutch looked forward to their annual journey with even more excitement than did the Japanese who played host to them. This visit to Edo to pay their respects to the Shogun was their one chance a year to see something of Japan. The rest of the time they were confined to Nagasaki, and chiefly to a tiny islet in the harbor. Only rarely were they allowed to visit Nagasaki city, and then under offensively heavy escort, all of whom had to be treated to a very expensive dinner.

It was the same story on their trip to Edo. To escort, attend, and guard four Hollanders there were a hundred Japanese, all traveling at the expense of the Netherlands East-India Company. But this drain on the corporate purse was not enough to dampen the thrill of getting out of Nagasaki.

The first of their annual visits had come in 1642, when the third Shogun took occasion to lay down the law. The Dutch would make port at Nagasaki and nowhere else; they would instantly report any Christians entering Japan on any ship; and they would render to the Shogunate complete reports of what was going on in the rest of the world. Failure to comply would mean being kicked out as the Spanish and Portuguese had been, and so the Dutch undertook to please.

Every year they carried to the Shogun and his court a heavy load of gifts, carefully selected for their value. These, in effect, were their annual taxes, and the Dutch considered them reasonable enough, in view of the profits they made on their trade.

Their journey took about three months, a month going up, a month in Edo, and a month coming back. They went overland from Nagasaki to Kokura, by ship on the Inland Sea to Osaka, and then up the Tokaido to Edo. They were carefully routed around Kyoto, it having been made clear to them that the cloistered Emperor was only the country's head priest, too sacred to be disturbed: the Shogun wanted no doubts cast on his own right to govern. On the Tokaido their party increased to about a hundred and fifty, for the baggage sent ahead from Nagasaki to Osaka by boat now had to be carried on men's shoulders.

Reminded that his alien visitors were almost upon him, Hanzo took leave of his friend Denzaemon and returned to the Minaguchi-ya. There was work to be done.

It was unlikely that the Hollanders would notice any difference between Mochizuki's inn and a *honjin*. Just ten years earlier, fire had swept Okitsu station, destroying the Minaguchi-ya along with most of the rest of the town. Ichikawa, Tezuka, and Mochizuki had received government grants to put them back in business, and the whole town had helped them rebuild, for *honjin* and *waki-honjin* were, after all, public utilities of a sort. Using the government's money, Hanzo had blandly defied its regulations and built an inn exactly like a *honjin*. (There had been some sputtering over his presumption, but Hanzo had a way with him and the sputtering had died away.) This meant that, unlike common inns whose front was hospitably open to the street, the Minaguchi-ya boasted an imposing gate and entrance which gave it a striking resemblance to a temple.

Hanzo was particularly proud of the gate and of the tile dolphins which sported at each end of its massive tile roof. He had commissioned these dolphins especially, and he maintained that each flipped his tail with unique grace.

Behind the gate stretched a long areaway, paved with white sand, leading to the second feature supposedly reserved to *honjin*, the big entry. This was the size of a small house, almost twenty-five feet square, with an elaborately gabled roof, an alcove for spears and halberds, and a berth for the chief guest's palanquin.

Adjoining the gate was a large storeroom for luggage and kago. In front of this was a pit to make loading easier, overhung by deep eaves for protection in rainy weather. Past the storeroom was the entrance to the family's living quarters, which occupied a modest corner of the property. Through this doorway Hanzo bustled now, mentally listing things to be done.

Playing host to the Dutch presented special problems. Chief among them was that the inn had to be converted into a kind of jail. The Hollanders traveled under close surveillance and on no account were they allowed to wander alone. Hanzo had received strict instructions to seal any doors and windows opening their apartment to the outside. They would be allowed to walk in the garden, but there must be no possibility of their seeing over the wall. Hanzo knew that Dutchmen were very tall, and he prudently ordered his carpenter to add masking which would raise the wall to ten feet. There was nothing to be seen over the top except Suruga Bay and Miho, but rules were rules.

It was past noon the next day before Hanzo decided that the Minaguchi-ya was at last ready for the Red-hairs. Then he retired to dress. His wife shaved his forehead and his crown, carefully combed his heavily pomaded hair which grew long at the sides and back of his head, and trimmed it where it lay forward in a thick lock over his shaved pate. She brought out a fine dark kimono of figured silk, whose only decoration, high in the middle of the back, was a small embroidered crest. She helped him into *hakama*, skirt-like trousers which enveloped his kimono up to the waist, and adjusted his wide flaring shoulder pieces of starched silk, which, like the kimono, bore his crest.

He was now in the full dress called *kamishimo*, and the only thing to distinguish him from a samurai was that he slipped under his sash not two swords but one.

His chief clerk, similarly dressed but swordless, joined him, and with a servant they set out for Seikenji, where they would meet their guests. They were early. It would have been unthinkable to be late.

Seeing them approach, the owner of Seikenji's big medicine shop called Fuji-no-maru invited them to wait in his shop. Hanzo sent his servant up the highway to speed back word as soon as the Dutch were sighted, and then he and his chief clerk sat on cushions placed at the front of the shop's platform floor, sipped the inevitable tea, and chatted happily with Fuji-no-maru's owner about the busy and profitable night that each looked forward to. The shrill cries of the salve-sellers, which had so disconcerted young Ito, seemed to bother Hanzo not at all.

The Dutch, now nearing Okitsu, had been on the road since dawn. One of their number, each time they made the trip to Edo, was their own physician, for the cautious Hollanders did not propose to deliver themselves into the hands of Japanese doctors. In this year of 1691 he was Englebert Kaempfer, M.D., who busied himself throughout the journey by taking copious notes, and whose observations have come down to us in his fat and fascinating *History of Japan.* A stranger's eyes are often sharper than a native's, so it is not surprising that we owe to Dr. Kaempfer many of the best descriptions of the Tokaido and the bustle of life upon it.

The Tokaido, he wrote, was a highway "so broad and large, that two companies, tho' never so great, can conveniently and without hindrance, pass by one another." It was built of sand and stone, banked up in the middle for good drainage, and, since wheeled vehicles were taboo, it was not cut by ruts.

"Every where upon Tokaido," Kaempfer went on, "between the towns and villages there is a streight row of firrs planted on each side of the road, which by their agreeable shade make the journey both pleasant and convenient. . . . The neighbouring villages must jointly keep [the roads] in repair, and take care, that they be swept and clean'd every day . . . The inspectors . . . are at no great trouble to get people to clear them; for whatever makes the roads dirty and nasty, is of some use to the neighbouring country people, so that they rather strive, who should first carry it away. The pine-nuts, branches and leaves, which fall down daily from the firrs, are gather'd for fewel. . . . Nor doth horses dung lie long upon the ground but it is soon taken up by poor country children and serves to manure the fields. For the same reason care is taken, that the filth of travellers be not lost, and there are in several places, near country people's houses, or in their fields, houses of office built for them to do their needs."

Kaempfer noted difficulties, too: "hills and mountains, which are sometimes so steep and high, that travellers are necessitated to get themselves carried over in kago, because they cannot without great difficulty and danger pass them on horseback"; rivers which "run with so impetuous a rapidity towards the sea, that they will bear no bridge or boat"; and those man-made impediments, the barrier-gates flung across the highway as checkpoints. The barrier in the Hakone Mountains was a mere nuisance for the Dutch, who traveled with an official escort, but it was a dreaded ordeal for many Japanese. It was snugly situated in the heart of the mountains, where the highway bordered the lake, and there was no easy way to bypass it. Traffic was often congested there, and it was frustrating to reach it after it had closed for the night, but it took a hardy soul to risk going around. If he was caught, the penalty was crucifixion

Women, especially, were given a bad time, for the Shogunate was vigilant against the escape of its hostages, and the higher the class, the worse the ordeal. Every woman had to carry an official certificate which authorized her travel and carefully identified her. First, she was classified, whether nun, priestess, pilgrim, widow, wife, young girl, or prostitute. Then she was described: if pregnant, injured, blind or demented; if marked by tumors, wounds, or cautery; if distinguished by a bald spot or thinning hair.

When she approached the barrier-gate, she first produced her certificate for a quick check of its validity. Then she was obliged to pay a handsome tip to a teahouse woman who had established herself in the lucrative position of a go-between, after which she was ushered in to the officials. Lord help her at this point if her pass was smudged or the writing hard to read.

If she was traveling from Edo, and looked to be of high station, she was turned over to female examiners. Young women had to submit to examination in a special smock, and this meant a big fee to a special concessionaire who rented them.

If any discrepancies were discovered, the unfortunate woman was taken into custody until the whole thing could be cleared up with the authority who had issued her certificate, a matter of several days at least; but if everything was unquestionably in order, the necessary stamps were affixed, and she was on her way at last.

This was the Tokaido, with its conveniences and its obstacles. It was the world's busiest highway, linking what were probably the world's largest cities: lusty young Edo, seat of government if not the capital; proud old Kyoto, still the capital even if it had no power to govern; and hustling, money-loving, shrewd Osaka, the commercial (without qualification) capital of the country. Between these cities, on this highway, under its firs, across its rivers, and through its barrier-gates, surged a motley traffic.

There were businessmen. There were great merchants like Ito, with their eye on the market that was Edo; their goods moved by sea but they went by land—it was far more fun. There were peddlers: patent-medicine men, sellers of almanacs and charms, of ink and utensils.

There were religious pilgrims, a happy crew mostly, singing and clapping their way on a light-hearted jaunt to some famous shrine or temple.

There were great daimyo, swashbuckling their way with massive entourage from home fief to Edo or back again. They were the reason for *honjin* and *waki-honjin*. They were the greatest boost to business since peace, for most of them had to use the Tokaido, and a lord of any importance could hardly keep face with a parade of less than two or three thousand men.

Kaempfer saw many of their processions, processions like the two that were converging on Okitsu that same day. And he probably got a better look at them than did the ordinary people of Japan, who, if they found themselves near such a cortege, were obliged to kneel with their faces in the roadway. Listen as the doctor catalogs the paraphernalia of pomp displayed by a daimyo of middling grade:

"1. Numerous troops of fore-runners, harbingers, clerks, cooks, and other inferior officers, begin the march, they being to provide lodgings, victuals and other necessary things, for the entertainment of their prince and master, and his court. They are follow'd by,

"2. The prince's heavy baggage . . . with his coat of arms . . . carried upon horses, each with a banner . . . or upon men's shoulders, with multitudes of inspectors to look after them.

"3. Great numbers of smaller retinues, belonging to the chief officers and noblemen attending the prince . . . some in . . . palanquins, others on horseback.

"4. The prince's own numerous train, marching in an admirable and curious order, and divided into several troops, each headed by a proper commanding officer: As

> "*1.* Five, more or less, fine led-horses, led each by two grooms, one on each side, two footmen walking behind.
>
> "*2.* Five, or six, and sometimes more porters, richly clad walking one by one, and carrying . . . lacker'd chests, and japan'd neat trunks and baskets upon their shoulders, wherein are kept the gowns, cloaths, wearing apparel, and other necessaries for the daily use of the prince; each porter is attended by two footmen, who take up his charge by turns.
>
> "*3.* Ten, or more fellows walking again one by one, and carrying rich scymeters, pikes of state . . . and other weapons in lacker'd wooden cases, as also quivers with bows and arrows . . . .
>
> "*4.* Two, three, or more men, who carry the pikes of state, as badges of the prince's power and authority, adorn'd at the upper end with bunches of cockfeathers . . . or other particular ornaments . . . .
>
> "*5.* A gentleman carrying the prince's hat, which he wears to shelter himself from the heat of the sun, and which is cover'd with black velvet. He is attended likewise by two footmen.
>
> "*6.* A gentleman carrying the prince's sombreiro or umbrello which is cover'd in like manner with black velvet, attended by two footmen.

"*7.* Some more . . . trunks, with the prince's coat of arms upon them, each with two men to take care of it.

"*8.* Sixteen, more or less, of the prince's pages, and gentlemen of his bed-chamber, richly clad, walking two by two before his palanquin. They are taken out from among the first quality of his court.

"*9.* The prince himself sitting in a stately . . . palanquin, carried by six or eight men, clad in rich liveries, with several others walking at the palanquin's sides, to take it up by turns. Two or three gentlemen of the prince's bed-chamber walk at the palanquin's side, to give him what he wants and asks for, and to assist and support him in going in or out of the palanquin.

"*10.* Two, or three horses of state, the saddles cover'd with black. One of these horses carries a large elbow-chair, which is sometimes cover'd with black velvet. . . . These horses are attended each by several grooms and footmen in liveries, and some are led by the prince's own pages.

"*11.* Two pike-bearers.

"*12.* Ten or more people, carrying each two baskets of a monstrous large size, fix'd to the ends of a pole, which they lay on their shoulders in such a manner, that one basket hangs down before, another behind them. These baskets are more for state, than for any use. . . . In this order marches the prince's own train, which is follow'd by

"5. Six to twelve led-horses, with their leaders, grooms, and footmen, all in liveries.

"6. A multitude of the prince's domesticks, and other officers of his court, with their own very numerous trains and attendants, pike-bearers, chest-bearers, and footmen in liveries . . . the whole troop is headed by the prince's high-steward carried in a palanquin. . . .

"It is a sight exceedingly curious and worthy of admiration, to see all the persons, who compose the numerous train of a great prince . . . marching in an elegant order, with a decent becoming gravity, and keeping so profound a silence, that not the least noise is to be heard, save what must necessarily arise from the motion and rushing of their habits, and the trampling of the horses and men."

The Tokaido's travelers were certainly intriguing, even spectacular. But it is not difficult to understand why Dr. Kaempfer was equally fascinated by the weird and wonderful types who made the highway their home and their life.

At any time of day there might be a mountain priest, long-haired, black-hatted, ponderous rosary looped over rough hemp uniform, pacing beside the Dutchman's horse, thumping the ground with a great staff, rattling its iron rings, and flinging out a windy speech capped by a "frightful noise" blown upon a "trumpet made of a large shell."

Incantations and prayers were the business of his kind, austerities in the mountains the key to their powers. They were able to command both native Shinto and imported Buddhist gods, "to conjure and drive out evil spirits, . . . to recover stolen goods, and to discover the thieves, to fortel future events, to explain dreams, to cure desperate distempers, to find out the guilt, or innocence, of persons accused of crimes and misdemeanors." In pursuing the last they would likely require that the accused walk over burning coals: no innocent man, they asserted, would char.

Kaempfer was cool to these zealots, but he warmed to the *bikuni*, begging nuns. When one of them singled him out, approached him, and sang him "a rural song," he dug into his pockets, for if a gentleman "proves very liberal and charitable, she will keep him company and divert him for some hours," and they were "much the handsomest girls we saw in Japan."

Once these *bikuni* had used song to propagate Buddhism among housewives, but they had slipped from ancient standards. Now they seldom bothered with housewives and their songs seemed little concerned with Buddhism. They painted their faces and wore attractive kimonos. True, they shaved their heads, but they took care to cover them with comely hoods of silk. Their manners were delightful, said Kaempfer, and "seemingly modest. However not to extol their modesty beyond what it deserves, it must be observ'd, that they make nothing of laying their bosoms quite bare to the view of charitable travellers, all the while they keep them company, under pretence of its being customary in the country, and . . . for ought I know, they may be, tho' never so religiously shav'd, full as impudent and lascivious, as any whore in a publick bawdy-house."

Kaempfer was not far off in his surmise, if surmise it was. Assault on a nun was considered one of the five heinous crimes, but *bikuni* invited a certain amount of assault and seldom complained about it afterward.

Children there were, too, sometimes the offspring of mountain priests, who brought them along to help in begging. "These little bastards are exceedingly troublesome. . . . In some places they and their fathers accost travellers in company with a troop of *bikuni* and with their rattling, singing, trumpeting, chattering, and crying, make such a horrid, frightful noise, as would make one mad or deaf. . . .

"There are many more beggars . . . some sick, some stout and lusty enough, who get people's charity by praying, singing, playing upon fiddles, guitars, and other musical instruments, or performing some juggler's tricks . . . [some] sit upon the road all day long upon a small coarse mat. They have a flat bell . . . lying before them, and . . . with a lamentable singing-tune . . . address the God Amida, as the patron and advocate of departed souls. Mean while they beat almost continually with a small wooden hammer upon the aforesaid bell, and this they say, in order to be the sooner heard by Amida, and I am apt to think, . . . by passengers too. . . .

"The crowd and throng upon the roads in this country is not a little encreas'd by numberless small retail-merchants and children of country people, who run about from morning to night, following travellers, and offering them . . . their poor . . . merchandise; such as for instance several cakes and sweetmeats, wherein the quantity of sugar is so inconsiderable, that it is scarce perceptible . . . or else all sorts of roots boil'd in water and salt, road-books, straw-shoes for horses and men, ropes, tooth-pickers, and a multitude of other trifles. . . ."

At the edge of Okitsu, Dr. Kaempfer kept right on taking notes: "This town being situate not far from the sea, the inhabitants make very good salt out of the sand on the coasts, after they have pour'd sea-water upon it at repeated times."

The Dutchmen's train had reached the town, and now it halted. Hanzo was kneeling before them, bidding them welcome. Wrote Kaempfer: "The landlord observes the same customs upon our arrival, which he doth upon the arrival of the princes and lords of the empire . . . he addresses every one of us, making his compliments with a low bow, which before the palanquins of the chief Japanese, and our resident, is so low, that he touches the ground with his hands, and almost with his forehead." Hanzo rose, dusted his knees, and fell in at the head of the troop to lead it into town.

On his way from Seikenji to the Minaguchi-ya, Kaempfer, having lost his begging nun at the edge of Okitsu, now turned his eye to the painted females in front of each general inn. "Walk in, walk in," they cried, "walk right in, gentlemen. You'll find warm welcome here." "They make," the doctor remarked, "no inconsiderable noise. . . ."

There was noise, too, in front of the Minaguchi-ya, where a curious crowd had gathered to stare at the Red-hairs. Urchins made faces and screamed, "Koreans!"—an epithet that exhausted their concept of foreigners.

It was a brief show. The Dutch dismounted quickly and, screened by their Japanese escort, passed through the dolphin-topped gate into the raked-sand areaway. Hanzo repeated his welcome, his compliments, and his low bows. The guests removed their boots and stepped up onto the matted floor.

The Minaguchi-ya had four rows of rooms but at the moment all their sliding doors were opened and the handsomely painted landscapes which they bore had given way to the cool green vista of the garden, seen straight through the building. The innermost quarters were the finest, and there the Dutch were led, as rows of doors closed shut behind them. They were penned for the night, and it irked them, but it was a pleasant prison. The garden lay before them and swept round on the left, as intimate with their room as sea to ship. Behind the wall on their right was a privy (immaculately fresh and fragrant with flowers), a dressing room, and a bath. There a big tub of satin-smooth, sweet-scented pine, brimming with steamy water, faced the open doors of its own small garden.

Not all the party, of course, could stay at the Minaguchi-ya. The four Hollanders and the chief Japanese were installed there. Hanzo had made arrangements for forty lesser Japanese to stay in general inns, and his friend Denzaemon had assisted by nominating several farmhouses to sleep the porters. With daimyo and Dutch, Okitsu bulged that night.

Now it was time for Hanzo's brief moment with his exotic guests. "As soon as we have taken possession of our apartment," Kaempfer recorded, "in comes the landlord with some of his chief male domesticks, each with a dish of tea in his hand, which they present to every one of us with a low bow, according to his rank and dignity. . . . This done, the necessary apparatus for smoaking is brought in, consisting of a board of wood or brass, . . . upon which are plac'd a small fire pan with coals, a pot to spit in, a small box fill'd with tobacco cut small, and some long pipes with small brass heads; as also another japan'd board or dish, with . . . something to eat, as for instance, several sorts of fruits, figs, nuts, several sorts of cakes . . . and other trumperies of this kind." Had he and his associates been Japanese, Kaempfer noted enviously, other necessaries would have been served by the maids of the establishment. "These wenches also lay the cloth, and wait at table, taking this opportunity to engage their guests to farther favors. But 'tis quite otherwise with us. For the landlords themselves, and their . . . domesticks, after they have presented us with a dish of tea, as abovesaid, are not suffer'd, upon any account whatever, to approach or to enter our appartments, but whatever we want, 'tis the sole business of our own servants to provide us with the same." Hanzo had had his last look at the Dutchmen until they were to leave.

He was, however, kept busy. The Japanese in the party demanded service, and the kitchen had to be looked after. The Dutch, throughout their journey, insisted on "dishes dress'd after the European manner" and so they brought their own cooks from Nagasaki. Hanzo's cooks had to prepare supper for the Japanese escort, and the innkeeper did not have to be told that two sets of artists in one kitchen was an invitation to riot. He intervened several times to smooth ruffled temperament.

While two culinary cliques made Hanzo's kitchen a danger spot, two daimyo's trains were doing as much for the whole town. One was already installed at Tezuka's *honjin*, the other was at the moment strutting slowly towards Ichikawa's.

Dr. Kaempfer, corked up in the Minaguchi-ya, did not see this approach, but he had seen many on the road. The palanquins of the daimyo and his chief officers were raised high in the air, "whilst the bearers by their short deliberate steps and stiff knees, affect a ridiculous fear and circumspection." And all the while, pages, pike-bearers, umbrella- and hat-bearers, chest-bearers and footmen in livery performed that strange dance reserved for great towns, their meetings with another lord, or, as now, their approach to a post station where they would pass the night. "Every step they make they draw up their foot quite to their back, in the mean time stretching out the arm on the opposite side as far as they can, and putting themselves in such a posture, as if they had a mind to swim through the air. Mean while the pikes, hats, umbrellos, chests, boxes, baskets, and whatever else they carry, are danced and toss'd about in a very singular manner, answering the motion of their bodies."

Thus they came to Ichikawa's *honjin*, its entrance screened with curtains blazoning their lord's crest. That worthy disappeared into the interior, the noisy work of posting guards and unloading the baggage went forward, and the village elders, looking harassed, checked the fire watch and uttered little prayers that there would be no clashes tonight between rival groups.

At the Minaguchi-ya, dinner was served. The Dutch had brought their own serving ware, chairs, even a dining table. On that table appeared foods carried from Nagasaki, including European wines foggy from being jogged up the Tokaido. Hanzo added odds and ends: one pheasant, one halibut, one sea bass, twenty-three eggs (most of these disappeared at breakfast), tangerines, and hot saké. It would seem that the Dutch were fair trenchermen, but Dr. Kaempfer insisted that their Japanese escort exhibited far greater capacity. Dinner for the Japanese that night was supplemented by rice cooked with red beans, that ceremonial dish having been ordered for them by the Dutch as a pretty compliment.

Dinner in the Japanese apartment was lively: " . . . They sit after meals drinking and singing some songs to make one another merry, or else they propose some riddles round, or play at some other game, and he that cannot explain the riddle, or loses the game, is oblig'd to drink a glass. 'Tis again quite otherwise with us in this respect for we sit at table and eat our victuals very quietly."

Okitsu went on a binge that night. Gambling was wide open and frenzied. Inns rocked with songs and drunken laughter and women's squeals. The Minaguchi-ya reverberated to the Japanese party and its raucous game of forfeits. And in the midst of it all, four sobersided

Dutchmen faced each other across their table and stolidly stowed away pheasant, halibut, and sea bass.

The Minaguchi-ya finally quieted down but the town sizzled until dawn set all three cavalcades in motion again. By arrangement never put into words, the lesser daimyo stayed in his *honjin* until the greater had passed, and thus avoided a dignity-bruising encounter. By then, the Dutch had consumed the last of Hanzo's twenty-three eggs.

"When everything is ready for us to set out again," wrote Kaempfer, diagramming Hanzo's second appearance before his guests, "the landlord is call'd, and our resident, in presence of the two interpreters, pays him the reckoning in gold, laid upon a small board. He draws near in a creeping posture, kneeling, holding his hands down to the floor, and when he takes the table which the money is laid upon, he bows down his forehead almost quite to the ground, in token of submission and gratitude, uttering with a deep voice the word, ah, ah, ah! whereby in this country inferiors shew their deference and respect to their superiors." Hanzo was, however, registering more than deference and respect. It was with genuine pleasure that he laid hands on some gold. Many Japanese officials traveled at government expense, which meant troublesome requisitions and almost endless red tape before payment appeared. The fact that the Dutch paid cash did not lessen their popularity with innkeepers.

"It is a custom in this country, which we likewise observe," Kaempfer adds, "that guests before they quit the inn, order their servants to sweep the room they lodged in, not to leave any dirt or ungrateful dust behind them."

Hanzo escorted his guests out of Okitsu as he had escorted them in, basking in glory as he strode along the highway. At the edge of the station he bowed them on their way, wishing mightily that he might continue with them right into Edo.

The last of the great guests gone, and without a single untoward incident, the town relaxed, sprawling lazily in the spring sunshine. Hanzo, Ichikawa, Tezuka—all were pleased with the night's business. Daimyo, like the Dutch, paid cash, and there had been generous tips all around, plus what their men had dropped in individual pursuit of pleasure. From the owners of Seikenji's salve shops to the river-crossing coolies, Okitsu's townsmen jingled coins and smiled.

Not that it was all profit, as old Tezuka would have been the first to tell you. A *honjin* or *waki-honjin* had the same problem that has plagued innkeepers since the first inn. "Most annoying of all is to lose things—tableware, candlesticks, smoking sets, etc. If fifty smoking pipes are offered, scarcely ten are returned. Tea cups and other small things are carried away under clothing. All this occurs because there are so many people milling around, including the daily-hire bearers, and everything is hustle and bustle. Some throw away their straw sandals and demand new ones. When it rains, straw mats are taken away as raincoats. Many of the things we lose were hired for the occasion from other places." But the people of Okitsu had heard this speech before.

The Dutch went on to Edo. There they lodged in an inn appropriately named Nagasaki-ya. Lodged is perhaps not the right word, for again they were closely confined. In the teeming city, but not able to roam it, their greatest thrills came from watching the "flowers of Edo," the fires that almost nightly scarred the city before its intrepid firemen put them out.

It was astonishing, though, how many kinsmen their innkeeper suddenly acquired, all of whom found it imperative to call on him while the Dutch were in his house. It was even more astonishing how many of these were noted scholars and great daimyo. True to character, the scholars sought information about medicine, physics, botany, and astronomy, while the lords of the empire wanted to talk politics, geography, history, and the art of war. The innkeeper applied himself to study of the stars and world affairs.

After more than two weeks of this, the day arrived for the Dutch to make their trip to Edo Castle. Their gifts were formally laid out in the audience chamber, and they waited, interminably it seemed, in various anterooms until finally the resident-director was summoned. He crawled on hands and knees to a designated spot in front of the Shogun, bowed his forehead to the floor, and retreated, crab-like, in the same position.

Once, that had been all there was to it. But in Kaempfer's day the Dutchmen were not let off so easily. All four of them were led deeper into the palace. In an inner chamber the Shogun's ladies and his several offspring were secreted behind a bamboo screen. Before this audience, which could see without being seen, Dr. Kaempfer and the two secretaries were required to perform: "... To walk, to stand still, to compliment each other, to dance, to jump, to play the drunkard, to speak broken Japanese, to read Dutch, to paint, to sing, to put our cloaks on and off... [and to] kiss one another, like man and wife, which the ladies particularly shew'd by their laughter to be well pleas'd with.... I joined to my dance a love-song in high German. In this manner, and with innumerable such apish tricks, we must suffer ourselves to contribute to the court's diversion." Only the director, by looking exceedingly solemn, managed to escape performing.

On their journey back to Nagasaki, the ordeal at court behind them, their guards were a little more lenient. It was on their return visit to the Minaguchi-ya that Hanzo managed to smuggle in a few visitors. Physicians, particularly, were eager to learn the latest European methods. Dr. Kaempfer's evenings were usually busy with clandestine visitors, and eighty-five years later another Dutch physician, C. P. Thunberg, introduced the mercury treatment for syphilis. Along the Tokaido, medicine and surgery profited from these visits of the Dutch.

And many Japanese journeyed to Nagasaki to study there, perhaps to earn a certificate of proficiency from the Red-hairs. Some of them wrote treatises based on what they had learned, like the early one called *Komo Geka* ("Red-hair Surgery"). All over Japan men were learning Dutch as the one remaining avenue to the achievements of Western science. There was even a poem written about it:

> Dutch letters
> Running sideways
> Are like a line of wild geese
> Flying in the sky.

OSCAR LEWIS

A day in the life

Oscar Lewis, a professor of anthropology at the University of Illinois, has done fieldwork in Mexico, India, and the United States. His other writings include: *Village Life in Northern India*, *Pedro Martínez*, *Children of Sanchez*, and *La Vida*, for which he received the National Book Award.

Cast of Characters

PEDRO MARTÍNEZ, age 59, *the father*
ESPERANZA GARCÍA, about 54, *the mother*
CONCHITA MARTÍNEZ, age 29, *the eldest daughter, married and living with her husband, Juan*
FELIPE MARTÍNEZ, age 23, *the eldest son*
MARTIN MARTÍNEZ, age 22, *the second son*
RICARDO MARTÍNEZ, age 18, *the third son*
MACHRINA MARTÍNEZ, age 17, *the youngest daughter*
MOISÉS MARTÍNEZ, age 13, *the youngest son*
HERMAN MARTÍNEZ, age 7, *Conchita's illegitimate son*

The ancient highland village of Azteca lay quiet and serene on the mountain slope in the early morning darkness. The air was cool and fresh after the long night rain. Spreading from the top of the slope to the broad valley below, eight barrios, each with its own chapel and patron saint, formed little communities within the larger village. A paved road connecting Azteca with the main highway cut across the village and ended abruptly at the plaza. Here were the municipal building, the central church, the mill, a few small shops, and a bare park. Extending up and down the slope the old terraced streets, laboriously constructed of blue-gray volcanic rock, were lined by small, one-story adobe houses with their patios of semi-tropical plants and trees set behind low stone walls.

In the barrio of San José, halfway between the highest and lowest point in the village, stood the house of Pedro Martínez, almost hidden by the overhanging branches of the native plum trees in his orchard. The tile-roofed house was typical of those in San José, the poorest of the eight barrios, and consisted of one windowless room and an attached kitchen flimsily built of cane stalks. The house site was still called by its pre-Hispanic Nahuatl name, *Tlatlapancan*, or "the place where much was broken," referring to a local legend which told how the village god Azteco, said to be the son of the Virgin Mary, had broken one of his clay toys on this site. Forty-three years before, Pedro had thought the house site would be a propitious one and had bought it for fifty pesos.

Over the years Pedro had carefully worked on the little house and its neglected plot of ground, planting guave, coffee, avocado, hog plums, and other plants, all of which contributed to the family diet. Five years ago he and his sons had built the kitchen and had moved the simple hearth of three large stones from the smoky adobe room to the more airy kitchen where the smoke could filter through the spaces between the cane stalk of the walls. For all of its simplicity, it was the best house Pedro and his wife Esperanza had ever lived in.

It was still dark on this July morning when Esperanza opened her eyes. The house was quiet and no sounds came from the street. Esperanza got out of the hard bed in which she and Pedro slept, smoothed her dress, and wrapped a thin dark blue cotton shawl about her head and shoulders to ward off the morning chill. She walked barefoot across the dirt floor, found the big clay water jug, and dashed some cold water on her face; then she dried herself with the edge of her shawl.

Kneeling at the hearth, Esperanza uncovered the ashes of last night's fire and fanned some still glowing chunks of charcoal into flames. She didn't want to use a match to light the fire for a box of matches cost five centavos and was still a luxury. Now the big clock in the plaza struck four. It was a half-hour earlier than she had thought. Well, her daughter Machrina could sleep a little longer. It was the time of year when the men planted and cultivated the corn, and the women had to rise early to prepare food for them. In the winter months, during the harvest, when the men sometimes worked all night and the women had to give them food at any hour, Esperanza and her daughter had to snatch sleep sitting on the low stools. It was only in September and October when the men were harvesting plums that the women could stay in bed as late as six o'clock.

Esperanza filled the clay pot and set the cinnamon tea to boil. Over a hundred *tortillas* had to be made—twenty-five each for Pedro and for Felipe, Martin, and Ricardo, the three oldest sons who worked in the fields, and ten more for Pedro's dog. Esperanza lifted down one of the tin cans hanging from the rafters where she kept her supplies of food. It contained corn which had been ground at the mill the previous night. Before the coming of the mill, a few years back, Esperanza had got up at two in the morning during the farming season to grind soaked corn into a fine dough. Now the mill did most of that work for her; she had only to regrind the dough a bit to make it smoother and to give it the taste of the grinding stone. The men of the village had opposed the corn mill because, they said, hand-ground corn tasted better. But the women had won out; the mill was a success. Yes, it was good to have the mill. But all the same it was expensive. The thirty-four centavos paid to the miller would have bought half enough corn to feed the whole family for a meal. Machrina should do more grinding at home, Esperanza thought as she knelt before the grinding stone.

The first slapping of the *tortillas* into shape caused Pedro to stir, but the reassuring sound lulled him back to sleep. Their bed stood in the far corner of the kitchen behind an improvised wall of empty plum crates. The wall did not protect him from the noises of the kitchen but it did provide some privacy from the grown children, except during the plum season when the crates were used to haul plums. Until a year ago the whole Martínez family had slept in the other room, but Pedro had recently moved the metal, springless bed into the kitchen. It was embarrassing, he had come to realize, to lie down with one's wife in the presence of one's grown children. And the bed, which he had acquired almost as a gift from a soldier he had met when they were both patients in the military hospital, showed off to better advantage in the kitchen.

Pedro's wish for privacy, however, had been partially thwarted when Machrina announced that she too wanted to sleep in the kitchen "since it was not nice for a girl to sleep all alone with her grown brothers." Machrina and little Herman, who had shared her bed since infancy, now slept in a cold and draughty corner of the kitchen. The four sons slept undisturbed in the adobe room.

When the plaza clock struck five Esperanza awakened her daughter who quickly jumped up, fully dressed in a slip, plain cotton dress, and apron, and took her mother's place at the grinding stone. Machrina looked younger than her seventeen years. Her brown hair was parted in the middle and worn in two braids; her face was quiet and serious but during the day, when she chatted with a friend or with her brothers, it was often lighted up by a smile that revealed her tiny, childlike teeth. Now she tucked her bare feet under her short, plump body and began to grind the corn. Esperanza, too, was short and round, but she rarely smiled and her face generally had a drawn, dull expression.

Esperanza next woke Martin since it was his turn to go for water. He slipped into his soiled cotton pants and huaraches, washed his face in the cold water, and without a word shouldered the yoke with the two water cans and left for the fountain. The daily rains now watered the fruit trees and the garden, so Martin had to make only eight trips back and forth to fill the family water jug. In the dry season the boys had to make twenty trips.

Felipe, the eldest son, awoke before Martin had finished his chore. Felipe was the most fastidious member of the family and took longest to dress. At night he took almost all his clothes off under his blanket and hung them on a nail. He brushed his teeth (without toothpaste), washed his face and hands with soap every day, and used a rag to dry himself with instead of his shirttail. He had a small pocket mirror which he let no one else use. All this had come about since Felipe had found a sweetheart, a widow much older than himself. Now, seated on the iron cot frame which supported the *otate*, a hard mat made of bamboo-like stalks placed crosswise and lashed together, Felipe groped for his huaraches. His left eye was blind, due to a childhood fall from a plum tree, and he turned his head in a rather exaggerated manner to see to the left.

As the eldest son, Felipe tried to dominate his brothers and sister, but was generally unsuccessful, particularly with Martin, who was taller and stronger than Felipe and almost the same age. Martin had flatly refused to obey Felipe or to show him the respect due an older brother. For this Felipe blamed his father, who had never permitted him to exercise authority.

Pedro and his third son, Ricardo, were now getting up. Pedro was short and stocky and his paunch bulged as he dressed in his homemade, dirty, patched shirt and white, pyjama-like *calzones*. He slipped his blackened, calloused feet into heavy huaraches cut from an old rubber tire. A sparse, untrimmed mustache covered his upper lip and he almost always looked unshaven. On Saturdays when he bathed and changed into clean clothes or on the days he went to town or to Mexico City, Pedro wore a pair of dark store-bought trousers and looked more sophisticated. He usually wore his straw sombrero tilted down over his eyes, a rather cocky angle for a man of fifty-nine.

Felipe, Martin, and Ricardo all looked like their father and until recently had dressed as he did. Now they wore factory-made shirts which they had demanded, but none of them owned dark trousers. The youngest son and the grandson wore old-style, homemade white *calzones* and shirts, used small sombreros, and always went barefoot.

Esperanza began to serve the men cinnamon tea, *tortillas*, chile, and salt, while Machrina filled four hemp shoulder bags with the same food for their midday meal. She added a handful of acacia pods to each bag and poured tea into four gourds. The men ate quickly, without conversation. Speaking in Nahuatl, Esperanza asked Pedro to bring home some squash for the evening meal. When Ricardo coughed over his food she warned him to wrap himself well in his blanket when they passed the stream, the abode of *los aires*, the spirits of the air.

The Martínez family had good reason to avoid these malign spirits; some years before Esperanza had become ill with a fever and had suffered a partial paralysis of the legs after having washed clothes in the stream. *Los aires*, as everyone in her village knew, could sometimes take the shape of winds, sometimes spirits, sometimes little malign people who could cause sores, pimples, paralysis, and other illnesses. One had to be on one's guard against offending them near ant-hills, stream beds, ravines, in stagnant pools, and atop the highest hills. Sometimes it helped to ask their permission in Nahuatl before taking water from a stream, but in any case it was safest not to venture too near them without being well wrapped up. Many men took a morning drink of alcohol to protect them from *los aires* before they started out to the fields, but Pedro preferred to take his when he came home at night.

By five-thirty the men were ready to leave. Each slung a bag and a serape over his shoulder. Pedro called to his dog in Nahuatl, "Now let's go." He used the old tongue with his wife and his dog, but he spoke to the children in Spanish except when he was angry. When Martin, on the other hand, said, "We're going, mamá," it was in Spanish.

The men set off in silence. Pedro walked with his dog a few paces behind the boys. When the neighbors saw them walking along in this formation they would say that Pedro looked like a veritable *patrón* striding behind his peons. Yet there were mornings when Pedro talked to the boys in the course of their two-hour walk to the fields, giving advice or telling what work had to be done. The boys, however, spoke only in answer to a question. Out of their father's earshot they would joke about their sweethearts or visits to the saloons of Cuahnahuac. But this morning they moved silently down the road.

It was still barely light. All around them, just beyond the far edges of the fields, the blue-green slopes of the pine-covered mountains rose through the morning mist. Pedro and Ricardo were headed for the mountain slope cornfield which they had cleared the year before. This was communal land belonging to the municipality which consisted of seven villages; anyone could work it. New clearings had to be made every two or three years, for heavy rains washed the topsoil away. To acquire new fields Pedro and his sons burned the brush and weeds, cut down young trees, and built new stone fences. The boys worked well; they had the largest mountain clearing in Azteca. But the crops could supply enough corn and beans for only three or four months. So Pedro had to try other means of earning a living as well—making rope from maguey fiber, selling plums, hiring out his sons as farm-hands. One thing he would not do to earn money was to make charcoal for sale, as so many of his neighbors did. This practice, he knew, was wasteful of the precious oak and pine forests and ultimately ruined the land. He had been one of the leaders in the struggle for the preservation of the communal forest lands. So he made charcoal only once a year and only for the use of his family.

Felipe and Martin were on their way to Don Porfirio's fields where they were working as peons. These fields, located on fairly level ground, were cultivated by plow rather than by the ancient *coa* or hoe which Pedro used on his mountain strip. The land was easier to work than the mountain clearing and Don Porfirio was less of a taskmaster than Pedro. So the boys were glad of a chance to work for Don Porfirio and to earn some cash for the family. Pedro could be expected to give them something later on—a new shirt or a sombrero or some pocket money.

When they got to Don Porfirio's field the two older boys left the road. Pedro nodded in parting and walked on in silence with Ricardo, absorbed in his own thoughts. He had sold a mule to Don Gonzalo the day before in order to pay off his debt to Doña Conde, and it infuriated him to think that he had to sell it for only 300 pesos when it was easily worth 450. And now he had only one mule left. This meant that the boys could only bring half the usual amount of wood down the mountains and that there would be little left to sell after Esperanza took what she needed. Besides, during the plum season the boys could earn only half of what they had the year before hauling crates of fruit to the railway station. And at harvest twice as many trips would have to be made to bring the corn down from the fields.

Pedro couldn't remember a time when he hadn't been in debt. Early this past year, after he had come out of the hospital where he had had surgery, he had borrowed 300 pesos from the widow Isabel to pay medical bills. Then, finding his indebtedness to her irksome because she expected free "legal" advice from him, he had borrowed 150 pesos from a wealthy politico to help pay her back, and 300 pesos from Asunción to pay other bills. And all this time he was paying back, at eight per cent monthly interest, a loan of 200 pesos from the previous year. At times it seemed as if he were walking forever in a treadmill of old obligations. "The debt remains; only the creditors change."

For Pedro as for most of the inhabitants of Azteca, getting enough money for food and clothing from one harvest to another was the all-absorbing, never-solved problem. At best Pedro, with the assistance of his wife and sons, earned 2,400 pesos a year ($300 at the 1948 rate of exchange). The boys earned about half of this by hiring out as peons and by gathering and selling firewood. Another third came from plums, rope-making, and corn. A small amount, hardly more than 60 pesos, came from fees the villagers paid to Pedro for going with them to see a lawyer or to attend a court session in Cuahnahuac. Pedro had learned something about legal matters during his years of political activity and had gained the reputation of being "half a lawyer." However, his income from "legal" advice was no greater than that from Esperanza's occasional small sales. Pedro could have doubled his income if he and the boys had worked as peons throughout the year at the local rate of four pesos a day, but he refused to work or permit his sons to work on haciendas which were still a symbol of oppression to him. Steady, year-round work was not available in the village, and in any case Pedro preferred to work as an independent peasant.

It was to become an independent peasant with a parcel of land of his own that Pedro had fought with Zapata in the Revolution. Pedro had worked for others since he was eight years old, first tending cattle for his Uncle Agustín who often beat him, then from age ten until after his marriage as a servant and peon on haciendas where he also had been beaten. Even during the brief, happy period when his mother had brought him and his sister to live with her and their stepfather in the large town of Tepetate and he had entered a public school, Pedro had had to defend himself from his "superiors." At that time he spoke only Nahuatl, the language of the Aztecs, and he would get into fights because his schoolmates called him "Indian," in an insulting manner.

"I did not know how to speak Spanish, but I knew how to fight. Then they would go crying to the teacher and he would come out and give me more strokes. I had a lot of trouble but I really liked school. One day when it was almost time to go home at noon the teacher was out of the room and the boys began to say to me in low voices, 'Indian, Indian.' I just raised my elbow up a little and hit one of them right where it hurt. Uy! He began to yell and the teacher came running, saying, 'What's going on here?'

"Well, all of them told on me and he hit me twelve times with a stick. Zas! Poor me! He even pushed me around on the floor. He threw me around until I urinated. Then, since it was time to go and the doors were being closed, he took me and made me kneel on a table with my arms stretched out and a stone on each hand. I tell you I was scared. They were leaving me a prisoner! But just as the last teacher was leaving I jumped off that table and began to yell and ran all the way to my house. I told my mother and stepfather what had happened. My mother said, 'Well, you may be ignorant, but you *did* stand up for yourself.' "

Pedro did not finish the first grade and barely learned to read because his stepfather took him out of school to begin to earn eighteen centavos a day at a nearby hacienda. When the Revolution came Pedro was already married and the father of a child; it was natural for him to sympathize with Zapata and he joined the fight. Later, he worked for the improvement of his own village, taking part in the rebuilding, in the new elections, in the local government, in the fight for the conservation of the forests, and in the construction of the road. And old abuses had been ended. The village regained the right to use its communal hillside land and some fortunate peasants received *ejido* land reclaimed from the haciendas. Indebtedness and acute poverty were lessened, the pawning of children as servants was abolished, school attendance increased, and there was more personal freedom. But for Pedro the Revolution was a failure. He believed that he did not live much better than he had under the pre-Revolutionary government of Porfirio Díaz. High prices and the increasing need for cash made life difficult. "What good is it to have freedom if we don't have enough to eat? Before it was the hacienda owners who exploited us, now it's the government and the bankers. It's all the same."

Yes, Pedro felt defeated. For him the Revolution had ended with the death of Zapata. His twenty-five years as a politico had gained him little more than prestige. His laborious effort to teach himself to read and write and to educate his eldest daughter had not "raised up" the family as he had hoped. Even his conversion, fifteen years ago, from Catholicism to Seventh-Day Adventism had left him dissatisfied. Pedro's life had been a search for ideals and causes rather than a struggle for personal aggrandizement. He did not understand the changing times, the money economy, or the business values of post-Revolutionary Mexico. He knew only that he was still a poor, landless peasant who depended heavily upon the labor of his sons to make ends meet.

Pedro was worried because his two older sons had begun to resist his plans for them. Felipe complained that too hard work was ruining his health. He wanted to learn a trade! Martin wanted to become a baker. When he had turned eighteen his godmother had offered to take him as an apprentice in her bakery and he had been eager to accept. Pedro had firmly forbidden it. He needed his sons to work in the fields. But as soon as Martin became of age he apprenticed himself to the godmother without consulting anyone. He had worked for six months without wages, and Pedro had scolded him until Martin wept in desperation. Whenever Martin missed a meal at home Pedro became enraged and shouted, "I don't want you to work for that piece of *tortilla* they give you." He ordered Martin to refuse all food at the bakery and to take his meals in his father's house. When the planting season started Martin returned to work in the fields, but Pedro feared that he intended to go back to the bakery when the harvest was over.

Pedro had different plans for his youngest son, Moisés, who was too delicate to bear up under the life of a peasant. With God's permission and the help of his older sons, Pedro hoped to educate Moisés to be a teacher "or perhaps even a lawyer." Pedro would be happy if one of his children could have a "career." It would benefit the whole family.

The path was lighter now and Pedro came out of his reverie to realize that the walk to his field was nearly over. He caught up with Ricardo and began to tell him just where to begin the weeding for the day.

When the men had gone Esperanza took stock of the day's food supply. There was only a little corn dough left, barely enough for the two boys still asleep, and some chile, cinnamon, sugar, and salt. There was no money because Pedro had used the mule money to buy huaraches for Felipe, a sombrero for himself, and a machete for Ricardo—all badly needed for work in the fields. The rest of the money had gone to the hateful Doña Conde. Where could she borrow now? What small thing could she sell?

These were the questions that faced Esperanza nearly every day. Yesterday's money was usually gone by the next morning except when she put away a small sum in one of her hiding places around the house. Even when Pedro gave her larger sums it would usually be spent quickly, either to repay debts or to buy something they urgently needed. But the really bad times were when there was a serious illness in the family. Then they had to sell nearly everything, sometimes all their young turkeys or a grinding stone, sometimes a mule.

Esperanza wondered from whom she could borrow. She could not ask her cousin Maria for a loan, for she had not paid back the ten pesos borrowed a few days ago. Nor could she approach her Aunt Gloria: she had herself stopped by yesterday to ask for a small loan. They were her neighbors to the right but they had spoken badly about Pedro ever since he had become a politico. Why they were so resentful Esperanza could not see, for his political activity had certainly not made the family "even a little rich." No one else nearby ever had enough money to lend, and Esperanza did not want to borrow a small sum at interest from those who had plenty. It was better to sell the turkey even though it would be a long time before she would be able to buy another baby turkey to raise. Esperanza drank her cinnamon tea and went to look for the bird. It was seven when she put on her shawl, hiding her turkey under it (why should her neighbors know her business?) and left for the barrio of San Martín where she knew of several houses where they ate well.

Machrina went out to the back of the orchard. The younger boys were still asleep and there was no danger that they would spy on her through the bushes as they sometimes did. Like most of the villagers, the Martínez had no toilet and no outhouse. When she came back Machrina washed her hands before she knelt at the grinding stone to begin making *tortillas*. She called sharply to Moisés and Herman and told them to wash. She generally adopted a scolding tone toward the younger boys, particularly to Herman, her special charge. She had taken care of him ever since her sister Conchita had come home from school and given birth to the fatherless boy. Even during the six months when Conchita was nursing him and still stayed at home, it was Machrina (then ten years old) who had carried Herman about, bathed him every three days, swaddled him carefully so that he would grow up to be quiet and well-mannered, and washed his soiled clothes. But during the past few years Machrina had gradually stopped playing with him and picking him up and had begun to scold him often. When he misbehaved she spanked him. It didn't trouble Machrina that Herman now avoided her and seemed to prefer Moisés' company to hers; it was right that he should keep his distance and respect her.

The boys had finished eating and were playing in the patio when Esperanza returned an hour later, still carrying the turkey. While she ate the two *tortillas* Machrina had made for her, she told her daughter she had been offered only two and a half pesos for the turkey. There was nothing to do now but go to Señor Don Porfirio and ask for an advance on the boys' wages.

Before she left again Esperanza reminded Moisés to bring water from the fountain and then to go to school. She sent Herman to her cousin's house to bring back the scissors she had borrowed. Machrina knew her work and needed no instructions. Ever since Esperanza's illness of the year before Machrina had shown that she could be depended upon. To show her family, particularly her father, that she could be depended on seemed in fact to be Machrina's only goal nowadays. She had gone to the local school through the fifth grade and had wanted to become a teacher, or at least a seamstress. But suddenly Pedro took her out of school to help her mother and no one dared say a word in protest. It was true that Esperanza had not been well and that looking after so many men and her little grandson seemed to be too much for her.

Alone now, Machrina folded the blankets on the two beds, then picked up the twig broom and began to sweep the dirt floor. She swept unhurriedly, taking special pains with the corners, for her father noticed whether or not the work was well done. She had often heard him speak, half jokingly, half scornfully, of how ignorant her mother had been when he had married her: "She didn't know how to sew, nor sweep, nor iron, nor wash clothes. She hardly knew how to grind corn or make *tortillas*." Pedro had showed Esperanza how to do much of the housework; he had taught her even how to sweep because at first she always missed the corners. When she had tried to make him his first pair of *calzones* she had had to call in her mother to help. Actually, as Pedro himself knew, this was not Esperanza's fault. Formerly parents did not teach their daughters many domestic skills because girls married very young and the mother-in-law was obliged to teach the daughter-in-law. Esperanza was about fourteen when she married and her mother-in-law was dead.

Machrina went to clean the room where her brothers slept. She folded the blanket and straightened the straw mat on the *otate* shared by Martin and Moisés. The other boys had taken their blankets with them. The blankets were almost the most expensive things in the house; each one had cost about fifty pesos. She then piled up the rough plum crates which served as a bed for Ricardo. For a while he had shared the cot with Felipe, but Felipe had wanted it all to himself and had quarreled and complained so much every time Ricardo lay down on it that he had finally rigged up eight plum crates, two across and four down, to make a bed of his own. With a straw mat and a rag-stuffed pillow under him, and a blanket, this new bed was only a little more uncomfortable than the cot. But the crates were heavy and made more work for Machrina; they had to be piled one upon the other during the day because they took up too much space.

The adobe walls, papered here and there with old newspapers, religious posters, and calendars, had nails jutting out to hold extra clothes and sombreros. The room had little furniture and did not take long to clean. Machrina dusted the wooden chest where her father kept his most prized religious books, a copy of the Constitution of Mexico, and the Civil Code of Morelos that he referred to when neighbors consulted him about legal problems. Here too were kept important papers and a few pieces of good clothing. Machrina lined up against the wall seven stools and two reed chairs that her father had bought in the past few years. Formerly the family had used the plum crates as chairs. She also arranged three small benches that Martin had made when he studied carpentry in a class held by a recent government cultural mission.

Machrina dusted the remaining piece of furniture, a wooden table that had served as an altar when the family was Catholic. It now held small piles of old, worn school texts that Conchita had used when she taught school, some religious pamphlets, and a little frivolous reading matter which Pedro hardly approved of: several sheets of popular songs, the comic books "Chamaco" and "Paquín," and three paper-covered novels which the older children had read and reread. This was more reading matter than could be found in most Aztecan homes. In addition, there was a special pile of six Bibles, one for each member of the family who could read. Machrina carefully dusted these and when she lifted Felipe's copy a folded paper, a note from the widow, fell to the floor. "Widows are bold," she thought as she put back the note. "With no man at home to tell them what to do they can have lovers and go to all the fiestas."

Machrina went back into the kitchen, wiped the low table where

Pedro and the three oldest boys ate, and picked up some plum pits from the floor. From force of habit she looked into the table drawer to see if there was a little money that Esperanza could use for food. There was nothing, not even Pedro's toothpicks or the aspirins that Esperanza took for her headaches.

At half past nine Esperanza returned empty-handed. Don Porfirio had gone to the courthouse and would not be back until about ten. It would have been humiliating to wait for him so Esperanza returned home, sat and talked with her daughter for fifteen minutes, and then climbed the steep hill once more to Don Porfirio's house. At ten-thirty she was back again, this time with four pesos in cash and twelve *cuartillos* of corn which Don Porfirio had given her. Tired from having walked so much, she lay down to rest for half an hour.

Esperanza had noticed that she tired more easily than she used to. Maybe she was getting old, but in truth she could not say what her real age was since her mother had never told her just when she was born. Or perhaps she drank too much alcohol, as her Aunt Gloria thought she did. The tiredness had grown upon her since her long illness of the year before. Perhaps she was being bewitched by some enemy of hers or Pedro's. Pedro, who studied the Bible, had taught her not to believe in that sort of thing unless it was an absolutely clear case of sorcery. She always tried to please her husband, but if it were sorcery should she not go to a *curandero* before it was too late?

While her mother rested Machrina washed the few breakfast dishes, cleaned the grinding stone, and prepared half of the corn by soaking it in water and lime. She revived the fire with a straw fan and placed two iron bars across the hearth to hold the tin can in which the corn would be boiled.

At eleven Esperanza got up and left for the plaza to do the day's marketing. She hurried down the hill, turned left, and walked along an unpaved street heedless of the mud and deep puddles of water left by the daily heavy rains. In fact the water felt good to her bare feet for it was almost noon and the ground was getting hot. At the end of this long street she turned right onto a steep, stone-paved street that was lined with houses, several of which had windows and were smoothly plastered and whitewashed and much finer than any in her barrio. She was now in the larger barrio of San Martín where some well-to-do peasants lived.

Esperanza quickened her step, pulled her shawl more tightly around her shoulders, and, as any good Aztecan wife would, kept her eyes to the ground except for an occasional swift glance when she passed a house or looked up to see who was coming her way. The street was quiet and empty except for a few pigs and chickens. Two women, still in the distance, were returning from the plaza. Esperanza could hear the slapping of *tortillas* in the houses and regretted that she had made such a late start. Her head ached, she was thirsty; and for the first time in a long while she felt that she wanted a drink of alcohol.

Actually, things at home had been peaceful for a time. Pedro had not scolded her since he had taken the widow Eulalia of the barrio of Santo Domingo to the fair two weeks ago. Esperanza had been resentful when Pedro told her to prepare food for the widow and she couldn't hide how she felt when she was serving him his dinner. Pedro had picked up the plate and thrown it at her, food and all, scattering beans and *tortillas* on the floor. And the flow of ugly words that followed! He had said that she was ignorant and he didn't know how he had come to marry her. He needed a woman who could read and write and who was able to earn money—like Eulalia! He said that he was a man and had the right to do what he pleased, that she, being a woman and a very stupid one, would have to bear anything he did or said to her, even if he should decide to bring the widow to live in the same house. Better yet, he would go away with the widow who also knew how to cook and serve him and who would be of more help to him because she was clever. Then Pedro had forced Esperanza to scrape up the beans and eat them while he sat and watched her. After he left she cried and took out her bottle and drank. The children didn't like to see her drink alcohol but sometimes she had to. Three days later Pedro returned and ever since he had been quiet and had not lost his temper. He had brought home some sweet chile, dried cod, salt, and sugar, and everyone had been pleased.

Esperanza knew her husband was hot-tempered and sometimes treated her and the children unjustly. But he was kind too, and she knew he loved her. When they were young he used to console her after he had made her cry by taking her in his arms and saying, "Come on, don't get mad." Yes, she had had a better life with him than with her mother and elder half brother.

"In my house my brother scolded me and my mother hit me and I never talked back. Once I said, 'You hit me so much that I would rather go to my godmother.' My *madrina* liked me a lot and gave me many things. Then my mother hit me more, hard with a rope. I ran out into the street to look for my *madrina's* house. My mother followed me and threw a stone at me. Possibly she just wanted to frighten me for it fell to one side. Later my brother came and defended me. 'Why do you hit her so much?' he said to my mother. I had no liberty whatsoever then. In truth I never went anywhere. Many times people wanted to hire me to watch their children but my brother never wanted me to. He never wanted me even to go to school."

Esperanza had never learned to read or write and could not defend herself when Pedro accused her of being ignorant and stupid. But she would say, "Didn't you know what I was when you sent your mother to ask for me?" Indeed, when Pedro had looked about for a wife he had decided that the young Esperanza, who was virtuous and innocent and poorer than he, was the ideal girl for him. Esperanza had not wanted to marry him or anyone else, but when his mother died and he was left an orphan with no one to make his *tortillas*, she took pity on him and consented.

A few days before the marriage her mother had given her advice: "Now that you are going to marry you must have a different character. Here you have one character but there you must have the character of your husband. If he scolds you, do not answer. If he beats you, bear it because if not your husband is going to say, 'What kind of upbringing did we give?' " Esperanza had followed her mother's advice. "And I was always that way," she thought. "When Pedro hit me I only sat down and cried."

The marriage took place in the village church in 1910. Pedro gave Esperanza the first dress she had ever had (before that she had always worn a blouse and long skirt). He gave her a fifty-centavo piece to spend. He took her to live with him and his aunt in his one-room house.

"I remember the night we married. I was terribly afraid. Pedro still bothers me sometimes when he says jokingly, 'Why were you so frightened that night?' In reality I do not know what it was that troubled me. Chills came over me. I was terribly afraid, for never, never had we spoken to one another. After we ate dinner Pedro's aunt went to bed and so did he. He had gone to bed with his clothes on. He has always done that. I also always go to bed with my clothes on. The aunt told me that for this I had got married and that I should go to bed. I was very afraid and ashamed. Pedro covered me with the blanket and then began to embrace me and touch my breasts. Then he went on top of me. I didn't know what the men did to one, and I said to myself, 'Maybe it's like this.' I felt like crying or going to my mother, but I remembered that they had married me and then I said, 'If I die, I'll die. I have to go through it here even though he kills me.' And I closed my eyes and waited for the worst. Pedro already knew how these things were done because he had even had a daughter by a married woman. I don't remember that I bled, but I know that it hurt a lot, and I didn't cry because there was someone else there and it would make me ashamed if she heard.

"Two weeks later I was still afraid. Little by little one picks up confidence. I didn't even tell anything to my mother. I only told a cousin of my husband. I said: 'Men only play with one. Why do they have to get married?' Then she said, 'That's the way they are and you have to let him.' After about two months I was feeling pleasure and then I began to love my husband."

Esperanza hurried down the street and without slackening her pace said "*Buenos dias*" to two women whom she passed. One of the women was her former *comadre*, the godmother of her little dead son Angel, the last of her children to have been baptized in the Catholic faith. When Pedro turned Protestant all their Catholic *compadres* had broken off the relationship with them. Esperanza had become Protestant because of Pedro's insistence and because "no one recognizes me any more anyway." That had been eighteen years before but it still upset Esperanza to meet her former *comadres* and *compadres*.

Why Pedro, when he was forty years old, had decided to abandon his old faith and incur the wrath of the village, Esperanza had never clearly understood. She was only dimly aware that he had been disillusioned with the Mexican Revolution and that his defeats in the post-Revolutionary political struggles in Azteca had been hard for him to bear. Then several things had happened all at once which led to his conversion. He was given a Bible which seemed to him the great revelation of his life. He treated it "like a saint," and when a Protestant missionary came to the village he was ready to listen to him. One night at a wake he denounced priests and Catholicism to his Uncle Agustín who was a devout Catholic and who, moreover, had treated Pedro cruelly as a child. When Agustín berated Pedro for his anti-Catholicism and taunted him about his ignorance, Pedro vowed to make a serious study of one of the Evangelical faiths. After a year the two met again for a debate which lasted throughout a night, and Pedro argued down this uncle who had once been such an authoritarian figure to him. He told his wife, "I really gave it to him good. I showed him all the lies. I fought my uncle with his own books. I showed him that the dead don't return, that Sunday isn't the day of rest, that baptism is done by immersion, that confession and communion are useful but not if done to another human being, that purgatory and hell are lies, all lies. The saints, too, these pictures before which they cross themselves, it's all a lie." He was so hard on his uncle that "the poor old man even cried."

Then Esperanza, Pedro, and a daughter Rufina fell ill. The villagers interpreted these calamities as his punishment from God and Pedro grew angry. "Now that people are talking so much," he had said, "I'm going to become a Protestant so that they will be speaking the truth. I'm going to take down all the religious pictures and saints we have. In this way once and for all we'll die or we'll be saved."

Rumor of Pedro's intention to "burn the saints" traveled through the village. Friends and relatives came to protest; other people stopped speaking to the family. This was the beginning of several years of ostracism. The Martínez boys had to sell their firewood in Tepetate; Esperanza went to more distant parts of the village to sell her chickens and eggs.

Pedro was once stoned, and when Rufina died her godfather refused to make her coffin. At school the children were shunned or tormented. Conchita's classmates once dragged her by her hair toward the church to force her to kiss the priest's hand, and two boys nearly strangled her with her own braids because, they said, she had been trying to convert them. One rumor which persisted for many years was that Pedro had been seen kneeling before his eldest daughter who stood on a table "like a saint" surrounded by flowers.

Although Esperanza was greatly disturbed when she realized that her husband was approaching conversion, she felt helpless to prevent it. She did nothing but weep and avoid people. Her relatives came and warned her not to leave the religion of their fathers. "Protestantism has just come out," they told her. "It is something new. Besides, Protestants don't believe in God." Pedro's sister urged her to leave Pedro. "It's awful, what he has done," she said, "to remove the saints and have those devils meeting in my mother's house. Leave him and his children and then you'll see how he will leave the Seventh-Day Adventists." But Esperanza had answered, "What can I do? He's the boss."

It had been more difficult for Esperanza to adjust to the change of religion than it had been for Pedro. He had always been ardently interested in religion and as a Catholic had been a prayer-maker and twice a *mayordomo* of the barrio. He was used to going to church often, especially on all the feast days. He had prayed all night on Good Fridays, fasted during Holy Week, and confessed and took communion once a year. When he became an Adventist, he threw himself into it just as passionately, reading and joining a study group, converting others, and conducting services in their home. He even seemed to enjoy standing up against the whole village!

Esperanza, who believed in a vague mixture of Catholic and pagan concepts, had never been deeply involved in the Christian religion. Once when she needed firewood in a hurry she had burned a cross which Pedro had set up in their patio to protect the house! She actually saw little difference between the new and old Christian faiths and even after her conversion she did not make a clear separation between them. Once, on the Day of the Dead, she "felt sorry for our dead little ones" and put a candle and flowers in the barrio chapel for them. Another time she went to the chapel of San José "to pray to God to give me peace in my home because Pedro was insupportable. And he really did calm down after that." On the whole the conversion brought Esperanza only confusion, inconvenience, and ostracism, and made it less possible for her to find comfort in her old folk beliefs.

The family did benefit, however, from a spiritual change in Pedro and for this reason was able to accept his conversion in spite of the severe social disapproval. Pedro dropped out of politics, stopped drinking, and turned to work and religion. As part of his faith he tried to control his temper and speak humbly in the face of provocation. "If we fight, everyone criticizes us." The family began to eat better and to have a more peaceful domestic life. In fact, at no time was the family so united and contented as during this period when Pedro devoted himself to their physical and spiritual well-being. For his part he was repaid for his efforts by the support and admiration of his children and, to some extent, of his wife.

In recent years Esperanza had been aware that Pedro was slowly but unmistakably drifting back toward Catholicism. He had become disillusioned, little by little, by the behavior of some of his co-religionists. He had hoped that the high moral principles of the Adventists and their emphasis upon brotherhood would give him the trust and love he wanted. The first jolt came when the man who had converted him attempted to seduce his daughter, Conchita, while he was a guest of the family for a night. Pedro also had been hurt by being treated as an inferior by some of the Protestant ministers. One incident had been crucial and stood out as a turning point. Conchita wanted to study in Mexico City and Pedro had taken her to the city to the home of the Protestant pastor who had promised to give her room and board in exchange for work.

"Conchita had malaria at the time," Pedro said, "but she was so enthusiastic about studying that she wanted to go anyway. So I brought her. It was a two-story house. It was beautiful, like heaven. I only saw it from a distance, like Moses when he went to . . . just from a distance, that's as much as I saw of it. Yes, the house was pretty but they took me into the kitchen and I never got any further than that. The so-and-so treated me like dirt. My poor daughter started right in helping his wife even though she was very sick. I said to her, 'Come on, let's go. I don't like this man's character and you're sick. I can tell he's very harsh and his two children are even worse.' She answered, 'I'm not leaving even though I die here.' Hmmm, what could I do? The pastor invited us to the evening service and said I could sleep there that night. They gave me a cup of coffee and when it was time to go to bed they took Conchita upstairs to sleep on a dirty carpet in their daughter's room. The pastor told me to make myself comfortable. But how could I make myself comfortable? They didn't give me anything, not even an old rug did they throw at me. The floor was made of cement and was still wet from being washed. It was very cold. I thought, '*Caray!* Are these people Christians?' That's how I began to lose faith.

"So I said to myself, 'This isn't right but what can I do? I'll stay this once. After all, it means her future.' Well, I suffered through it. I didn't sleep the whole night long. I just sat down on my pack and leaned against the edge of the charcoal burner. As bad luck would have it I had to go to the toilet but I couldn't find a place to go. There was a great big dog outside the kitchen door in the patio and as soon as I opened the door a bit he would start to growl. He was an enormous dog and angry. That was worse. Now I was a prisoner! The animals there were just as bad as their master. God was punishing me, I was really in a fix.

"At about four-thirty in the morning the mother came downstairs to sweep the street. She was so much of an Indian that the children treated her like a servant. Just imagine! The children and the husband sleeping and the poor mother out in the street sprinkling and sweeping. And these people were Christians! The son came into the kitchen at night and didn't even speak to me. Just walked past me. What kind of upbringing do these people have? At five o'clock my daughter came down. She saw me sitting there and said, 'Papá, let's go.' I said, 'Yes, these bourgeois! the kind who won't work!'

"That was the way they treated me. It entered like a big thorn and hurt a lot. The man a Christian? A lie! That man a brother? A lie! I hated him. May God forgive me but I still hate him. I wrote him a strong letter saying, 'You are not a Christian, you are a king bee who doesn't work. You are nourished by the health of the faithful. You are even worse than the priests.' "

After that Pedro participated less in the affairs of the Adventist church, although he continued to attend Saturday services fairly regularly. In 1943 he stopped contributing tithes (one-tenth of his crop) to the church. He prayed but no longer underwent penitential fasting. He drifted back into politics and because of politics began to drink again. Also "because of politics," he began to attend wakes and fiestas with his Catholic supporters. He grew more tolerant of Catholicism and in fact took pleasure at being accepted again by the Catholic community. Yet he believed at the same time that his Protestant faith and his high standard of morality had gained him more respect from the villagers than they had had for him before.

But it was too late for Esperanza. She was too far withdrawn from social and community life to pick it up where she had left it eighteen years before. She was unprepared to build anything new. Her conversion had been one more traumatic experience in a lifetime of traumas. She would be content, so long as God gave her life, to keep on working for her family, accepting whatever fate brought her and asking for nothing.

From the paved road Esperanza made another left turn and walked quickly past a few more houses, past the park, and across the plaza to the archway where the women waited in the shade to sell their little piles of food. From them Esperanza carefully made her small purchases—one-fourth of a kilo of rice at thirty-five centavos, ten centavos' worth of coffee, fifteen centavos' worth of lard, fifteen centavos for tomatoes, and twenty for chile. The rice and lard were wrapped in little cones of paper which Esperanza placed along with the other articles in the basket which she carried under her shawl. She then went into one of the small dark stores under the archway and bought one-tenth of a liter of drinking alcohol and twenty centavos' worth of kerosene for the lamp. On the way home she stopped at the drugstore for two aspirin.

The noon church bells were ringing when she reached home after the long climb up the hill. Without sitting down to rest she gave the basket of food to Machrina, took up the can of boiled corn, and hurried back to the plaza, this time to the corn mill. The corn was still too hot to be ground but it was already late, and even though the dough would be tough and rubbery it was needed for the noon meal for those at home. Machrina had put aside some corn to cool for the evening meal. It meant another trip to the mill but that was better than giving the men inferior *tortillas*. Like all men, they had bad tempers and had to be served properly.

Esperanza looked expectantly at the mill entrance to see who was waiting there. She enjoyed standing in the long queue; it was one of her few chances to chat with the women she knew. But at this hour the mill was empty and the miller put her corn through the noisy machine without delay.

Machrina was preparing the rice when Moisés came home from school. Without greeting his sister he sought out Herman, who had been playing quietly in the patio all morning. Herman's face lit up when he saw Moisés, but he did not move away from the little pile of stones he had gathered. When Esperanza came in she called to Moisés to take the mule to pasture. This was one of his daily chores. He also brought some water from the fountain every morning, picked fruit for his mother, ran errands, and every afternoon after school he went back to the plaza with a small can of corn for the mill. During school vacations he had more responsible jobs, selling a little corn or wood, cleaning the maguey fiber, and helping his brothers make rope.

Herman also had regular chores since everyone was expected to work. He had to make five daily trips to the fountain with two small water pails, bring in firewood as it was needed, and run errands for Machrina or his grandmother. Herman liked to go with Moisés to pasture the mule and asked Machrina to let him go. She said no because it looked like rain. Herman then appealed to Esperanza, who said yes. Since the food was not quite ready, the boys were sent to pick a few hog plums to stay everyone's hunger. Then, after a lunch of rice, *tortillas*, and coffee, the boys set out with the mule. Machrina shouted to them from the door not to loiter because if they came home wet she was going to hit them.

At one o'clock the two women sat down to eat. Esperanza was too tired to talk about the people she had seen in the plaza and fell asleep, still seated on the low bench. Machrina washed the few dishes and then took a can to fill at the fountain. The men of the barrio had built a new fountain near the house. Machrina was proud of it because it was largely due to her father's efforts that the fountain had been built. He was the only man in the barrio who wanted to advance and who could get things done. It had taken him more than a year to persuade his neighbors to form a *cuatequitl* (a cooperative work party) to build the fountain. Pedro might be poor, but he was a man of importance not only in his own barrio but in the village. Machrina had often heard her father call men who did not take part in politics "stones," "balls of flesh with eyes," or simply "women!" and she judged her neighbors by his standards.

Machrina was too young to remember how the family had suffered because of Pedro's political activity. He had been jailed three times and twice he had had to flee the village for his life. When he worked during elections he forgot his family entirely and left them to shift for themselves. He drank with his friends, had love affairs, and got into debt. That was why Esperanza said that, "Politics only grinds one into dust."

Down the street Machrina saw Elena, the daughter of the widow Gloria, sweeping her patio. Elena put down her twig broom and leaned over the stone wall. "I have something to show you," she said. She pulled a folded letter from her blouse. "A little girl ran over and gave me this letter at the mill this morning. It's a love letter." Love letters were very much prized by the young people in Azteca and severely frowned upon by the adults. This form of courtship, indeed courtship itself, was a recent phenomenon.

"Who sent it?"

"Who knows? There is no name."

Machrina read the letter carefully:

Most Beautiful Señorita:

It is impossible to see you and not to love you and that is what has happened to me. Your beautiful image is engraved on my heart, so deeply do I see you everywhere and, in the same way, I hear your sweet harmonious voice which shatters my whole being. If I contemplate the countryside, it appears to resemble you, so beautiful is it; its odor carries a memory of a divine vision. Upon looking straight at the sun, my eyes become wounded; so do your beautiful eyes equally wound me. When I hear the song of the birds, it seems that I hear your divine voice. I beg only one word of you to indicate that you are not indifferent to the sensations of my heart; tell me this word which will make me think of myself as the happiest man on earth and which will make me fall upon my knees at your feet. If you are utterly disinterested, then I will die little by little as a flower dies on being plucked. But in my agony I shall always say I love you, I adore you.

"He must be very cultured," Machrina said.

"*Que va?* He probably copied it out of a book." Elena, who was eighteen, had a reputation of being *loca*, crazy about men. The year before she had gone to Cuahnahuac to be a servant in a doctor's house, but it was not long before the doctor's wife had managed to send her back home.

Machrina went on to the fountain to fill her water can. She thought about the letter and wondered whether she would ever receive one like it. And would she ever marry? Machrina was not sure. Where would she meet a young man who was not a Catholic? She would be glad to marry a Protestant and be able to keep her father's religion. If she married a Catholic she would have to become a Catholic and go to church to confess. She didn't want to do that. Better to stay at home with her parents.

When Machrina came home her mother was asleep in bed. Machrina poured the water into the water jug and sat down to read the Bible. The conversation with Elena had somehow disturbed her and reading the Bible made her feel better. She dozed off; with a start she heard the village clock strike three. She got up to sweep the patio and was watering the plants when Esperanza joined her, yawning and combing her hair. Esperanza said there was some mending to do. Without a word Machrina went into the kitchen for needle and thread and brought out the clothes. She always sewed under a tree in the patio because it was too dark to sew in the house. From the patio she could also see what was going on in the street.

Esperanza left to visit Conchita, her oldest daughter. During the morning she had twice passed Conchita's house on the way to the plaza, but she hadn't gone in because Juan, her son-in-law, might still have been home. He had forbidden Conchita to see her family, and Pedro had forbidden anyone in the family to visit Conchita. So Esperanza had to choose her hours carefully.

Conchita's troubles had begun eight years before when she left home to study to become a teacher. She had attended the State Normal School and a lot of money had gone into her education—for books, clothing, and transportation. For three years her father had given up planting and worked as a peon to earn cash for her expenses. Of course the neighbors had been critical from the very beginning. They had warned Pedro that he was striving too high for a poor man. They said that a girl could not be trusted away from home and least of all Conchita, who was "hot-blooded." Pedro ignored them. He had faith in his favorite daughter. Conchita had been born after the first children had died, and for five years she was an only child. Both Esperanza and Pedro had babied her, played with her, and enjoyed her more than they did any of their later children. Pedro gladly spent the money on her schooling in the hope that when she became a teacher she would help raise the economic and social standing of the entire family. Then she had had to come home from her very first position even before she had begun to earn any money. The school principal had made her pregnant.

It was a terrible blow to Pedro. He gave Conchita a merciless beating and did not speak to her for months. But he let her stay home and have her baby. After Herman was born Pedro ignored his presence; even now he seldom spoke to his grandson. Conchita went off to teach again when she was well and sent home thirty pesos a month to help with expenses. She also brought little gifts from time to time, and everyone liked her for that. Pedro had begun to forgive her too. She had her father's temperament, he said; she couldn't help herself.

About a year before Conchita had first gone away to study, Pedro had met a young man named Juan who was an orphan born out of wedlock and unrecognized by the relatives of both his dead parents. At twenty-two Juan was still a bachelor with no home of his own. Pedro took a liking to the young man and invited him to live with the family for a year. Conchita was fourteen then and soon became Juan's secret sweetheart. The following year Conchita left the village, but for the next ten years she and Juan managed to be together whenever she returned home. Meanwhile he had other sweethearts and began to have children by several women. Conchita too had other sweethearts at school, but she liked Juan best. When her high status as a teacher was diminished by the appearance of Herman, Juan felt that he could ask her to marry him. She agreed, and her father quickly accepted. After a civil marriage ceremony the couple went to live with Juan's married half sister, leaving Herman with his grandparents.

But things had not gone well. Conchita could not adjust herself to being the wife of a peasant and there were many quarrels. When Conchita became pregnant she felt that Juan did not take proper care of her. He refused to hire a servant when the baby was born and she was not able to rest for the traditional forty days. The baby was only a month old when Conchita asked her father to take her home because Juan was neglecting her. Pedro took her home and because of his experience with legal matters he had his son-in-law brought to court on a charge of neglect. All this, of course, caused antagonism between the two men. Conchita later returned to her husband, but he began to get drunk frequently and to beat her. Just before the birth of their second baby he beat her so badly that Pedro took her home again. Pedro said, "While I live, your husband won't abuse you." Again there was a reconciliation and again Conchita became pregnant. Now her husband was even more violent and she went back to her father's house. This time Pedro demanded that

Juan pay for the children's maintenance. Juan refused. Pedro had him arrested. Juan charged Conchita with abandonment.

Conchita gave birth to a healthy looking girl who died in a few days. The midwife accused Esperanza of having killed the baby through carelessness—she had attended a wake and then had sat in the kitchen near the baby without first having washed and changed clothing. Juan heard the accusation and refused to go to the child's funeral or to contribute to the expense.

Pedro wanted his daughter to stay home for good, and she seemed to agree. Actually she was not happy in her parents' home. Pedro made her work all the time and sometimes struck her in her children's presence. Conchita got in touch with her husband and he consented to take her back provided she would never again speak to her family. When Pedro came in from the fields one day and found that Conchita and her children were gone, he disowned her in a rage and forbade the rest of the family ever to see her again.

That was why Esperanza had to make secret visits to her daughter nowadays. And not only she: Machrina and the boys visited her too, for everyone missed Conchita at home. She had helped with the housework, had sympathized with her brothers, and had given each of them gifts. From Conchita, Esperanza had received her first silk dress, Machrina her first pair of shoes, Felipe a mirror, Martin a flashlight, Ricardo a pocket comb, Moisés his first toy. And Conchita had never come without a present for her son Herman.

When the dogs announced Esperanza's arrival, Conchita came out of her dark little one-room house with her sons beside her. Her long hair was uncombed, her clothes looked old and torn, and she limped from an infection in her foot. Partly because of her husband's jealousy and partly from pride, Conchita seldom left the house. She preferred to grind corn on her own grinding stone rather than walk to the mill.

"Come, greet your little grandmother," Conchita said to her sons.

With no change in expression each boy walked up to Esperanza, pressed his lips to her outstretched hand, then ran off to the rear of the patio to play among the chickens. Esperanza wiped the back of her hand with her shawl and, still standing, said, "Just imagine, I could not sell the turkey today. They offered only two and a half pesos for it." Conchita went into the house and came out a moment later with a sardine tin full of beans. Esperanza dropped the beans into her shawl and returned the measuring tin. They exchanged a few words, Esperanza said, "Thanks, little daughter," and quickly left.

It was five o'clock, not much time to prepare the beans for the men. At home Esperanza found that Machrina had stirred up the fire and put on the large bean pot full of water. Esperanza picked over the beans, washed them, and dropped them into the boiling water. Machrina went on mending clothes.

At five-thirty Moisés and Herman came back with the mule. Moisés was sent off at once to the mill with the can of boiled corn which this time was properly cooled. Herman went back to play with his pile of stones in the patio. Esperanza put up water for coffee, stirred the beans, added some *epazote* leaves and salt for taste, and prepared a sauce of onion, tomato, and chile to be eaten with the *tortillas*. Then she sat beside her daughter to mend an old shirt. They talked about Conchita, the evening meal, and what new clothing each might receive at harvest time.

When Moisés came back with the ground corn an hour later it was Machrina's turn to get up and make the *tortillas*. She complained that Moisés had taken so long she wouldn't have the *tortillas* ready in time. To make matters worse the corn was poorly ground and would have to be reground by hand. Esperanza went on calmly sewing. "Don't upset yourself, little daughter," she said. "There's no help for it. That's how it is."

Machrina was still grinding corn when her father and three brothers walked in at seven o'clock. Obviously tired, they went to lie down. Esperanza went to sit on a plum crate beside Pedro's bed, to recount to him her efforts to get money for the day's food. Pedro nodded approvingly when she told him that she had refused to let the turkey go at the low price offered and that she had succeeded in getting an advance on the boys' wages from Don Porfirio. She said nothing about her visit to Conchita and the gift of beans. She complained that her head ached and Pedro told her to go to bed early to avoid getting ill. She got out the alcohol and gave her husband his evening drink; this was to guard him from the ill effects of the winds which had blown against him as he had walked home hot and tired. She too took a short drink and then joined her daughter.

Machrina was kneeling at the grinding stone, working quickly now because the men did not like to be kept waiting long for their meal. She already had a little pile of *tortillas* which she kept warm in a napkin near the hearth. For each *tortilla* Machrina rolled a ball of corn dough between her hands, then slapped it out flat with a quick pat-a-cake movement. She was justly proud of her ability to make fine *tortillas*. When she was only eleven she had made them better than her older sister, and now her father and brothers said that she made them better than her mother.

Esperanza examined the young squash her husband had brought home from the field and prepared it for cooking. By eight o'clock it was done, and by then also Machrina had a large pile of toasted *tortillas*. Esperanza called out, "Pedro, come to eat!" More affectionately she said to the boys, "Come, little fathers, it's ready." Pedro and his sons washed, then straggled into the kitchen one by one, still drying their hands on their shirttails. The four men sat down on low benches on either side of the small table. Esperanza placed a pile of *tortillas* in the center of the table and handed each one a plate of beans. The boys waited for their father to take a *tortilla* before they took one, rolled it, and expertly scooped up mouthfuls of beans with it. The only sounds in the kitchen for some time were the noises of chewing, the slap of Machrina's hands making more hot *tortillas*, the crackle of the fire, and Moisés and Herman laughing in the patio. The older boys had talked and joked with each other in their bedroom, but now they sat eating soberly, as though wrapped in their private thoughts.

Pedro gave full attention to his food but he took everything in with his alert, small eyes. He noticed the pile of unmended clothes, the swept floor, the marketing basket with its little rolled paper packages, the basket of corn from Don Porfirio, and he mentally checked these things with Esperanza's tale of the day. He saw the Bible still opened on Machrina's bed in the corner and for a brief moment he permitted himself to glance affectionately at his youngest daughter. She was a good girl and a serious one, he reflected. She accepted wholeheartedly her father's new religion. She worked hard and was obedient. She might not be as intelligent or well educated as her sister but at least she would stay out of trouble and behave as a woman should. "Little daughter, how good these *tortillas* are!" Pedro said.

Machrina smiled. The boys nodded assent. Esperanza added some hot *tortillas* to the pile. Everyone was at ease for Pedro was in a good mood. There would be no ugly words tonight. Esperanza gave a dish of rice to Pedro, then one to her eldest son. Felipe was annoyed if she served any of his brothers before him. For Martin, her favorite, she spooned out a little more rice. Little was said. While the men drank their coffee Esperanza called to Moisés and Herman to come in, wash their hands, and be quiet. Before eating the two boys greeted Pedro silently, brushing their lips against his outstretched hand. They ate their beans, rice, and squash sitting on the floor near the hearth where Esperanza also sat.

The three older boys left the kitchen as soon as they had finished eating and went to lie down on their cots. They lay talking and laughing together. Moisés and Herman soon followed them. Martin and Felipe took out little bags of candy which they had bought on their way home from work. Machrina, who ate last since she had to keep providing hot *tortillas* for the others, hurried through her meal in order to join them before all the candy was gone. Soon Esperanza and Pedro were left alone in the kitchen. They listened to their children, who were now singing songs from the song sheet that Machrina had borrowed from her friend Elena. Pedro made a move of displeasure.

"Let them sing," Esperanza said. "It makes me feel a little happy."

But Pedro went to the boys' room. As soon as his children saw him in the doorway the singing stopped. "There is always High Mass among my poor children when he appears," Esperanza thought.

"Be quiet," Pedro said sternly. "The people will think we are a house of crazy ones. If you want to sing, sing a hymn. Let them see that we take our religion seriously." But when Pedro left there was no more singing. Herman came out and went to bed. Machrina helped her mother with the dishes. Felipe said that he was going out for a walk. Now that he was twenty-three years old he no longer asked his father for permission to go out. Nor did either of his parents demand to know where he was going as they had formerly done. Pedro merely called after him not to stay out late. Felipe did not reply.

At about nine o'clock Machrina climbed into bed and settled herself next to Herman, who was already asleep. She covered her face with the blanket and lay quietly on her back with her legs demurely stretched out before her as her mother had taught her to do when she was a little girl. Pedro and Esperanza sat near the fire occasionally saying something in a low voice. "Do you have money for tomorrow?" asked Pedro. "Who knows if it will be enough?" Esperanza said. They heard the sound of coughing in the other room. "Ricardo has a cough," said Esperanza. "I'll rub his chest with alcohol." She took the bottle and went into the boys' room. A few minutes later she came out. "He says that his lungs hurt. His body is hot. I think the spirits have hit him." Esperanza was worried; for her illness in the family was always a serious matter. She had given birth to twelve children and only six were alive. Their first child had died at eight "of the stomach," the second at eight months of smallpox, the third at two of a scorpion bite. Later two more children, aged seven and three, died "of the stomach." The last child, a daughter born in 1940, had died at ten months of "bronchitis."

Pedro was impatient with his wife. "It's a little thing. Don't make a woman out of him. Just give him some lemon tea and he will be better by tomorrow."

Esperanza stirred up the dying fire and put on the water to boil. She took a candle out with her into the garden and after groping about for a moment came back with a few blades of lemon grass which she dropped into the water. When the tea was ready she added some drinking alcohol and took it to her son. "That will cure him," Pedro said when she returned. But Esperanza said, "He has chills now. Let him stay in bed tomorrow. He is barely eighteen and still but a boy." Pedro looked at her with annoyance. "Be quiet!" he said. "What do you know, woman? When I was ten, I was working like a man, supporting my mother and my sister. He must learn what it means to be a man."

At nine-thirty Felipe walked in. His father said, "Now you are here."

Felipe nodded and went to bed. He had never been one to talk much but for the past two weeks he hadn't addressed a word to his father. "He is angry again," observed Esperanza. "Who knows why?" Pedro knew why. It was because of the girl in Mexico City whom Felipe had decided he wanted to marry. He had met the girl only once for a few moments when he and his father had gone to the city to arrange for a sale of plums. She was an Aztecan girl but she had gone to school in Mexico City and was now a "lady of fashion." She wore shoes and stockings all the time and had cut off her braids. But she had smiled at Felipe and although he was a poor country boy he had dared to hope that she liked him. Felipe did not sleep well for a whole week after he had seen her. Finally he had asked his father to arrange the marriage with the girl's family.

Pedro had been against it from the start. "Think well," he had argued. "She lives in the city and we don't know her habits. She might even be a street woman and we wouldn't know." Pedro had really been taken aback by Felipe's request. Nowadays young people arranged their own marriages in secret before their parents were called in to carry out the traditional steps. If the parents objected the young couple usually eloped and made peace with their families later. But Felipe, who had never been fortunate with girls, did not smooth out the path for his father, and Pedro, although he had agreed to ask for the girl's hand, kept putting it off. Sometimes he growled at Felipe, "Do you still want to marry that girl in Mexico City?" He succeeded in turning the whole thing into a joke and Felipe was furious. So now the boy wouldn't speak to his father at all.

Pedro did not mind. The financial burden of the wedding, the gifts to the bride and her family, the support of his daughter-in-law while Felipe lived with them—all this would be more than he could manage. In the old days a son might live on with his father and more than repay these expenses by working for him, but nowadays young couples generally moved away after a year, leaving the parents with all their debts. The worst blow of all would be to lose a good worker. So Pedro kept his sons under close watch and saw to it that they worked hard and did not spend much time in the streets with the other young men. He discouraged them from thinking of having a good time or spending money on clothes, diversions, or other vanities. He also discouraged Machrina's attempts to look smart and pretty. Actually, marriage was the last thing he wanted for his children. Esperanza had much the same attitude. If she had needed a daughter-in-law to help take care of the menfolk, it might have been different. But she had a good worker in Machrina.

At ten o'clock Esperanza and Pedro got up from the low kitchen benches and went to bed, carrying a lighted candle. Pedro adjusted the wooden board which served as a door at night to keep out the animals. Without removing their clothes they got into bed and were soon asleep.

THEODORA KROEBER

A Yurok success story

Theodora Kroeber has long been a student of the Indians of California. She is the author of *Ishi in Two Worlds*, a biography of "the last wild Indian in North America," and is presently completing a biography of her late husband, Alfred L. Kroeber, whose obituary appears in Part IV of this book.

The house Pekwoi is in the village of Kotep, close to the Center of the World. It is the custom among the River People for the wealthy and aristocratic to give names to their houses, and such a house is Pekwoi.

The pattern of Kotep, which is in the canyon, is that its named houses are built in rows high above the river, with sun and view. Below them, the rows begin to straggle and only an occasional house will have a name. And at the sunless bottom of the canyon cluster the mean and ramshackle and nameless houses of the poor.

Pekwoi's sunny terrace of matched stone looks upriver as far as the bend and downriver as far as eye can see. Its round doorframe is carefully carved; the redwood planks of its walls and roof bear marks of the finest adzing. Inside, it is dry against the rains, tight against the winds.

Long, long ago, for Pekwoi is old, a fire burned night and day in the pit. Around the four sides on the main floor and on the shelves under the eaves were stored the long boxes filled with treasure and the great baskets filled with the fruits of ocean, river, bush, and tree, fresh and dried. In the pit close to the fire lay the deerskin blankets for sitting comfortably or for sleeping warmly.

Such was Pekwoi in the time when Nenem and Nenem's father and mother and grandparents lived there. Nenem and her proud and aristocratic family were known and respected all up and down the river. No Jumping Dance took place in Nenem's time without the wolfskin headbands and the civet aprons from Pekwoi; no Deerskin Dance was complete without the priceless pure white deerskin of Pekwoi.

Theodora Kroeber, *The Inland Whale* (Bloomington: Indiana University Press, 1959), pp. 17–38. Reprinted by permission of the publisher.

Nenem herself had a tender, rhythmic sort of beauty. Her heavy hair, parted in the middle and held with minkskin ties, lay straight and shining over her shoulders and breasts. Ear disks of polished abalone shell framed a gentle face, high-bred in its modeling, with long eyes and crescent-moon eyebrows and a gracious mouth. She was small and she moved with a light proud step, so smoothly that the many-stranded shell beads around her neck and the hundreds of strings of seeds in her apron and the heavy polished abalone and obsidian pendants which hung from her buckskin skirt made only a soft shu-shu-shu-shu accompaniment to her walk.

Her father expected to receive the highest bride price for Nenem when she should choose to marry, and he expected her choice to be made from among the most eligible. It came out quite otherwise, however. Nenem fell in love with a young man there in the village, the son of a widowed and impoverished mother, obscure and without family. He and his mother lived in one of the most primitive of the shacks along the river's edge. They were so poor and so little known that at this distance of time not even the name of the young man is preserved to us.

Nenem's nameless lover must, nonetheless, have been a person of some positive attributes of person and character for Nenem truly and wholly loved him. When she knew that she was to have a child by him, he and she went to her family and told them and said they wished to be man and wife. Nenem's parents and family were shocked and outraged. Her lover could not pay a bride price that would have been other than insulting to this family.

He knew this and he said to Nenem's father, "It is my wish to be full-married to your daughter; to earn her and to deserve her. I will, if you will have it so, work faithfully for you and do whatever you order me to do and be a good son to you. If you will not have it so—here I am—kill me. This is your right." But the father was too proud to kill one whom he considered so far beneath him. "Then take me as your slave—do with me what you will," he said.

But it was intolerable to the father to so much as look at his daughter's lover. He could not bear to have him at Pekwoi or even in Kotep.

Nenem, in deep disgrace, was not allowed to leave Pekwoi. Her lover, without money or powerful friends, was quite helpless. In despair, he left the village and was lost to Nenem and to his mother. Neither they nor anyone ever heard of him again. It is believed in Kotep that he was murdered in the lonely hills beyond the river.

Her parents' fury turned full on Nenem as soon as her lover was gone from Kotep. In their hurt pride and the disappointment of all their hopes for her, they drove her out of Pekwoi and declared her to be no longer their daughter.

What the distracted Nenem might have done, one can only imagine. Before there was time for her to make any of the desperate decisions of the disgraced and abandoned, the mother of her lover, the old woman Hunè, took her home to the shabby dwelling by the river's edge where she and her son had always lived. There she cared for Nenem and comforted her and loved her as her own daughter. And in the same humble house, Nenem bore a son after some moons, and Hunè was mother and midwife and nurse to her. And not even in Pekwoi would the elaborate ritual of the birth and first moon of a son have been more rigidly enacted than it was in this same house.

Nenem called the baby Toàn. He was a strong, happy baby. Hunè cared for him and his mother, and she had the joy of recognizing his first words and of watching him learn to take his first steps on his short sturdy legs. The moons waxed and waned and the seasons were new and grew old and went and came again. Toàn lost his first roundness and the sturdy legs grew longer and carried him, running, tireless, at her side.

The river gave them salmon to eat fresh and to smoke and dry. Hunè's storage baskets bulged with fat acorns gathered from the oak trees that the people of Kotep harvest. Hunè and Nenem searched the sunny hillsides of late spring and early summer for the grasses with which to weave hats and cooking and serving baskets, and they picked up any pieces of pine root they found for repairing the heavy old storage baskets. They kept themselves decently and cleanly dressed in fresh bark skirts and aprons. They set snares for rabbits and they were warm in winter under rabbit-skin blankets.

With no man to care for it, Hunè's house was becoming little more than a patchwork of old planks somehow renewed when she and Nenem found a discarded board along the river or when a canoe broke up and they were able to salvage parts of it for a new door ledge or other replacement. The noonday sun shone through holes in the roof now.

Hunè lived for one more World Renewal ceremony and then before spring came, she died. This was a heavy grief and loneliness to Nenem, and as long as she lived she missed Hunè and cried in loving memory of her.

The summer after Hunè's death came and went without event and it was time for the World Renewal ceremony again. The dancing was to be upriver from Kotep this year and almost everyone in Kotep was already on his way there, either by canoe or trail. Only Nenem and Toàn remained at home. Nenem was leaching acorns by the river, when several canoes filled with people from downriver came by and the people recognized her. Their voices carried to her across the water, "Nenem, Nenem! Come along with us—we've plenty of room!"

"Oh—thank you—thank you!—I can't go—I'm not ready—I—" Nenem's answering call showed her reluctance.

One of them who knew her well, called out coaxingly, "Nenem! Surely you are not staying away from the dancing!"

Nenem hesitated to admit that indeed she had meant not to go at all. Instead, she answered, "I'll be a little late. You mustn't wait—I'm coming—I'll be there in time for the Ending Dances!"

Her friends in the canoes went on since she seemed really to wish it so. When they were gone, Nenem, having said she was coming, did get herself and Toàn ready and, taking some food and such other things as they might need, she set off by foot trail upriver.

She reached the dancing place in time for the Ending Dances as she had said she would. Everyone was there. It was evening and the fire illumined the faces of the dancers and of the onlookers equally. There were four dance teams. One of them was dancing and the other three were standing in formal lines, waiting their turn.

The onlookers were arranged with equal formality. Closest to the dancers on the right side sat the men of the great families of the river; and on the left side, the women of these families. The common people stood behind, but separated in the same manner—the men on the right and the women on the left. Nenem joined the group of standing women. She was gentle-mannered and gracious as always and thanks to Hunè's example, she and her small son were as carefully groomed and dressed as though they had been carried by canoe straight from Pekwoi itself.

There was a slight rustle as the women in the front row moved over so that Nenem might join them there. They motioned to her to come up with them and one of them took her arm and guided her to her seat and made her sit among them. They all greeted her, and between the dances they showed her the customary courtesies of friendliness and the special and formal ones due the honored daughter of a first family.

Nenem's own blood relatives ignored her—her coming—her son—her being seated.

Nenem did not know how to refuse the kindnesses and courtesies shown her by everyone except her family. She was already upset and when she saw the white deerskin of Pekwoi on its pole in the dance, she could not bear to sit there, so close, and in her old natural place. She slipped quietly away, little Toàn asleep in her arms. It did not occur to her friends that she was leaving for more than the moment. No one saw her start back down the trail toward Kotep, carrying Toàn and crying bitterly, bitterly.

Nenem kept to the river trail as far as Atsìpul Creek where there is a fork. Here she left the river, taking the fork which leads back through the hills and around Kewet Mountain and rejoins the river trail only a little above Kotep. This is a rough and steep way to go. Nenem chose it because it is not much used and it would bring her home without going through any of the larger villages along the river. In her present unhappy state she dreaded meeting anyone.

Toàn wakened and wondered much at his mother's tears, for she continued to cry. It was a clear night with a moon. Nenem put Toàn down and let him walk and the two of them wandered on up through the hills as far as a small mountain lake called Fish Lake. By this time Nenem was quite worn out and she made camp. They slept there the rest of the night by the lake.

To a world in balance, the flat earth's rise and fall, as it floats on Underneath Ocean, is almost imperceptible, and nothing is disturbed by it. Doctors know that to keep this balance, the people must dance the World Renewal dances, bringing their feet down strong and hard on the earth. If they are careless about this, it tips up and if it tips more than a very little, there are strange and terrible misplacements. One of the worst of these occurred before Nenem's grandparents' time and her unhappy father traced his own troubles to it. Most people along the river would agree with him.

This was the time when the earth tipped so far that Downriver Ocean came over the bar and flowed up the river, filling and overflowing the canyon, carrying its waters and its fish and other sea life far inland, past even the Center of the World—farther than it had ever penetrated before. With prayers and dancing, balance was eventually restored and the ocean flowed back down the canyon and outside the bar, carrying the fish and other sea life with it, except for a young female whale who had been washed all the way into Fish Lake and was left stranded there.

Ninawa, the whale, had lain there all this while, scarcely able to move, for she reached almost from one side of the lake to the other; and when she slapped her tail as whales do, she threw mud as far as the encircling meadow.

She was quiet the night Nenem and Toàn slept beside her. She listened to Nenem's crying in the night and in the morning, for Nenem's tears started again as soon as she wakened. And she heard what Nenem said through her tears. Then Ninawa knew why Nenem cried and she was glad that the ocean had brought her and left her stranded here. For Ninawa was no ordinary whale. These things about her were special: she had great power; she was compassionate to all suffering but particularly to Nenem's suffering. And this was because Ninawa was a bastard like Toàn.

Ninawa dared not move, lest she frighten Nenem and Toàn, and she had determined to help them. She lay still, making herself look as much as possible like a log fallen across the lake, and thinking and willing one thing all of the time: that Toàn should sit on her or climb on her; that he should somehow come and touch her if only for a moment, so that some of her power might flow into him.

Nenem would have followed the Kewet trail around the lake when she was ready to leave in the morning, except that Toàn distracted her from doing so. He had been playing at the water's edge all morning, and now he went a little farther and a little farther, until he was wading in water quite deep for him. And there beside him was Ninawa—something solid and rough and most tempting to climb. Toàn climbed; and when Nenem looked around for him, he was on top of what she, through her tears, took to be an enormous old water-soaked log, lying like a bridge across the lake.

Nenem was frightened, realizing how easily Toàn might slip or stumble. She had the wisdom not to cry out or startle him. She merely waded out as he had done and climbed up on Ninawa, following after him as fast as she could go. She knew that if anything were to happen to Toàn, she had no wish to live. But nothing happened to Toàn. He ran along ahead of her, on Ninawa's broad back, and when they came to the other end of their "log," they climbed down, waded to shore and went on their way to Kewet Mountain.

Ninawa shook ever so slightly when Toàn first touched her and she trembled as he left her. Toàn would recall this many moons from now, but he and his mother did not think much about it at the time.

Nenem had never been inland before. It was a long day's walk for her, carrying Toàn much of the time, around Kewet Mountain. She was relieved when the trail finally came back to the river and she knew she had not lost her way.

It was after dark when she and Toàn reached home. They ate a cold supper and went to bed without lighting a fire. As soon as her neighbors saw the smoke from her morning fire, they came to make sure she and Toàn had come to no harm. After all, no one had seen them, either at Kotep or at any of the villages along the river for two nights, and they were fearful for them. They did not press Nenem to talk—they saw her tears were yet too close. But her sore heart was eased; she knew she had come home to friends.

Nenem and Toàn had another friend—Nenem's father's father, Toàn's great-grandfather. It is not the way of the aged, if they are wise, to raise their voices against the decisions and actions of the household. And this great-grandfather was wise. He watched Nenem and Toàn and waited.

The day came when great-grandfather took his tools and the wood he was carving and sat down close to Hunè's house where Toàn was playing. Toàn, full of interest and curiosity, came and sat beside him and watched him carve. Great-grandfather appeared to be making a boat. He explained that it was not to be a boat, however, but a box; a hollowed-out box with a cover that would lash on and close tight. Toàn wanted to make a hollowed-out box, too. With great-grandfather's help, he gouged and cut and whittled until, by the end of the afternoon, Toàn's box was finished. It was a very small box, but it was complete with its own small lid and lashings. (Great-grandfather had contributed a piece of moccasin lace.)

Great-grandfather suggested that, having a box, he might collect pretty bird feathers and store them in his box. Toàn collected fallen feathers and soon the box was full and he and great-grandfather carved out a bigger box. To fill this one, they no longer contented themselves with collecting feathers. Great-grandfather made bow and arrows and brought light sharp arrow points from his store of them. Then he taught Toàn to shoot and to hunt.

As Toàn grew older and went hunting alone or with other boys, he continued to bring to his great-grandfather little birds, then bigger birds, and especially the red-headed woodpecker, and then the fur animals—whatever he could hunt or trap. Together, they cleaned the feathers and scraped the skins and stored them away in their boxes. As they needed them, they made more boxes, always bigger and handsomer ones, and these, too, began to be filled with treasure.

Toàn sometimes hunted inland on Kewet Mountain and as far as Fish Lake. Whenever he was at the lake, he wondered what had become of the log on which he had climbed that first time, with his mother, for it was no longer there. He recalled how it had trembled under his touch and he thought again of how his mother had cried. He had not known there were such tears in the world until that day.

All this great-grandfather did for Toàn without once raising his voice against his son or his daughter-in-law in Pekwoi.

Great-grandfather died as Toàn was coming to his first manhood. He left a great-grandson looking forward to a different sort of world from that Nenem had feared he would be facing. For there in Hunè's house were many, many boxes, carved by a sure young hand and filled with the prowess of a remarkably skilled young hunter.

Great-grandfather was dead. There was the funeral and there was the mourning. Toàn went to Fish Lake alone, for he was bereft and grieved by this death. He lay down by the lake and went to sleep. As he slept, he dreamed.

Ninawa came to him in his dream, and she told him many things. She told him that she, Ninawa, was the Inland Whale; that she was the "log" on which he and his mother had crossed Fish Lake; and that, after they were gone, the Inland Spirits came and carried her to another lake. She did not tell him where the lake is, for it is not given to anyone but an occasional Doctor in trance or, briefly, to a specially purified person, to see or know this lake. Ninawa said of it only that it is far, far inland, that it is big enough for a whale to live in comfortably and to slap her tail without striking mud, that it is boat-shaped and ringed round with oak trees.

In the dream, Ninawa slapped her tail as whales do, and spoke. "Toàn," she said, "Toàn, you should know that the winter moons are children of no-marriages—bastards like you and me. I listened to your mother crying over you for a night and a day, when you were too young to know why she cried, and I pitied you.

"Then I remembered—it is the bastard winter moons that bring the rains and the strength to the Earth for the budding and blooming and gathering of the full-marriage moons of spring and summer and autumn. And I determined that you, too, should have the strength of a winter moon, and I willed you to come to me. You came to me, and when you touched me, I trembled. Do you remember, Toàn? That was because I so much wanted you to come and dreaded lest I with my great size might frighten you away. But you had no fear and you climbed up and walked on my back. Do you remember that, Toàn? Here in Fish Lake it was. You walked from my tail to my head, and while you walked, I made my power flow through you.

"You will go on as you are. You will be a good man as you are a good boy; you will be a great hunter; you will own much treasure and wealth, and you will be remembered as the greatest of the sons of Pekwoi.

"Remember all that great-grandfather taught you. Cry also to the bastard winter moons when you pray. And never forget that once you walked on Ninawa's back." This is what Ninawa said to Toàn.

When Toàn wakened, hours later, Ninawa was not there. He lay still, recalling her words, memorizing them so that as long as he lived, he remembered them.

Nenem taught Toàn the words and gestures of greetings and of leave-takings, the ways of holding the elk-horn spoon and the basket when eating, what to do with the hands and the arms and the body, how to speak and to modulate the voice, the rules of precedence—the whole complicated etiquette of the aristocrat. He learned from her example the courtesy and graciousness and openness of the well-born.

One thing more Nenem taught Toàn before he was big enough to go to the sweat house: the severe and rigid code of a proud house. Toàn learned earlier than do most boys to fast and to purify himself and to practice control so that pain, anger, greed, excessive feeling of any sort did not show in his expression or in his actions.

By the time he went from Nenem's instruction to that of the sweat house, he was well accustomed to discipline and restraint. And once he went to the sweat house, he followed its pattern of behavior. He went far off to gather wood for the ceremonies there; he prayed long and exhausting hours at the shrines in the hills; he adhered to the rules of fasting, chastity, and purification imposed on the hunter. When he fasted and prayed, he cried out to his great-grandfather and to the bastard winter moons as Ninawa had said to do, and through it all, Toàn never forgot that once he had walked on Ninawa's back.

Five times the moons of the winter rains gave way to the moons of the first green buds. Nenem looked at her son. She saw that he was a proud and brave and good man as Ninawa had said he would be, and Nenem was satisfied.

Toàn was scarcely full grown when his bulging boxes could outfit a Deerskin Dance upriver and a Jumping Dance downriver at the same time. Such an accumulation of treasure by one so young had not happened before on the river and perhaps has not happened since. And it was the more remarkable, since the power and wealth and prestige of Pekwoi were denied him. Ninawa had supplied, in her own way, more even than Pekwoi withheld.

Ninawa's power sent his arrows farther and straighter, but the tireless hunter was Toàn. From hummingbird to blackbird to woodpecker to eagle to condor; from weasel to mink to civet cat to wolf to deer—Toàn snared and netted and trapped and decoyed and hunted. He cleaned and tanned and glued and cut and sewed as great-grandfather and his mother had taught him to do.

It was Ninawa's power that spread the word of this hunter who might sell or trade his surplus. She started the flow of those with money for purchasing and those with sea lion tusks and rare obsidian and flint, who sought him out. But the buyers and traders came again and again because they were pleased with him and with what he offered. Trading and selling far upriver and downriver to the sea, Toàn gradually filled a large box with the precious long strings of dentalium shell money.

At last Toàn could afford to hire the skilled old craftsmen of Kotep to work moon after moon after moon, making up his feathers and furs and skins and ivories and flints and obsidians into treasure of incredible beauty and value. And Toàn was free to go farther and farther afield, searching out the rare, the unique, and the beautiful, in bird and animal and rock and shell.

Meanwhile Pekwoi stood—a proud house—whose present occupants fed their pride on its past.

Nenem's father died, the last of the older generations.

Then the younger men of Pekwoi, Nenem's brother and his two sons, came with all of the principal men of Kotep, to Hunè's house. The brother was their spokesman; in their name and his own, he invited Toàn to live in Pekwoi and to be the head of the house. When he was finished speaking, the others urged Toàn to accept his uncle's invitation.

Toàn turned to his mother. "What should I do, mother? What do you want me to do?" he asked her.

"You should go, Toàn. I wish you to go," was what Nenem answered.

That is how it was that Toàn came home to Pekwoi, and the people of Kotep and of the other villages felt this to be a right and good thing. And far away in a boat-shaped lake ringed round with oak trees, a bastard female whale trembled and slapped her tail as whales do. And Nenem gazed up the steep canyon side to where Pekwoi stood, its round carved door open to the sun, and she smiled from a serene and grateful heart; then Nenem turned and went inside Hunè's house.

The boxes and treasure and money went with Toàn to Pekwoi. But Nenem did not go. Her brother invited her and everyone at Pekwoi wanted and expected her and Toàn urged her almost frantically. It was no use. Toàn had to leave her where she was.

She told him, "You must go. What would you do here—how could you live here? It is no sort of place for the First Man of the village and the family you will have one day soon. But this is my home and I have no wish to live anywhere else—ever."

So Nenem lived on in the house which had sheltered her and her baby. Its shabby walls, its old baskets and keepsakes were home to her, her near neighbors were her dear friends. Toàn understood this but he was never wholly reconciled to her staying there, and he asked her over and over to come to Pekwoi; and when Toàn bought himself a wife from one of the great houses of Olegel, upriver, his wife too urged her mother-in-law to come to them, and after a while there were grandchildren, and they asked her to come.

She always answered the same way, "Some day, some day," putting them off.

She protested when Toàn wanted to give her house a solid roof. She loved the briar and manroot vines which had grown up the sides of the house and over the roof, filtering the noon sun which shone in briefly through the holes and screening them from the rain. She and her friends called the house "Briar Roof" and she would say coaxingly to Toàn, "Don't you see? I too live in a named house now!"

Toàn did as much as his mother would let him do to make the house more habitable for one no longer young, and to keep it in some sort of repair. But after many winter moons had shone on "Briar Roof," he said firmly she must come to them before another season of storms, else he must certainly build her a new house on the site of Hunè's old one.

Nenem did not want that. She said, "No! I will come to your house—to Pekwoi—with you."

So, at last, Nenem, too, came home to Pekwoi.

Nenem fitted Pekwoi and completed it. She was the grandmother it had been missing. Toàn saw how his children liked to be near her. He watched her going up and down the little ladder to the pit and in and out of the low round door, her step smooth and light as always. He liked best to find her sitting, feet tucked under, on the sunny terrace, working at one of her perfect basketry pieces. Then he would sit on a redwood block, close by, carving or watching her. He would have been at peace then—there really was nothing more he desired—except that he sensed something not wholly right in his mother.

One day, they were sitting so and Toàn said to her, "What is it that troubles you, my mother? Can you tell me?"

In her usual, quiet voice Nenem tried to tell him, "It is that I know I won't live much longer, and . . . and . . ."

But Toàn, dreading lest his mother see that in his heart he knew this to be true, interrupted her, speaking as lightly as he could, "You must wait awhile till I kill a very special deer so you can have the most beautiful skirt in the world to wear when you die . . . would you like that?"

Nenem reached over and put her arms around him. "No . . . no . . . Toàn . . . that is what I've been wanting to tell you . . . in my grave I wish to wear a maple bark skirt and apron like the ones your father's mother always wore—nothing else. Will you dress me so when I die?"

"If that is what you wish . . . "

"And . . . one thing more . . . I want to be buried beside her. Will you do that, Toàn?"

"I will bury you beside her," Toàn promised.

"There is nothing else, my son." Nenem smiled her tender smile and Toàn no longer saw the look of trouble in her eyes.

Before the last moon of winter was full, Nenem was dead.

Alone, Toàn observed the full burial ritual. This was his wish. His wife and Nenem's close friends, who helped him dress her and make her ready, took the grapevine cord which was used to lower her into her grave, and passing it slowly down over their bodies, handed it to Toàn, thus passing on to him their contamination from the dead.

Alone, Toàn cried and fasted for five days, speaking to no one, drinking no water, eating only a little thin acorn gruel. Each night, he made a fire on his mother's grave to warm her until she should have had time to make her journey to the land of the dead.

At the end of the five days, he went to the sweat house where an old man of Kotep performed the ceremony of burial purification. He washed Toàn with an infusion of roots and aromatic herbs, meanwhile praying to each of the Inland Spirits who live along the river and blowing a puff of the sacred tobacco smoke from his pipe toward each of them in turn. And so he came finally to the Spirit who lives at the mouth of the river, just inside the bar. The ritual response of this One, after the prayer and the smoke offering, was that the corpse contamination was removed. Toàn's purification was now complete, and he was free to return to his wife in Pekwoi and to go hunting once more.

Toàn had remembered his promise to his mother. He dressed her only in a fresh maple bark skirt and apron and he buried her beside the mother of her lover. Their graves are still there today, at the river's edge, close to a grassy hollow which is all that is left of Hunè's house. Toàn cared for them and kept the tops clean as long as he lived, as did his children and his children's children, after him.

Nenem had taught Toàn, long ago, that it is wrong to grieve too much for the dead, that it is dangerous for those near to you even to think too much about one who has died; and Toàn remembered this teaching. He passed his mother's grave whenever he went to the river, and sometimes he took his carving and sat near where she lay while he worked, as he had sat near her all his life. He cried to her sometimes, but for the most part, her tender smile and the shu-shu-shu-shu rustle of her step came into his memory and out again, soft and passing as a river breeze.

PART THREE

Technology

We may view a cultural system as a series of three horizontal strata: the technological layer on the bottom, the philosophical [ideological] on the top, the sociological stratum in between. These positions express their respective roles in the culture process. The technological system is basic and primary. Social systems are functions of technologies; and philosophies express technological forces and reflect social systems. The technological factor is therefore the *determinant of a cultural system as a whole.*

LESLIE A. WHITE

INTRODUCTION

Every culture has a set of beliefs concerning the nature of the physical environment and the ways in which changes in this environment can be effectively produced. This part of culture is known as *technology*. Technology mediates man's relations with his environment by instructing the members of a society in the proper (that is, traditional and expected) uses of their bodies and of those bodily extensions known as *tools*. Just as a social system defines the significant categories of persons and associates with each a plan for action, technology defines categories of tools and associates with each a *technique*: a plan for its use to achieve a given end. Under the guidance of experienced teachers, members of a society learn the techniques appropriate to their social roles and develop the *skills* that enable them to employ appropriate tools and techniques effectively.

Technology is intimately related to the social system and the ideology of a culture. One need not be a Marxist to recognize the importance of productive techniques to social relations. Peoples who hunt and gather wild foods for their subsistence are necessarily limited to certain social arrangements by the availability of food sources and by the cooperative techniques necessary for survival. Peoples who have mastered the techniques of food production (horticulture, agriculture, or pastoralism) may have a somewhat more assured food supply, but they too are implicated in a network of ecological relations which affect their mobility and the forms of social life that are possible for them.

Technology, then, provides the tools and techniques for satisfying man's biological and social needs. It includes plans and devices for making shelter, clothing, and other necessary objects; ways of obtaining food and water, harnessing energy, curing illness, and communicating messages or objects as needed. In complex societies, various kinds of technological knowledge and skills are distributed among a large number of specialized roles. Each specialist is responsible for his own trade or profession, and he depends upon other specialists with whom he exchanges goods and services. Some such *division of labor* is found in even the most primitive society, though it tends to be very limited as compared with that in modern, industrial society. In the very simplest societies, every man and woman must master all of the skills appropriate to his or her sex; and the presence of ritual, craft, or political specialists is a mark of social development and differentiation.

The selections that follow offer a sample of the subsistence, craft, and curing techniques used by a few peoples. John M. Campbell describes a modern Eskimo caribou hunt and reflects on the passing of a way of life reminiscent of late ice-age Europe. Elizabeth Thomas presents a first-hand account of the Kung Bushmen in their daily search for vegetable food, showing how their minimal tool kit is supplemented by their intimate knowledge of the desert environment. (See Part V for an account by the same author of Bushman hunting techniques.)

Bernard L. Fontana and his collaborators describe contemporary techniques of making pottery among the Papago Indians of Arizona. Their description covers all phases of this craft, from gathering the raw materials through the ways in which the completed artifacts are used. They also comment on innovations in pottery techniques, giving an unusually clear picture of the degree of individual variation that exists among the women who practice this craft.

The description of canoe building provided by Fang-Kuei Li serves several purposes of this section: it shows how a Chipewyan Indian thinks about one of his crafts, and it exemplifies the kinds of materials and analyses used by the anthropological linguist. (Because Chipewyan is related to the Navaho language, many of the grammatical features described in the selection by Kluckhohn and Leighton in Part I may be seen in this text.)

The selection from *Moby Dick* is included partly because of Melville's evocation of the "subculture" of an American whaling ship, but also to provoke reflection on the role of hunting in our own society only one hundred years ago. The roles described are obviously highly specialized and skillful; but the need for whale oil as a source of energy (in the days before Standard Oil) stemmed from the larger society, and its demands created these roles. The practical use made of the whales' teeth, bones, and other body parts are reminiscent of the Plains Indian approach to the bison.

Linguistic analysis also plays an important part in Duane Metzger and Gerald Williams' description of the Tenejapa curer. The authors treat the curer and his clients as part of the Tenejapa social system. The native view of illness and basic techniques of diagnosis and curing are brought out through detailed comparison of questions and answers in the native language—in this case a Mayan dialect.

Still other kinds of technology are described in previous selections, for example in Mead's account of the sexual division of labor in Samoa, in Lewis' description of food preparation in a Mexican household, in Statler's observations on Japanese transportation, in Bennett's account of English agriculture and in Kroeber's description of Yurok crafts. The relationship between technology and ideology will be explored in several articles in Part V.

JOHN M. CAMPBELL

The hungry summer

John M. Campbell is a professor of anthropology and department chairman at the University of New Mexico. His specialty is Arctic archaeology and the ethnology of hunting peoples; he is now editing a series of drawings by one of the Eskimo hunters described below.

It is nearly impossible for modern man to imagine what it is like to live by hunting. The life of a hunter is one of hard, seemingly continuous overland travel. It is a life that involves carrying one's possessions to an endless series of temporary camps; of constant traveling with and caring for wife and children, and perhaps one's widowed mother or the orphaned children of a brother. A life of frequent concerns that the next interception may not work, that the trap or the drive will fail, or that the herds will not appear this season. Above all, the life of a hunter carries with it the threat of deprivation and death by starvation.

These conditions have not applied with equal intensity to every hunting society, but endless roving and the specter of famine have been the age-old companions of most true hunters. The reasons for this lie in the habits of large, herding herbivores and the nature of the environments they occupy. Big game such as bison, horses, or reindeer is invariably migratory. A given herd commonly travels hundreds of miles in the course of each year, moving in response to breeding requirements, predators, or seasonally changing conditions of pasture and climate. To exploit such a population, hunters must either follow the animals or intercept them by traveling from one locality to another on their known migration routes.

Until very recently, numerous societies supported themselves to some degree by killing one or more species of mammalian game. However, during the past several thousand years hunting has been a secondary food-getting pursuit for almost all societies. For example, at the time of Columbus only a handful of the several hundred North American tribes

---

This account was written especially for the present volume.

were truly hunting societies whose members depended on game animals for more than fifty percent of their total annual diets. For all of the rest, hunting was only an adjunct or supplement to horticulture, fishing, or gathering wild plant and animal foods.

Two crucial faunal requirements must be met to permit a human society to base more than half of its subsistence economy on land mammal hunting. First, the mammals must be large, and second, they must be extraordinarily numerous and gregarious. In practice, this second requirement means that these mammals typically are found in herds and that (at least at certain seasons of the year) these herds number hundreds or thousands of individual animals. It follows that such mammals must be herbivores, and because of the food requirements of the animals themselves, they must dwell on open lands, not in forests.

Once a human society has become economically dependent upon big game hunting, the society often comes to occupy an environmental niche that provides relatively little else in the way of sustaining food resources. Historically, many of the prairie lands of the world, perhaps most of them, have not contained abundant *varieties* of wild food plants and animals. A human community committed to big game hunting is thus likely to fall upon very hard times indeed, if for any reason it fails in its continuous quest for one or a few major prey species. Furthermore, the greater the distance from the equator, the fewer the varieties of plants and animals. Thus, the hunting way of life is more hazardous in those open lands lying farther away from the tropical zone, and hunters of the arctic plains have led the most precarious lives of all.

Such a group of arctic hunters were the Nunamiut Eskimos. In A.D. 1875, before European-Americans had reached them, the Nunamiut numbered perhaps 1,400 individuals who lived in an area containing more than 65,000 square miles. Their environment was an immense tundra prairie which, in north Alaska, extends southward from the shore of the Arctic Ocean to the barren canyons of the front of the Brooks Range and beyond to the edge of the boreal forest. The Nunamiut tribe, consisting of fifteen to twenty bands, based its living on caribou (*Rangifer arcticus*), a mammal very little different from the Old World reindeer (*Rangifer tarandus*). The Nunamiut ate fish and other animals and plants, but their mainstay was the caribou; in fact, without this single species of big game, interior northernmost Alaska would have been uninhabitable in aboriginal times.

When I first met the Nunamiut, in 1956, the tribe had been reduced to one combined band numbering fewer than 100 people. They had established their main camp in Anaktuvuk Pass, one of the barren mountain valleys in the central Brooks Range. Although, by 1956, the Nunamiut had long since acquired rifles and many other trappings of civilization, they still dwelt 200 air miles from the end of the nearest road, and their lives still depended on killing caribou. In the few years that were left before their culture was to be suddenly and enormously changed by the outside world, I traveled with them each summer, participating in a way of life that no longer exists. After one such season I wrote in my notebook the following account of what I saw and felt when for a moment I became a Nunamiut, a caribou hunter.

From the northern gate to the place where the walls close in above the last great tributary valley to the south, Anaktuvuk Pass is about twenty miles long. Right at the summit, which is nearly midway through the Pass, the valley floor is only 2,000 feet above sea level; but for all of its length it is bounded by mountains of sedimentary rock, which rise straight up on either side for another 2,000 to 4,000 feet. Seen from the perspective of the enormous mass of the Brooks Range, which spreads outward east and west for hundreds of miles, Anaktuvuk is a very small crevice. But to the earthly eye of a caribou or a man it is a magnificent corridor that promises safe travel through a world of mountains. Its effect on the senses is strengthened by the contrast between the cold sheerness of its rocky walls and the velvety softness of its grassy floor. In some places one can stand on the top of its eastern or western rim and throw a rock clear to the valley. Soakpuk is such a place, and according to legend, a man once jumped to his death from this part of the western scarp.

Now, in late August, it is through this passage that the great herd must come, the cows and their calves walking up over the Arctic Slope from the north, the bulls falling in with them. For the Eskimos it has been a poor summer, "a hungry country," as Paneak puts it. It *has* been hungry, more than usual, even though to the Nunamiut the whole universe is chronically hungry. They catalog the world according to its degrees of edibility: "lots to eat," "something good to eat," "pretty good to eat," "spoil your belly," are the sorts of phrases that I have heard so many hundreds of times that more than once I have found myself pointing to a three ounce sandpiper on the tundra, and vacantly saying, "something good to eat." The gelatinous, watery shoots of willows are pretty good to eat, and so are the maggots of the bot fly and a kind of clay.

The world is a hungry place, and the Nunamiut can prove it. They carry the proof in their minds as well as in their hearts. One man has told me several times about finding the stinking corpses of his uncle and his uncle's family one spring, dead in their camp of starvation. Another tells of eating sled harness, and another of digging for mice. It is not that such awful occurrences happen every year, or even every five or ten years, but they have happened and they continue to happen often enough.

We are waiting for *tuktu*, caribou, good fat caribou, and we have waited all summer—one old man, his teeth worn to the gums, four babies less than two years old, and about eighty other people. We have eaten what there has been to eat: a few grayling from Kayuk Creek, ground squirrels, a single porcupine found wandering here, thirty walking miles from the nearest trees. Caribou are fine looking, dark with light bellies and white throats—possibly the most beautiful deer in the world. On the hoof a big bull will weigh 350 pounds. It has been said that the Brooks Range caribou herd is the largest gathering of land mammals of a single species anywhere to be found, not excepting Africa's game. I don't know. There are tens of thousands of caribou in the Range. I have seen that many with my own eyes. But now there is nothing, not a single animal. Sometimes in the summer we find stragglers, or even a small band of deer. Once in July, in another hungry year, we found 800 bulls, all together. We still talk about it. This summer we have searched for weeks, two or three of us at a time scouting thirty and forty miles to the north, northeast and northwest: *pesuk*, nothing.

This is because the annual migration of these animals takes them away from the mountains for a large part of the summer. Simply stated, the great herd may be characterized as summering on the Arctic Slope and Arctic Coastal Plain, and as wintering on the lower slopes and among the forested valleys south of the Brooks Range divide. The seasonal ranging of the herd is thus a cyclical thing, and it is to the rhythm of its wanderings that the Nunamiut have adjusted their own lives. So we wait, hoping that in the early autumn the animals will pour southward through the mountains, where, with luck, they can be killed as they funnel between the enclosing valley walls.

The natural world impresses some people more than others. It continually impresses me. I am easily awed by things in nature, but never by anything else as much as by the caribou in Anaktuvuk Pass. One day the earth is empty. The next, if it is a good year, the caribou come. They come in endless, sinuous masses which, traveling the clock around, take five days or a week to pass a given point. Once the migration is well under way, the Pass is literally filled from end to end with the caribou. The animals walk southward along two routes, one on either side of the valley floor. They travel every hour of the day, and while they are there, there is absolutely no end to them.

If a man gets up on a knoll so that his horizon is, say, five miles in one direction and seven miles in the other, there are caribou, north and south, as far as he can see. If he is right down on the valley floor he will, depending on where he is, see from 50 to 5,000 caribou. Urged on by instinct and season, the herd can hardly be diverted from its course. As I sit beside my fire in the willows, caribou crash past me on either side for a whole afternoon. They are so close I can hit them with clods of dirt. When I stand and yell, and wave my arms, the ones already past break into a trot; the ones behind hold back, milling and uncertain. When I sit down again the herd comes on, snorting and prancing at the scent and sight of me. My fire and I are like an island in a river. If a lake lies athwart its track the herd swims buoyantly across, cows, calves and bulls driving from shore to shore in an unending stream. Wolves follow it, killing the laggards, and grizzly bears and wolverines devour the feeble and the sick. These predators, if left alone, help control the herd's size and keep the stock healthy and robust, but the herd goes its predestined way in spite of all of them.

The Nunamiut camp lies directly in the path of the migration. In these last weeks anticipation is nearly unbearable. At last a foraging party coming in from the north reports that caribou are gathering in front of the Pass. This triggers frenzied activity in camp. A twenty-four hour round-robin of loading ammunition begins. (Among all the hunters there are just two cartridge reloading tools, and no one has gotten around to using them earlier.)

The vanguard of the herd is allowed to pass camp unmolested. The Eskimos claim that caribou on migration follow the scent of the first animals and that letting the pioneers go by assures that all the rest will come behind. Then we begin waiting for the big herd, scattered out in groups of four or five over three square miles of tundra. Four of us have chosen a little defile on the east side of the valley. It is 200 yards across, with low, rocky walls on either side, and we are hidden, a few feet apart, against a pile of boulders, each man in a good place from which to shoot, with extra cartridges on the ground beside him.

They come into our view over a rise of ground half a mile north strung out 400 abreast; and after the first of them come down off the skyline we see that the knoll behind is solidly blanketed with moving caribou. The excitement is so physically overwhelming that each man in turn scurries off to urinate. That accomplished, we sit as still as we can against the lichen-covered stones.

From off to the northeast, nearly a mile across and down the tundra, we hear a single pealing call. It is the raven, *tuluak*. Then closer, from the west, we hear him again. But *tuluak* this time is dressed in caribou skins and dirty canvas; the first call is actually from Paneak and his partners, who have gotten behind this part of the herd, and the second is from Kakinya, and Naiyuk, and Putu, who have flanked it on the west.

How many animals are now between us? Worlds of them, that's how many; a universe of caribou. They come closer. We can now feel their feet, striking into the soft tundra, and we can smell them too, fresh urine and wet hides. Now they are so close that we can hear the strange little noises they make with their hooves and see the tendons moving in their shoulders and rumps.

Our rifles are up. There is no word spoken, no sound, as we each work our magic, Ahgook, Okiotak, Kavik, and the *tannik*, the white man. "Eee" (yes), breathes Ahgook. A cow falls first. Her little calf, terrified by her kicking, runs right up to us. We laugh, but no one shoots it. We will kill it soon for its soft hide and its brains, but now we are killing the bulls, the big fat ones. Fat meat is what we must have. The herd stops, milling, and then three animals break out, trotting in front. We shoot them as quickly as we can to turn the herd and drive it back to the other hunters, and we keep shooting until *tuktu* is out of range.

In a few moments the shots will come rolling up from the north. Meanwhile, we watch the herd, marking the wounded as they drop behind. One big bull running swiftly beside the herd suddenly drops stone dead 500 yards away. Another stands with its head down and then slowly turns and turns, six times around like a dog making a bed, before it falls. Ahgook goes off after a young bull shot through the intestines which is painfully staggering up a rise of ground to the right. Kavik walks toward the little calf. For a few yards it followed the herd, but it is waiting now, as if for help. Kavik hums a little and talks softly to it, and when he is close he shoots it low behind the ears in order to spoil neither its brains nor its hide. When we take count, the four of us have killed fourteen caribou.

Hours later, in the Nunamiut camp at midnight, we have each eaten pounds of fat meat and drunk hot tea and cold water. A few of the people are asleep in this, old Maptirak's, tent. They will awaken long before morning and eat some more. The little boy Tulakana, four years old, is sucking a marrow bone. He is as gaunt as a wolf, and as he sucks I watch his eyes. They are threatening and I wonder if he will growl if I move closer to him. He has not slept, and he has vomited twice, but he will eat until he falls asleep eating. His mother touches him, saying no words, but saying just the same how good it is, her Tulakana being sick from too much food. The hungry summer is over.

ELIZABETH M. THOMAS

Food quest of the African Bushman

Elizabeth M. Thomas has accompanied three anthropological expeditions to South Africa to make studies and films of the Kung Bushmen. Her most recent book is *Wandering Herdsmen*, a study of another nomadic African tribe, the Dodoth.

There are many kinds of wild roots which can be eaten in winter, and each is marked among the grass blades by an almost invisible dry thread of a vine. The roots are swollen with liquid by which the plants preserve their life during the drought. When the plants feel the onset of spring, warm air and raindrops, the dry vines suck moisture out of the watery roots, turn green, and put out tiny leaves, and in this way, if the false spring lasts, the roots are soon sucked dry entirely. Bushmen cannot get enough water from eating the vines and leaves. The plants do not bear fruit until summer; the spring-season vegetables, such as little onions, pods like pea pods, and leafy green vegetables that taste like rhubarb, have not grown in yet; and so the Bushmen must go thirsty. People have died of thirst in these false seasons.

Gathering veld food is the work of the Bushman women, and I used to go with them quite often on their trips. We sometimes stayed in the veld all day eating roots instead of drinking water. One day my brother came along to film the gathering of veld food, and as we were getting ready to leave, Gai also joined us. It is customary for Bushmen never to let a group of their women go anywhere with a Bantu or a European man unless a Bushman man goes with them to protect them. Gai sauntered along behind us in his role of guardian, quite unhampered, as he had nothing with him but his loincloth. Dasina, Twikwe, and Tsetchwe walked in front, each with a digging-stick thrust in her belt like an enormous knife, each wearing a heavy cape, and Tsetchwe carrying her

---

From *The Harmless People* by Elizabeth Marshall Thomas (New York: Alfred A. Knopf, Inc., 1958), pp. 102–113. Reprinted by permission of Alfred A. Knopf, Inc., and Marie Rodell.

baby, who rode, carefree and swinging his feet, on her shoulder. John and I walked in the middle of the procession, and at the end came the three young boys, who did not stay in single file but ran all over the veld, ran circles around us, and shouted to each other happily.

We walked across the pan of Ai a ha'o through the fine, soft grass, which left tiny, barbed seeds sticking to our legs. We walked through the brush on the opposite side and then over a wide plain, where we saw a herd of wildebeest. No one was armed, and when the wildebeest saw us, put down their heads, and ran, we could only watch helplessly as all that meat galloped away.

We walked until we came to a patch of tsama melons, perhaps twenty of them lying together, shiny, smooth, and green in the grass. The vine that once had nourished them had dried away and already some of the melons were turning yellow, overripe, ready to open and release their seeds.

The women stopped and began to gather up the green melons, Twikwe picking them with a mechanical, stereotyped gesture. She first slipped her hand under a melon; then, twisting her elbow, she lifted the melon and held it pinched between the heel of her hand and her forearm, and with a scoop slipped it into the pocket of her kaross on the side. In a moment the side of her kaross was full, and she stood erect for an instant, looked at the sky, shifted her weight, and suddenly the melons rolled to the back of her kaross, leaving the side free for more. She was very efficient. In a moment she had a load. I was a little surprised at her, however, for now she would have to carry the melons with her all day whereas she might have gathered them on the way home. But Bushman women do not seem to mind this.

The women left behind the yellow melons which would have been bitter and rotten, touching them disappointedly with their toes instead. The false spring was hastening the time when all the melons would be gone, forcing the Bushmen to eat roots as a staple diet, not as desirable because of the uses that tsama melons have. Melons are eaten as both food and water, their pulp is added to meat which needs liquid for boiling, their seeds are roasted and eaten or ground into powder and used as flour, their rinds serve as mixing-bowls, as containers for small, loose objects, as cooking-pots with or without the pulp inside, as urine-containers for curing hides, as targets for the children's shooting practice, as children's drums, as resonators for musical instruments, and all this amounts to a serious loss for Bushmen when the melons rot or dry.

We went on until we were about two miles from camp. We were going to an almost imperceptible small hill, a place, said Twikwe, where a great deal of veld food grew. On the way a moving shadow caught our attention, and we looked up to see a white-breasted, black-winged vulture sailing not far above our heads, not stirring himself but riding the drafts and currents of the air. He was looking at us with hard eyes, his red face turned to look down, and suddenly he closed his great wings under his body, sweeping them down so far that the long wing feathers brushed together four feet under his belly. Then his wings swept up again and bore him on. I had never seen a vulture do that before. He did it only once, then made a circle all around us, looking down at us, his eyes cool in their red wrinkles; he rose higher and higher and soon he was gone. All over Africa the sky is full of vultures, but so high that you can seldom see them; any time you look up with binoculars, however, you will probably be able to see one sailing, waiting up there for a disaster.

We were going particularly to look for *bi*, a fibrous, watery root that is the mainstay of the Bushmen's diet during the hot season when the melons are gone. From the end of August, when the spring begins, the heat increases in intensity until December and January, when the rains come, relieving the drought. During this hot, dry season the sand reflects the sun until the air all over the veld shudders and dances, until human beings and animals alike gasp for air and water. This is the hardest season of all for the Bushmen, yet most of them remain alive by going into the veld early in the morning in the cooler light of dawn to gather bi. The bi they find is brought back to the werf before the sun is hot; it is scraped, and the scrapings are squeezed dry. The people drink the juice they squeeze. Then they dig shallow pits like graves for themselves in the shade. They urinate on the bi scrapings and line the pits with the now moist pulp, then lie in the pits and spend the day letting the moisture evaporating from the urine preserve the moisture in their bodies. They lie still all day and at dusk go into the veld again to gather food, perhaps a few roots or cucumbers, returning to their werf before it is utterly dark, for in the hot season the big snakes, too, move only at night, the mambas and the cobras out of their holes.

By the end of the season the Gikwe are emaciated from hunger and thirst, and it is because of this season that the Gikwe hear the jackals on the plains cry "Water, water."

When we reached the little hill Twikwe had mentioned we found no bi root, but we found other kinds of veld food: a bush with red berries, several kinds of roots, and a spiny cucumber not three inches long, round and bristling with its spines like a sea urchin, handsome in its light-brown, yellow-striped skin. The young boys found five of these cucumbers lying in a crooked row on the sand, all put there by a vine which had mostly dried and shriveled away. We picked them and ate them. They have a watery green flesh which looks just like the flesh of a cucumber as we know it but which is sweet.

Witabe, noting the direction of the vine by the way it had deposited its cucumbers, traced it to its source and found a bit of it left above the ground, below the branches of a whitethorn bush. He said there would be an edible root there, and when he dug, there was.

Meanwhile, Gai had found a solid, stiff vine like a stalk among the roots of a gray bush which was the home of a small flock of birds. Just for fun, Gai chased the birds out; they would have gone anyway, but, frightened by him, they flew like little pellets in every direction, leaving behind a pale, soft grass nest blowing in the wind. Gai sat down facing the bush with the branch shadows all over him and dug with a digging-stick in the sand between his legs. The branches around his head got in his way, tickling his ears, causing him to slash impatiently at them with his digging-stick, and when this did no good he endured the nuisance for a moment, then flung himself down on his back, put up his long legs like a fighting cock, and kicked the branches down.

He dug out a great deal of earth, throwing it behind him, and finally uncovered a *ga* root, big and dark with a warty surface all covered with lumps like a toad or a stone; a fascinating thing, for although it was large and nondescript, brownish gray in brown-gray sand, marked only by an old dry vine, it was life itself to Bushmen, bitter but quite moist even in the hottest season. Tsetchwe put the root in her kaross and we went off, Gai generously carrying the baby, taking him from Tsetchwe by the forearm and swinging him up to his shoulder. The baby rode astride Gai's neck with the soft kaross he wore draped over Gai's head. From the rear they were an apparition, as this made the baby's head, not much higher than Gai's, look like a tiny head on a man's tall, slender body.

We wanted very much to find a bi root, and while Gai, the baby, and my brother went off to look for one I waited behind with the women. We rested in a small circle in the dim shade of the grass, which, when we were sitting, came high above our heads so that all we could see was a circle of sky and, in the circle, the ragged, waxing moon. It had risen luxuriously in the daytime and was a pale, large crescent, pearl-colored in the sun. The moon is a root with a climbing stalk, a vine. It can be eaten.

Giamakwe began to urinate right in our midst, crouching and pulling his loincloth aside. Although the adults are slightly inhibited about this the children are not, sometimes simply turning aside to urinate as one might turn aside to cough. Presently the young boys got up and ran away, and when they did Tsetchwe herself got to her feet, stepped aside and urinated also, standing up but leaning forward. Bushman women sometimes do this, but Bushman men crouch to urinate. "It is our law," they say.

While the women rested they had refreshed themselves with one of Twikwe's melons which Twikwe chopped for them by holding the melon between the soles of both feet and mashing its pulp with her digging-stick, which she held in both hands. Then they got up from their grass nest, sharpened their digging-sticks with Twikwe's knife, and set out to begin the search for food. They each chose a different direction and soon they were out of sight. I followed Twikwe to see what she would find, hurrying to keep up as she trampled ahead of me on those spindly, awkward legs of hers, which she kicked out with each step in a walk like the walk of a clown. She kept her back straight, for it was still early and the load in her kaross was light.

As I could not speak many words of Gikwe, she didn't even try to talk, but paused from time to time instead to show me things. Once she crouched among the branches of a thorn bush and beckoned to me to show me a tiny vine winding around the bush's trunk. I nodded. It marked an edible root. She pinched the base of the vine where there was a faint touch of green, then, grasping her digging-stick, began to dig. The ground was quite hard, but she dug rapidly, her slender back curved as she squatted over the hole and the muscles of her thin arms swelling. After a long time she threw down her digging-stick and tugged at something in the bottom of the hole. She sat back, and in her hands was a huge stone, which she heaved aside.

"Look," she said, and I crawled beside her into the bush. She had made a hole three feet deep, a foot across, and at the bottom, dim in shadow, lay an immense gray root wedged securely between two stones. "Ga," she said. She ripped the severed vine from the bush it clung to and tossed it into the sunlight. "Look," she said again, assuming that I would now recognize a ga vine when I saw one; but although I examined it closely, it still looked like any other vine to me.

Again she bent over the hole, leaning over so far that her head came between her knees, and grasped the huge root with both hands. She tugged so hard that I heard her joints crack, but the root was wedged and she couldn't move it. She took up her digging-stick again, panting now, and struck the rocks, and the point of her digging-stick splintered.

"Ai," she said, exasperated, sitting back on her heels to carve a new point with her knife. She bent again, pried at the rocks, pried at the root, but it was useless, she couldn't move it. Then she relaxed, resting for a moment as she rubbed her sore shoulders before she got to her feet and walked away, beckoning with her head for me to follow. We would leave it.

We wandered about haphazardly for a time, looking for a vine, and presently I saw one twisted around some grass blades, binding them together in a tuft. I pointed it out to her, but she smiled and shook her head, turning her hands palm upward in the gesture for nothing. She meant that it was a useless species of vine, marking nothing below. Later, as we walked along, she laughed. Twikwe was charmed by the mistakes the members of our expedition made, for they were always elementary and, to her, very diverting.

Keeping her eyes on the ground, Twikwe noticed a tiny crack in the sand. She scooped at it with the point of her digging-stick, tipped out a truffle, and picked it up almost without stopping. As we walked on she broke it in half, put half in her kaross, and offered half to me. I ate it. It was light brown and had a delicious, salty flavor. Truffles grow an inch or so below hard-surfaced ground and have no leaf nor stalk nor vine to show where they are, only the tiny crack made by the truffle swelling, which the Bushmen notice.

We had crossed a barren stretch of plain where only grass was growing and were in another patch of low bushes where veld food also grew. The great plains of the Kalahari may seem undiversified, but really they are divided into countless little patches, some barren, some fertile, depending probably on the soil. In this veld-food patch Twikwe found another vine tangled in the lower branches of a thorn bush and she crawled in after it and began to dig. The thorns around her head, all smooth and shining white like jewels, were tickling her, but, unlike Gai, she delicately put up just one hand and picked off the very thorns that pricked her.

She resumed her digging and after perhaps twenty minutes as she followed down the vine she uncovered another ga root also wedged among stones. This ga was not as large as the other one, nor was it wedged as tightly, and when she grasped it, arched her back, and tugged, clenching her teeth and straining her thin arms, the rocks suddenly gave way and the ga flew loose, sending Twikwe crashing back among the thorns. She wiped the perspiration from her forehead with her thumb before she crawled out of the bush, dragging her root and her digging-stick. I noticed that the root was very wrinkled, as if it had shrunk. Twikwe struck at it with the point of her digging-stick, chipping out a fragment, which she put in her mouth. Then she spat, stood up, and walked away from it. When I, too, tasted it to see what was the matter I found that it was flaccid, dry, and very bitter, quite inedible. I looked inside the bush and saw that its vine had begun to turn a little green.

We went on, and passed a few dry melons on our way, yellow and empty, perhaps bitten by an antelope some time ago. I kicked at one of them and a gray lizard ran out, straight and fast as an arrow. Then it turned around and ran back in again, having no place else to go.

Soon Twikwe found a third root and, after digging it out and tasting it, found it quite acceptable; putting it in her kaross, she went on to find a fourth. We found old, dry holes where Bushman women had dug out roots seasons ago, a few dry vines with bitter, useless roots below, and three more roots that proved to be edible, as well as two more melons a few spiny cucumbers, a handful of berries from a tiny bush, and one more truffle. This would feed Twikwe and her two sons for one or two days, or perhaps would be shared with Ukwane and Kutera because Kutera, that day, had not felt well enough to gather food of her own. Bushmen help each other, each Bushman woman contributing to the support of her own family and perhaps to the well-being of some very old people as well.

When Twikwe considered that she had enough, we turned back to find the others, and presently we came to the plain where we had left them. Twikwe called, and was answered by three or four voices very near by. Then, right in front of us as if from nowhere, the three boys, Tsetchwe, and Dasina appeared standing, having been crouching in the long grass. Twikwe and I joined them, and the Bushmen passed Twikwe's pipe, the short, wide antelope bone stuffed with tobacco. When it was passed to me I puffed it, too, but it was so strong and rank that it made me dizzy.

Soon we heard a wail, a sad crying out in the veld, and it was Gai and John returning with Nhwakwe, who had begun to miss his mother or want to go home. Gai looked cross and walked rapidly with his little burden riding on his shoulder, and even John seemed somewhat annoyed because of the noise and because they had not found a bi root. When they came up to us Gai swung Nhwakwe down, dangling him by the arm as he handed him to Tsetchwe, who took him at once and let him nurse. Bushman babies do not like to go for veld food because the sun is hot, there is nothing to eat except the raw roots, and there is nobody to play with, yet they do not like to be left at home alone either. This is a constant and insoluble problem for Bushman mothers.

After asking Gai more questions and, at his suggestion, roaming from one point to another over the veld in search of a bi, it came to John and me that he did not want to show us where one was growing. We understood this, for the bi roots of the veld are naturally limited and if we took one when the Bushmen did not need it, it would not be there when they did. We assured Gai that we did not want to eat it, only to see its vine, and at last he remembered, he said, where one was, far out in the veld and on the way to Okwa. But we were not discouraged and set off in that direction, and after a while we found it far away but not as far as Gai had said. It took us an hour to reach it, but we had traveled slowly because the women had stopped to gather melons along the way.

When we came to the center of an enormous plain with no tree or bush to mark the place, Gai stopped and, glancing around for a moment, pointed suddenly with his toe. After trying hard to see, we noticed a tiny shred of a vine wound around a grass blade; no part of the vine still touched the ground, as the vine had dried and parts of it had blown away. Gai had known where the bi was, he told us, because he had walked by it months ago in the last rainy season when the vine was still green, and he had remembered. He had assumed that it was still there because only his own people used the territory around it and if one of them had taken it he would have heard. Bushmen talk all the time about such things. He had had it in his mind to come back and get it when the tsama melons were gone, but now, perhaps when he saw its vine there and thought about it under the ground, he changed his mind. Squatting near the vine and digging with his hands, he soon had exposed it, two feet down and dark in shadow. He seized it and tore it from the earth.

It was shaped like a monstrous beet, with its vine coming from the top like a little stalk and its root bristling from the bottom like a tassel. It had a hard, bark-like crust and it was gray and hairy. Gai held it daintily by its vine, and, as dirt was still dropping off it he slapped and brushed it to clean it; then he held it high above the big cavity it had filled, looked at it with a rather satisfied smile, and said what nice water it would be.

We went home then, walking again in single file in a straight course over the veld, veering only once toward a fallen tree, where the women stopped to gather firewood. The women, walking first, were heavily loaded now with melons, roots, and firewood, Tsetchwe loaded most heavily of all because the baby rode on her shoulder. The women used their digging-sticks as canes because their knees were bending, and walked quickly, trying to get home as soon as possible. After the women came the young boys carrying nothing, and last of all came Gai, holding his bi by its tassel of root. Before long he hurried and caught up to Tsetchwe, and once again he took a turn with Nhwakwe, swinging him from Tsetchwe's shoulders to his own, where Nhwakwe rode happily, his tiny hands pressed over his father's eyes.

BERNARD L. FONTANA,
WILLIAM J. ROBINSON,
CHARLES W. CORMACK,
and ERNEST E. LEAVITT, JR.

Techniques of pottery manufacture of the Papago Indians

Bernard L. Fontana is a professor of anthropology at the University of Arizona. He and his three co-authors collaborated on a study of ancient and modern Papago pottery, but Fontana and Cormack, both ethnologists, are primarily responsible for this description of contemporary pottery techniques. (The original edition is illustrated with photographs of each step and each type of pottery.)

Potters go for clay in the early or late spring, usually just before it is hot enough to make pottery. Generally a male relative accompanies the potter to help her with the clay-gathering chores. When they arrive at the deposit, the topsoil is first cleared away with the use of a shovel, rake, hoe, or any other handy tool they might have. When the clay is exposed beneath the topsoil, the potter or her helper digs that clay loose with a pick, a hoe, a long knife, or a shovel—again using anything that will do the job. The large chunks of clay thus picked loose are carried in a sack or can to a cleared place on the ground, sometimes in the middle of the old part of the pit that has already been dug. The potter then crushes the chunks of clay by pounding them on the ground with a stick. The pounded clay is further refined by sifting it into a can through a screen. When the potter has her can filled with ground and sifted clay, she sacks the remaining large chunks and returns with both coarse and sifted clay to her home.

The amount of clay gathered varies, of course, from potter to potter and from time to time. In general the rule seems to be that one gathers all one can conveniently carry, perhaps fifty to one hundred pounds. The clay is hauled either in a wagon or a modern automobile or truck. We recorded no instances of a potter carrying the clay herself, although there is no reason to believe that this does not occur. Usually it is the male, if there is one along, who does the heavy lifting.

Bernard L. Fontana *et al., Papago Indian Pottery* (Seattle: University of Washington Press and The American Ethnological Society, 1962), pp. 55–83. Reprinted by permission of the publisher.

There is also no way to generalize about the number of trips a potter may make for clay in one season. We doubt that any makes more than three or four trips at the most, and some doubtless make do with the supply from one trip.

What has been said about clay is also true for the hematite used as slip, except that it is not crushed on the spot and it is brought back in relatively small amounts. A little hematite can go a long way.

PREPARING THE CLAY BODY When the potter returns to her home, she mixes her finely ground clay with water "in just the right amount," as potters will explain. The clay is placed in a pan or other container and water is added a little at a time; between pourings the potter mixes the clay with her hand. When the clay has been mixed into what the potter considers to be the right consistency, it is placed in a wet rag and stored away either in a tin can kept in the shade or in an olla buried in the ground.

The clay is kept damp to "cure" for from three to five days before it is ready to use. One of the effects of such curing is doubtless to wet all the particles.

. . .

Although we have not analyzed the various clays collected for their properties, and granting that their properties are indeed variable, we found that all the potters we questioned on the subject agree on three to five days' soaking time for the clay.

Sometimes the clay that has been prepared into paste is allowed to dry completely, and is stored dry over the winter season to be used the following summer. The clay is repounded and sifted and again mixed with water, but whether or not this clay is required to "cure" we cannot say. It seems likely, since the same necessity to moisten all the fine particles still exists.

What we have been describing thus far is "pure" clay to which no temper is added. This clay already contains various inclusions that make further tempering unnecessary. If temper is required, however, it is added to the sifted clay before water is added. Papago potters use a wide range of tempering materials, the most popular among them being dried and sifted horse manure. Fired, manure-tempered pottery shows a heavy carbon streak in the center of a sherd when viewed in cross section. Horse manure is the only vegetal temper we found in use among Papagos, and since the horse was introduced by the Spaniards, sherds showing the heavy black carbon streak are more likely to be historic than prehistoric. Potters add horse manure and other tempers in varying amounts, depending on the properties of the clay and on individual experience and preference.

We failed to find any potters who, when adding temper, added more than one kind to a batch of clay, and in general, a potter will use only one kind of temper at all. A few said that they have used both horse manure and mineral tempers on different occasions.

In addition to horse manure, Papagos also use coarse sand from desert washes as well as sand that is sifted through a screen; ground rock, both granite and schist; and ground potsherds. Very often no temper is added at all: Alvina Ignacio adds ground schist to clay used for water jars "to make the water cooler" (because of more porous clay), but not to the clay intended for other forms.

It is likely that "curing" the clay body is an empirical matter, learned by potters on the basis of experience. Listiana Francisco told us about a Papago from Tucson who came to her for clay. She laughingly told us how the Tucson woman's attempt at making pottery failed because "...she used the clay right away after mixing it with water—without curing it."

Similarly, the matter of adding temper appears to be based on individual experience. Listiana Francisco uses two clay deposits near her village: to one she says she must add horse manure to give the body the right consistency; to the other, with its gold mica inclusions, she adds nothing. She says too, that if what she is making is very small, such as a little bowl or small plate, she will add no temper to the clay of the first deposit either. It is when she makes large pots, pots that have to stand up and hold their shape while she is working on them, that she adds the tempering material.

FORMING THE POT When the clay body has been prepared and aged for a few days, the potter prepares to form the pot. There seems to be no special significance attached to a working place, except that in all cases the potters work in their yards at home seated either on a cloth on the ground or on the ground itself.

The first part of the process, molding the base of the pot, is generally done under shade, either in a shed or *ramada*, or perhaps in the shade of a building or under a tree, both because it is cooler for the potter and because the potter does not want her clay to become too dry at this point.

She first surrounds herself with the materials she will need: the container of wet clay, wooden paddle and stone anvil, rag ring and cloth, a pan of water, the pot to be used as a mold for the base, and perhaps a pan of ashes or fine dirt.

With her materials close at hand she seats herself on the ground, legs usually crossed under her (sitting positions vary somewhat), and removes a fistful of wet clay from its container. This she puts on the cloth in front of her and begins to pat it into a bun. As soon as the ball of clay is round and flat, she adds ashes or dirt to the stone anvil with which she pats the bun, or to the mold, to prevent the clay from sticking to her hands. Some potters, rather than add ashes or dirt, simply keep their hands and anvil wet or use nothing at all. The circular bun is thinned and rounded by hand.

The potter then places the bun over the base of the inverted pot that is being used as a mold. She may first put ashes on the base of the mold to prevent the bun from sticking to it, or she may use dirt, water, or, as one potter told us, nothing. Another potter, Rita Valenzuela, places a cloth over the base of the mold, with the result that cloth imprints show in the interior of the base of the new pot even after it is fired.

With the bun over the mold, the potter proceeds by using the stone anvil to pat the clay thin. She turns the mold in front of her from time to time, using only her hands to do so. When the bun has been pressed over the base of the mold for a short distance by the use of the anvil, the potter then uses a wooden paddle (generally carved from mesquite or fashioned from a barrel stave) to spread it farther, gently patting the clay; the concave curvature of the paddle fits the convex curvature of the mold pot. This continues until the clay is spread evenly to approximately one-quarter of the way down the walls of the mold.

Then the potter wets her hands, washing off any clay that might be stuck to them, and smooths the molded clay with her wet hands until the surface is quite shiny. She then lifts the clay from the mold and sets the new base upside down on a cloth on the ground, wrapping a second cloth around the rim as she does so. It is set in the sunshine, and the cloth is placed around the rim of the base to prevent it from becoming dry while the very bottom of the base is drying.

After the base of the pot has dried to a leatherlike texture, the potter turns the base upright, setting it down in the center of a rag ring under a cloth. The rag ring, sometimes made with plain rags tied in a circle or with rags wrapped over thin tree branches or dried yucca blades, is in effect the stand or base upon which the potter supports and turns her pot. It is usually hidden from view under a cloth, which further facilitates turning the base, and keeps it free of dirt.

At this point the potter now moistens her right hand and with it dampens the interior of the base as well as its rim, smoothing them out, removing rough particles with thumbnail and forefinger, and filling small holes either with removed rough particles or with pieces from a wet ball of clay that is kept at her side. When she has smoothed the base to her satisfaction, she then dips a curved wooden paddle into a pan of water, wets a stone anvil with it, holds the stone anvil on the interior of the rim in her left hand, and strikes against the rim of the base opposite the anvil with the paddle held in her right hand. She keeps the anvil and the paddle damp continually, and employs this paddle-and-anvil process all the way around the rim of the base. The result of this staccato patting, using no more than a three- or four-inch rapid stroke with the paddle (wrist action alone), is to thin the wall of the base of the pot and to increase its height....

The potter then smooths off the rim with a moistened right hand and tears off a small handful of wet clay to make the first clay coil. The coil is formed of the same material from which the rest of the pot has been made, and is shaped into a rope simply by spinning the clay between the palms of the hands. The length of clay rope is stuck to the rim of the base by placing four fingers behind it on the interior of the pot and pinching in and down against the coil in front of the fingers with the thumb....

When the coils for the body have been added, they are made to blend into the base of the pot first by sealing the seam by hand where the coils join the rim, and then by pounding smooth with the paddle-and-anvil technique. The coils for the neck are next added and treated in the same way, except that the paddle used is no longer a large, curved paddle, but rather one which is straight, flat, and narrow. This is better adapted to the inverted neck.

. . .

We observed that in the process of adding the rim to a pot, the same potter never makes two rims that are identical in every detail. Some will be more or less everted than others; some are thick and some are thin; and in general, the rims lack the character of having been treated mechanically as with paddle-and-anvil or with a mold. Being modeled entirely by hand as they are, rims display a great deal of individual variation when viewed in cross section, variation which seems to lack cultural or chronological significance.

SMOOTHING AND SLIPPING THE SURFACE When the pot has been brought to its desired form, it is allowed to dry in the sun for a few minutes. Then the potter rubs over the entire surface with a waterworn pebble or other smooth object. While the waterworn pebble is the usual smoothing implement, one potter (Victoria Marqueta) used a glass insulator fragment of the kind used on electric power poles.

The amount of rubbing given to the surface of the pot varies considerably from potter to potter. The end results range from a "smoothed" effect to a "polished" or burnished appearance. Potters such as Susie Miguel, who specialize in black-on-red tourist wares, take great pains to bring the surface of their pottery to a high gloss. A few potters, such as Dolores Chico, rub the surface only cursorily. The majority of potters, of whom Mary Sue Carmen is an example, finish the surface in such a way that it lies midway between "smoothed" and "polished."

Mrs. Domingo, at San Xavier, ordinarily smooths the surface of her pottery, but in the case of one piggy bank no smoothing whatsoever was done. She explained that this was the idea of a man watching her make it, who told her that if she did not rub the form with a stone the surface texture would look like hair. And because her clay contains particles of dried horse manure temper that have burned out on the surface in firing, the surface does have a "hairy" appearance.

It is difficult to correlate the amount of surface smoothing with regional or cultural differences among Papagos. Like the rims added by hand, the amount of smoothing done seems to be a matter of individual preference, depending to a certain extent on the demands of the market. One makes what one can sell, and sometimes one makes what a specific customer has ordered. It is certainly true that it is the pottery made for sale on the non-Indian market, the black-on-red and black-on-white ware, that is highly polished, while traditional Papago forms tend to be less so. But occasionally even Papago forms, such as the bean pots made by Susie Miguel for sale to other Indians, are polished.

The preparation and application of slip is likewise not a universal feature of Papago pottery, and again we run into individual preferences and individual variations.

There are only two kinds of slip added to the surface of Papago pottery: red (hematite, called *hūt* in Papago) and, more rarely, white. The white slip is simply a thin paste made of the white clay that is itself used for some types of pottery.

Unfortunately, we never witnessed the preparation of slip nor its gathering from the natural deposit. We did, however, collect samples in the field that had already been gathered and we obtained several verbal descriptions of how slip is prepared. The usual means is to let small chunks of the slip material, usually hematite, soak in a small can for several hours. Excess water is then poured off, the hematite is crushed in a little water in the can either by hand or with a stick, and the resulting fine paste is the slip.

. . .

Among Papagos, slip is universally applied with a cloth. We failed to record a single instance of its having been applied by hand. The coat is added after the pot has been smoothed, and in all cases, the slip is allowed to dry and the pot is again smoothed with a smooth stone.

Whether the pot is slipped or not is also a matter of individual taste except that again the non-Indian ware, the black-on-red, is all slipped.

Listiana Francisco slips pottery made from the clay of one pit but not from the clay of another. There seems to be some kind of Papago cultural standard which requires that most pottery be either a kind of brown or a red after it is fired, and if the clay alone will not produce this result, slip is used. An exception is white pottery. We cannot state the conditions under which white slip is added to white clay and when it is not. In no instance have we found white slip added to any other than white clay pots.

Susie Miguel applies slip to all her pottery, utility ware and otherwise; there are some potters who apparently never apply slip to any pot that will be used for cooking over an open flame, reserving the red color for water jars and storage vessels.

When a sherd of pottery is viewed in cross section it is not always possible to say whether a slip has been applied or if the color change on the surface has been caused by the compacting of the clay in polishing.... As a general rule, we suspect that slipped Papago pottery appears clearly to be so, and the "red" pottery that does not obviously seem to have been slipped, probably was not.

A second phenomenon, that of "scumming," has been discussed by Malcolm Rogers. According to Rogers, scumming results when gypsum salts (calcium sulphate) migrate to the surface of the pot during firing. The finished appearance of such a pot is much like that of one with added slip, and Rogers contends that often what is really scumming has been mistaken for slip. We have seen pots, especially those made by Savilla Miguel, that definitely were not slipped but whose surfaces have a kind of tan, creamy appearance that might be mistaken for a buff slip. Moreover, her clay is gathered within a mile of a gypsum mine, and it is possible that her clay does indeed contain gypsum salts.

Because we lack further data on the point, we do not feel we can reply intelligently to Rogers' arguments contending that there is such a process as scumming. We do believe it is possible, however, and feel that it is worthwhile mentioning here.

FIRING After the pot has been formed, polished, and possibly slipped and polished again, it is allowed to dry—usually in the shade—from two to three days depending on the weather.

When the potter decides the pot is fully dried, it is ready to be fired. Papagos use a wide variety of fuels and in varying combinations, and interviews indicate that each potter apparently has experimented with various fuels during her pot-making lifetime. For example, some potters told us cottonwood is no good for fuel because it burns too fast, adding that they tried it and did not like it. Similarly, ironwood is said to burn with too hot a flame.

The fuels most generally used are mesquite, palo verde, and cow manure. Ocotillo stalks, saguaro ribs, and simply "sticks" are also listed as fuels, and Mrs. Domingo at San Xavier uses cottonwood despite objections made to its use by other potters. Cholla wood is also used.

Laura Kermen fires her pottery in an electric kiln, and Susie Miguel fires hers in a large can placed over hot coals burning in a washtub. The rest of the potters fire their pottery in shallow pits scooped out of the ground, whose walls have been built up by the deposition of successive layers of burned coals and ashes.

Although we saw nearly every potter's firing pit, and although we collected thorough verbal descriptions from each potter concerning her method of firing, we observed only Listiana Francisco in action. Her firing method . . . is the one we describe here. Our field notes indicate that her firing method is typical for other Papago potters, and that aside from different choice of fuels and length of burning, her firing is no different from that of anyone else except Laura Kermen and Susie Miguel.

At 5:00 A.M., the potter lights a small fire of palo verde wood in the bottom of her pit. (All potters fire their pottery in the early morning, when it is cooler.) She then returns the 200 or 300 feet to her house to eat breakfast. When breakfast is done, she goes back to her pit, arriving between 5:30 and 5:45. By this time the palo verde has burned down to a few hot coals and white ashes. The potter sets three fist-size rocks down in the coals, places a sheet of tin on its side, and rests one large pot (such as a water jar or feast-size bean pot) on its side on the rocks. She then completes building the tin oven, roofing it with a final piece of tin.

Next she places more palo verde sticks at the outside base of the oven where they promptly catch fire from the heat of the coals inside the oven. She adds numerous cakes of dried cow manure, finishing the fueling by tossing on—or more properly, setting on—sticks of mesquite.

The potter then waits until the fire has burned down to coals. Before she tears down the tin oven with a stick, the potter first removes the lid and checks to see if the pot looks fired. If it is not ready, she adds a few more mesquite sticks and fires it as long as necessary.

If the pot seems to be ready, the potter knocks down as much of the tin oven as is necessary to be able to reach into the mouth of the pot with a stick and thus to remove it by lifting the pot off its three-rock stand in the coals. She uses the stick to set the pot down on its side on three additional rocks laid there for that purpose about 12 feet or more from the fire. The pot is a rather dark gray, almost black color as it comes hot from the coals, but turns to a rich, light brown as it cools in the air. (This is Listiana's unslipped pottery.)

When the pot has cooled sufficiently to be handled, she sets it on the ground and wipes off the ashes and dirt with a cloth before taking it back to her house where it will be stored to await a buyer.

She then rebuilds her fire, this time placing two small saguaro-sirup jars on rocks in the coals to be fired. By 8:00 A.M., these two jars have been fired, and she is through working on pottery for the day.

A single large pot fired in this manner requires about 1½ hours to be fired properly; the two small pots require 30 to 45 minutes. The potter says that if the pot is a bluish color inside, then it is cooked completely and ready to be taken from the heat. After the pot has cooled, she tests it for serious fractures by striking it with her knuckles and listening to the ring. A clear ring indicates a well-made pot, with no cracks caused by firing.

We were unable to measure the intensity of the firing heat, lacking both the equipment and the potter's willingness to let us add anything foreign to her fire. It is possible to see the pot through the juncture of the oven roof and wall during firing, and at one point the pottery walls were absolutely red from the heat.

Susie Miguel, as we mentioned above, fires her pottery a different way. She places her fuel—formerly dried cow manure and mesquite, but only mesquite today—in a large washtub. A smaller can rests on flat cross-pieces of iron immediately over the washtub, and it is in this second can that her pots are placed. She keeps the firing going for a half day to fire the small pots; all day to fire the large pots. Her "small" pots are tourist-trade miniatures; her "large" pots are regular family-sized bean pots.

Unless a potter is making miniature pots, she will generally fire only a single pot the size of an olla or two pots the size of a family-sized bean pot. She may, however, fire several pots in one morning by repeated firings, perhaps as many as six or seven. If the pots are miniatures, as many as 15 to 20 might be fired in a single day, four to six at a time.

PAINTING Today Papago potters use only two colors with which to paint designs on pottery: black and red. We were unable to locate a single potter with the exception of Mrs. Domingo at San Xavier who has actually painted designs with red paint, and it would appear that for all practical purposes this art is no longer practiced by living Papagos. We interviewed several Indians whose mothers had painted with red paint, but our study appears to have been begun from three to ten years too late to find living painters of the past generation.

Mrs. Domingo has painted a few pieces of pottery with red, using merely the red slip, or *hūt*, just as she uses it for slip. Informants in the Santa Rosa–Anegam area told us that potters used to prepare red paint by mixing red hematite (*hūt*) with mesquite gum in the same way black paint is prepared with black mesquite bark.

Potter Lucy Stevens from Big Fields said that her mother prepared red paint from "a black rock collected from a pit near Covered Wells," again mixing this ground pigment with mesquite gum. Investigation at Covered Wells disclosed the fact that the Papagos there, especially the young boys, are aware of a deposit black in outward appearance which contains a lot of red pigment when it is ground. The boys at Covered Wells used the ground pigment to make red streaks on their faces in playing games. This magnetite is almost certainly the material to which Lucy Stevens refers, and it most certainly would turn red when fired in an oxidizing atmosphere.

Black paint ... is made with mesquite bark that has blackened on the tree where sap has oozed out, and with mesquite gum.

The potter strips the black bark from mesquite trees with the help of a knife, and takes it, along with balls of clear golden mesquite gum picked from the branches, back to her house. She boils water in a small can, perhaps ½- to 1-gallon size, adding five or six strips of the black mesquite bark while the water is heating. She allows the water with the bark in it to come to a full boil, then removes it from the heat. At this juncture she adds a small handful of mesquite gum, three or four balls, to the brew. She puts the can back on the heat and brings the paint to a boil from three to five more times.

When the paint nears readiness, the potter tests the color and consistency by dipping a stick into the can of paint and making a streak on a pot kept handy for this purpose. If the paint is not too runny, and if it has what seems to the potter to be the right color, she removes the can from the heat for the last time.

Some painters use feathers for a paint brush, but most use the unaltered tip of a devil's-claw (*Martynia*). They do not chew the tip or in other ways make it more brushlike. The painting implement is dipped into the paint, and a design is applied. ... All strokes are completed with the tip of the applicator remaining bent only in one direction.

In all cases paint is applied to fired pottery which is generally, but not always, slipped. When the painting job is done, the pot is fired a second time to fix the paint. This final firing consists only of putting the painted surface of the pot directly on hot coals or in revolving the pot over flames for three to four minutes. Not only does this turn the mesquite paint a coal black color, giving it a shiny appearance where properly fired, but it tends to alter the color of the pot slightly, darkening it.

In former times, another decorative technique consisted of using a pigmented glaze to make lines in addition to nonglaze red lines on the surface. These glazes were both green (copper) and white (lead). ... Very few Papagos interviewed knew anything more about these glazes other than that they were once made. The generally agreed-on term for glaze is *wá-chuk*, and one old man told us that it was made from "blue-green" rocks. This is doubly interesting because it suggests a copper ore and green glaze, and because *wá-chuk* sounds suspiciously like *Huachuca*, the mountain range in southern Arizona from which glaze-manufacturing materials may have been collected.

MODELING POTTERY Although Papagos do not make a great number of modeled forms of pottery, some potters, such as Susie Miguel, almost specialize in them. For the most part, modeled forms such as coffee cups, piggy banks, and ashtrays are formed by a combination of hand and mold work. Piggy banks, for example, are made by first molding the upper and lower longitudinal halves of the four-legged standing pig over a rock or other suitable mold that is the approximate shape. Then by poking with sticks or fingers and by adding hand-modeled bits of clay for legs, head, and tail, the pig begins to take shape. He is joined in the longitudinal section by bringing the upper and lower halves together and smoothing the juncture with wet fingers.

Although a clay effigy figure was found at Batki [Arizona], and despite the fact that modeled effigy vessels and figurines doubtless have considerable antiquity among Papagos, modeled pottery has never really been popular among Papago potters. Susie Miguel models pottery more than anyone else, but her work is a response primarily to a non-Indian market. The result is that there are no ironclad procedures or cultural rules to prescribe how modeled pottery is to be fashioned. Consequently, any means that will give the desired effect, hands, sticks, molds, or whatever, are the means used.

The *Ee-ee-toy* figurines that appear to be a family tradition are interesting from the standpoint of manufacture because of their eyes. The eyelids on these figurines protrude in such a way that when viewed in lateral cross section the effect is that of a triangle with the apex in front on the face side. It would be impossible to achieve such an effect by incising with a tool. Information from Goldie Richmond, who knew Frances Montaña well, tells us that these eyes were formed by pinching a little of the face clay around a small piece of straw or stick. The stick is burned out in the firing, leaving the eye slits.

BOWLS In addition to figurines that are at least partially hand-modeled, Papagos also make bowls whose manufacture requires no coiling and thus offers a variation on standard procedure.

Larger bowls, such as serving dishes, are made exactly in the same way as water jars and other forms of this kind, except that the process stops with the paddle-and-anvil application to the molded base.

Smaller bowls that are sometimes made simply as miscellaneous containers or for sale to non-Indians are molded over stones, gourds, or, in the case of Victoria Marqueta, over a croquet ball or the iron ball from an end post of a Cyclone fence. In this case the clay is simply formed into a small bun, placed over the mold, and pounded into bowl shape by hand or with a small paddle or stone anvil.

RE-USING CLAY When we went to interview potter Alvina Ignacio at Anegam, she had before her on the ground a large water jar fully formed but in which a wide crack had opened on one side before she had a chance to polish it. She informed us that she would destroy the form, make a large ball of the clay and use it again, starting the entire process over once more beginning with making a bun for the pot's base.

We recorded no other case of a potter re-using prepared clay in this way, but it is a question we failed to ask. There is no reason to suppose that most, if not all, Papago potters do not do the same thing. An experienced potter is less likely to attribute such a failure to her mixture of clay than to wind-sun drying conditions. Potters feel that the humidity-temperature conditions are critical, and once a pot formation is begun, the potter continues at a steady pace without stopping for anything.

Using the pottery

Just as there is a technique for the manufacture of pottery, so is there a technique for its use. Newly made pottery is not ready for immediate use, but must be further "cured" by the consumer.

Water jars are prepared by first pouring enough water in them to cover only the bottom. The porous, blotterlike quality of the clay body draws the water into the walls, capillary action bringing the moisture all the way to the rim of the pot. When the entire pot has been moistened in this way, more water is added each day until the rapid dripping of water through the bottom (new water jars are so porous they almost always leak) slows to a small drip. The evaporation slows down when calcium and other minerals in the water have taken their part in a sealing effect. At this point, the jar is ready for use. Water is kept at the one-half to two-thirds level, seldom higher. Papagos very often wrap the water jars with gunny sacks or burlap strips to aid in the evaporating-cooling action, and place tin containers under the bottoms to catch dripping water. Tin or wooden lids are placed on water jars when not in use to keep foreign matter out of the water. Thirsty birds will sometimes fall and drown themselves in water jars without lids.

Eventually water jars will seal completely, thus losing their effectiveness as water coolers. At this point they are either discarded or converted into cooking pots.

A new cooking pot, before it can be put into full use, must be heated over an open flame or over intense heat for about 15 minutes. This fires out any possible remaining unfired particles, especially vegetal temper that may be present. This final firing readies it for use. Beans, or whatever else may be cooked in it, are seldom added to more than two-thirds of the capacity of the pot.

Papago cooking pots can withstand extreme temperatures. We saw one new pot being cured, placed over an open fire until it was red hot. Into this same hot pot a woman poured room-temperature saguaro fruit, and the pot did not shatter or even crack.

Occasionally a user will first test a pot for leaks by adding a little water. Bean pots are sometimes allowed to seal with water before they are used for cooking.

If a pot should chip, develop a small crack, have a small piece broken out of the rim, or if for some reason it should acquire a hole in its wall, it may be mended by the user. For this purpose Papagos use lac gathered from the stems of the creosote bush (*Larrea tridentata*, Cav.), sometimes called greasewood, found so abundantly in their desert region. Lac is produced by a minute insect, *Tachardiella larrea*, and Papagos boil a preparation of this red material to make a black mending glue. . . .

Unhappily, we were never able to see glue being prepared and applied to pottery, although we collected samples of raw lac still attached to the creosote bush branches and brought them into the Arizona State Museum. At South Komelik we found a pot mended with what appeared to be lac, only to discover that it was roofing tar collected by the user of the pot from a nearby chapel roof which was being repaired. We found no instance of any other glue being used for pottery mending.

The potter as an innovator

During the course of conducting our research we had an opportunity to make several observations concerning innovations in Papago pottery.

We brought potters Listiana Francisco from Coyote Village and [Mrs.] Raphael Domingo from San Xavier to the Arizona State Museum. Here they both saw prehistoric and historic pottery from the entire Southwest: Anasazi, Mogollon, Hohokam, Salado, Sinagua, Maricopa, Pima, Mohave, Yuma, Navajo, and Hopi, as well as pottery from the New Mexico Pueblo Indian groups. We also showed these potters movies of Hopi pottery being made, and of Maria of San Ildefonso making her famous black-on-black wares. Both Papago women were intensely interested in all they saw, and both asked many questions about techniques, painting, firing, and the like. We suggested to both of them that it might be nice if they would try, at least once, to make some black pottery or to decorate the surface of the pot by incising, scoring, punching, leaving the coils unsmoothed, or by using some other simple texture treatment. Both listened politely, but neither made any comment concerning the suggestion.

That neither potter had made any changes in her techniques was evident after a year had elapsed. Listiana said she thought about the black pottery, but pointed out that making even the one pot is work, and that it would be needless to risk spoiling it. Similarly, Mrs. Domingo could see no need to change her pottery technique since she sells all she makes as it is.

A second point was made when Lambert Fremdling, O.F.M., asked Savilla Miguel if she made any effigy forms: horses, cows, sheep, pigs, or the like. It was evident from her response that while she may have made some effigy form or other at one time or another, she certainly had never made animal figurines of the range suggested by Father Lambert. Nonetheless, she said she would make anything, and asked the priest what he wanted. He said he would like to have a horse, and she said she would make one for him. Similarly, Rosa Antone of Hickiwan has been willing to make forms of pottery on order for the priest stationed at Ajo, Arizona. . . .

Although Listiana Francisco does not paint her pottery, she told us that once a customer insisted on having a decorated pot. She complied, using black mesquite paint and "the very finest feather from a road runner" for a paint brush. It was her one and only attempt at painting pottery.

The point of all this, it seems to us, is that pottery forms manufactured primarily for sale to non-Indians are not bound by tradition, but rather are governed by the demands of the market. If a priest wants a pottery thurible* or a horse, there are no strictures against making either. If a tourist wants a painted pot, a potter who ordinarily does not paint will comply, but will use a traditional Papago technique.

Traditional Papago forms, on the other hand, change but little. The potter does not experiment with the forms, forms that have been tested for countless generations by Indian users. And the techniques for slipping, decorating, and firing also change little.

What is most interesting is that Papago potters who have been "trained" in traditional Papago pottery techniques adhere to those techniques even when shown others. There is no limit to the range of forms that

* A container for incense used in the Roman Catholic Mass. [Ed.]

might be produced on demand; and also on demand, a potter would probably be willing to paint a bean pot. But non-traditional forms are made in traditional ways. The gathering and preparation of clay is the same; the modeling or molding with paddle-and-anvil and coiling are the same; the slipping is the same; and the firing is the same. If a decorated pot is requested, the paint will be either black mesquite paint or red paint, and there will be no texture treatment of the surface.

Papago pottery changes, to be sure, and there is an extensive allowable range in forms, clays, tempers, firing fuels, and so on. But the changes, like the range in techniques and materials, all occur within a framework that is distinctively Papago and beyond whose bounds no true Papago potter will go.

Finally, however, we must point out that there may always be potters like Laura Kermen who, although assuredly a Papago Indian, learned to make pottery primarily from non-Indians and as a result, her pottery is only barely Papago. Her innovating tendencies, unlike those of most Papago potters, know almost no bounds.

FANG-KUEI LI

How to build a canoe

Fang-Kuei Li is a professor of linguistics at The University of Washington. He has done work in Sino-Tibetan as well as American Indian languages. This text was obtained in 1928 from Francois Mandeville at Fort Chipewyan. The Chipewyan language is a member of the Athapascan family, as is Navaho (see Part I, "The Language of the Navaho Indians").

The text is divided into paragraphs (**1.1.1, 1.2.1, 1.3.1, 1.4.1, 1.5.1, 1.6.1**), somewhat arbitrarily for the sake of convenience. Each paragraph is followed by its translation (**1.1.2, 1.2.2, 1.3.2, 1.4.2, 1.5.2, 1.6.2**) and its notes (**1.1.3, 1.2.3, 1.3.3, 1.4.3, 1.5.3, 1.6.3**).

1. The title of the text is: ṫą·ṫŭ·ṫsi θiłtsį *How I Made A Canoe.*

1.1.1. ˀįłá ṫsi θiłtsį ˀɛkú· ṫsi-yúγwɛ́ híłtcú. ˀɛyi hų́ṫłɛ́δɛ́ bɛγą ˀɛγálaγi·ná. ṫaht· θɛhį́ṫŭ· ḱeih daγiłṫcel hų́łdų́u hodelyų̆· ṫsi-dɛtcinɛ́ híłtcú. ˀɛγwoz-xa ˀįłáγɛ dɛtcin hɛ̨γi·tθel. kúlú ˀɛyi dɛtcin ˀɛłṫθi dɛzúz kúlú ˀoteyɛ́ hɛṫcel-hílɛ. ˀɛyiṫá ṫθi dɛtcin nɛtcâ· nąhiłxɛ́z. ˀɛyi dɛtcin bɛṫsį ˀɛγwoz γiłṫcel. ṫθi nahî· ṫsi-yúγwɛ́ bɛṫsį híłtcú.

1.1.2. *Once I made a canoe. So I began to get the material for the canoe I worked hard at it. First of all I tore off the birch bark from the upper par of the tree, and then I got all the wood for the canoe. For the canoe rib I chopped one tree down. However, that tree* [*ought to*] *split straight, but i did not split well. Therefore I knocked down another big tree. From that tre I made* (*split*) *the canoe ribs. I also got some other parts of the canoe from it*

1.1.3. ṫa·ṫŭ· *how* is probably derived from *ṫah-hįṫɛ-ú, cf. ṫah- in ṫah *that which,* ṫahi *the one who*; -ṫɛ *to be so,* and -ú *gerundive suffix.* Th analysis of such stereotyped particles is, however, not certain.

ṫsi *canoe* is not used with the pronominal possessive prefixes, thus *m canoe* is usually given as ṫsi sɛṫsį *canoe from me*, i.e., *my canoe.*

θiłtsį, *1st person perfective* of the verb *to make one object.* The use c perfective active verbs, transitive or intransitive is normal in narratives

---

Fang-Kuei Li, "A Chipewyan Ethnological Text," *International Journal American Linguistics*, 30, 2 (1965), 132–136. Reprinted by permission of th publisher.

but for neuter verbs, etc., the imperfective is used, thus, a few lines below ʔεłṫθi dεzúz *it splits straight*, and ʔoteyέ hεṫcel *it tears or splits well*.

ʔεkú or kú· *then, so*.

ṫsi-yúγwέ is a compound of ṫsi- *canoe* and -yúγwέ (poss.) *its garment*, meaning *the material used to make a canoe or canoe parts*; similarly below, ṫsi-dεtcinέ *canoe-its wood*, i.e., *canoe frame or material used to make the frame of a canoe*.

ʔεyi *that, it*.

hų́ṫłέδέ *much, hard*, from *hú-nε-ṫłέδ-έ, cf. nεṫłέδ *it is strong*.

bεγą *at it*.

k̇eih *birch, birch bark*.

daγiłṫcel, 1st pers. perf. of -ṫcuł, -ṫcel, -ṫcuł *to tear apart, off*, with da- *up*, referring to the position of the bark on the tree. The reason for preferring the bark on the upper part of the tree is that it is usually in a better condition, without cracks or holes.

ʔεγwoz-xa *for the canoe ribs*. xa is a variant form of the postposition -a *for* when the object immediately precedes. All postpositions beginning with a vowel take the consonant x-, while all postpositions beginning with a consonant are simply attached to the preceding object.

hę- in hęγi·tθel *I chopped it down*, . . . referring to the upright position of the tree.

ʔεyiṫá *therefore* comes from ʔεyi *that*, and -ṫá *with*.

ṫθi *also*, together with the following numeral one means *another*, and a few lines below with nahî· *some* means *some other*.

nεtcâ· is contracted from *netcá-i *that which is big*. In rapid speech the -i is often assimilated to the preceding a, giving a long vowel.

ʔεyi dεtcin bεṫsį *that tree from it*, i.e., *from that tree*, is unusual in having bε- *it* before -ṫsį *from*. Perhaps after ʔεyi dεtcin there is a long pause, so that a redundant 3rd pers. pronominal object prefix is introduced before the postposition -ṫsį.

nąhiłxέz is from *na-hęhiłxέz, *I knocked it down again*.

nahî· *some*, is a contracted variant of nahε̂i.

1.2.1. kú· hodεlyų̆u ṫsi-yúγwέ γi·γą hų́łdų́u ṫsi-k̇έ hóθiłtsį. kú· k̇eih-k̇ε θε nį́ni·la. k̇eih híγwułú ṫsi hołε̂· nεzų-hílε. k̇eih ʔoteyέ ʔεłṫθirέδʔa-yį́-ṫá si nεzų nastsi-nį-ṫá. ʔoteyέ nį́ ʔεłṫθihodέδʔa ʔasłâi ʔεyi-k̇ε k̇eih εłkέdεyi·la. bεk̇ε dεtcin nį́ni·la hų́łdų́u tθε bεk̇ε nį́ni·la, ʔεkwą́ṫŭ· k̇eih εłṫθi dáhílk̇as-ixa.

1.2.2. *Then after I made all the parts of the canoe, I made the canoe-lace. Then I laid rocks on the birch bark. If the birch bark got warped, the canoe, thus made, would not be good. For only with well-stretched birch bark made good canoes. On the ground which I made very level I spread the* *birch bark. I laid logs of wood on it, and then I laid rocks on it, so that the birch bark would thus get stiff and flat.*

1.2.3. γi·γą *I made several objects*. The canoe parts are considered as several objects while the canoe as a whole is conceived as one object, thus ṫsi θiłtį *I made a canoe.*

ṫsi-k̇έ *canoe-place* refers to the ground which was leveled and made into the shape of a canoe, and on which the birch bark was laid.

hóθiłtsį *I made it*, where hó- is the pronominal object referring to place, time, or event, i.e., on the canoe-place. The high pitch is due to the following θ(ε)-perfective.

k̇eih-k̇ε *birch bark-on*, i.e., *on the birch bark.*

tθε *rock, rocks* does not indicate plurality, it is the verb nį́ni·la *I put down several objects* which indicates that we are dealing into several rocks.

hołε̂·, contracted and assimilated from *hołέ-i *that which is made.* The verb seems to be the causative of the verb -lέ, -lį, -lέ *to be, become* with the ł-classifier.

'εłṫθirέδ'a *it stretches straight*, from εłṫθi *straight*, incorporated as a prefix, and dέδˀa *it extends*, -yį́ *only*, suffixed to the verb, and -ṫá *by means of, because of, for*. The whole phrase literally means *by means of the birch bark which was well stretched only.*

nastsi-nį-ṫá *I customarily make it—in the past—for, i.e., for I usually made it*. The stem -tsi is the customary form, with the iterative prefix na-, and the verbal suffix -nį, followed by the postposition -ṫá.

nį́ˀεłṫθihodέδˀa *the ground or place stretches straight or level*, with nį́- terminative, referring to the ground, and ho- 3rd pers. pron. subj. referring to place, cf. ˀεłṫθirέδˀa *it (birch bark) stretches straight.*

ˀasłâi from ˀasłá-i *that which I made so*. ˀasłá is often used after a verb to form a sort of paraphrastic causative. The phrase here literally means *very much—the ground stretches straight—I made it so—that, i.e., the ground which I made very level.*

ˀεłkέdεγi·la *I spread them one by the side of the other*, with ˀεłkέ- *one by the side of the other*, dε-, and -la, perfective of the stem *to handle several objects.*

ˀεkwą́ṫû *in that way*, probably from ˀεkwá- *thus* -hį-ṫε-ú.

dáhílk̇as-ixa *in order that all of them get stiff and flat*. dá- *distributive* hí- *inchoative*, l-classifier, -k̇as *to become stiff (active, intransitive)*, and -ixa, a verbal suffix to indicate *future* or *future purpose.*

1.3.1. hų́łdų́ú xai xádáθiłṫcel. ˀεyi ṫθi hodεlyų̂u dáγiłṫcel. hų́łdų́ú ˀεṫła nį́ni·tą. ˀoteyέ 'εṫła θiłṫaδú ṫsέkuyi sa nádáyįnέłką́. hų́łdų́ú ṫsi-zírέ xa k̇eih nį́ni·la. ˀεyi dεtcin-hotsáł-ṫá ˀoteyε nániłtsáγ. ˀεkwâ·slá hų́łdų́ú ṫsέkuyi sa ṫsi-zírέ nádáhunέłką́. hų́łdų́ú ˀεγí bεk̇ε nį́ni·tą. ˀεyi ṫθ bεγárέ ṫsi-daγa θiłṫaδ. hų́łdų́ú ṫsέkuyi sa ˀεγí-k̇ε náhurέδdeδ hų́łdų́ú ˀįθęł ṫθi ṫsi yέγi·la. ˀεyi ṫθi ṫsεkuyi sa ˀįtθęł-k̇ε nádâunέłką́.

1.3.2. *Then I tore the roots out (from the ground) here and there. I also tore them all up. Then I put the bottom of the canoe down. When I had cut the bottom out, the woman sewed (the pieces of birch bark) up for me. Then I laid the birch bark down for the canoe-side. With wood nails I nailed it well. After I did that, the woman sewed the canoe-side for me. Then I put the gunwale on it. I also cut off (the sides of the canoe) along the gunwale above the canoe. Then after the woman wound (the bark) around the gunwale, I put the bow posts in the canoe. The woman sewed also the bow posts down for me.*

1.3.3. xádáθiłṫcel, see xá- *out*, dá- *distributive*, referring to the roots of many plants, θ(ε)- *perfective*. Notice the different perfectives used with the same stem -ṫcel.

ˀεṫła *bottom of the canoe*, cf. sį́łaṫłaγá *palm of my hand*. Here it refers rather to the birch bark used to make the bottom of the canoe.

nį́ni·tą *I put down a long object.*

sa, from s-a *for me.*

nádáyįnέłką́ *She sewed them up*, see ná- *along, continuative* (?); dá- *distributive*, referring to the pieces of bark; yį- nasalized on account of the following nε- from yε- *3rd person obj., sing. or pl.*; nέ- prefix constantly used with this verb stem; the high pitch is from the influence of the θε-perfective which is coalesced with the following ł-classifier.

dεtcin-hotsáł- ṫá *wood-nails-with, i.e. with wood nails.* Presumably iron nails were not known or used.

nániłtsáγ *I nailed them up*, from ná- n(ε-θε)- i-ł-tsáγ, cf. náyįnέłtsáγ *he nailed them up*, similar in structure to nádáyįnέłką́ above, only without the dá- prefix, which is often optional unless the distributive or plural sense is emphasized.

ˀεkwâ·słá *I did that, in that way*, from ’εkwá-ˀasłá.

ˀεγí bεk̇ε *gunwale-on it, i.e. gunwale on the canoe side*, cf. below, ’εγí-k̇ε *on or around the gunwale.*

ṫsi yέγi·la *canoe—in I put them, i.e. I put them in the canoe.* yέ- *incorporated postposition* would normally take a pronominal object, thus bεyέγi·la *I put them in it*, unless the object of the postposition immediately precedes.

1.4.1. hų́łdų́u ˀεṫłatθíγali ṫsi yέγi·tą. kú· ˀεṫłatθíγalitsele ṫθi ṫsi yέγi·la. bεk̇ε ˀįtθęłtcăiˀa nį́ni·tą. kú· ˀεṫłatθíγali ˀεdį́ hoˀą́zį́ nεnέθ θiłtsį. ˀεyiṫá bek̇εnani·ṫaδ hų́łdų́u súγwá ˀaγįłnεθ ˀadjá. kú· ṫsi-yέ-dεtcinέ, ṫsi yέγi·la. ˀεłεhunέlyą ˀasłău hų́łdų́· ˀεγwɔz ṫsi yέγi·la. kú· tu-łel-ṫá bεk̇ε tahęsłε. ˀεkwą́ṫŭ ˀoteyέ k̇eih γaˀεnįłθíl. hų́łdų́u ˀεγwoz ˀɛłɛna ṫséθiyę̨ bɛγɛcéł. yaze bɛnádánăɛcíł. ˀɛkwâ·sˀį-hįṫŭ· ˀɛtsį́naθé ṫahi bɛk̇é bɛnį́dâ·θiłcel. ˀɛkwâ·słá-hiṫá ṫsi ˀoteyé k̇eih bek̇ɛ dɛnįtiy ˀasłá.

1.4.2. *Then I put the inside-keel in the canoe. Then I put the small pieces (on both ends of the keel) also in the canoe. On them I put that which propped the bow posts. Then I made the keel much too long. Therefore I cut a part of it off, then it became of the correct length. Then I put the frame in the canoe. After I made them all fit each other, I put the ribs in the canoe. Then I spread hot water over it. In that way the birch bark was heated through. I knocked at the ribs one after the other carefully. I moved them little by little by knocking. While I was doing thus, I knocked them finally to their proper place. Because I did so, I made the birch bark stretch quite tight on the canoe.*

1.4.3. ˀɛdį́ hoˀą́zį́ nɛnéθ θiłtsį—*too-beyond-it is long-I made it, i.e., I made it much too long.*

bɛk̇ɛnani·ṫaδ—*on it-again-I made a cut, i.e., I cut off a part of it.*

súγwá *good, correct.*

ˀaγįłnɛθ—*it has such a length*, cf. -néθ *to be long.*

ˀadjá *so it became.* The stem -djá (*perfective*) is probably a coalescence of the d-classifier (medio-passive) plus the stem -yá *to do, act.* The imperfective is -nɛ, cf. -lɛ, -lá *to make, to cause*, causative derived *-ł-nɛ, *-ł-yá.

ṫsi-yé-dɛtcin-é, a compound of *canoe-inside-its wood, i.e. the canoe frame.*

ˀɛłɛhunélyą *each other-toward-it has the size, i.e. it fits each other.*

tu-δel-ṫá *water-hot-with, i.e., with hot water.*

tahęsłɛ *I spread water on it*, ta- referring to water, probably an incorporated noun stem related to tu *water*. The stem is -lɛ, -la, -lɛł, *to handle several objects.*

γaˀɛnįłθíl *it was heated through*, γa- *through*, with the perfective of the stem -θił, -θíl, -θił *to heat up*, cf. -δel *to be warm.*

'ɛłɛna *each other-in place of, i.e. one after the other.*

bɛγɛcéł—*at them-I kept on knocking.* This is the progressive form of -cúł, -cel, -cúł *to hit, knock with a stone.*

bɛnádánăɛcíł *I knock (cust.) again and again at them to move them.*
bɛnį́dâ·θiłcel *I knocked them to their proper places.* dâ·- must be a contraction of dá- *distributive* plus another prefix difficult to determine.

dɛnįtiy *It is stretched tight.*

1.5.1. hų́łdų́· dzé káθiya. dzé náγi·gé. 'ɛyi ˀąniłtą. ˀɛyi θiłtcáz. kú· dzé hɛtcɛs-húk̇ɛ ṫes bɛtadéni·yis ˀɛkwą́ṫŭ· dɛlzen ˀasłá hų́łdų́· ṫsékuyi sa ṫsi θɛdzɛγ. hų́łdų́· ṫoθé dɛγɛstsį hų́łdų́· ṫsi-gwóδé-yé dzéréγi·kkeih. dɛgwóδ ṫų·ṫɛ-hiṫá bɛyé tu húlɛ. ṫθi náltła. ṫsi-dɛtciné ṫsɛṫalɛ ˀarásłá-hiṫá ṫsi nɛdδaγa.

1.5.2. *Then I went to look for the gum. I poked it down. I brought it home in a sack. I boiled it. Then while the gum was boiling, I crumbled charcoal into it. In that way I made it black, afterwards the woman put the pitch on the canoe for me. Then I made a paddle for myself, and then I paddled around in the new canoe. As it was new, there was no water in it. Also it moved fast. Because I made every part of the canoe frame thin, the canoe was light.*

1.5.3. dzɛ́ káθi·ya *I went to look for the gum.* ká- is a prefixed postposition, the pronominal object is omitted as its object immediately precedes, cf. bɛkahɛsaih *I go to look for it*, bɛkáθi·ya *I went to look for it.*

náγi·gɛ́ *I poked down with a stick*, from the verb -gɛr, -gɛ́, gɛr *to spear at, to poke.*

ˀąniįłtą *I brought it home in a sack.* ˀą- *back home*, n(ɛ)- *momentaneous*, -tą *to handle a stick-like object.* The peculiar use of the ł-classifier here changes the meaning of the stem to *handling something in a sack, vessel, etc.*

θiłtcáz *I boiled it*, 1st pers. perfective causative of the neuter verb θɛtcáz *it is boiling.* hɛtcɛs *it boils* (*imperfective*).

-húk̓ɛ- *while*, a verbal suffix, probably from -hú, *gerundive suffix*, and postposition -k̓ɛ *on.*

bɛtadɛ́ni·yis *I crumbled* (*charcoal*) *into it*, with bɛ- *pron. obj.* of the prefixed postposition ta- *among*, dɛ́, and n(ɛ)- *momentaneous.*

dɛγɛstsį *I made it for myself*; cf. dɛ- *reflexive*, γɛ- *perfective*, s- coalescence of -s-l-. Notice the different perfective prefix used in θiłtsi, *I made it.*

ṫsi-gwóδɛ́-yɛ́, *canoe-new-in, i.e. in the new canoe.*

dzɛ́rɛ́γi·keih *I paddle* (*a canoe*) *around*, with dzɛ́rɛ́-, which requires the customary form of the verb -kéih, -kį, -kɛł, *to paddle a canoe.*

ṫų·ṫɛ *it is so.*

húlɛ *there is not*, cf. hílɛ *not.*

ˀarásłá *I made them so.* Cf. ˀa- *so*, rá- from dá- *distributive.*

dɛlzen *it is black*, dɛgwóδ *it is new*, nɛdδaγa *it is light*, and ṫsɛṫalɛ *it is thin* are all neuter verbs.

1.6.1. ˀɛṫθá yį́ dɛyɛ́r ˀarááłá, ˀɛyi bɛṫázį́ ṫsi dzɛ́rɛ́stį-ixa. dɛyɛ́r hílɛ ˀasˀuį, nahɛ́k̓e ˀįγą́ ṫsi-yɛ́ nį́ɛsaih ˀɛṫθá k̓ɛ́snįu, ˀɛṫθá bɛk̓ɛhɛteih. ˀɛyiṫá ˀɛṫθá dɛyɛ́r ˀalˀįu bɛhorɛłni-hílɛ. ṫsi nɛzų θiłtsį́, kúlú ˀį́łáγe ˀɛγwoz-tsele nɛdúwɛ ˀasłá- hiṫá ṫsi-yɛ́ dɛ́dɛnįṫiy-hílɛ. kúlú ˀɛyi bąłṫɛ-hílɛ. ˀɛyi ṫsi θá ṫsi γɛsṫį.

1.6.2. *I made only the thwarts strong, so that I might carry the canoe around by means of them. If I do not make them strong, sometimes when I get up quickly in the canoe, pressing on the thwart, the thwart will usually break. Therefore, when the thwart is made strong, there is no danger.*

I made a good canoe, because I made but one small rib short, there was one place in the canoe not tight. But that was not a fault. I used that canoe for a long time.

1.6.3. bɛt̓ázį *by means of them.*

dzɛ́rɛ́stį *I carry it around*, with dzɛ́rɛ́- *around*, and -tį́, customary form of the verb -tį́, -tą, -tą́, *to handle a long object.*

From dɛyɛ́r hílɛ ʔasʔį́u ... *If I do not make them strong* ... on for a couple of sentences, the aspect is imperfective, as the sentences here refer to a general situation, not a part of the narration.

nahɛ́k̓ɛ *sometimes*, from nahɛ́- *some* and -k̓ɛ *on.*

nį́ɛsaih, from *ni-hɛ́saih *I get up*, ni- *up*, hí- *inchoative*, and the verb stem for *one person goes.*

k̓ɛ́sníu *when I press on* (*the thwarts*), cf. k̓ɛ́- *on to*, and -ni *to push with hands.*

bɛk̓ɛhɛteih *on it there is customarily a break, i.e. it customarily breaks*, from the verb -tɛ, -tɛ́, -tɛ *to break.*

dɛ́dɛnįt̓iy *it is tight in one place*, cf. dɛnįt̓iy *it is tight.*

t̓si γɛst̓į *I used it as a canoe* (*but no longer*), perfective of -ʔį *to do, make* with the d-classifier.

HERMAN MELVILLE

Life on an American whaler

Herman Melville (1819–1891) was one of America's greatest novelists. He worked aboard several merchant ships and whalers in the mid-nineteenth century and many of his stories tell of life at sea. In this excerpt from what is probably his greatest work, he describes part of the technology by which useful parts were extracted from the heads of captured whales, and the highly specialized skills involved in these activities.

The Sperm Whale's head—contrasted view

Of the grand order of folio leviathans, the Sperm Whale and the Right Whale are by far the most noteworthy. They are the only whales regularly hunted by man. To the Nantucketer, they present the two extremes of all the known varieties of the whale. As the external difference between them is mainly observable in their heads; and as a head of each is this moment hanging from the Pequod's side; and as we may freely go from one to the other, by merely stepping across the deck:—where, I should like to know, will you obtain a better chance to study practical cetology than here?

In the first place, you are struck by the general contrast between these heads. Both are massive enough in all conscience; but there is a certain mathematical symmetry in the Sperm Whale's which the Right Whale's sadly lacks. There is more character in the Sperm Whale's head. As you behold it, you involuntarily yield the immense superiority to him, in point of pervading dignity. In the present instance, too, this dignity is heightened by the pepper and salt colour of his head at the summit, giving token of advanced age and large experience. In short, he is what the fishermen technically call a "grey-headed whale."

Let us now note what is least dissimilar in these heads—namely, the two most important organs, the eye and the ear. Far back on the side of the head, and low down, near the angle of either whale's jaw, if you narrowly search, you will at last see a lashless eye, which you would

---

Herman Melville, *Moby Dick* (New York: Modern Library, 1930), pp. 475–484, 491–499. First published, 1851.

fancy to be a young colt's eye; so out of all proportion is it to the magnitude of the head.

Now, from this peculiar sideway position of the whale's eyes, it is plain that he can never see an object which is exactly ahead, no more than he can one exactly astern. In a word, the position of the whale's eyes corresponds to that of a man's ears; and you may fancy for yourself, how it would fare with you, did you sideways survey objects through your ears. You would find that you could only command some thirty degrees of vision in advance of the straight side-line of sight; and about thirty more behind it. If your bitterest foe were walking straight towards you, with dagger uplifted in broad day, you would not be able to see him, any more than if he were stealing upon you from behind. In a word, you would have two backs, so to speak; but, at the same time also, two fronts (side fronts): for what is it that makes the front of a man—what, indeed, but his eyes?

Moreover, while in most other animals that I can now think of, the eyes are so planted as imperceptibly to blend their visual power, so as to produce one picture and not two to the brain; the peculiar position of the whale's eyes, effectually divided as they are by many cubic feet of solid head, which towers between them like a great mountain separating two lakes in valleys; this, of course, must wholly separate the impressions which each independent organ imparts. The whale, therefore, must see one distinct picture on this side, and another distinct picture on that side; while all between must be profound darkness and nothingness to him. Man may, in effect, be said to look out on the world from a sentry-box with two joined sashes for his window. But with the whale, these two sashes are separately inserted, making two distinct windows, but sadly impairing the view. This peculiarity of the whale's eyes is a thing always to be borne in mind in the fishery; and to be remembered by the reader in some subsequent scenes.

. . .

It may be but an idle whim, but it has always seemed to me, that the extraordinary vacillations of movement displayed by some whales when beset by three or four boats; the timidity and liability to queer frights, so common to such whales; I think that all this indirectly proceeds from the helpless perplexity of volition, in which their divided and diametrically opposite powers of vision must involve them.

But the ear of the whale is full as curious as the eye. If you are an entire stranger to their race, you might hunt over these two heads for hours, and never discover that organ. The ear has no external leaf whatever; and into the hole itself you can hardly insert a quill, so wondrously minute it is. It is lodged a little behind the eye. With respect to their ears, this important difference is to be observed between the Sperm Whale and the Right. While the ear of the former has an external opening, that of the latter is entirely and evenly covered over with a membrane, so as to be quite imperceptible from without.

Is it not curious, that so vast a being as the whale should see the world through so small an eye, and hear the thunder through an ear which is smaller than a hare's? But if his eyes were broad as the lens of Herschel's great telescope; and his ears capacious as the porches of cathedrals; would that make him any longer of sight, or sharper of hearing? Not at all.—Why then do you try to "enlarge" your mind? Subtilize it.

Let us now with whatever levers and steam-engines we have at hand, cant over the Sperm Whale's head, that it may lie bottom up; then, ascending by a ladder to the summit, have a peep down the mouth; and were it not that the body is now completely separated from it, with a lantern we might descend into the great Kentucky Mammoth Cave of his stomach. But let us hold on here by this tooth, and look about us where we are. What a really beautiful and chaste-looking mouth! from floor to ceiling, lined, or rather papered with a glistening white membrane, glossy as bridal satins.

But come out now, and look at this portentous lower jaw, which seems like the long narrow lid of an immense snuff-box, with the hinge at one end instead of one side. If you pry it up, so as to get it overhead, and expose its rows of teeth, it seems a terrific portcullis; and such, alas! it proves to many a poor wight in the fishery, upon whom these spikes fall with impaling force. But far more terrible is it to behold, when fathoms down in the sea, you see some sulky whale, floating there suspended, with his prodigious jaw, some fifteen feet long, hanging straight down at right angles with his body, for all the world like a ship's jibboom. This whale is not dead; he is only dispirited; out of sorts, perhaps; hypochondriac; and so supine, that the hinges of his jaw have relaxed, leaving him there in that ungainly sort of plight, a reproach to all his tribe, who must, no doubt, imprecate lock-jaws upon him.

In most cases this lower jaw—being easily unhinged by a practised artist—is disengaged and hoisted on deck for the purpose of extracting the ivory teeth, and furnishing a supply of that hard, white whalebone with which the fishermen fashion all sorts of curious articles, including canes, umbrella-stocks, and handles to riding-whips.

With a long, weary hoist the jaw is dragged on board, as if it were an anchor; and when the proper time comes—some few days after the other work—Queequeg, Daggoo, and Tashtego, being all accomplished dentists, are set to drawing teeth. With a keen cutting-spade, Queequeg lances the gums; then the jaw is lashed down to ringbolts, and a tackle being rigged from aloft, they drag out these teeth, as Michigan oxen drag stumps of old oaks out of wild wood-lands. There are generally forty-two teeth in all; in old whales, much worn down, but undecayed; nor filled after our artificial fashion. The jaw is afterwards sawn into slabs, and piled away like joists for building houses.

The Right Whale's head—contrasted view

Crossing the deck, let us now have a good long look at the Right Whale's head.

As in general shape the noble Sperm Whale's head may be compared to a Roman war-chariot (especially in front, where it is so broadly rounded); so, at a broad view, the Right Whale's head bears a rather inelegant resemblance to a gigantic galliot-toed shoe. Two hundred years ago an old Dutch voyager likened its shape to that of a shoemaker's last. And in this same last or shoe, that old woman of the nursery tale, with the swarming brood, might very comfortably be lodged, she and all her progeny.

But as you come nearer to this great head it begins to assume different aspects, according to your point of view. If you stand on its summit and look at these two *f*-shaped spout-holes, you would take the whole head for an enormous bass-viol, and these spiracles, the apertures in its sounding-board. Then, again, if you fix your eye upon this strange, crested, comb-like incrustation on the top of the mass—this green, barnacled thing, which the Greenlanders call the "crown," and the Southern fishers the "bonnet" of the Right Whale; fixing your eyes solely on this, you would take the head for the trunk of some huge oak, with a bird's nest in its crotch. At any rate, when you watch those live crabs that nestle here on this bonnet, such an idea will be almost sure to occur to you; unless, indeed, your fancy has been fixed by the technical term "crown" also bestowed upon it; in which case you will take great interest in thinking how this mighty monster is actually a diademed king of the sea, whose green crown has been put together for him in this marvellous manner. But if this whale be a king, he is a very sulky-looking fellow to grace a diadem. Look at that hanging lower lip! what a huge sulk and pout is there! a sulk and pout, by carpenter's measurements, about twenty feet long and five feet deep, a sulk and pout that will yield you some 500 gallons of oil and more.

A great pity, now, that this unfortunate whale should be hare-lipped. The fissure is about a foot across. Probably the mother during an important interval was sailing down the Peruvian coast, when earthquakes caused the beach to gape. Over this lip, as over a slippery threshold, we now slide into the mouth. Upon my word, were I at Mackinaw, I should take this to be the inside of an Indian wigwam. Good Lord! is this the road that Jonah went? The roof is about twelve feet high, and runs to a pretty sharp angle, as if there were a regular ridgepole there; while these ribbed, arched, hairy sides present us with those wondrous, half-vertical, scimetar-shaped slats of whalebone, say three hundred on a side, which depending from the upper part of the head or crown bone, form those Venetian blinds which have elsewhere been cursorily mentioned. The edges of these bones are fringed with hairy fibres, through which the Right Whale strains the water, and in whose intricacies he retains the small fish, when open-mouthed he goes through the seas of brit in feeding-time. In the central blinds of bone, as they stand in their natural order, there are certain curious marks, curves, hollows, and ridges, whereby some whalemen calculate the creature's age, as the age of an oak by its circular rings. Though the certainty of this criterion is far from demonstrable, yet it has the savour of analogical probability. At any rate, if we yield to it, we must grant a far greater age to the Right Whale than at first glance will seem reasonable.

In old times, there seems to have prevailed the most curious fancies concerning these blinds. One voyager in Purchas calls them the wondrous "whiskers" inside of the whale's mouth; another, "hogs' bristles;" a third old gentleman in Hackluyt uses the following elegant language: "There are about two hundred and fifty fins growing on each side of his upper *chop*, which reach over his tongue on each side of his mouth."

As every one knows, these same "hogs' bristles," "fins," "whiskers," "blinds," or whatever you please, furnish to the ladies their busks and other stiffening contrivances. But in this particular, the demand has long been on the decline. It was in Queen Anne's time that the bone was in its glory, the farthingale being then all the fashion. And as those ancient dames moved about gaily, though in the jaws of the whale, as you may say; even so, in a shower, with the like thoughtlessness, do we nowadays fly under the same jaws for protection; the umbrella being a tent spread over the same bone.

But now forget all about blinds and whiskers for a moment, and, standing in the Right Whale's mouth, look around you afresh. Seeing all these colonnades of bone so methodically ranged about, would you not think you were inside of the great Haarlem organ, and gazing upon its thousand pipes? For a carpet to the organ we have a rug of the softest Turkey—the tongue, which is glued, as it were, to the floor of the mouth. It is very fat and tender, and apt to tear in pieces in hoisting it on deck. This particular tongue now before us; at a passing glance I should say it was a six-barreler; that is, it will yield you about that amount of oil.

Ere this, you must have plainly seen the truth of what I started with—that the Sperm Whale and the Right Whale have almost entirely different heads. To sum up, then: in the Right Whale's there is no great well of sperm; no ivory teeth at all; no long, slender mandible of a lower jaw, like the Sperm Whale's. Nor in the Sperm Whale are there any of these blinds of bone; no huge lower lip; and scarcely anything of a tongue. Again the Right Whale has two external spout-holes, the Sperm Whale only one.

. . .

The great Heidelburgh Tun

Now comes the Baling of the Case. But to comprehend it aright, you must know something of the curious internal structure of the thing operated upon.

Regarding the Sperm Whale's head as a solid oblong, you may on an inclined plane sideways divide it into two quoins,* whereof the lower is the bony structure, forming the cranium and jaws, and the upper an unctuous mass wholly free from bones: its broad forward end forming the expanded vertical apparent forehead of the whale. At the middle of the forehead horizontally subdivide this upper quoin, and then you have two almost equal parts, which before were naturally divided by an internal wall of a thick tendinous substance.

The lower subdivided part, called the junk, is one immense honeycomb of oil, formed by the crossing and re-crossing, into ten thousand infiltrated cells, of tough elastic white fibres throughout its whole extent. The upper part, known as the Case, may be regarded as the great Heidelburgh Tun of the Sperm Whale. And as that famous great tierce is mystically carved in front, so the whale's vast plaited forehead forms innumerable strange devices for the emblematical adornment of his wondrous Tun. Moreover, as that of Heidelburgh was always replenished with the most excellent of the wines of the Rhenish valleys, so the Tun of the whale contains by far the most precious of all his oily vintages; namely, the highly prized spermaceti, in its absolutely pure, limpid, and odoriferous state. Nor is this precious substance found unalloyed in any other part of the creature. Though in life it remains perfectly fluid, yet, upon exposure to the air, after death, it soon begins to concrete; sending forth

* Quoin is not a Euclidean term. It belongs to the pure nautical mathematics. I know not that it has been defined before. A quoin is a solid which differs from a wedge in having its sharp end formed by the steep inclination of one side, instead of the mutual tapering of both sides.

beautiful crystalline shoots, as when the first thin delicate ice is just forming in water. A large whale's case generally yields about five hundred gallons of sperm, though from unavoidable circumstances, considerable of it is spilled, leaks, and dribbles away, or is otherwise irrevocably lost in the ticklish business of securing what you can.

I know not with what fine and costly material the Heidelburgh Tun was coated within, but in superlative richness that coating could not possibly have compared with the silken pearl-coloured membrane, like the lining of a fine pelisse, forming the inner surface of the Sperm Whale's case.

It will have been seen that the Heidelburgh Tun of the Sperm Whale embraces the entire length of the entire top of the head; and since—as has been elsewhere set forth—the head embraces one-third of the whole length of the creature, then setting that length down at eighty feet for a good-sized whale, you have more than twenty-six feet for the depth of the Tun, when it is lengthwise hoisted up and down against a ship's side.

As in decapitating the whale, the operator's instrument is brought close to the spot where an entrance is subsequently forced into the spermaceti magazine; he has, therefore, to be uncommonly heedful, lest a careless, untimely stroke should invade the sanctuary and wastingly let out its invaluable contents. It is this decapitated end of the head, also, which is at last elevated out of the water, and retained in that position by the enormous cutting tackles, whose hempen combinations on one side make quite a wilderness of ropes in that quarter.

Thus much being said, attend now, I pray you, to that marvellous and —in this particular instance—almost fatal operation whereby the Sperm Whale's great Heidelburgh Tun is tapped.

Cistern and buckets

Nimble as a cat, Tashtego mounts aloft; and without altering his erect posture, runs straight out upon the overhanging main-yard-arm, to the part where it exactly projects over the hoisted Tun. He has carried with him a light tackle called a whip, consisting of only two parts, travelling through a single-sheaved block. Securing this block, so that it hangs down from the yard-arm, he swings one end of the rope, till it is caught and firmly held by a hand on deck. Then, hand-over-hand, down the other part, the Indian drops through the air, till dexterously he lands on the summit of the head. There—still high elevated above the rest of the company, to whom he vivaciously cries—he seems some Turkish Muezzin calling the good people to prayers from the top of a tower. A short-handled sharp spade being sent up to him, he diligently searches for the proper place to begin breaking into the Tun. In this business he proceeds very heedfully, like a treasure-hunter in some old house, sounding the walls to find where the gold is masoned in. By the time this cautious search is over, a stout iron-bound bucket, precisely like a well-bucket, has been attached to one end of the whip; while the other end, being stretched across the deck, is there held by two or three alert hands. These last now hoist the bucket within grasp of the Indian, to whom another person has reached up a very long pole. Inserting this pole into the bucket, Tashtego downward guides the bucket into the Tun, till it entirely disappears; then giving the word to the seamen at the whip, up comes the bucket again, all bubbling like a dairy-maid's pail of new milk. Carefully lowered from its height, the full-freighted vessel is caught by an appointed hand, and quickly emptied into a large tub. Then re-mounting aloft, it again goes through the same round until the deep cistern will yield no more. Towards the end, Tashtego has to ram his long pole harder and harder, and deeper and deeper into the Tun, until some twenty feet of the pole have gone down.

Now, the people of the Pequod had been baling some time in this way; several tubs had been filled with the fragrant sperm; when all at once a queer accident happened. Whether it was that Tashtego, that wild Indian, was so heedless and reckless as to let go for a moment his one-handed hold on the great cabled tackles suspending the head; or whether the place where he stood was so treacherous and oozy; or whether the Evil One himself would have it to fall out so, without stating his particular reasons; how it was exactly, there is no telling now; but, on a sudden, as the eightieth or ninetieth bucket came suckingly up—my God! poor Tashtego—like the twin reciprocating bucket in a veritable well, dropped head-foremost down into this great Tun of Heidelburgh, and with a horrible oily gurgling went clean out of sight!

"Man overboard!" cried Daggoo, who amid the general consternation first came to his senses. "Swing the bucket this way!" and putting one foot into it, so as the better to secure his slippery hand-hold on the whip itself, the hoisters ran him high up to the top of the head, almost before Tashtego could have reached its interior bottom. Meantime, there was a terrible tumult. Looking over the side, they saw the before lifeless head throbbing and heaving just below the surface of the sea, as if that moment seized with some momentous idea; whereas it was only the poor Indian unconsciously revealing by those struggles the perilous depth to which he had sunk.

At this instant, while Daggoo, on the summit of the head, was clearing the whip—which had somehow got foul of the great cutting tackles—a sharp, cracking noise was heard; and to the unspeakable horror of all, one of the two enormous hooks suspending the head tore out, and with a vast vibration the enormous mass sideways swung, till the drunk ship reeled and shook as if smitten by an iceberg. The one remaining hook, upon which the entire strain now depended, seemed every instant to be on the point of giving way; an event still more likely from the violent motions of the head.

"Come down, come down!" yelled the seamen to Daggoo, but with one hand holding on to the heavy tackles, so that if the head should drop, he would still remain suspended; the negro having cleared the foul line, rammed down the bucket into the now collapsed well, meaning that the buried harpooner should grasp it, and so be hoisted out.

"In heaven's name, man," cried Stubb, "are you ramming home a cartridge there?—Avast! How will that help him; jamming that iron-bound bucket on top of his head? Avast, will ye!"

"Stand clear of the tackle!" cried a voice like the bursting of a rocket.

Almost in the same instant, with a thunder-boom, the enormous mass dropped into the sea, like Niagara's Table-Rock into the whirlpool; the suddenly relieved hull rolled away from it, to far down her glittering copper; and all caught their breath, as half-swinging—now over the sailor's heads, and now over the water—Daggoo, through a thick mist of spray, was dimly beheld clinging to the pendulous tackles, while poor, buried-alive Tashtego was sinking utterly down to the bottom of the sea! But hardly had the blinding vapour cleared away, when a naked figure with a boarding-sword in its hand, was for one swift moment seen hovering over the bulwarks. The next, a loud splash announced that my brave Queequeg had dived to the rescue. One packed rush was made to the side, and every eye counted every ripple, as moment followed moment, and no sign of either the sinker or the diver could be seen. Some hands now jumped into a boat alongside, and pushed a little off from the ship.

"Ha! ha!" cried Daggoo, all at once, from his now quiet, swinging perch overhead; and looking farther off from the side, we saw an arm thrust upright from the blue waves; a sight strange to see, as an arm thrust forth from the grass over a grave.

"Both! both!—it is both!"—cried Daggoo again with a joyful shout; and soon after, Queequeg was seen boldly striking out with one hand, and with the other clutching the long hair of the Indian. Drawn into the waiting boat, they were quickly brought to the deck; but Tashtego was long in coming to, and Queequeg did not look very brisk.

Now, how had this noble rescue been accomplished? Why, diving after the slowly descending head, Queequeg with his keen sword had made side lunges near its bottom, so as to scuttle a large hole there; then, dropping his sword, had thrust his long arm far inwards and upwards, and so hauled out our poor Tash by the head. He averred, that upon first thrusting in for him, a leg was presented; but well knowing that that was not as it ought to be, and might occasion great trouble;—he had thrust back the leg, and by a dexterous heave and toss, had wrought a somerset upon the Indian; so that with the next trial, he came forth in the good old way—head foremost. As for the great head itself, that was doing as well as could be expected.

And thus, through the courage and great skill in obstetrics of Queequeg, the deliverance, or rather, delivery of Tashtego, was successfully accomplished, in the teeth, too, of the most untoward and apparently hopeless impediments; which is a lesson by no means to be forgotten. Midwifery should be taught in the same course with fencing and boxing, riding and rowing.

I know that this queer adventure of the Gay-Header's will be sure to seem incredible to some landsmen, though they themselves may have either seen or heard of some one's falling into a cistern ashore; an accident which not seldom happens, and with much less reason too than the Indian's, considering the exceeding slipperiness of the curb of the Sperm Whale's well.

But, peradventure, it may be sagaciously urged, how is this? We thought the tissued, infiltrated head of the Sperm Whale, was the lightest and most corky part about him; and yet thou makest it sink in an element of a far greater specific gravity than itself. We have thee there. Not at all, but I have ye; for at the time poor Tash fell in, the case had been nearly emptied of its lighter contents, leaving little but the dense tendinous wall of the well—a double-welded, hammered substance, as I have before said, much heavier than the sea water, and a lump of which sinks in it like lead almost. But the tendency to rapid sinking in this substance was in the present instance materially counteracted by the other parts of the head remaining undetached from it, so that it sank very slowly and deliberately indeed, affording Queequeg a fair chance for performing his agile dexterities on the run, as you may say. Yes, it was a running delivery, so it was.

Now, had Tashtego perished in that head, it had been a very precious perishing; smothered in the very whitest and daintiest of fragrant spermaceti; coffined, hearsed, and tombed in the secret inner chamber and sanctum sanctorum of the whale. Only one sweeter end can readily be recalled—the delicious death of an Ohio honey-hunter, who seeking honey in the crotch of a hollow tree, found such exceeding store of it, that leaning too far over, it sucked him in, so that he died embalmed. How many, think ye, have likewise fallen into Plato's honey head, and sweetly perished there?

DUANE METZGER *and* GERALD WILLIAMS

Curers and curing in southern Mexico

Duane Metzger was a Junior Fellow at Harvard University and has taught at Stanford and at the University of Illinois. Gerald Williams is presently with the Department of Anthropology at the University of Rochester, New York. This selection is taken from one of a series of papers by Metzger and others dealing with Tenejapa culture from the native point of view.

The treatment of serious illness in Tenejapa—a Tzeltal-speaking community in the Chiapas highlands—is primarily the province of the /hpošil/, "curer." We propose to examine the role of the curer, placing particular emphasis on the characteristics and performances which not only define the role but which also, in their internal variation, are the basis for evaluation of curers and selection of one curer rather than another.

The procedures employed in the collection of the data and in the descriptive analysis of it are in part revealed in the body of the paper where eliciting frames and typical responses have been shown. The establishment and employment of specifiable eliciting frames, formulated in the informants' language and in terms "entertainable" by informants, constrains their response in some great degree to a focus or foci which are in turn defined in the informants' terms, rather than by the categories of the investigator. In this sense the description stems from the material itself. The structure and limits of the description bear a significant relation to structure and limits of the informants' "knowledge."

The role of the curer

Working with seven Tenejapa informants from six *parajes*, we were able to compile a list of some three hundred curers known to them. The approximate population of all Tenejapa *parajes* being about 10,000 (1960

Duane Metzger and Gerald Williams, "Tenejapa Medicine: the Curer," *Southwestern Journal of Anthropology*, 19, 2 (1963), 216–225, 228–234. Reprinted by permission of the publisher.

Census) and calculating a population of curers of two or three times the size of the list obtained, since our informants' acquaintance did not extend over the whole of the *municipio*, it appears that the ratio of curers to total population is somewhere between one to ten and one to twenty-five. This ratio indicates something of the importance of the performances engaged in by curers and of the situations which call up these performances. It may be observed as well that the variety and frequency of illness are equally of a large order and that, though we have not attempted any sort of statistical confirmation, the subject of illness figures with great frequency in conversation.

Virtually anything that upsets the Tenejapaneco's equanimity is a potential source of illness, while the maintenance of the health of the members of the family is a major drain upon available resources. It is the curer whose role is central to these concerns and who exercises major control over the disposition of these resources. Also, it appears, at least in some instances, it is the curer who decides whether an illness may be treated or not, and thus, at least indirectly, has some power of decision over the life or death of the patient. An illustration of two of these points is the curer's recommendation in instances of apparent imminent death to refrain from great expenditure in a hopeless attempt at a cure. The curer who fails to show such concern for the welfare of the patient's family is accused of avarice and failure to fulfill his obligation to /ya školta te muk' b'ik'it/, "watch over the people." Derogation of this duty leads to punishment in the form of illness.

Being known as a curer confers a status which overrides other status achieved, such as that of great age. It is usual for a respected elder to address even young curers as /tatik pošil/, /tatik/ being the most respectful, reverential term of address available, and, in general, curers are so addressed rather than by name.

Attributes of curers

Curers may be of any age (including children) or sex (though male curers are more numerous than female). No formal training is provided for those who fill the role.

The primary distinguishing characteristics of curers is their ability to "pulse" (/ya snaʔik lek ʔaʔy k'ab'al/, "They know well how to 'feel of the hand.' "). /ʔaʔy k'ab'al/ or /pik k'ab'al/ or /¢ahtae k'ab'al/, which refers to the process of pulsing, and thereby sensing, the movement of the blood of the patient, allows the identification of the illness, its etiology, cure, etc. This skill comes to the curer only as a "gift of God," usually discovered in himself by the curer (even while still a child). It is said that by praying to God in the church and burning candles, it is possible to obtain the necessary power to cure for the asking and without danger. Informants, though reporting this to be the case, cannot name any person who has become a curer in this way. More generally, persons attempting to acquire without the gift the knowledge of pulsing that characterizes curers run the danger of being punished by a visitation of illness.

In contrast to pulsing, a second performance characteristic of curers is not limited to them but is shared by non-curers of high status. This is the "true prayer," /b'a¢'il č'ab'/, which is an integral part of the public performances of the civil and religious officials as well as of heads of families, whose perceived function is to /sk'anel kušlehal/, "ask for the life (of the *pueblo* or household)." Public prayer, occurring at conventionally appropriate times, anticipates a potentially great number of dangers to the community and its individual members; within the context of curing, the focus of prayer is upon the life of an individual in relation to a single specific danger to that life.

While any non-curer who is skilled in praying (/ya snaˀ lek č'ab'/, "he knows how to pray well") may attempt, and sometimes succeed at, curing, the curer's ability to pulse makes his use of prayer more surely effective. Since there are many varieties of /b'a¢'il č'ab'/, differentiated by the god to whom addressed and specific to the disease, the ability to identify the disease (by pulsing) and the knowledge, which is essentially restricted to curers, of the association between specific diseases and gods is crucial. The would-be curer, like anyone else in the community, can learn these associations by closely observing curers at work when there is illness in his household. However, he must be circumspect in his learning. Attempts at acquiring such knowledge are generally punished by illness /ya stikun tal te hč'ultatik ~ te ryos/, "sent by God," because /ya htohb'e ryos tame ya hk'an ya hnop pošile/, "God punishes me if I want to learn to cure."

Like prayer, skill in the use of medicinal plants, which is characteristic of curers, is shared in a general sense by non-curers but becomes unique in the hands of curers because of its association with their other attributes. Medicinal plants are known by all adults in Tenejapa, and association of specific plant remedies with common illnesses is well-known. The curer's use of these plants is special in that, first he alone can surely identify the illness. Then, once the illness is identified, knowledge of the specific herbal remedy for the illness is more or less restricted (as in the case of prayer) to the curer. Finally, /tuhtael/, the preparation and administration of the remedy, involves prayer and spitting into the mixture, both of which invest the medicine with the curer's power.

Other curing skills are exclusive to curers but not common to all of them. Among these are blood-letting, and the curing of various specific types of diseases. Still other curing skills are neither common to all curers nor exclusive to them. These coincide with a set of infirmities which are not /čamel/, "illness(es)": /tiˀb'en čan/, "snake bite," /k'asem sb'akel/, "broken bones," /k'ahk'et/, "burns," /b'e¢'em/, "sprains," and /mahel/, "bruises."

Another somewhat peripheral phenomenon sometimes associated with curers is the /sánto/ or /hč'ultatik/, the "talking saint." These generally are in boxes in the house of their owner and may not be seen, though the more reliable are audible, sometimes "speaking" in a high-pitched whining noise, sometimes in recognizable words. The most highly regarded instance reported is that of one which can be heard speaking from inside the house while the listeners remain outside. The primary function of the saint is divinatory and ranges beyond divining the causes of illness and the identification of witches to the finding of lost objects.

The man who owns a saint is the /yahwal hč'ultatik/ or /b'ankilal mučáču yuˀun hč'ultatik/, "dueño del santo," and need not be a curer at all. The curer who has a saint, /ˀay hč'ultatik ta sna/, "there's a saint in his house," may employ his saint as a substitute for his own pulsing, but more generally uses it to confirm pulsing. The saint, then, is a supplement or substitute for more traditional (and generally more respected) modes of obtaining information; it has no apparent function in other segments of the cure.

Classes of curers

Having established the attributes of /hpošil/ we asked the question /hay ten hpošiletik ˀay ta b'alamilal/, "How many kinds of curers are there in the world?" One reply was /ˀay čaˀten/, "There are two kinds," specified as /b'ankilal hpošil/, "(literally, older brother curer) master curer" and /ˀih¢'inal hpošil/, "(literally, younger sibling curer) junior curer."

In respect to knowledge, these two classes contrast on several interrelated dimensions. One of these dimensions is the types of knowledge attributed to them. The ability to treat specific illnesses distinguishes all /b'ankilal hpošil/ and some /ˀih¢'inal hpošil/ from all others. For example, /spisil b'ankilal hpošiletik ya snaˀik te *hulawe*/, "All master curers know how to let blood (specifically from the head)," but /ˀay ˀolil ˀih¢'inal hpošiletik ma snaˀik te *hulawe*/, "There are some curers who do not know how to let blood."

The presentation of the names of other illnesses or modes of treatment elicited further differentiated statements of the same kind in which the following were some of the items substitutable for /hulaw/ in the statements above:

(1) /ya snaʔik lek č'ab'/	"they know how to pray well"
(2) /ya snaʔik tuhtawaneh/	"they know how to prepare and bless medicine"
(3) /ya snaʔik čonaw/*or* /ya snaʔik suhtesel čonel/	"they know how to send an illness back (to the hostile person who caused it)"
(4) /ya snaʔik poštawan yuʔun meʔtik tatik/	"they know the cure for /meʔtik tatik/"
(5) /ya snaʔik špoštael ʔak'b'il čamel/	"they know the cure for illness caused by witchcraft"

This knowledge, while characteristic of /b'ankilal hpošil/, may be possessed as well by individual /ˀihȼ'inal hpošil/, but the latter as a class cannot be said to be characterized by the knowledge. It will be noted that at least some abilities are clearly matters of degree (see 1 above), while in other cases the master curer and junior curer are distinguishable by the types of illness they are competent to cure; thus, of a junior curer who pretends to cure a /tulan čamel/, "a strong illness" such as /meˀtik tatik/, it is said /ya špoštawan haˀte ma lom sˀuȼub' yuˀun te mač'a ya špoštae/, "he cures (treats), but the person treated does not recover well." There are attributed to the /ˀihȼ'inal hpošil/, who knows the limits of his ability, such statements as /ha ˀin čamel ˀaˀwuˀuni ma šhuˀ kuˀun lek špoštael melel lom tulan čamel ˀaˀtaohi/, "This illness of yours, I cannot cure, because (you have) met with a very strong illness" or /haˀlek leaiktal te mač'a ya snaˀ lek špoštael te tulan čamele/, "Better summon someone who knows well the cures of serious illnesses."

A general statement of the difference may be seen in the following regarding the /ˀihȼ'inal hpošil/: /maˀma spisil ˀak'b'il ta yok ta sk'ab' yu'un hč'ultatik/, "Not all is given into his hands by God"—while of the /b'ankilal hpošil/ it is said, /spisil ˀak'b'il ta yok ta sk'ab'/, "All is given into his hands."

It will be noted that among the abilities characteristic of /b'ankilal hpošil/ is that of curing /ˀak'b'il čamel/, "given illness," i.e., illness attributed to an act of will of a /hˀak' čamel/, "giver of illness." The classes /hˀak' čamel/ and /hpošil/ intersect in some of the same persons. However, not all /haˀak' čamel/ are /hpošil/, and while all /b'ankilal hpošil/ may be able to cure such illness, not all master curers can induce illness. Those who are so able are said to /čaˀten ya snaˀ/, "he knows two kinds (classes)." A master curer never induces illness in this way in his role as curer, and the cure for /ˀak'b'il čamel/ does not include counter-measures of the same kind.

"Sending the illness back," /suhtesel čonel/, another ability characteristic of the master curer, is concerned not with /ˀak'b'il čamel/, but /čamel yuˀun čonel/, "illness induced through ritual 'sale' (of the victim)." This illness is attributed to a /hčohawal/, who implements his ill will by cutting candles into small pieces and praying over them as they burn. The master curer performs the same ritual as an integral part of the cure for /čamel yuˀun čonel/. Thus, while not all /hčonawal/ are /hpošil/, all /b'ankilal hpošil/ are /hčonawal/; moreover, the latter, unlike the role of /hˀak' čamel/, is entailed in the master curer's role.

One type of specialized knowledge which is characteristic of /b'ankilal hpošil/ is not common to all of them. The ability to handle /čamel yuˀun ˀalahel/, "childbirth," is more or less restricted to women;* while there are a few men who share this ability, they are reportedly little used because women are "embarrassed" to be attended by men in childbirth. The knowledge of such curers is not restricted to the problem of childbirth; they are general practitioners as well. The curing skills mentioned earlier as neither exclusive to curers nor shared by all of them—e.g., bone-setting—do not distinguish between /b'ankilal/ and /ˀih¢'inal/ curers, for many master curers lack some or all of these skills.

The knowledge attributed to the master curer which distinguishes him from the junior curer is manifest in his performances in the curing setting. The /b'ankilal/-/ˀih¢'inal/ contrast, previously defined in general terms of reputation, is carried out on another level in the performances which contribute to—and which at the same time reflect—that reputation.

Within the performances of the curer and others involved in the cure there may be distinguished (1) pulsing: /ˀaˀy k'ab'al/-/¢ahtae k'ab'al/, and (2) praying: /č'ab'atael/.

Previous to performances differentiating curers from other visitors who are not curers, the usual formulae of greeting are exchanged by the visiting curer and the family of the /čamel/, "sick person."

Differentiation of the curer's reception begins with the request of the family that he "pulse" the patient: Head of the family: /maˀyuk šˀob'ol b'ahat šaˀ ¢ahtab'en sk'ab'in hčamel kuˀuni/, "Would you not do me the favor of feeling for him his hand?"

Pulsing generally consists indeed of taking the pulse of both wrists for lengths of time ranging from five minutes to a half-hour per wrist. In *extremis*, the pulse at the wrist being too weak to "hear," pulsing may be done inside the elbow joint or inside the upper arm. This stage in the

* This is the only area in which sex distinguishes curers in any way. Age is reported to have no correlates in knowledge or evaluation, although the experience of old curers might be expected to lead to high evaluation of them if the age of all curers were known.

cure and its constituent performances are much more than diagnostic, leading not only to the identification of the illness, but to a variety of other information regarding the illness as well.

Among the information extracted by the master curer from his pulsing are the following:

/ya yal šč'ič'el te hčamel te b'i čamelil ya šti?wan ya ya?ye/
"The blood of the patient says what illness it is he is suffering"

/te b'i čamelil ya štaot te hčamele/
"... what illness has seized him, the patient"

/te b'anti ya štaot te hčamele/
"... where it seized him, the patient"

/te b'a č'ab'atael ya sk'ane/
"... which prayer is required"

/ta me ?ay čuhkem šč'ulele/
"... if his soul has been captured"

/ta me ?ay skape/
"... if there is a combination (of illnesses)"

/ta me ?ay ščohe/
"... if there is envy (involved)"

/ta me ?ay sme? šwiše/
"... if the soul is not well guarded (by the old woman who is responsible for it)"

Thus, virtually everything concerning a disease, from its provenience, etiology, to specific medicines and locations in which specific prayers must be said, is available to the curer through pulsing. The curer can also point the finger of guilt at the person whose misbehavior has resulted in the illness, even to parents and ancestors:

/ya sna?b'e lek ya?yel šč'ič'el te hčamel te b'i smul skola?al hahčemtal yu?un te hmam hme?čuntike/
"The blood of the patient knows well what sins of parents (or ancestors)"

During the course of the pulsing, the curer may carry on conversation with the family, the subject of conversation being unlimited, and the occasion not necessarily excluding jokes and laughter. If, during this conversation, the curer makes obvious attempts to elicit from the patient or the attending family the information which is properly forthcoming from pulsing, it is likely to be said that he is /ihȼ'inal/and not /b'ankilal/.

/te me ya sna? ya?yel k'ab'ale ma ya shohk'o/
" 'If he knew how to pulse, he would not ask questions,' he said"

In such a situation, the family may deliberately withhold information:

Curer: /b'it'il ʔaʔ lihk te sčamel te ʔan¢e/
"How did the illness of the woman begin?" *or*
/b'anti ʔaʔ s¢akat te čamele/
"Where did the illness grasp you?"

Family: /hič naš ʔaʔ ¢akot/
"It just grasped."

Curer: /maʔyuk b'a t'ušah/
"Couldn't it be she has fallen?"

Family: /maʔyuk/
"No."

In contrast, the /b'ankilal hpošil/ displays his lack of concern by engaging in small talk, gossip, and jokes. Silence, or any other apparent sign of concern on the part of the curer (e.g., trembling of the hand while pulsing, /ya šnihk/, "[his hand] trembles") is negatively evaluated.

Duration of the pulsing constitutes another potential point on which differentiation between /b'ankilal/ and /ˀih¢'inal hpošil/ is based. Thus a short pulsing (followed by a clear, unhesitating explication) is characteristic of the master curer, while a long pulsing (and hesitation in explaining the results) indicates skill of a lesser order.

Family: /b'i yael te sk'ab'e/
"What says his hand?"

Curer: /ma škil mama ya yal ʔaʔ kaʔy te sk'ab'e/
"I don't know. His hand does not speak, I feel."

The pulsing completed, the curer is expected to explain what he has learned. The master curer's explication of the circumstances antecedent to the disease generally conforms to what the family and patient know of them, while the junior curer's may not.

An instance of a highly evaluated set of performances by a curer will be seen in this example: The curer, a woman in this case, was called to a "gravely" ill patient. Without asking questions, and after a brief pulsing, she indicated that the patient was suffering illness as a punishment for complaining of the rigors and inconveniences of the *cargo*, "public office," he had recently assumed. The /ryos/ of his cargo was punishing the cargo-holder for remarks which he admitted to having made, the remarks being known as well to the family.*

* This underlines one way in which medical beliefs relate to the social structure, specifically the recruitment to and maintenance of the governing apparatus.

Further, the contrast between master and junior curers extends to the curer's statements with respect to the severity of the disease and the possibility of curing it. Accuracy of such estimation, as evidenced in subsequent developments and in the costs involved in the cure, is characteristic of the master curer. Informants report that /ʔihȼ'inal hpošil/ are prone to underestimate the severity of disease, while the confidence of the /b'ankilal hpošil/ does not deter him from staking his reputation on an extended and expensive cure. The /b'ankilal hpošil/ admits the gravity of the illness and characteristically undertakes the cure with due humility: /sk'an ryos ya šʔuȼub'/, "With the help of God he will recover."

The conclusion of the pulsing is the point of selection between alternative courses in the cure, depending upon the identification of the disease, perceived cause of the disease, etc. The curer may rest while preparations are made for whatever course is to be followed in the subsequent segment, and he will generally be fed.

The succeeding segment of the curing sequence consists of the components directed toward the curing itself. The constituent components depend upon the results of the preceding segment. Among possible components are the preparation and administration of medicine or other physical attempts at curing, the burning of incense and candles, the saying of prayers to appropriate gods (the prayers being said in specific places depending on the illness and its provenience), and possibly a ceremonial meal. Among these potential components, there are relations of mutual exclusion, of sequential order, of co-occurrence, the description of which will constitute a subsequent account of Tenejapa Tzeltal curing practices.

We will confine ourselves here to an outline of the general sequence of performances which constitute this segment.

Encompassing the variability arising from different results of pulsing and the variability arising from apparent changes as the cure proceeds, the three highest order sequential components appear to be as follows: (1) /b'aȼ'il č'ab'/, "prayer," (2) /tuhtael/, "preparation and administration of blessed medicine" and (3) /hulaw/, "blood letting." The time span of a single sequence (there is always the possibility of the iteration of the sequence) can be as long as four days. If the pulsing segment indicated that /b'aȼ'il č'ab'/ is appropriate, it will be anterior to other co-occurring components, if any. The /b'aȼ'il č'ab'/ itself is divided into four or six parts (practice appears to vary from one *paraje* to another), the parts being distributed in sequence on succeeding mornings and evenings, the first occurring in the evening. Special routines, however, may be accorded severe illness, or certain specific illnesses such as /meʔtik catik/, and the requisite number of prayers may be said in sequence without interruption. Severity may also dictate simultaneity of several segments, requiring the participation of a person other than the curer. This person, the /hč'ab'owil/, "prayer sayer," is not a curer, but one who can recite the appropriate prayer as determined by the curer. A prayer cycle, once begun, must be carried to its conclusion by the person reciting it without his engaging in any other curing component; thus, in order for other components to be simultaneous with the prayer, the latter must be said by another person (the /hč'ab'owil/) while the other component is carried out by the curer. Prayer, in this sense, is the only component which may be delegated.

. . .

If the cure is to be continued, the repetition of the cycle will be limited to /b'a¢'il č'ab'/, given that the cure is continued by the same curer. Where a different curer is called in, however, the complete cycle may be begun again.

The components of the curing segment proper also show variation in terms of which evaluation of the curer may be made. In prayer, whether the /b'a¢'il č'ab'/ or that of /tuhtael/, the performance of the /b'ankilal hpošil/ shows variety, that of the /ʔih¢'inal/ repetitiveness; and the repertory of the /b'ankilal/ allows him to continue longer, with consequent greater effectiveness.

In the preparation and administration of medicines the /ʔih¢'inal hpošil/ may always rely on the same medicine; /ma lom snaʔb'e sb'a spisil pošiletike/, "He doesn't know all the kinds of medicines." To the /b'ankilal/ there is attributed, at least, the knowledge of "all classes (of medicine)," /ya snaʔb'e sb'a spisil stukel/.

The physical manipulations of /hulaw/, "blood letting," make clear the curer's confidence or lack thereof, in that the incisions made should be regular and the hand steady, while the trembling hand of the incompetent leads to ragged incisions.

Upon termination of the curing segments, the curer is offered a gift of 10–30 ears of corn. The amount of corn varies neither with his status nor with the success of the cure (although he may decline it if the patient has died), but with the wealth of the patient's family. Daily consumption of corn is estimated at five ears per person per day.

Throughout the curing sequence, then, there are opportunities to evaluate—or to re-evaluate—the curer in terms of the /b'ankilal/ /ʔih¢'inal/ contrast. (In the course of the cure, a curer who has claimed master's knowledge and skill may betray his junior status by injudiciou eliciting of information, trembling hands, etc.; or, even in the absence o these signs of lesser status, he may incorrectly predict the course of th illness, e.g., the patient may fail to recover or die in contradiction of favorable prognosis.) An informant's evaluation of a curer is primarily based on the personal observations which he or his close associates have made of that curer. The relative lack of consensus in such evaluations by our informants suggests that these experiences vary greatly and that the classes of /b'ankilal hpošil/ and /ˀihȼ'inal hpošil/ are, in general, not to be regarded as groups with fixed memberships. Where multiple judgments were obtained as to the ability of various curers, there was disagreement between the informants in two-thirds of the cases. However, in the remaining third of the cases, where there was agreement, the overwhelming majority of curers were evaluated as /b'ankilal/, a fact which suggests that there may be a certain amount of consensus at the highly skilled end of the scale. The apparent lack of consensus below this level makes the selection of a curer problematic and involves the trial-and-error employment of /ˀihȼ'inal hpošil/ (labelled after the fact), as well as masters. In any case, there is a floor, as it were, underlying any evaluation, a level below which the definition of a person as a curer will not permit evaluation to go. Thus, an obviously poor curer can still, despite negatively evaluated performances, produce reactions of fear in the family of the patient by a prediction of death. Informants confirm that, in the position of patient, they find themselves vacillating between belief and disbelief of such predictions.

Conditions appropriate to the summoning of the curer

The curer is not summoned in every instance in which a person defines himself as /ˀayon ta čamel/ or /čamelon/, "I am sick," or is defined as such by others, /ˀay ta čamel/, "he/she is sick." The criteria which appear to operate in distinguishing between occasions appropriate and inappropriate to calling the curer generally involve the contrast between (1) /muk'ul čamel/, "great illness," /ˀip čamel/, "powerful illness," /tulan čamel/, "hard illness," versus (2)/ solel k'ašlel čamel/, "illness which passes," /č'uhč'ul čamel/, "a little illness."

In reply to the question, /b'it'il ya šb'aht taluk te hpošile/, "When do you call the curer?" there emerges the following family of responses:

/haʔ hič ya šb'a yič' tal ʔik'el hpošil/
"One is going to call a curer,"

(A) /te me ʔay muk'ul čamele/
"if there is a great illness"
/te me ʔay ʔip čamele/
"if there is a powerful illness"
/te me ʔay tulan čamele/
"if there is a strong illness"

We take this one level further by asking, /b'inti ˀut'il ˀay te ˀip čamele/, "How is (what is) a powerful illness?" and eliciting the response:

> /haʔ ʔip čamel ta me ʔay ma sk'an šhelaw ta ʔora te čamele/
> "It is a powerful illness if it does not (wish to) be cured in (normal) course, the illness."

Other conditions for calling the curer include:

(B) /ta me ʔay b'ayel k'uš hkok k'ab'tike/
"if there is great pain in our bodies"
/ta me ʔay me š¢'ihk' stiʔaw te čamel ya kaʔytike/
"if we cannot bear the pain of the illness we feel"

Other conditions require anticipation of illness, as:

(C) /haʔ lek ta nail ya šb'aht tal ta ʔik'el te hpošile/
"It is best first to call the curer" *or*
/haʔ lek te ʔalan ya kak'hb'ahtik ta poštaele/
"It is best to send for curing beforehand"
/ta me ʔay b'i šiʔotike/
"if we are *espantado*" *or*
/ya kaʔytik ta me ʔay mač'a ya ščap hk'olaltik ta ʔak'b'il čamele/
"We feel that there is someone trying to give illness (through witchcraft)"

Sometimes the calling of a curer follows the failure of another curer to restore the patient to health. Indeed, the lay diagnosis of "powerful" illness may follow—as the definition in A suggests—from an unsuccessful attempt to cure it; along with the diagnosis goes the after-the-fact evaluation of the curer as /ˀih¢'inal hpošil/.

Obtaining the services of the curer

The recognition of the above conditions within the household is up to the head of the house, and the decision to obtain the services of the curer is his. If the head of the house himself is the patient, it may be his wife or one among the children of the household who will make the decision to call the curer, if the head of the house is perceived to be ill but does not act himself. In general, if the patient is perceived as ill, but in such a condition as to refuse or be unable to recognize it, the curer will be called, even against the will of the patient.

Occasionally, if the illness is defined as "powerful" but the patient is not too sick to walk, the patient may go himself to the curer's house with a keg of *chicha* (a fermented sugar cane beverage) to request and participate in the cure. Usually, however, the curer is summoned to the patient's house.

The actual performance of going to request the services falls under the general heading of /ˀabat/, "errand," a performance mutually exclusive with the performances appropriate to the senior members of the household, and particularly to those of the senior male, generally the father in the predominantly nuclear family household. A child or young adult is usually sent, though he (or she) may be reluctant or afraid if he has not done such an errand before. The informants were encouraged to supply hypothetical but appropriate instances of verbal behavior to fit this situation. We constructed the interaction by setting up the question frames used by the person requiring information, in this case the young person who is to run the errand. Thus,

Child: /meʔ b'inti mahtanalil ya kič'b'el yuʔun ¢'in hpošile/
"Mother, what is the gift I should take for the curer?"

Parent: /haʔ ʔič'a b'el htab'uk ʔišimi/
"Take these twenty ears of corn."

The parent's response constitutes a substitution frame for the eliciting of other appropriate gifts:

/haʔ ʔič'a b'el hunuk pulatu čenek'i/
"Take this one bowl of beans." *or*
/haʔ ʔič'a b'el čeb'uk pulatu čenek'i/
"Take those two bowls of beans." *or*
/haʔ ʔič'ab'el hunuk pulatu ʔiči/
"Take this one bowl of *chiles*." *or*
/haʔ ʔič'a b'el čeb'uk pulatu ʔiči/
"Take these two bowls of *chiles*."

Child: /b'inti ya šk'o kalb'e ¢'in hpošile/
"What shall I say (on coming) to the curer?"

Parent: /haʔ ya šk'o walb'e ¢'in te ʔay hčamel kuʔuntike/
"Arriving, tell him that we have a sick person."

Child: /b'inti ya kalb'e ¢'in ta me ʔay ma sk'an štale/
"What shall I say if he does not wish to come?"

Parent: /yaniš ʔaʔwokol k'opta tal ta pórsa ¢'in/
"Ask him please to come under any circumstances." *or*
/te ʔay šʔob'oi b'a štal yilotike melel ʔip hčamel kuʔuntik yaʔwil/
"That he do us the favor of coming to see us, because our sick person is serious(ly ill)."

The errand-boy is quite likely to find the curer is away from home, as curers of good reputation are often employed, and a single cure may require as much as four full days if travelling time to distant patients is included. Moreover, while no curer is busy curing every day, all of them carry on the usual adult occupations as well—the men in the cornfields, the women in their kitchens and courtyards. There are no full-time specialists in curing; the meager fees paid for curer's services are incommensurable with such specialization, and the time that curing subtracts from subsistence activities is so great as to cause curing to be considered a somewhat sacrificial vocation.

The response of the curer to the request and gift may be one of three: (1) he may come as requested, and at once; (2) he may protest a previous obligation, undertaking to come later; or (3) he may refuse the "gift" and thus decline to undertake the cure. The second may be interpreted as a disguised attempt to pursue some work of his own, and the third may indicate some history of conflict between curer and the family of the patient. In both types of situation, the curer places himself in jeopardy of supernatural punishment in that he is refusing what is considered an obligation contingent upon his role as curer.

The selection of a curer

First and foremost, the curer selected by the patient's household is generally one with whom they have had favorable first-hand experience in previous curing situations; at least initially, curers known only by hearsay are not considered. Proximity is a factor important in the initial stages and often associated with his acquaintance, except that normally the curer does not treat his own children or members of his own household. Proximity may also be crucial in emergency. Given these guiding principles, the selection of a curer takes into account the household's guess diagnosis of the illness and involves an attempt to match the illness and the curer's skills as they have observed them. A "powerful" illness requires a known /b'ankilal hpošil/, while for a "little" illness an /ˀihȼ'inal hpošil/ may be chosen. The guesswork involved both in identifying the illness and in evaluating the curer often means that the first curer called will not be the last. However, the ideal rationalization of the selection of a curer is phrased in firm, positively evaluative terms:

/mač'a hunuk hpošilil ya šb'a kik'tik tal/
"Which curer shall we send for to come?"

/haʔ ya šba kik'tik tal te hʔaluš lopis howil ȼ'iʔe melel haʔ ya snaʔ ššiknatesel spisil te b'i ya štʔwan ya kaʔytike/
"Let us summon Alonso López 'Mad Dog' because he knows how to explain all the things that we suffer."

Conclusion

In this paper, some aspects of the role of the Tenejapa Tzeltal curer have been described in terms consistent with discriminations made by the Tenejapa Tzeltal themselves; the discrimination of curers from non-curers, the evaluation of and distinction between curers, the establishment of recognized units within the curing performance (and their relation to the evaluation of the curer), the relation of evaluation to the selection of the curer, etc.

The techniques here employed seem to us to be applicable in ethnographic description generally. Whether through these or other techniques, the arrival at cultural descriptions which mirror the discriminations made by informants is a desirable end for ethnography. The present paper is, of course, only a sample; Tzeltal curers and their activities constitute a focus which if articulated with a number of other such foci will place the Tzeltal curers within a potentially ever-widening description, having as its end a Tzeltal-centered "whole-culture" description of the Tenejapa Tzeltal community.

PART FOUR

The anthropologist at work

An anthropologist has failed unless, when he says goodbye to the natives, there is on both sides the sorrow of parting. It is evident that he can only establish this intimacy if he makes himself in some degree a member of their society and lives, thinks, and feels in their culture since only he, and not they, can make the necessary transference.

E. E. EVANS-PRITCHARD

INTRODUCTION

Anthropologists have many different kinds of interests. Some are teachers in liberal arts colleges. Others devote their lives to research in connection with museums or research institutes. Most achieve a compromise between these extremes by teaching in a university and pursuing their research interests in the field and library on a part-time basis. In this section we shall consider some of the kinds of work that anthropologists engage in and the problems and delights that are peculiar to this discipline.

The selections that follow are relatively self-explanatory. Harold C. Conklin and John Adair each tell about one of their informants (not to be confused with informers) from whom they learned important lessons about Hanunóo and Pueblo culture, respectively. The obituary of Alfred L. Kroeber conveys a vivid picture of the intellectual activities of the late dean of American anthropology; it also tells a good deal about its distinguished author, Julian H. Steward. Laura Bohannan recounts one humorous and informative story-telling session that occurred during her work with the Tiv.

The other selection, by Stewart Peckham, calls for a bit more explanation. It is an archaeological site report, fairly typical of hundreds of such reports prepared each year by excavators all over the country. I have included it here so that the reader can see exactly what kinds of observations the field archaeologist makes and how he records them for future use by himself and others. (Peckham's reports are models of clarity in this regard.) Although the report is primarily descriptive, you will find that inferences are drawn regarding the temporal position and cultural connections of the site. Finally, this report is an example of "salvage archaeology"; and it shows how scholars cooperate with private firms and government agencies in quickly excavating sites and recording data that are threatened with destruction by industrial advance. In its first nine years of existence, the New Mexico Highway Salvage Program recorded over 350 sites and excavated 110 of them, salvaging a great deal of valuable data. Incidentally, many of these sites would have gone undiscovered without the road-building activities that also threatened them. As Grahame Clark observed in *Archaeology and Society*:

> The growth of urban life, the increased demands of industry, and the immense development in communications have each in their own way tended to extend and deepen all manner of excavations and in so doing to bring antiquities to light in unprecedented numbers.

Other selections that describe the anthropologist at work will be found in Part V. In addition, the article by Metzger and Williams in Part III includes information on the techniques and goals of the "new ethnography"—a descriptive approach which relies heavily on the native language as a key to culture.

HAROLD C. CONKLIN

Getting to know a Hanunóo girl

Harold C. Conklin is a professor of anthropology at Yale University. He has done intensive fieldwork in the Philippines, and his numerous publications deal with linguistic, ethnographic, and ecological problems. In this section, we find both the anthropologist and his young informant learning about Hanunóo culture. For the former it is an explicit, systematic kind of learning; but what Maling learns she will have to use fluently and unconsciously as a member of the society.

Just before dawn, one day in late September, 1953, seven-year-old Maling tiptoed to the edge of my sleeping mat to wake me with a short but sad announcement: "*namatay yi kanmi 'āri*'" (our younger brother is dead). Still an infant, Gawid had succumbed to an unknown malady during the night. On his death, the Mt. Yagaw Hanunóo family with whom I had been residing in the small hamlet of Parina for almost a year immediately arranged for his burial and began the observance of a five-day religious restriction on agricultural work, bathing, and travel. To understand how Maling interpreted this turn of events as she waited for me to get up and help with the preparations, it is necessary to know the part she had played in the activities connected with Gawid's birth eighteen days earlier.

For that occasion, Maling's father, Panday, had rethatched a small, dilapidated annex to the family house and had built a sturdy rail fence around its wooden piles and storm props to keep the foraging pigs away from the space under the bamboo slat floor. Although the period of pregnancy had not been marked by any of the anomalies recognized by the Hanunóo, the customary magical precautions such as refraining from unnecessary binding, tying, or planting activities had been strictly observed for the preceding week by both Panday and his wife, Sukub. On the day before the birth, after a brief final weeding of the maturing

---

Harold C. Conklin, "Maling: A Hanunóo Girl from the Philippines," from Joseph B. Casagrande (ed.), *In the Company of Man*, pp. 101–118.

rice crop in her steep jungle clearing, Sukub harvested enough bananas for the next two days and returned to Parina to spend most of the afternoon and evening in her rattan hammock-swing.

Maling came to tell me of these things and of how she had helped mend an old buri mat which her father had set up as a screen to shut off the annex from the rest of the house. Her older sister, Hanap, was responsible for most of the family cooking and during this period often relieved Sukub in caring for two-year-old Iyang. Thus, Maling was relatively free to visit the other four households in our small settlement and occasionally to discuss her views on daily events with me. While I made more systematic attempts to elicit adult interpretations of such events, Maling often volunteered crucial details which her elders deemed either too obvious or too intimate to be mentioned. It was partly for this reason and partly because of her cheerful disposition and youthful enthusiasm that I was immediately drawn to her. Despite her childish exuberance, Maling was an obedient and respectful child, capable of almost infinite patience and concentration if necessary. She was one of those children who felt equally at ease whether sitting for an hour quietly watching her grandfather carve intricate sigmoid curves into a bolo handle or publicly—though jokingly—chiding and poking him for ending a humorous tale with an excessively lewd remark. Her poise with both children and adults in quite varied situations (including even an ethnographer's presence), was a fortunate circumstance for which I became increasingly appreciative.

Early the next morning when I entered the refurbished room that served as the birth chamber, Maling and her two sisters were standing with their backs against the palm-leaf thatch on the side opposite the door, with their eyes glued on the scene directly in front of them. Panday had girth-hitched his loincloth around a low beam at a point only a foot above Maling's head. Sukub, who was facing her daughters in a kneeling position, had wrapped the loose ends of this white cotton fabric securely around her wrists and was pulling—almost hanging—on the taut webbing that stretched from her raised hands to the beam. Sitting on the same floor mat and just behind her, Panday was helping his wife through the first stages of labor by massaging her abdomen and applying arm pressure. No elaborate preparations had been made for the occasion. The usual commonplace objects were left in the room. In the corner beyond the couple were two buri rice sacks, some odd bits of clothing, and a blanket. Winnowing trays, coconut shell dishes, a pitch candle, two bundles of bark and roots used in making incense, and various medicinal herbs filled the remaining corners. Except for a blood-red scarf wrapped tightly around her waist and the broad rattan pocket belt at her side, Sukub was dressed as she had been the day before—in a short homespun sarong with three loose, plaited waist bands and numerous bead necklaces.

The three sisters were dressed like their mother in miniature, except for the addition of loose cotton blouses. Several medicinal charms and an old Spanish silver coin dangled from Maling's beaded necklace. In her tiny sensitive face one could easily read the signs of intense observation. Below a faintly wrinkled brow, her large, somber eyes remained motionless. She had almost succeeded in keeping most of her slightly tousled, shoulder-length hair back from her face with a tight-fitting beaded fillet. One stray lock, however, escaped the encirclement of this headband and fell in a wisp over her smooth brown cheek.

A few minutes after I had sat down next to Iyang, Panday asked Hanap to start heating some rice gruel in the next room. Maling prepared a betel quid for her mother, at the latter's request, and helped Hanap pour some water from a bamboo tube into an earthen cooking pot. By the time Maling returned, her mother had already uttered the first in a series of long, piercing cries, "Udu-u-u-u-y, udu-u-u-u-y, . . . ," which signaled to the settlement at large as well as to those in the room, that the second stage of labor was about to begin.

During the next hour, Maling continued watching every detail intently, often drawing my attention to particular points that differed from the way Iyang had been born in Alyun two years before. "Then," she explained, "Mother's contractions were delayed much longer. And she had to tug on a rough abacá cord instead of a homespun loincloth because Father's was being washed."

A little while later, Maling told me confidently that this looked as if it would be a normal delivery, pointedly adding that her granduncle had been a breech baby and still had the name Su'i (legs first) to prove it.

From the beginning, it was obvious that the family wanted a boy. Maling had told me how she envied her girl cousins who had younger brothers to take care of, and how her father would like to have at least one son who, as he grew older, could help with house construction and the felling of larger trees during the annual forest clearance. Even Sukub had once mentioned that she and a mother of three sons (but no daughters) had exchanged waist bands several months earlier to "switch their luck." More recently, Maling had confided to me that she was afraid her Aunt Agum was correct in saying that Sukub's buttocks seemed to be getting flatter—a sure sign that the unborn child was a girl. Consequently, right up to the time the baby was born, considerable anxiety over the sex of the expected offspring was combined with the usual concern about the condition of the mother.

It was a boy, and Maling had the pleasure of announcing the fact to three of her cousins who had gathered outside on the veranda. In a matter of seconds the word reached the rest of the hamlet and attention shifted abruptly from the untouched neonate in front of Sukub to Sukub herself. From previous questioning, I knew that no one would move the baby until the afterbirth was expelled, no matter how long this might take.

During the first hour, Sukub was given all of the comforting treatment customarily provided to induce a rapid expulsion of the afterbirth and to prevent any of the numerous kinds of relapse distinguished by the Hanunóo. Hot, liquid infusions were rubbed over her limbs which were then bathed in sweet pitch incense. She perspired heavily as the room filled with the fragrant smoke. Maling was asked to knot the ends of the loincloth so that Sukub could rest her elbows in the resulting loop.

Never leaving his wife's side, Panday efficiently supervised all of these activities, now in a soft voice asking Hanap or Maling to prepare a betel quid for their mother, now adjusting Sukub's waist band or wiping her forehead with an old shirt, and always checking to see that the requisite magical procedures designed to hasten this last stage of labor were properly carried out. Under his direction, Maling helped Hanap untie everything in the house that either of her parents had lashed, woven, or spliced together in the last few months so that the afterbirth would come "undone" likewise.

Hanap fed her mother some hot rice gruel and kept the fire going while Iyang and two of her cousins spun areca nut tops on a nearby winnowing tray. Periodically, Maling added hot embers to the shell bowl in which fresh scented herbs had been mixed and passed the vessel around her mother several times.

Still, there were no results, even after Sukub's older sister, Ampan, arrived from the settlement across the Silsig valley with additional rice gruel and a new supply of pitch. As the delay extended into the second hour, Sukub became noticeably weaker and even Iyang, who had become extraordinarily quiet—saying she no longer wanted to play outside—began to reflect the urgency of this situation for the entire family.

During the next few minutes, Panday, Hanap, and Ampan conferred hastily on the most effective steps to be taken to help free the afterbirth. Maling had witnessed several such discussions under similar circumstances during the last few years, but this was different. Previously, she had listened to older relatives talk about events which did not concern her directly. Now, however, she found herself involved in almost every activity mentioned.

She had been with her father, for example, when he had planted sweet potato vines three weeks past, and was the only other person present who knew exactly which area in the family clearing he had "seeded."

Furthermore, in regard to this particular incident, it was agreed unanimously that Panday should not have planted any new crops so near the end of his wife's pregnancy and that the vines would have to be uprooted. Knowing that Panday could not leave Sukub at this time, Maling offered to take Hanap to the sweet potato patch where both of them could perform this mechanical act of sympathetic magic in hopes of easing the passage of the placenta.

The two girls left almost immediately, stopping on the veranda just long enough to pick up two empty bamboo water tubes to be filled on their way back from the field. I decided to go with them, leaving Panday and his sister-in-law considering other possible sources of Sukub's difficulty. The baby remained untouched, and for the moment, unthought of.

Hanap, followed by her equally slight and even more diminutive younger sister, led the way down the 600 yards of mountain trail connecting Parina with Panday's clearing. As usual for this time of year, the steep, narrow path was muddy and slippery and, at several points where it led around the brim of a 40-foot ravine, even dangerous. Because of their daily trips to fetch water, however, the girls knew every inch of the route intimately. Where recent heavy rains had loosened rocks and made the footing precarious, Maling turned to warn me, adding at one point how only two nights before she had nearly tripped on a wild yam vine that had grown across the trail. Along the way we passed familiar stretches of bamboo forest and second-growth jungle, through two stands of coconut and other fruit trees, and across a small stream where the girls left their heavy containers.

Once in the field, Maling took us straight to the vines Panday had planted, and the girls began pulling them up. As soon as this task was done Hanap hastened back to Parina to inform the others.

Maling and I paused at the stream to talk briefly with one of her young cousins who had stopped there to prepare a betel chew. Before he went on his way Maling asked him to cut some coconuts for us from a nearby tree which belonged to her family. He appeared happy to do this, and while he was detaching nuts from the crown of the nearest palm she emphasized how useful it is to have a young man in the family who can climb such trees. By the time she had filled her water tube from a streamside spring, her cousin had opened three of the felled fruits for our immediate consumption, and was husking two other coconuts to make it easier for me to carry them back to Parina. Having had nothing to eat since early morning, we were greatly refreshed by this common midafternoon snack.

After our pause at the stream, Maling and I continued the trip back alone, and although it was a difficult climb most of the way, she kept up a lively conversation about the things she noticed along the trail. On numerous other occasions Parina children had amazed me with their precise knowledge of the plant environment. This was no exception. Before we reached Parina Maling had drawn my attention to five separate clumps of productive perennial crops—ranging from bananas to betel palms—each of which had been planted by her grandfather or by one of his sons, and she had shown me two wild herbs used for making *panrunas*, a medicinal preparation which, when accompanied by appropriate rituals, is believed to be a permanent oral contraceptive.

"They say," noted Maling, "that's the reason why Father doesn't have any younger sisters or brothers. Grandmother took the *panrunas* treatment soon after he was born because his had been such a difficult delivery."

"Do you know," I asked, "what other ingredients are needed to make *panrunas*?"

"I'm not sure," she replied, "but I think *tunawtunaw* weed is one. Hanap says parts of seven different plants are needed; she probably knows what the others are."

In the course of many similar conversations, Maling had demonstrated an astonishing maturity of interests and experience, richly illustrating the way in which a Hanunóo child, without formal instruction, acquires an increasingly detailed acquaintance—direct or vicarious—with all sectors of the local adult world. Geographically, this is a small universe, limited often to an area within ten kilometers of one's birthplace. (Maling had only once been farther than a half-hour's walk from Parina.) But this small orbit comprehends a comparatively vast realm of knowledge in all provinces of which any member of the society is expected to be at home. In this setting, Maling's parents never thought it particularly precocious that on some occasions she should be as interested in contraceptives as in learning to spin cotton or take care of her younger sister. Nevertheless, I was constantly impressed with her independent thinking and utter frankness which seemed to recognize no boundaries, except of degree, between child and adult knowledge. Her status as a child neither prevented her from occasionally accepting some of the responsibilities of her elders nor blocked her intuitive analysis of their adult roles.

As we approached the edge of our settlement, Maling suggested we pick an armload of the soft, leafy heads of the aromatic *'alībun* shrub, explaining that not only could we use some of them to wipe the mud from our feet, but that her mother would appreciate having a few in the room because of their fragrance.

After hanging her filled miniature water cylinder on the veranda rack Maling lifted the screen matting and quietly entered the room where her father, sisters, and aunt were watching Sukub and talking in very low tones. Maling sat quietly looking around the tiny room. Sukub and Panday had both undone their hair knots, and someone, probably Panday, had hung half a dozen untied lashings, unwound arrow bindings, and the like, over a low crossbeam. While we had been gone, many efforts had been made to recall and remedy any recent act by Maling's parents that might be the root of the trouble. Hanap leaned over to tell Maling that at Panday's behest, Aunt Agum had gone to a nearby banana grove to pull up the first and last of thirty banana sets which Sukub had planted in August. This had seemed to please Sukub, but the afterbirth still had not appeared.

Ampan remained attentively at Sukub's side while Panday looked once more through his betel bag, and Maling joined in the search for nooses, slip knots, balls of wound yarn, pegs, and other bound, joined, or fastened objects that might have been overlooked. The muffled voices from the adjoining houses and the occasional gusts of wind up from the Silsig valley only served to underscore the gravity of the quiet but intensive search inside. Maling broke the long silence by inquiring if anyone had undone the leash of the new wooden turtle that Panday had carved for Iyang. No one had, and it was agreed that perhaps this was the knot which was causing the delay.

Maling went into action swiftly, but calmly. By gentle questioning she learned from Iyang that she and her cousins had been playing with the toy turtle earlier in the day. Since their own house had already been thoroughly searched, Maling decided to check in the adjoining house where her cousins were still romping about. Her hunch was right; the toy was returned, and the leash carefully untied, completely unknotted, and thrown over the beam along with the other lines and cords. All eyes again turned to Sukub. After a few more minutes of anxious waiting, and much to everyone's relief, she indicated that the final contractions had begun.

With the expulsion of the afterbirth, the tension relaxed and things moved quickly. Hanap sponged her mother's forehead and adjusted blankets while Maling made her a fresh betel quid. Although Panday could cut the baby's navel cord, it was decided to have Yuktung act as the child's *gupas* (cord cutter) so that the boy would grow up, not only to be like his father, but also to be a good hunter and trapper like his uncle.

Panday cut the tip of an old arrow shaft into a long tapering blade and quickly fashioned one of Maling's empty water-carrying tubes into a small bucket-like vessel to hold the umbilicus and placenta. Maling joined me in the background and, knowing that this was the first time I had observed such a ritual, eagerly explained to me all that she knew about the procedure.

"See," she said, "we can't use an iron blade to cut the cord. Even an arrow shaft is dangerous if the poisoned tip has not first been removed because then the child would grow up to be easily angered. He might even fight his parents, and seriously injure them."

Finally, nine hours after Gawid's birth, and after both the bamboo container and reed knife were prepared, Panday placed the baby on its back and proceeded to tie the umbilicus close to the infant's belly with a piece of homespun yarn. Yuktung, who had been called in from his house, then took Panday's place and with a sawing motion, severed the cord just above the cotton binding with very deliberate short strokes. In rapid succession, he then touched the moist blade tip to the baby's lips, waved the shaft in a zigzag pattern over its head, and uttered a barely audible magical formula to insure rapid healing. As he stuck the shaft in the roof thatch, Maling leaned back to tell me that in a few days her father would shoot it into a tree so that her brother would be a good shot with a bow.

Sukub now handed the afterbirth to Panday who placed it in the bamboo container, filled the tube with earth, and then went off into the forest where, Maling said, he would hang it from a high limb out of reach of large animals. The bamboo floor in front of Sukub was cleared and spread with an unused homespun cloth on which the infant was placed for bathing. While this was Sukub's responsibility, Hanap and Maling helped by heating water and bringing it to their mother's side in large coconut shell bowls. Soon Sukub was holding her young son in a cotton wrap and discussing the events of the past day with her children. Hanap began to winnow rice for the evening meal, Iyang cried for her plaything, and the household gradually settled down to a more normal schedule. When I left, Maling and her mother were still talking about the knot around the turtle's neck.

For the next few weeks Maling was an enthusiastic observer and participant in the care of Parina's youngest resident. Within this settlement of independent nuclear families residing in two lines of veranda-linked dwellings, she served as the chief disseminator of news about the infant's progress. She spent some time in each of these households almost every day, ostensibly to borrow a shellful of salt or a needle, or to check on the identity of an unfamiliar visitor for the folks at home. On these small errands as well as during her casual visits, she could not resist the opportunity to talk about her brother. Her little cousins would sometimes go back with Maling to examine for themselves the various items of behavior and appearance which she had reported. First it was his feeding habits that drew their attention. Then his somewhat flattened head (which Aunt Agum assured Maling would grow "round again" in a few months), then his manual skills, and so on.

One day Maling was sent by her parents to see if the door had been finished on a nearby rice granary which was being built for the family by one of her uncles. She said she wasn't going to be gone long and wondered if I wouldn't walk along with her. On reaching the bamboo and wood storehouse which was hidden from our houseyard clearing by a few yards of low scrub and jungle, we climbed the inclined pole ladder and sat down on the door ledge.

Maling seemed to be in a talkative mood.

"Mother went down to the stream to bathe today," she began, "and left the baby all alone with Hanap. We were awfully worried that something might happen, but nothing did. He is six days old, and he doesn't have a name yet. Our grandparents are coming up here in a day or two and I suppose we will decide on a name then."

"What do you think would be a good name for your brother?" I queried.

"There are a lot of names that are good for boys, but some we don't like because they sound too much like those used by the lowland Christians. Others we can't use because they belonged to relatives who have been dead only a few years. I think the best name would be the one Father has suggested, Gawid. My great-great-grandfather's name was Gawid. See that peak beyond Alyun? I've never been there, but they say that's where old Gawid once shot two deer with the same arrow. When my brother gets Grandfather Andung to prepare some hunting medicine for him, he should be a good hunter too.

"You know, we used to have a brother, who was several years younger than Hanap, but he died of a sudden illness two rice harvests ago. It was really too bad. He was just learning how to trap and shoot. If he had lived we would now have fish and game to eat with our rice or bananas almost every day. And there are so many things he could have helped Father do. He could have operated the bellows while Father worked at the forge, and he could have built this granary. As it is now, Father will have to forge two bolo blades to repay my uncle for this job. And look there, the cogon thatch seems a bit thin over in that corner, and the lashing here on the floor is poorly knotted. It just isn't the same as having one's own son for a helper.

"With Mother it is different. Hanap already can do most household chores including cooking, and she is pretty good at spinning and weaving baskets. I haven't learned to do all these things yet, but by the time Hanap gets married, I'll be able to take her place."

Our conversation was interrupted at this point by Hanap's call for Maling to go with her to fetch water. As we walked down to the main settlement clearing, Maling asked if girls in America also carry water like the Hanunóo, and whether their brothers ever helped them. Before I had time to answer she had joined Hanap and two other Parina girls on their way to the spring.

The infant's ears were pierced the following day and, not unimpressed by Maling's (and her father's) enthusiasm, the family decided to name him Gawid. Sukub was now able to gather firewood, cook, harvest bananas and beans, and work in the family fields—never, however, without Gawid slung at her side, or in Hanap's care.

During the second week, Maling helped her mother tie small circlets of red and white beads around Gawid's wrists and legs, and a tiny medicinal amulet about his neck. He was now well on his way to becoming accepted as a full-fledged member of the community and Parinans stopped calling him "the infant" as they began to use his proper name.

Parina children were already including Gawid in their play activities, such as the mock feast they held one afternoon behind Panday's house. Sukub whispered to me that they had been dining on twig and turmeric stalk stew and a main dish of ashes for almost half an hour, as I followed her quietly to observe them from a natural blind. Iyang, Maling, their cousin Biru (Yuktung's son), and four other three-to-eight-year-olds had set out a row of banana leaf trays on which these foods had been placed. Mimicking their elders, they were exclaiming loudly about the quality of the meal and shouting for the men to fill up their shell bowls with more "stew." Maling and the gourmandizing tots demanded better service from Gawid and other males not actually present almost as often as they did of Biru and his older brother. This most entertaining make-believe meal ended in a round of laughter on all sides as Gawid himself betrayed our presence by beginning to cry.

Though no one would say so, it was obvious that there would be an abundant rice harvest. Maling evidently knew this should not be stated directly, but at the same time she found it difficult to ignore. Once, for example, she suggested that I visit "her" field in order to gather some cucumbers which were now ripe. "And," she added, "one of the two kinds of rice Father gave me is almost ready to be cut."

Maling was still too young, of course, to do much agricultural work of her own, but she took immense pride in the fact that she possessed some seed of her own which had actually been planted in a full-sized hillside clearing instead of only in a play garden such as the one she had helped Iyang make in their Parina houseyard.

That afternoon I accompanied Sukub and Maling on a brief cucumber-picking visit to their fields, during which I saw for myself that the rats and grubs had not done nearly so much damage as local farmers would have led one to think. In a few months there would be plenty of rice for a large community-wide feast.

Recalling that the last feast her family had sponsored was for the disinterment of her deceased brother's bones, Maling proposed that this year they should hold a post-harvest rite to celebrate Gawid's birth. On the way back, she composed, in the form of a familiar children's chant, a number of extemporaneous verses addressed to Gawid, informing him of the preparations which would soon be undertaken in his honor, how much rice his different kinsmen would contribute, how many people would participate, and how many pigs would be slaughtered:

'Anung 'ari'ari'an
kang di waydi sabīhan
dūru ti 'gdulud 'aban
balaw lāmang kalim'an
kay pāsung dūru hanggan
kay bābuy 'imaw diman!

Oh little brother
I must say again
That more than fifty
will attend,
And that our feast will
never end!

In a few words set to a very simple melody she expressed the spirit with which the whole family looked forward to the harvest season.

During the third week after his birth, however, Gawid caught a slight head cold which was evidently accompanied by complications other than those observed by his parents. Two days later, on the seventeenth night of his short life, he died quite unexpectedly—while the rest of the family was asleep.

Maling had seen death before. She knew only too well what would happen that morning when she woke me with the sad news. Her father would cut a digging stick and sufficient bamboo poles for the grave mats, while her mother would wash the baby and wrap it in cotton cloth and beads. Hanap would help her mother tie the corpse and carry it out through a hole in the wall on the eastern side of the room in which he died, while Maling herself would assemble some of the usual grave goods, including a small cooking pot, some rice, water, and vegetables in separate shell dishes, and a small betel basket with all essential ingredients —nuts, leaves, lime, and tobacco. Iyang would cry. Many rituals would be performed at the grave and the family would not be able to leave the settlement, even to visit their ripening grain fields for five days, lest all types of misfortune descend upon the already grief-stricken household.

However, there were no tears. While this was a very sad moment for a seven-year-old, Maling was well prepared to accept such events realistically. Her voice reflected sincere disappointment, but, with characteristic optimism, she added that perhaps her mother's next baby would also be a son. As we went to join the other members of her family, she said succinctly, "*mahal māna ti magkabalākih*" (it would be nice to have the same number of both boy and girl children).

This, then, was Maling as I knew her in 1953. Four years later, in the summer of 1957, I returned to the small Yagaw hamlet where she and her family were living. The Maling who greeted me in the houseyard had the same thoughtful eyes and modest smile but she stood at least a head taller than when I had last seen her. Her black hair, still held in place by a beaded band, now fell gracefully down her back to the top folds of her sarong. Her very short blouse was beginning to flare out slightly in front, and she had tightened her corsetlike rattan pocket belt about her otherwise bare midriff in an obvious attempt to accentuate her fast developing wasp-waisted ("ant-waisted" in Hanunóo) figure. And straddled on her now shapely hips was a new member of the family.

This particular pose was to become a familiar one. From early morning until shortly after the evening meal, Maling's time was almost entirely taken up in caring for her younger siblings. She was unassisted by Hanap, who had graduated from this type of surrogate motherhood several years before, and who, in fact after a long series of courtships, was about to leave the immediate family circle to establish one of her own. Iyang of course was still too young to be entrusted with such baby tending duties. And Sukub, except for the feeding and bathing of the youngest child, devoted most of her time to food-getting activities and heavy household chores.

Maling's two young charges were both boys. In 1954, within a year after the death of Gawid, Panday happily took a year-old orphaned baby (and distant cousin) as a foster son. Sukub nursed the infant whose name was Bilug, and Maling soon had the task of caring for him most of the time. When Bilug's mother's bones were ritually exhumed the following dry season, Maling proudly carried him at her side to the grave site several kilometers away. Then, in 1956, Sukub gave birth to a son of her own, Tabul, who immediately became the focus of the whole family's attention. After the first few months, and except for nursing and bathing, Tabul became Maling's main responsibility.

The constant care of two small children in a Hanunóo hamlet is by no means an uneventful or easy task. There are goats, pigs, chickens, cows, dogs, monkeys, and occasionally millipedes, lizards, snakes, and insects for them to watch, play with, or be harmed by. Flat areas being nonexistent on the eastern slopes of Mt. Yagaw, the houseyard itself is usually a steep incline down which a child may slide, tumble, or slip; and the fact that the raised verandas are frequently unrailed does not lessen the danger of falling. When one notes further that favorite playthings, even for a two-year-old, include such weapons as keen-edged meat knives and fire-hardened bamboo pokers, it is rather remarkable that Maling showed practically no outward signs of fatigue, impatience, or discontent with her lot. On the other hand, she seemed quite indifferent to the fact that her mother was again pregnant. And once I heard her say that when she got married she really wouldn't care if she didn't have any children at all!

Though her former enthusiasm for baby boys had waned, at least temporarily, her interest in older ones was rapidly taking its place. Soon she would become a full-fledged, marriageable young maiden, a status which is the acme of female social existence among the Hanunóo. With this change would come many new privileges and opportunities. Maling, as Hanap before her, would hand over what child care duties remained to her younger sister Iyang, set up living quarters in an adjacent but separate pile dwelling, and, for several—perhaps five or six—years, lead a relatively independent life dominated by the direct but intricate local patterns of courtship ending in pregnancy, or marriage, or both.

Maling was well along in preparing herself for the new role she would be playing. In addition to dressing in a more meticulous manner, she had begun to oil her hair regularly, to trim her eyebrows, and to bind her wrists and ankles with fine red beads. Hanap had given her several decorative tortoise shell combs and a round mirror small enough to be carried in her pocket belt. Whenever her father went to Alyun, she would ask him to dig fresh vetiver roots for her to use as a sachet to keep with her sleeping blanket and extra clothes. Many of these practices she had started years before, but refinements in them had been added more recently by virtue of close observation of Hanap's behavior.

She had also begun to acquire many of the domestic skills that Hanunóo women are expected to learn. During the late morning hours when the children were napping, and by the light of a pitch candle after they had fallen asleep exhausted from a busy day at play, Maling could often be seen weaving a small betel basket, spinning cotton, or repairing a torn blouse. In this way, during the past four years, Maling had found time to learn many of the steps of basket and mat weaving, of producing homespun yarn, and of cooking native dishes. She still was not skilled in tailoring and embroidery, nor could she yet set up a cloth loom by herself.

Maling had learned to conduct herself in a more reserved manner in public, to initiate conversation with male guests only when asking for betel leaf or areca nut, and to communicate simple messages effectively with a minimum of facial gesture. All phases of betel exchange etiquette, which I had first seen her practice with mock chews or red sugar cane four years before, were now perfected. She had become quite versatile with the bamboo jew's-harp and had already learned the rudiments of nose flute playing from her mother and Aunt Agum.

To go with these instrumental skills, however, Maling knew she would need to build up as large a repertoire as possible of chanted verses which form the basis for most serenading and courting activities. While, like all Hanunóo children, she could already sing some *'ambāhan* songs, she also knew that to memorize enough appropriate verses to participate successfully in extended repartée, it would be very helpful if she could record new lyrics solicited from her close relatives in some semi-permanent form. Hence, about the time I arrived, she was attempting to learn the Hanunóo syllabary.

Inasmuch as Maling's newly acquired reticence in talking openly with men outside the immediate family did not extend to me, I was able to observe and discuss with her at great length the details of these various preparations. The manner in which she learned to read and write, for example, afforded an intimate picture of how she managed to acquire this bit of useful but specialized knowledge without any formalized course or tutor.

From previous visits to the Hanunóo, I knew that their Indic-derived syllabary of forty-eight characters functioned primarily as a vehicle of amorous and often poetic communication, and not as a means of historical, religious, or legal documentation. There are, in fact, no permanent records in this script, the component symbols of which are scratched into the hard but perishable outer surface of bamboo with a sharp steel knife. But what of the actual process of learning how to use this script which is never arranged in an "alphabetic" order or formally taught?

One morning after she had shaped toy animals from a half cylinder of green banana sheathing for Tabul and Bilug, Maling grasped the tip of her small knife blade between her thumb and forefinger and began pushing it across one of the flooring slats with her other hand so that a series of lightly engraved marks were produced. In reply to my asking her what she was doing, Maling said, "Nothing, just scribbling," and left quickly to stop Tabul from twisting the tail off Bilug's "carabao." She had seemed a bit embarrassed by my question, so I did not press the matter at that time. But later, when I had a chance to examine her "scribbling," I found half a dozen clearly inscribed syllabic characters among what apparently were a good many false starts and scratch-out erasures. That night she admitted that she didn't know what all the characters she had written stood for; she had simply copied them from her mother's tobacco tube. Yet she seemed quite interested in learning and said she would get Hanap to read some of the *'ambāhan* their father had written on their lime containers so that she could memorize the words and compare them with characters.

A few weeks later, while her mother was bathing Tabul, Maling came to where I was typing and began to inscribe something along the edge of my large bamboo desk. From the halting way she was singing to herself, it was obvious that she was trying to write down the words:

kang ma-nuk sa bid-la-wan	My dear bidlawan bird,
nu ka-'in-da ma-'u-ran	In a storm like this
pī-san dap ti hu-ru-nan	We are perched together,
nu may...	But when...

Assuming that she had now learned to use some of the characters adequately, I gave her a simple "dictation test" covering the whole range of syllable types. After every word I paused while Maling inscribed the characters deliberately or told me she didn't yet know them. At the end, she had written eighteen characters correctly. These represented syllables of high frequency in simple conversation and children's *'ambāhan*, and included those symbols necessary to sign her own name.

At six to eight week intervals thereafter I made additional checks to note Maling's progress. Each time she had learned seven or eight new characters, until she had mastered all but those representing the five or six rarest syllable types in the language. By that time she had become quite skilled in rapid transcription, and could and did read almost any verse she could find. Inside of six months, and without giving up any of her family duties she had all but completed the technical training she would need to record and read innumerable songs and letters for the rest of her life. No one person had provided her with more than a fraction of the reading materials she had studied, although Hanap, who at this stage spent a good many leisure hours practicing *'ambāhan*, was most frequently consulted.

Although Maling's ability to read and write will probably prove to be very useful, it will not introduce her to any worlds beyond that which she can see from Mt. Yagaw. She has remained close to home all her life and with Hanunóo marriage residence rules as they stand, her future husband will undoubtedly help her set up a new household in Parina or in whatever nearby hamlet her parents are living at the time. He will probably be a distant cousin from one of the other Hanunóo regions near Mt. Yagaw. Several young men of this description have already begun to visit Parina rather frequently. Ostensibly these visits are for medicines or bolo handles, but no one in Parina is deceived.

JOHN ADAIR

Problems of a Pueblo ex-G.I.

John Adair teaches anthropology at San Francisco State College. His main research interest has been in the Indians of the Southwestern United States. He is the author of *Navaho Silversmiths*, among other works; and, with Evon Vogt, he has done a comparative study of Navaho and Zuni veterans.

Soon after arriving at the pueblo, I heard that Marcus Tafoya would make a good informant. He was a veteran of World War II, about 30 years of age, and married into a family prominent in the religious life of his pueblo. His wife belonged to a clan that "owned" many religious offices, including one of the high-priesthoods of the village.

With this tip about Marcus, I approached the house of his wife, Maud Arviso. It was an imposing one near the center of the village, built of morticed stone with the new style gabled roof and front porch. Venetian blinds at the windows gave the place a look of prosperity in contrast to the mud-plastered, flat-roofed houses next door.

A woman about 22 years old, whom I judged to be his wife, greeted me at the door.

"Come in and have a seat," she said in perfect English.

"Is Marcus here?" I asked as I sat down on an elaborate over-stuffed chair.

"No, he has gone to the store, but he will be right back. What do you want?"

Her boldness in meeting strangers set her apart from other Pueblo women I had met; however, her manner was quite in harmony with her house—in both there was a spirit of revolt, yet not so complete that the new fully replaced the old. On one side of the fireplace was a radio; resting on the far side of the mantle was a bowl of sacred corn meal. As my eyes roamed around the room, I spotted other evidences of Pueblo

---

John Adair, "A Pueblo G.I.," from Joseph B. Casagrande (ed.), *In the Company of Man*, pp. 101–118.

tradition: a cradleboard; a house-blessing fetish, tied to a ceiling beam; and out beyond, in the kitchen alongside the enameled gas range, a metate and mano. The traditional was there all right, but in this house the modern veneer was more blatant than in most.

"I have been talking to veterans here in the village, and I understand he is one," I answered.

She asked me to have some coffee while I waited, and as I drank, she sat down and we continued to talk.

"Where was I from? What was I doing? How long did I intend to stay? Had I got permission from the Governor to work in the pueblo?" These questions and a dozen others came pouring out. I was as noncommittal as I could be and still satisfy her curiosity. Then quite abruptly she asked, "Are you an anthropologist?"

"Yes, I'm a student from the University," I confessed.

"Do you know ———? He was in the village some years ago."

It was just as well that I answered "No," for she went on: "I never saw what he wrote, but it couldn't be any good. He worked with ———," and she named a bitter rival on the other side of the village who had befriended and worked with anthropologists.

I began to squirm in my chair. Would her husband ever come, I wondered. But with each lull in the conversation, Maud picked it up once more and engaged my attention. She was taking no chances on her husband losing out on informant's fees.

Finally, Marcus arrived, groceries in hand. He was not as short or stocky as most of the young Pueblo men, and a fineness of features gave him a Navaho look. He wore bluejeans, work shoes, and a G.I. shirt—like many of the veterans in the pueblo.

I repeated some of what I had already told his wife and added, "I would like to know how the veterans are getting on in the village, what kinds of jobs they have, and how it seems to be home after those years away in the service."

"I see you are wearing your sun-tans," he said. "At first I thought you were a recruiting sergeant here to sign me up for another hitch."

We both laughed. That led to our obliquely sounding each other out. In contrast to his wife, Marcus was almost bashful. As she was preparing supper, we each found out where the other had been in the service, for how long, and when discharged. Marcus, I learned, got out eighteen months ago. But as members of the family gathered for the evening meal, I decided to wait until another time to continue the interview. It was with some misgivings that I asked if I could see him on the next day. Other veterans had said "Yes," but hadn't shown up.

Marcus was there at the appointed time on the following day. After further exchange of war experiences, I asked him if he would be willing to take a test I was giving the veterans. He was too embarrassed to say "No," and not ready with an excuse, so he lamely said "Yes," and we sat down at a table in the back room.

The test was one of the projective type, the well-known Thematic Apperception Test. As we looked at the pictures and I asked him to tell me about each, I sensed an uneasiness even before he spoke.

"What am I supposed to say now? I'm not sure I know how to answer this one."

My explanation that there was no correct answer was not reassuring.

"I'm just a dumb Indian. I don't know all that stuff. You should go see Joe Mirabal. He'll give you the right answers. He's studying at the University."

I put the test back in its folder and there followed, much to my surprise, another barrage of questions. "Where was I staying in the pueblo? Did I live right in the house with the family?" And Maud, who had come in from time to time to see how we were doing, joined in.

"How much do they charge you for that room? For your meals? Do they give you enough to eat?" she asked.

"They are real stingy," she added. "At our last fiesta they hardly fed their guests a thing, and look at all the sheep they own."

After a brief pause, she continued, "You should have come here first. We wouldn't have charged you so much. My sister has a house with a couple of spare rooms. I am sure she would have been glad to rent them to you."

I told her I wished I had done so, and then switched back to Marcus and asked him if I could talk to him again another time. Before he answered, he glanced up at Maud and I knew by the set expression on her face that he could not have said "No." When I went out of the house to my car, Marcus followed. I told him I wanted to pay him for his time.

"You don't owe me a thing. I flunked that test," he said.

It didn't go so well in the household where I was staying. The annual *Indian Drums* tourist attraction at one of the towns on the highway had just closed. A few days later I learned that a rumor was going around the village that I had written a piece in the special edition of the local newspaper about the sacred clowns of the pueblo. The article was one from the paper's files based on an ethnologist's account of seventy years back. This they took out every few years and refurbished for a new crop of tourists.

As time passed, I learned that one of the men of the house where I was living had entered my room during my absence and looked through the notes which I had been careful to hide under the mattress. (I was becoming as secretive and suspicious as the Indians themselves.) There he had run across the native name for these clowns in a life history I was taking of one of the veterans.

Needless to say, this discovery didn't help me in my relations with my landlord or his veteran sons. I knew that they were looking for an excuse to be rid of me as they had begun to feel I was bringing shame to their house. Since my family was joining me in the pueblo, I needed larger quarters and this provided the "out" both my landlord and I were looking for.

The house Maud had mentioned would serve our needs if it were fixed up a bit, and when I approached her sister about the matter she was pleased at the prospect. We entered as careful a set of business transactions as any concierge with a promising tenant. These included an agreement that I would purchase all of our firewood from the men in her family.

A good share of the work fixing up the old house fell to Marcus and I assisted him in various ways. But I was of greatest use in driving him to town for supplies. As we drove along, we fell to talking about days in the service. We both had been in the Air Corps.

"I felt free as a bird when I was in the army," he said. "For the first time in my life, I could do just what I pleased. There was no one snooping into my business, no one gossiping about me. It sure felt good."

"Did your buddies from other parts of the country feel the same way?"

"Hell, no," he replied. "They did nothing but bitch all the time. There wasn't anything good about it—the food, the drills, inspection, it was all p—s poor according to them. But for me, it was sure a welcome change.

"Just before I went into the service, I decided the hell with it. I might just as well have some fun before I left. I didn't care what the people in the village would say after I left. I was going to be gone for a long time. Maybe I wouldn't even get home again.

"So I got hold of a case of wine and stayed drunk for two weeks. Me and some of the other fellows sure had fun with the girls. Shacked-up just about every night. We sure left plenty of gossip behind us when we did leave."

Maud and Marcus were not married until after the war. He had courted her some years earlier but she had married another fellow and he turned to another girl. However, Maud was still interested in Marcus, and wrote to him when he was in service camp.

"She got my address from my younger brother," Marcus said. "We wrote back and forth and those letters got hotter and hotter. Then one day her husband went to the Post Office and opened one of those letters. They busted up in 1943."

"Why?" I asked.

"He drank too much and was lazy," Marcus replied.

After several such talks, I asked Marcus if he would tell me the story of his life, saying that I could better tell how he felt about the village and his army life if I knew more about his family, his boyhood, his schooling, and the like.

His first reaction was like the time I gave him the test. I could tell before he replied that he didn't want to do so, yet he didn't want to turn me down. Finally, he agreed but only after I promised that we would work at my house and at night.

"If I were to come over here in the daytime, or if people saw us talking at my house, they would say that you were writing another piece for that paper on the religion of my people," he said with a nervous laugh. "Those old people don't know that there aren't any secrets left. All of that stuff was sold long ago," he added.

I agreed with him but said, "I know, but let's not add to the gossip. There are enough rumors going around about me as it is."

"And what about me," he said. "Already the people call me '*newista.*' "

"What's that?" I asked.

"White-lover," he replied.

Marcus was very self-conscious as he started to tell me of his life, and I was never sure he wouldn't find an excuse for breaking off. With each episode he would ask, "Is that the sort of thing you want me to tell you?"

The best reassurance I could give him was to ask that he tell me more. It was not long before he was back to his boyhood, living it over and enjoying the telling of it.

But these early years were recalled in a rather matter-of-fact way—as if that life was so foreign to me that sharing it was futile. It was easier to talk as we had on those trips to town about common experiences in the service. Even his initiation into the tribal dance cult was told stiffly, and in the second person, as if he were summarizing what he had read in some ethnologist's monograph rather than telling me about what had happened to him. The excitement he must have felt, the drama, the brilliantly costumed dancers, these were all omitted from his flat account:

"Now the dancers get in line in the middle of the plaza. They take the clothes off you and put on only two blankets with the canvas covering; this time you are on the back of your guardian again. They all go through, pass the line of dancers, each hits you four times now, this time you could feel the pain. Some boys cry for help. The people laugh."

But as the story of his life progressed, Marcus became more personally involved and that other person he was talking about eventually became him.

He told of his life at school, of fights with the other boys on the playground, and always with special interest he related the summer adventures at the ranch where his family lived, ten miles or more from the pueblo.

Every year when the school ends I went home to the family ranch. The same work each year, nothing new. One day, me and Robert was going through a pine forest, the rain really poured on us, we had to stop. We were riding horseback. Lightning almost struck us, it struck a pine tree about fifteen feet away. The horses kicked and wheeled. We smelled that lightning odor so knowing the Indian superstition we hurried home, on one horse, the other one ran away when I let loose the reins.

My father was out in the corral, and the first thing he asked me was if I was hurt. He thought the horse threw me off. We told him what happened and he didn't let us go in the house. He told us to stay outdoors. It was still raining then. We had to stay outside when he went out to the field to look for them black young beetles, stink-bugs, I think you call them. When he came back, he told us to strip down our clothes, let the rain wash us down. Then he told my mother to make tortillas half-done, also the meat half cooked. He put the black beetles in between the meat and between the tortillas. Before we ate he took us down to the small stream, it was one of those made by the rain. We bathed in there from head to toe and we went up to the house and we ate those stink-bug sandwiches. Boy they tasted bitter. Like chili, they were hot. He picked up some of that stuff, the twigs that come with the flood, made some prayer, and made a motion around in the air and threw the twigs away. After we ate then he let us into the house.

That summer there was an eagle, the same eagle that has his nest about two miles from our place. My dad and I were after that eagle, so one day, we went out to see if its young were ready to fly. There were two of them, she had her nest on top of the highest steep cliff. It was about four times as high as the highest pine tree. I made a strong sling shot, but the pebbles didn't reach. I tried to scare them down. There was a way of going up the west side. But when you get on top of the mesa, you see that tall monument-like cliff is separated from the mesa by a crevasse that is about 50 feet deep. A long time ago a Navaho tried to get across that 50-foot crevasse; he only climbed half way and he fell backwards. So from that time on no one tried to get across.

My father had a .38 revolver so the next day we took it with us. He shot about two feet away from that nest, until one of the young ones got scared and flew down. We watched her till she disappeared among the pine trees. We followed and searched about an hour before we found her. She flew when we got near her, then next time she tried to fly she only jumped ten or fifteen feet at a time. We caught her when she got tired. We tied her around the legs with string and carried her home. We made a cage with a post in the middle for her roost. Whenever it rained hard I used to go out and get prairie dogs by running the water into their holes and I fed them to the eagle. Or else I go out early in the morning and late in the evenings after the rabbits. The people use eagle feathers for their prayer sticks. My father was one of the Snake Society—he was their boss, their chief, he used many feathers on the prayer sticks. So we took care of the eagle well.

School started too soon. When I have a lot to do during the summer when school opens I hate to come to the pueblo. That's when I was always shy when school opens, especially among girls. Everybody seems to be all dressed up. So I had to look my best. Usually I have sunburn 'cause I was always out of doors during the summer. My eighth year in school Teddy, my older brother, went away to the Sante Fe Indian School, so did Dolores, my sister. I and Bill, my younger brother, were the only ones that went to school in the village that year.

I seemed to have chased around quite a bit. I didn't stay home during the evenings mostly. I got a quick bite of supper 'cause there were always some of my friends calling me out. Mrs. Umberto who I stayed with that year didn't like me fooling around late at night so I used to sneak out. Their folks don't want them out late at night so that is why they whistle at each other to come out. When they want to call each other they just whistle, or else they have a special place to meet at a certain time. Nowadays they can visit each other at their homes. That time I went to talk to my girl she has to make a good excuse to go out at night. Sometimes girls have funny excuses, such as if there isn't any washing to do she thinks of things she is going to wash so she can throw the water out. Like handkerchiefs, or bandannas or dishtowels. Just so she could go out to throw the water out and meet her boy friend. Else she tell her folks that she wants to chop some wood. Sometimes if it is all right she will let her boy friend do the chopping.

Those days we had hard times visiting our girl friends at night. During cold days in the winter time the boys always have their blankets on, they are usually dark for the purpose you can't be seen in the night I suppose. That is still the style among the people. They also put a pretty bandanna around their head.

After three or four such sessions at our house, Marcus said he woul[d] have to break off his story as he had to take his turn herding at the famil[y] sheep camp. I asked him if we could continue his story out there.

"That would be good. I get awfully bored herding those dumb sheep. I follow along just like one of them. I hate it. But I'm sure you wouldn't like it either. You're used to city ways. It's rough out there, just camp style."

I arrived at the sheep camp several days later, threw my bedroll down beside some sagebrush, and set out walking over the rolling range lan[d] that stretched to the horizon on all sides. A few piñon trees scattered here and there made the sweep seem more immense. Far to the south I spotted Marcus following the sheep as they headed toward the watering tank marked by a windmill against the sky.

I approached, greeted Marcus, and helped him fix some sandwiches which we ate sitting under a juniper tree close by the ranch house.

"Gee, I'm glad to see you, John. It's sure lonely out here—worse than any guard duty I ever had."

"Well," I said, "it seems good to get away from the village and out to the open country. I guess I'm getting to be like one of your people. I imagine others are gossiping about me all the time."

"That's a sure sign if you really feel that way," Marcus replied.

"But that's not all," I said. "Worse than that—after hearing all those stories about witches that you told us at our house, my wife has been uneasy. She said she heard someone prowling around in that empty room next door. In fact, she didn't like to stay home alone with the children when I came out here." (This I said in complete honesty.)

"My wife is just the same way. She's scared to death of witches. She won't stay in the house alone when I'm gone. She takes the children and goes over to stay with relatives. All of us are the same way. We are constantly watching for those jealous people. Just the other day, my wife was in the trading post and she heard a woman boasting about what a good crop of fat lambs her family had this year. My wife told me it just sent the shivers up her spine to hear her talk like that, because standing right behind her was one of the biggest witches in the whole village."

We talked more about the witches as we got up and moved off, following the sheep.

"That's another thing I liked about being in the army. There were no witches over there. It felt good to be away from all these worries. But they came back again as soon as I returned home."

"Do the people have any way of getting rid of those witches?" I asked.

"No, that's the trouble," Marcus answered. "In the old days they did. They'd string them up from the ceiling beams by their elbows until they confessed or died—at least that's what my folks told me."

"And today?"

"Today the government won't let us do that so these witches just keep multiplying."

"What do you do to try and forget about them?" I asked.

"Well, getting away from the village helps. But even out here you're not completely safe. Those witches go after the sheep, too. Just last month we had a medicine man come out here to suck some stuff out of one of the sheep. It had been placed there by one of those people. We think we know who it was that did it."

The sheep were all bunched up now, browsing in a place where the grass was long and thick.

"I see you brought your paper along. We better start in again on my story, or we'll never finish," Marcus said. "Where were we when we stopped? Oh, I remember now. I had reached England with the troops.

"Another thing I thought was funny, all those English people rode around on those bicycles; and when I first saw that village with all those chimneys in those houses, all just alike in a row. This village was called Little Stockton, and it was about twelve miles to Bedford. Another thing, the sergeant got each of us English bicycles. We used to go out riding on the country roads. It surprised me, all those country roads were paved, no dirt roads. About those English workmen, I got a kick out of them. Every morning at ten o'clock, teatime in those old style jugs. They squatted on the cement and had tea. There is another one at two o'clock in the afternoon. The workmen have those black clothes with narrow pants. That seemed funny. Also those small autos, not streamlined. And they told us that it was only a wealthy person who could own one."

As Marcus continued his story, he became increasingly absorbed in the telling of it. I thought back to the first halting beginning of only a few weeks ago. Now he was the one who urged me on. Each time we were interrupted by sheep straying off from the flock, he brought us back with that same, "Let's get on with the story." These breaks seemed almost painful to him, as if he wanted to remain there in England for a while longer.

"Then I used to go to Winchester to meet this girl, this 15-year-old girl. I met her at a carnival in Bedford, all that way she and her folks came to the fair; they call it a fair, sort of carnival like. I was standing there watching the merry-go-round. She was pretty dizzy. I asked her to go on a ride. She said we could take rides only as long as her mother and grandmother were there. They were about to go home. She gave me her address, and took mine. She wrote me first, the first one I guess you would call an introduction letter—where she lived and so on. The next one told me to meet her at Winchester Station. I had a two-day pass, and when I got there a lot of people were waiting. I didn't recognize her until she came over. We got out of the station and walked through town, a couple of miles. First I thought we would have something to eat, fish and chips, that was their main dish, and brussel sprouts. Those hard leaves—I didn't like that stuff.

"Then we went to a show, a picture about the 8th Air Force. She knew I was in the Air Force and I guess she felt pretty proud of me. When we got out it was getting dark. I asked her if she could go to a pub. She said she was under age, but we went to the outskirts of town where they let her in one pub. We had ale and light beer, got her dizzy, made me dizzy too.

I drank twice as much as she did. Then I said, 'I guess I'd better go home.' She suggested that I take her home on the ten o'clock train to her village five miles away. There were only three cars attached to that locomotive, took about half an hour for that five miles. Had the whole car to ourselves. At first I was very bashful towards her. I didn't get to feel her that time, but I did later at the station. She suggested I stay at Mrs. Hicks' that night. She said she could easily put me up. Mrs. Hicks' place was just like any farm cottage, grass roof, an old time cottage. Walls were green with moss. Those old English style furniture, fireplace. The bed was skreeky. She gave me tea before I went to bed. The next morning early she brought me breakfast in bed. It sure felt funny. I felt funny. I felt rotten that morning with a hangover and here she brings that breakfast on a big tray. But I enjoyed the fresh eggs she gave me. That night before she had said, 'What time are you going to get knocked up?' I said, 'What?' I only knew the other meaning."

"Did that girl or the other ones you dated in England know that you were an American Indian?" I asked.

"I used to tell them I was an Indian, but they wouldn't believe it."

"Why not?"

"They said I was too light to be an Indian. You know those Negroes were over there in England. They got there before we did and they told all those girls that *they* were Indians."

For some while now we had been herding the sheep back toward the corral. As Marcus drove them in and secured them for the night, I sat down and glanced over what I had been writing. This was a curious experience. Marcus, the Indian, was an eager informant on a way of life other than his own. Listening to his experiences in England was like hearing another anthropologist fresh home from the field. The remote was vivid and compelling. The immediate had not yet come back into focus.

Marcus told his story with such relish that I thought he would never end. He piled incident upon incident; he recounted the most minute details of barracks life and gave day by day accounts of each furlough he took.

He told me of a flight in a plane over Europe after hostilities ceased:

"We hit Aachen too, it was on the side of a hill, on the edge of a forest, all cut to pieces, skeletons of buildings, not a soul there, just long tracks passing. Boy, that place was studded with bomb craters, trenches along the hills. I wasn't air sick, but I had a hangover that day and got sleepy; after we passed Aachen I fell asleep. This friend of mine woke me up. He said we were coming to Cologne. We went over the Rhine River, real muddy water. I had seen pictures of that city, this was just like seeing a newsreel, all those ruins, on one side that cathedral—not a scratch on it, and railroad tracks with a lot of bomb craters around them. The people were probably burning a lot of that stuff that was crumbled. The bridge, we could see it plainly, broken in half. Then to Coblenz with the bridge in the water. Then from Cologne we went back along the Rhine. There were some other towns, I forget the names. I was feeling bad and dozed off for half an hour.

"Then we went over to Frankfurt; this is a big city—lots of factories. They told us about what the cities manufactured, why they bombed them. From there we headed for Münster where they built planes, and there was a shell industry there. That's where we turned around and came back to the Rhine; oh yes, we were along Hitler's superhighway. We could see the Alps off in the distance—it was a clear day. Somewhere along there we came to three or four German air fields. Saw a lot of crashed planes and B-17's broken up, crashed. All the runways full of bomb craters. We hit, what's the name of that famous concentration camp? We could see long grey buildings with an iron fence around, people milling around in there. Then we went back to Aachen again and flew back; got back around 6:30. That was a long day's trip."

We talked now as close friends and he told of his life in England as he might to a barracks mate, not to an anthropologist with a projective test in hand. He concluded the story of his days in the army with an account of the trip back to the States and across the country to the Southwest.

"Next afternoon I took a bus to ———. It seemed to me like a little village, all those Indians around, it seemed sort of strange. I forget how I felt. I was hiding from those people from my village. I just hid in the shops."

"Why?" I asked.

"Because of gossip," he replied.

"What sort of gossip could it be?"

"I don't know, I didn't want them to know I just got back. There was that Red Cross on First Street where I checked my bag. There were a lot of Mexican G.I.'s around. So I thought I'd walk up the street, and there was Jim S., first one I met. Right away he wanted to take me along. He told me that Robert and Mother were in town.

"When I met Robert, he didn't care about that old superstition, he just came up and greeted me. But when I saw my mother she just said, 'Son, I am glad to see you after all this time away from home, but according to the superstition I am not supposed to touch you until you have had that ceremony for the returned warriors. You didn't have that one when you went away, but you better have this one now. Lots of the veterans have returned home and had that.' I thought that was sort of funny. I never knew about that one before. So we came to the village and that man came out to the bridge and said those prayers. After that she was able to greet me."

Marcus had participated in only a few of the group fertility rituals which play such an important part in the religious life of the pueblo. I had noted this as his story unfolded but did not directly question him until now.

"Do you believe that the dancers bring rain?" I asked.

"No, I don't. I think that is just a dance, that there is no power to bring the rain. Weather is weather. It isn't man-made," he replied.

And then later, he added, "I'm not a religious man."

That evening in the ranch house, we had some rum to drink and as time passed the anxieties that bothered me in the pueblo melted away. I had not realized how tense I had become as a result of living constantly under surveillance.

As we talked more, and drank more, my understanding of Marcus increased. I felt I had never before been in such close contact with an Indian. His deeply private beliefs about witchcraft and the powers of the medicine men were clearly revealed to me, as we sat by the campfire and talked.

That night, as I crawled into my sleeping bag, I had an exhilarating sense of having gained a profound new insight into the mind and heart of Marcus and through him into the quality of life in the pueblo. When I woke the next morning, all of it was lost. I could remember very little of what we had talked about. But I did recall that the night before I had said to myself, "Write this down. Keep a record of what Marcus is saying." I got out my paper and began to write as I sat there groggy in the intense early morning light. But there was nothing now to record. All had vanished except the memory of the intense excitement I had experienced. Even this was a hollow thing. My only consolation was the hope that Marcus, too, had forgotten and would not suffer regrets at his lack of reticence.

I left the sheep camp the next day and returned to the pueblo. That wasn't the last time I saw Marcus. We went over his whole life story again and I questioned him in detail about all he had told me. But the easy comradeship of the sheep camp was gone. As we resumed work at my house, the same tensions built up once more in me, and I am sure, in him as well.

We had returned to the atmosphere of anxiety that pervades life in the pueblo and touches all within its reach. Communicated in many ways—by rumors, whisperings, suspicion, envy, secretiveness, and in silent watchful demeanor—this basic Pueblo characteristic is both a strong governing influence on village life and a powerful defense against the outsider. It is by such means that they have preserved their way of life and protected the inner workings of their religion, its medicine and fertility cults, from alien scrutiny.

One day a few weeks later, I went over to the trading post. As I stood there waiting my turn, I saw Marcus with some friends on the other side of the store. I greeted him, but he did not respond in any way—he just looked right through me without a flicker of recognition. Only then did I fully understand what it meant to be a Pueblo veteran. I represented that other world which they had individually enjoyed, but which had to be collectively renounced in order to hold on to that which was theirs.

STEWART PECKHAM

A Southwestern archaeological site

Stewart Peckham is curator of archaeology at the Museum of New Mexico. He is the author of many reports and interpretive works dealing with Southwestern archaeology.

Introduction

A preliminary archaeological survey of U.S. Highway 260, about twelve niles south of Reserve, New Mexico, revealed the presence of an early :eramic (Pine Lawn Phase) site which would be destroyed during the ealignment and construction of the highway. A request for assistance in alvaging the site was submitted to the New Mexico State Highway)epartment, and in December 1956, a crew of two men was provided y the Project Engineer, Ray Polk. Additional assistance was gratefully eceived from the project contractor, G. I. Martin, of Albuquerque, New Mexico. Although shallow, the pit house excavated required a total f four days digging due to the extremely hard fill.

'he area

'he site excavated, LA 3337, is located in Catron County, New Mexico, nd is about 800 feet south of what is known locally as the Luna Junction -the intersection of U.S. Highway 260 and State Highway 12. About ne-half mile north of the Luna Junction Site is the SU Site excavated y the Chicago Natural History Museum during the late 1930's and arly 1940's (Martin, 1943; Martin, Rinaldo, and Kelly, 1940; Martin ad Rinaldo, 1947).

The Luna Junction Site is situated on a broad, low, flat-topped hill of uaternary alluvium which forms a divide between the drainages of

---

ewart Peckham, "The Luna Junction Site: An Early Pit House in the Pine awn Valley, New Mexico," *Highway Salvage Archaeology*, 4, 17 (Santa Fe: ew Mexico State Highway Department and the Museum of New Mexico, 63), 41–55. Copyright © 1963, Museum of New Mexico Press.

Starkweather Canyon, which flow north and east into the San Francisco River near Reserve, and the Leggett drainage, which flows south to join the San Francisco River thirteen miles below Reserve. The resultant valley is bounded on the east by the Saliz Mountains and on the west by the San Francisco Mountains.

Once an area of great volcanic activity, the Pine Lawn Valley is characterized by long outcrops of basalt, rhyolite, andesite, and tuff, which together with constituent nodules of glassy minerals provided prehistoric inhabitants with an inexhaustible supply of raw materials for stone implements.

Vegetation in the area consists primarily of western yellow pine, juniper, and oak, with short grasses occurring sporadically in the shallow gravelly soil and providing the principal cover in adjacent open meadows. Animal life in the area included: "mule deer, white-tailed deer, black bear, rabbits, tree squirrels, ground squirrels, chipmunks, prairie dogs, wood rats, turkeys, quails, and doves" (Martin, Rinaldo, and Antevs, 1949, p. 43).

The excavations

When first visited, the only surface indications at the Luna Junction Site were a few sherds of Alma Plain, stone chips, and a topsoil which was darker than that found farther away from the site. No depressions were present to indicate subsurface architecture, and it was only through trenching that the single pit house was found. Topsoil was generally only a few inches deep and was underlain by a sterile deposit of sticky, brown gumbo. When this clayey material was not encountered almost immedi ately in a test trench, a man-made feature of some sort was considered to have been found.

There were two principal types of fill in the pit house. Adjacent to th walls the fill was a mixture of gumbo and darker trashy soil which tended to cling tenaciously to a pick, shovel, or trowel. This mixture als occurred on and near the floor and was removed most easily with hammer and chisel. The upper fill in the central portion of the pit hous was a softer, less sticky soil darkened by charcoal and ash.

Potsherds were not particularly numerous in the upper fill, and it wa only on and near the floor that sherds and stone artifacts becam abundant. Floor features, other than post holes, were few and wer readily discerned through the contrasts, in color and texture, betwee fill and sterile soil.

Trenching outside the pit house entry uncovered more sherds an artifacts, but no other architectural features were found. Perhaps th previous construction of U.S. Highway 260 destroyed other structures, but a single unit site is equally possible.

Conclusions

The sole architectural feature of the Luna Junction Site was a shallow, nearly round pit house (Fig. 1) with a southeasterly oriented, short,

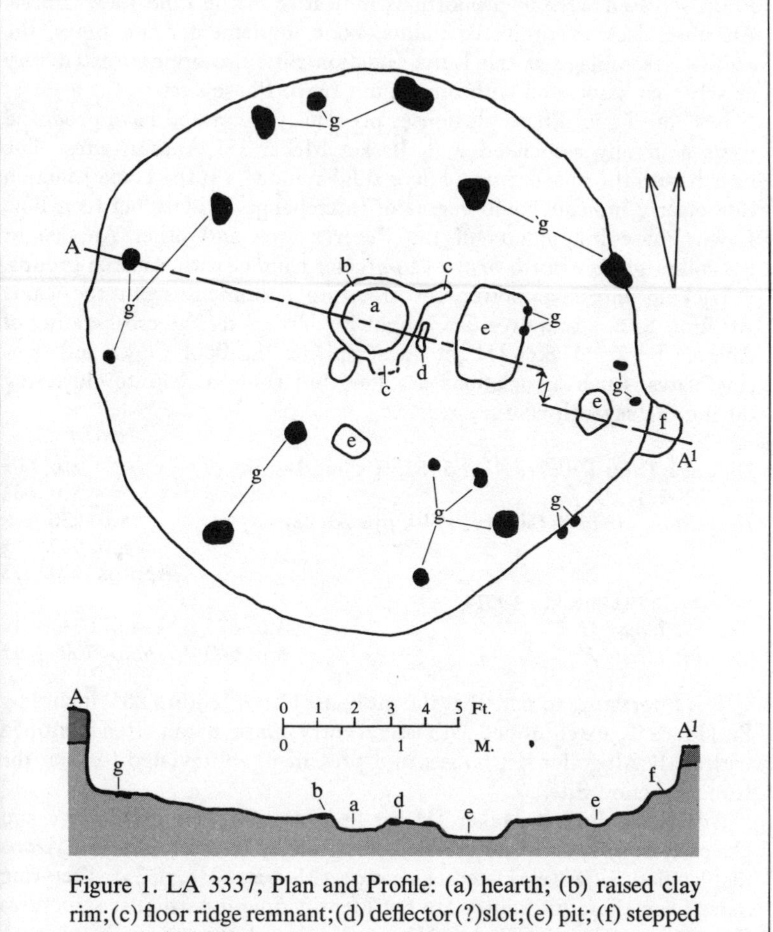

Figure 1. LA 3337, Plan and Profile: (a) hearth; (b) raised clay rim; (c) floor ridge remnant; (d) deflector(?)slot; (e) pit; (f) stepped entry; (g) posthole.

stepped entry. Depending on viewpoint, the primary roof support system was either four-post or five-post with a tendency toward placement of roof posts near the perimeter of the room. Subfloor pits, common and conspicuous at the nearby SU Site, were few and shallow at the Luna Junction Site. Most prominent and distinctive was the circular hearth whose raised clay rim and rudimentary raised floor ridges showed marked resemblance to similar features associated with Anasazi pit houses much farther north.

The three pottery types present: Alma Plain, Alma Rough, and San Francisco Red were in proportions indicative of the Pine Lawn Phase. Although lacking projectile points, bone implements, and pipes, the artifact assemblage at the Luna Junction Site also approximated very closely that associated with other Pine Lawn Phase sites in the area.

No Pine Lawn Phase pit houses previously excavated have produced traits generally associated with Basket Maker III Anasazi sites. The hearth with the raised rim and floor ridge remnants at the Luna Junction Site clearly indicate some degree of interchange of ideas between Pine Lawn Phase inhabitants of the Reserve area and other Anasazi or Mogollon groups north or west in greater contact with Anasazi groups.

Lacking intrusive pottery or tree-ring specimens from the Luna Junction Site, a tentative date might be derived by the cross-dating of Anasazi Basket Maker III pit houses possessing floor ridges and tree-ring dates. Such associations are few, but show a definite clustering during the seventh century A.D.

Durango Talus Village, Area 5 (Morris and Burgh, 1954, pp. 21–23)	A.D. 605 A.D. 631
Bear Ruin, House 1 (Haury, 1940, pp. 20–22)	A.D. 636 + x A.D. 667 + x Approx. A.D. 675
Jeddito 264 (Daifuku, 1961)	
Pit House B	A.D. 673 ± 1–A.D. 694 ± 1
Pit House F	A.D. 660 ± 1–A.D. 700 ± 15

It is interesting to note that the pit houses from Jeddito 264, including Pit House C, are equipped with lateral entry ramps, a trait often identified with early Mogollon pit houses and present in abbreviated form at the Luna Junction Site.

Additional Basket Maker III pit houses at Broken Flute Cave and Caves 1, 2, 6, 7, and 8 in the Red Rock Valley in northeastern Arizona display floor ridges and lateral entrances (Morris, 1936, p. 35). Tree-ring dates from these pit houses are not identified with particular structures (Douglass, 1936, p. 33), but show a similar clustering in the seventh century A.D. Other Basket Maker III dates from these cave sites extend backward to the fifth and sixth centuries as well, so that radial floor ridges and lateral entries may pre-date the better-established A.D. 600–700 time range for these features.

Admittedly, cross-dating on the basis of an architectural feature should be viewed with considerable caution. However, radial floor ridges are certainly more distinctive than post holes, floor pits, and fireplaces, and are not likely to have developed in widely separated areas independently. In this instance, perhaps, more weight can be placed on this chronologically unique feature.

If we accept a seventh-century date as valid for LA 3337, it raises the question of the upper termination date for the Pine Lawn Phase. Wheat (1955, p. 185) places the end of this phase at circa A.D. 600, yet the ceramic and stone artifact assemblage of the possibly later Luna Junction pit house is characteristic of the Pine Lawn Phase. The alternative is to assign the Luna Junction Site to the Georgetown Phase, whose presence in the Pine Lawn Valley has not been wholeheartedly accepted since its distinguishing traits as described for Mogollon Village and Harris Site (Haury, 1936, Fig. 30) are not consistently duplicated in the Reserve Area (Martin and Rinaldo, 1950a, pp. 268, 358, 381).

The Georgetown Phase in the Pine Lawn Valley has been characterized ceramically as "marked by the scarcity of Alma Rough and textured pottery and a preponderance of Alma Plain" (Martin and Rinaldo, 1950a, p. 375). If such is the case, then the ceramics at Luna Junction do not correspond, since textured pottery is completely absent, and we must look elsewhere for a cultural-chronological pigeonhole for the site. One solution would be to revise upward the end date for the Pine Lawn Phase by as much as fifty to seventy-five years to A.D. 650–675, which would not conflict with established dates for the succeeding San Francisco Phase (post-A.D. 700) (Smiley, 1951, p. 21). Another alternative would be to assign a pre-A.D. 600 date to the Luna Junction Site using as a basis the possible earlier presence of floor ridges and lateral entries in the Red Rock Valley.

Pottery

Only three pottery types were found at the Luna Junction Site: Alma Rough, a smoothed but not polished brown pottery; Alma Plain, a polished, presumed descendant, and, for a while, companion of Alma Rough; and San Francisco Red, a brown pottery having a fired-on, but often fugitive, pinkish red slip. Separated, but not constituting a pottery type, were those sherds whose surfaces were too weathered to classify into the above three types. No sherds were observed to have been textured by neck-banding or scoring, and there was no evidence of smudging of vessel interiors.

Of the sherds found on the floor of the pit house, over 71 per cent were Alma Plain. Alma Rough sherds constituted almost 21 per cent of the floor sherd total, San Francisco Red about 6 per cent, and Indeterminate Alma slightly more than 1 per cent. The percentages of these pottery types lie well within the limits of the ceramic makeup of the Pine Lawn Phase as described by Paul S. Martin (1943, pp. 120–121). Compared with the pottery seriation assembled by the Chicago Natural History Museum (Martin, Rinaldo, and Antevs, 1949, pp. 192–193), the sherd percentages from the Luna Junction Site seem to fit best near the middle of the Pine Lawn Phase seriation (between Pit House O and Pit House G).

Pottery Summary

Type	*Fill*	*Floor*	*Room total*	*Trenches and surface*	*Site total*	*Per cent*
Alma Plain	139	572	711	35	746	65.96%
Alma Rough	66	167	233	11	244	21.57
San Francisco Red	57	50	107	6	113	9.99
Indeterminate Alma	3	12	15	13	28	2.48
Totals	265	801	1066	65	1131	100.00%

Other artifacts

Basalt, andesite, and tuff were used for most grinding and hammering implements at the Luna Junction Site. Rhyolite, chert, quartzite, and chalcedony were the most common materials used for cutting and scraping tools. Most of the abrading stones and full-grooved mauls were made of an extremely coarse, fossiliferous, calcareous sandstone which is found only at two small outcrops northwest of Luna, New Mexico.

Projectile points, bone implements, and pipes were absent from the array of artifacts at the Luna Junction Site, although relatively common at the nearby SU Site. It is possible that these items were missed during the excavations, but it is more likely that they occur more frequently where a pit house village and its associated sample of artifacts are more extensive.

Although only slightly more than one-third of the artifacts recovered were on the floor of the pit house, the purity of the ceramic sample indicates a similar lack of contamination among other artifacts. Except for the above-mentioned absences, the artifacts resemble, both in type and material, Pine Lawn Phase assemblages from the SU Site, the Promontory Site, and Three Pines Pueblo (Martin, Rinaldo, and Kelly, 1940; Martin, 1943; Martin and Rinaldo, 1947; Martin, Rinaldo, and Antevs, 1949; Martin and Rinaldo, 1950b).

Artifact Summary

Artifacts	*Fill*	*Floor*	*Surface and trenches*	*Site total*
Metates	—	1	—	1
Manos	1	2	2	5
Metate-like stones	—	1	—	1
Abrading stones	—	6	2	8
Hammerstones	8	12	6	26
Cores	3	1	—	4
Full-grooved mauls	—	2	1	3
Choppers	4	1	1	6
Knives	11	—	4	15
Scrapers	13	1	7	21
Scraper-gravers	2	—	—	2
Gravers	2	1	—	3
Polishing stones	—	1	—	1
Stone bowls	—	2	—	2
Pestles	—	1	—	1
Worked slabs	—	2	—	2
Antler polishers	—	2	—	2
Crystals	1	—	—	1
Pottery bowls	—	1	—	1
Totals	45	37	23	105

METATES (1) Natural slab with grinding surfaces on both sides, each occupying approximately three-fifths of the total available surface. One grinding surface basin shape and the other concave lengthwise and relatively flat widthwise. Length, 21.5 inches; width, 8.9 inches; thickness, 3.1 inches. Trachyte.

MANOS (5) *a.* Oval with a single grinding surface convex lengthwise and crosswise. Lengths, 5.5 and 5.7 inches; widths, 4.3 and 4.7 inches;

thicknesses, 2.9 and 1.6 inches, respectively. Trachyte and andesite. (2). *b.* Rectangular with rounded sides and ends and a single grinding surface convex both ways. Lengths, 6.8 and 7.8 inches; widths, 4.4 and 4.7 inches; thicknesses, 1.2 and 1.6 inches, respectively. Fragment thickness, 1.6 inches. Basalt and andesite. (3).

METATE-LIKE STONES (1) Small slab with single grinding surface concave lengthwise and crosswise. Length, 9.6 inches; width, 5.6 inches; thickness, 2.6 inches. Trachyte.

ABRADING STONES (8) Irregular gritty stones having one or more flat use surfaces. Length, 2.2 to 5.0 inches; width, 2.0 to 3.9 inches; thickness, 0.7 to 2.3 inches. Average: length, 4.0 inches; width, 3.1 inches; thickness, 1.6 inches. Calcareous sandstone, sandstone, tuff.

HAMMER STONES (26) Battered and pitted cobbles, pebbles, and nodules of stone. Length, 1.2 to 4.6 inches; width, 1.0 to 4.0 inches; thickness, 0.9 to 3.0 inches; weight, 0.88 to 41.51 ounces. Average: length, 2.8 inches; width, 2.2 inches; thickness, 1.8 inches; weight (bimodal), 0 to 10.58 ounces, average 5.75 ounces; over 17.54 ounces, average 27.19 ounces. Basalt, rhyolite, chert, quartzite, chalcedony, limestone.

CORES (4) Stones showing random removal of flakes with no further signs of use. Length, 1.4 to 2.9 inches; width, 1.3 to 2.4 inches; thickness, 0.8 to 1.8 inches; weight, 0.92 to 8.22 ounces. Average: length, 2.1 inches; width, 1.7 inches; thickness, 1.2 inches; weight, 3.77 ounces. Chert, chalcedony, basalt, quartzite.

FULL-GROOVED MAULS (3) Oval stones with rounded ends and having a shallow to deep groove around the middle. Lengths, 3.1, 5.4, and 5.5 inches; widths, 1.8, 3.1, and 3.3 inches; thicknesses, 1.4, 2.2, and 2.6 inches; weights, 5.89, 33.72, and 35.34 ounces. Calcareous sandstone, syenite.

CHOPPERS (6) Thick to moderately thin cores or cobbles having unifacial or bifacial chipping along one edge. Length, 1.8 to 4.1 inches; width, 1.3 to 2.8 inches; thickness, 0.7 to 2.4 inches. Average: length, 3.0 inches; width, 2.6 inches; thickness, 1.3 inches. Quartzite, rhyolite, basalt.

KNIVES (15) Thin random flakes with one or two nearly straight to slightly curved cutting edges showing unifacial or bifacial retouching.

Length, 1.1 to 3.2 inches; width, 0.6 to 1.7 inches; thickness, 0.1 to 0.7 inches. Average: length, 2.0 inches; width, 1.3 inches; thickness, 0.4 inches. Chert, quartzite, basalt, rhyolite.

SCRAPERS (21) Thin to thick random flakes with some unifacial retouching along one edge. Length, 0.8 to 2.4 inches; width, 0.6 to 1.9 inches; thickness, 0.1 to 0.8 inches. Average: length, 1.5 inches; width, 1.1 inches; thickness, 0.3 inches. Basalt, rhyolite, chert, quartzite, chalcedony.

SCRAPER-GRAVERS (2) Random flake scrapers with local retouching to produce a sharp projecting point. Lengths, 0.9 to 1.7 inches; widths, 0.7 to 0.6 inches; thicknesses, 0.3 to 0.3 inches, respectively. Chert, rhyolite.

GRAVERS (3) Random flakes with a sharp projecting point produced by local retouching. Lengths, 1.1, 1.4, and 1.1 inches; widths, 1.0, 1.2, and 0.7 inches; thicknesses, 0.2, 0.2, and 0.3 inches. Chert, rhyolite.

POLISHING STONES (1) Small pebble with polished facet; re-used as a hammerstone. Length, 2.4 inches; width, 2.1 inches; thickness, 0.7 inches. Basalt.

STONE BOWLS (2) Rough-shaped boulders with relatively smooth but pitted concave interior. Exterior dimensions: lengths, 7.1 and 9.6 inches; widths, 5.7 and 8.5 inches; thicknesses, 2.7 and 3.5 inches, respectively. Interior dimensions: lengths, 4.2 and 5.9 inches; widths, 3.0 and 5.9 inches; depths, 1.4 and 1.6 inches, respectively. Tuff, syenite.

PESTLES (1) Long tapering cylinder showing battering at one end. Length, 5.9 inches; width, 2.6 inches; thickness, 2.0 inches. Syenite.

WORKED SLABS (2) Thick, irregular slabs showing pecking around circumference. Lengths, 7.3 and 9.8 inches; widths, 6.1 and 5.9 inches; thicknesses, 1.8 and 2.4 inches, respectively. Trachyte.

POLISHERS OR RUBBERS (2) Short sections of antler (deer) having one or more rounded and abraded edges. Length, 2.1 inches; width, 1.3 inches; thickness, 0.9 inches. One fragment.

CRYSTALS (1) Small quartz crystal showing much wear at each end and at junctures of facets. Length, 0.9 inches; width, 0.6 inches; thickness, 0.4 inches.

Discussion

In the Reserve area of New Mexico, the developmental unit which marks the earliest known simultaneous occurrence of architecture, ceramics, certain non-ceramic artifacts, and some implied socio-economic traits is called the Pine Lawn Phase. The catalog of traits of the Pine Lawn Phase is remarkably complex—so complex as to lead one to expect that an even earlier manifestation of architecture and ceramics may yet be found in, or not far from, the Reserve area.

Although defined primarily from material excavated in the Pine Lawn Valley, west of Reserve, the Pine Lawn Phase also has been recognized along the Tularosa Valley, north of Reserve, at Tularosa Cave (Martin, *et al.*, 1952) and at LA 2948 (Wendorf, 1956). Probably neither of these two sites do justice to the extent of the Pine Lawn Phase occupation of the Tularosa Valley, and it is likely that this locality, with its abundance of water and arable land was more receptive to settlement and cultivation than the comparatively marginal conditions of much of the Pine Lawn Valley. Presumably, later large sites and recent European settlement have obliterated or obscured other sites of the Pine Lawn and earlier phases in the Tularosa Valley.

The presence of maize, beans, and squash in pre-pottery levels at Tularosa Cave (Martin, *et al.*, 1952, p. 470) indicates the early existence of a sedentary way of life with the means for supporting a population greater than that which could occupy the available natural shelter (caves) in the area. From this we might deduce the presence of a number of nearby open sites having some form of pit house architecture. The Cochise dwelling near Wet Leggett Pueblo (Martin and Rinaldo, 1950b, pp. 430–431) is ample evidence of early architecture in the vicinity and indirectly suggests, by its distance from Tularosa Cave, an already scattered, even if small, population in the Reserve area. Lack of other examples prevents us from knowing whether or not Cochise architecture was undergoing change or remained relatively static. If we can use an example from another area, the Cave Creek Village of the San Simon Branch of the Mogollon (Sayles, 1945, pp. 5–14), a bare minimum in shelter prevailed in pre-pottery periods, and not until some time after the introduction of pottery did refinements in architecture begin.

Unless the lack of a distinctive ceremonial structure at Cave Creek Village indicates a closer relationship of that site to Hohokam cultural developments, we may also infer that the advent of the Mogollon Great Kiva postdates that of pottery. Although dated as earliest at the SU Site in the Pine Lawn Valley, Pit House A, a Great Kiva, not only is associated with pottery, but also reveals by its size, symmetry, and construction that it is neither the earliest of ceremonial structures nor early in terms of architectural developments in the Reserve area.

Pine Lawn Phase domiciliary architecture at the SU Site also shows sufficient standardization in method of entry, orientation, roof support systems, and the like to indicate that ancestral forms must exist. Although variability is prominent at the SU Site, the architectural consistencies in a well-established village with a communal, rather than family, oriented religious structure substantiate the postulation, based on a ceramic seriation, that there are sites and pit houses with pottery in the Reserve area that are earlier than at the SU Site (Martin, Rinaldo, and Antevs, 1949, p. 199). To the writer, these sites would assume characteristics that would distinguish them from both the Pine Lawn Phase and a preceding pre-pottery phase.

At this point it might be worthy to note the rather striking similarities between Pit House A at the SU Site and several of the so-called "ring" and "non-ring" structures of the Los Pinos Phase in the Navajo Reservoir area of north-central New Mexico (Eddy and Dickey, 1961, Figs. 9, 30, 45). The structures in the latter area usually have ante-chambers and a cobblestone pavement encircling the room, but they often exhibit bean-shape outline, lateral entry, central hearth, profusion of interior storage pits, and horizontal logs around the perimeter of the room. Although they contained no logs, the half-log-shape grooves in Pit House A were assumed to have once held them (Martin, Rinaldo, and Kelly, 1940, p. 14) and suggest that the use of a cribbed-log dome roof, like those indicated at Los Pinos Phase sites and the Durango Basket Maker II structures (Morris and Burgh, 1954, pp. 11, 15, 50), was an early, but soon abandoned, trait in Mogollon architecture. Peripheral floor grooves have also been noted at the Bear Ruin (Haury, 1940, pp. 28, 30) and the Bluff Site (Haury and Sayles, 1947, pp. 22, 24) in the Forest-dale Valley in east-central Arizona. A remote possibility exists that the log-shape grooves which surround hearths in some later Mogollon Great Kivas represent vestiges of the earlier peripheral floor grooves retained in the same manner as the sipapu and other features of pit houses and kivas in the Anasazi area to the north.

The Los Pinos Phase structures show other indications of possible contacts with groups much farther south in the form of intrusive sherds of brown paste fired pottery finished with the paddle and anvil technique. Adamana Brown, from the Petrified Forest area of eastern Arizona, shows this finishing technique, and is the nearest known occurrence of it to the Los Pinos sites. Differences in paste and/or method of finishing distinguish the relatively contemporary sherds of the Reserve, Los Pinos, and Petrified Forest areas, but when considered together with their architectural contexts they lend further support to Dittert's recent postulation of an "early pan-Southwestern brownware horizon" (Anonymous, 1961, p. 2).

BIBLIOGRAPHY

Anonymous

1961 *Third Southwestern Ceramic Seminar*. Museum of Northern Arizona. Flagstaff.

Daifuku, H.

1961 *Jeddito 264: A Report on the Excavation of a Basket Maker III–Pueblo I Site in Northeastern Arizona with a Review of Some Current Theories in Southwestern Archaeology*. Papers of the Peabody Museum of Archaeology and Ethnology, Harvard University, Vol. 23, No. 1. Cambridge.

Douglass, A. E.

1936 "The Central Pueblo Chronology," *Tree Ring Bulletin*, Vol. 2, No. 4. Tucson.

Eddy, F. W., and B. L. Dickey

1961 *Excavations at Los Pinos Phase Sites in the Navajo Reservoir District*. Museum of New Mexico Papers in Anthropology, No. 4. Santa Fe.

Haury, E. W.

1936 *The Mogollon Culture of Southwestern New Mexico*. Medallion Papers, No. 20. Globe, Arizona.

1940 *Excavations in the Forestdale Valley, East-central Arizona. University of Arizona Social Science Bulletin*, No. 12. Tucson.

Haury, E. W., and E. B. Sayles

1947 *An Early Pit House Village of the Mogollon Culture, Forestdale Valley, Arizona. University of Arizona Social Science Bulletin*, No. 16. Tucson.

Martin, P. S.

1943 *The SU Site: Excavations at a Mogollon Village, Western New Mexico, Second Season, 1941*. Field Museum of Natural History, Anthropological Series, Vol. 32, No. 2. Chicago.

Martin, P. S., and J. B. Rinaldo

1947 *The SU Site: Excavations at a Mogollon Village, Western New Mexico, Third Season, 1946*. Field Museum of Natural History, Anthropological Series, Vol. 32, No. 3. Chicago.

1950a *Turkey Foot Ridge Site: A Mogollon Village, Pine Lawn Valley, Western New Mexico. Fieldiana: Anthropology*, Vol. 38, No. 2. Chicago.

1950b *Sites of the Reserve Phase, Pine Lawn Valley, Western New Mexico. Fieldiana: Anthropology*, Vol. 38, No. 3. Chicago.

Martin, P. S., J. B. Rinaldo, and J. B. Antevs

1949 *Cochise and Mogollon Sites, Pine Lawn Valley, Western New Mexico. Fieldiana: Anthropology*, Vol. 38, No. 1. Chicago.

Martin, P.S., J.B. Rinaldo, E. Bluhm, H.C. Cutler, and R. Grange, Jr.
1952 *Mogollon Cultural Continuity and Change: The Stratigraphic Analysis of Tularosa and Cordova Caves. Fieldiana: Anthropology*, Vol. 42. Chicago.

Martin, P.S., J. Rinaldo, and M. Kelly
1940 *The SU Site: Excavations at a Mogollon Village, Western New Mexico*. Field Museum of Natural History, Anthropological Series, Vol. 32, No. 1. Chicago.

Morris, E.H.
1936 "Archaeological Background of Dates in Early Arizona Chronology," *Tree Ring Bulletin*, Vol. 2, No. 4. Tucson.

Morris, E.H., and R.F. Burgh
1954 *Basket Maker II Sites near Durango, Colorado*. Carnegie Institution of Washington, Publication 604. Washington, D.C.

Sayles, E.B.
1945 *The San Simon Branch: Excavations at Cave Creek and in the San Simon Valley: I, Material Culture*. Medallion Papers, No. 34. Globe, Arizona.

Smiley, Terah L.
1951 *A Summary of Tree-Ring Dates from some Southwestern Archaeological Sites. Laboratory Bulletin of Tree-Ring Research*, University of Arizona Bulletin, Vol. 22, No. 4.

Wendorf, F.
1956 "Excavations of LA 2948," *Highway Salvage Archaeology*, Vol. 2, No. 8. Santa Fe.

Wheat, J.B.
1955 *Mogollon Culture Prior to A.D.* 1000. Memoirs of the Society for American Archaeology, No. 10. Menasha.

JULIAN H. STEWARD

The life and work of Alfred L. Kroeber

Julian H. Steward, research professor of anthropology at the University of Illinois, served as editor of the four-volume *Handbook of South American Indians*. He is the author of many studies including *Theory of Culture Change* and, with L. C. Faron, *Native Peoples of South America*. His relationship to Kroeber is described in the obituary. In its original form, the obituary was followed by a twenty-seven-page bibliography of Kroeber's writings: more than 530 separate items. This listing should be consulted for an appreciation of Kroeber's massive contribution to American anthropology.

The last day

On October 5, 1960, at fifteen minutes past midnight, Alfred Kroeber died in Paris in his 85th year, ending six decades of continuous and brilliant productivity which earned him a professional reputation second to none and the warm respect of his colleagues as the dean of anthropology.

. . .

The fullness of Kroeber's life was manifest in many ways. He played a major role in developing American anthropology from the rather random endeavors of amateurs and self-trained men to a coherent, scientific, and academic discipline. His contributions to knowledge included extensive ethnographic investigations in California and the Great Plains, archeological studies in Mexico and Peru, linguistic research, especially in California, theory of communications in the animal world generally, historical syntheses which often had world scope, and a large number of papers on the nature of culture.

Kroeber developed one of the world's great research museums and teaching departments of anthropology. As the impact of his influence was felt, kudos accrued to him. He was the recipient of five honorary degrees (Yale, California, Harvard, Columbia, Chicago), two gold medals, and honorary membership in sixteen scientific societies. He held offices in innumerable professional organizations. These kudos resulted from

---

Julian H. Steward, "Alfred Louis Kroeber, 1876–1960." Reproduced by permission of the American Anthropological Association from *American Anthropologist*, 63, 5 (October 1961), 1038–1060.

undeviating dedication to scholarship. He never sought to popularize, he wrote little that was not on a serious anthropological subject, and he avoided the lecture circuits.

. . .

The man

As an adult, Kroeber's acts were always well considered and his behavior impeccable. Anthropology somehow had more than its share of unorthodox, colorful individuals, and, during the twenties, some of the University's graduate students showed slightly more zeal than the youth of that decade in breaking with traditional mores. Kroeber never judged these people from a moral point of view, but his own course was to avoid entanglement. Occasionally he advised, even admonished, but always he sympathized and understood. There was a perpetual twinkle in his perceptive grey eyes.

During the thirty-five years that I knew Kroeber he always seemed a miraculously well-integrated, smoothly functioning man. It was hard to imagine a person who evidenced fewer internal conflicts, worked with less lost motion, and managed more felicitously to combine an extremely happy family life with monumental professional accomplishments. His economy of effort was manifest in his ability to read at high speed and absorb essentials, and to write with an extraordinary cogency, conciseness, and choice of words.

Kroeber's adult life was a continuation of the childhood and teenage pattern, which had created a rare singleness of purpose. He always had boundless curiosity and would discuss new ideas for hours, whether he agreed or not. He had an uncanny grasp of the essential qualities of poetry, art, music, and religious and philosophical ideas, which were of major importance in his characterization of cultural styles. And he had little time for the trivia of modern life—for television, moving pictures, who-dunnits, and other distractions, which Americans today either rationalize as necessary escapes or accept as essential fare. Kroeber was always self-sufficient; he had no need to cultivate hobbies in order to relax from the pressures of serious affairs. His basic interests were at once the substance and spice of life. He was always earnest and dedicated, but not solemn; intensely purposeful but not oppressively or domineeringly so. In fact, he always accepted life exuberantly and enjoyed people and gossip enormously.

Another facet of the same character was a slowness to anger. The usual irritations of life seemed to roll off him. I knew him to be thoroughly angry only a few times, and then owing to unfair treatment of friends rather than on his own account. By the same token, he was intensely loyal to his friends, sometimes long after it was evident that his loyalty had been misplaced.

Choosing a profession

When Kroeber was an undergraduate, anthropology did not exist as a distinct, unified academic discipline at Columbia University. A crucial event in the history of American anthropology, and in Kroeber's life, was the appointment of Franz Boas to the faculty in 1896, which was Kroeber's senior year.

. . .

In 1899, anthropology, along with philosophy, education, and psychology was incorporated in a department and Boas was made a full professor, but the contributory offerings to anthropology remained for years in different departments and even faculties of the University. Columbia was not very different from other universities of that era, when anthropology, which had earlier been represented only in museums, and largely by amateurs, was introduced into universities by diverse expediencies and did not at once achieve the unity we know today. To choose a career in anthropology at the turn of the century, therefore, was to commit oneself to a nebulous and insecure future. Kroeber's later efforts to build anthropology at California confronted similar difficulties.

Kroeber entered Columbia College with interest in English and literature, in which he was encouraged by George E. Woodberry, poet and critic, who became his intimate friend by his sophomore year. Kroeber went on to take an M.A. degree in English in 1897 (thesis: "The English Heroic Play"), served as teaching assistant for two years, 1897–99, and taught a course in eighteenth-century English literature.

Kroeber's conversion to anthropology was in part a gradual intellectual seduction.... Sheer curiosity led him to take Boas' language seminar in 1896, but this flamed into enthusiasm the next year when the students worked with Eskimo and Chinook informants. Especially interesting were six Eskimo whom Lt. Robert Peary brought to New York from the Central Arctic. Original research with them on language and culture led to Kroeber's first publications: Eskimo folklore in 1898 and 1899, and Eskimo ethnology in 1900. Kroeber went on to take other courses in anthropology, and he became more deeply involved in the subject after a three months' field trip to the Arapaho in 1899. The clincher was a trip in 1900 to the Arapaho, Ute, Shoshone, and Bannock. In 1899–1900, he committed himself when he accepted a fellowship in anthropology and elected psychology as his minor. Another field trip of a few months for the California Academy of Sciences was followed by the preparation and defense of his Ph.D. dissertation in the spring of 1901.

Kroeber's gradual immersion in anthropology via his linguistic and natural history interests has something of the inevitable. But Alsberg, his closest friend at this time, discloses another motivation for his choosing anthropology and thereby an important, although largely covert, idealism. Alsberg, a chemist, argued against Kroeber's going into research in a subject so "vague, inchoate and intangible," to which Kroeber replied that "a result in chemistry or physics . . . was not likely to affect men's thinking and to make for progress in the only way that was worth while . . . to free men intellectually. The confused thinking about religion was perhaps the most important bar to man's progress and freedom." Kroeber's interest in cultural values many years later was more than a humanist's view of styles or contexts. He treated the questions of objective or scientific criteria of progress quite explicitly in several papers, and yet he eschewed programs of research aimed at social reform. While I cannot quite fathom Kroeber's genuine intent, I surmise that he wished to create a perspective and to destroy ethnocentric thinking without committing himself to problems of human welfare.

. . .

Building anthropology at California

Kroeber began his professional career at the University of California in Berkeley in 1901. The achievements in building a department and museum in the face of the uncertainties, insecurities, and frustrations that confronted a young anthropologist at the turn of the century merit honors as great as those from scholarly accomplishments. The secure academic and scientific niche which anthropology holds today was won through considerable pioneering toil, sacrifice, and imagination by the first generation of Boas' students. Kroeber and his contemporaries went to academic positions that were vaguely defined and offered meager and uncertain financial support.

. . .

In 1901, Kroeber and P. E. Goddard, who had been a lay missionary among the Hupa Indians, were appointed university instructors, and Mrs. [Phoebe] Hearst paid their salaries for five years at $1,200 per annum. Each taught one semester, but their principal jobs were to investigate the diversified and little-known languages and cultures of native California. Some five or six years later they taught both semesters, and Kroeber was appointed assistant professor and paid from university funds. Teaching accumulated such momentum that they were able to award Samuel Barrett a Ph.D. in anthropology in 1908.

An important achievement during these early years . . . was the establishment of the "University of California Publications in American Archaeology and Ethnology." Goddard's *Life and Culture of the Hupa*, in 1903, was the first paper. Later volumes contained papers by Kroeber and many others, giving priority to California Indians but eventually covering a much wider area. This series is perhaps second in volume only to the publications of the Bureau of American Ethnology, which was begun some thirty years earlier.

. . .

After joining the university staff in 1901, Kroeber divided his time between Berkeley and San Francisco. He became Secretary of Anthropology and eventually Head of the Department. At Putnam's retirement in 1909, he became Curator of the Museum. His principal activities, however, centered in San Francisco, where he lived until 1917.

The San Francisco period was productive in research and in building museum collections from the artifacts of the Indians of California, but it was a time of personal tragedy. Kroeber married Henrietta Rothschild in 1906, but she contracted tuberculosis and died in 1913 after five years of lingering illness. His meager salary had barely sufficed to meet doctors' bills. Three years later the death of Ishi also had a strong personal impact on Kroeber. Ishi was a Yana Indian, the last survivor of his tribe, who had been found in a completely wild and aboriginal state in the Sierra foothills and housed for a number of years at the Museum, where he contracted tuberculosis.

Kroeber moved to the Faculty Club on the Berkeley campus in 1917, when the teaching department had so grown as to demand more attention. Various people came and went before the permanent staff was established. N. C. Nelson succeeded Goddard in 1909 and remained two years. T. T. Waterman, whose colorful personality and vivid teaching made him one of the legendary figures of his time, served in various capacities between 1907 and 1918, when he entered the army. By 1920, Boas, Wallis, Sapir, Spier, Radin, Barrows and others had taught for brief periods.

Lowie, who had been visiting lecturer in 1917–18, was permanently appointed in 1921, the year that Kroeber sets as California's serious advent into graduate teaching. Lowie provided a complement, and in some ways a foil, to Kroeber's basic feeling for substantive data; for it was Lowie who took students into theory and who argued with Malinowski, Radcliffe-Brown, and others when, as visiting lecturers, they proselytized their own views.

The third member of anthropology's threesome throughout the nineteen-twenties was Edward W. Gifford. Gifford's original interest was in ornithology, and he had served as Associate Curator of Ornithology in the California Academy of Sciences from 1904 to 1912, when he was employed by the Museum of Anthropology, which he finally served as Director. Gifford also added substantially to the teaching of the Department.

Prior to 1926, California had given only two Ph.D.s in anthropology. When I entered the graduate school in the fall of 1925 on the advice of Livingston Farrand, then President of Cornell University, William Duncan Strong, Forrest Clements, Anna Gayton, Theodora Krakow Brown, and Lloyd Warner were well into graduate work. Ralph Beals, Ronald Olson, Lila O'Neale, and I were starting, and W. W. Hill, Isabel Kelly, Theodore McCown and others were interested seniors.

Theodora, or Krakie, was an attractive widow with two young sons, Clifton and Theodore. In Kroeber's seminar during the spring of 1926 she and I were assigned jointly the problem of working out element distributions on North American Indian hockey and other field games. I was never quite sure what became of our intellectual endeavors, for Kroeber continued this seminar for many years to train students in organizing data. The semester, however, terminated in the marriage of Kroeber and Krakie, to the delight of everyone.

. . .

During the thirties, the number of students at Berkeley, including candidates for higher degrees, increased rapidly and the faculty expanded. Previously, the Department had taught basic fact and theory but offered little specialized training for graduate students. Kroeber liked especially to deal with civilizations in which archeology and ethnology were not distinguished. Despite his tremendous interest in linguistics, he offered no formal courses in the subject. His reason for not giving special courses was that of Boas, whom he quoted, "If they have shown that they are good men, they should be given their degrees, after which they will learn what they need." If, owing to limited teaching personnel, a choice had to be made between basic knowledge and specialized skills, wisdom favored the former. It must be confessed, however, that several of us made a considerable hash of our first attempts to do archeology and that nearly all of us avoided linguistic field work.

The need for more specialized skills was remedied in the thirties.

Ronald Olson was appointed especially to take charge of the large introductory course. Later, Theodore McCown joined the faculty to teach Old World archeology and physical anthropology. New World archeology, including California which had been rather neglected, was accorded due attention after the appointment of Robert Heizer. Eventually, the Department filled out with specialists in other topics and areas.

Its offering continued to attract graduate students. Between 1926 and 1930, California awarded seven Ph.D.s in anthropology, and between 1931 and Kroeber's retirement in 1946, it gave twenty-five. Since 1946, it has given fifty-seven.

In 1936, when Kroeber's sixtieth birthday was celebrated with a festschrift volume, his professional accomplishments were more than sufficient to insure a lasting reputation. But twenty-five more productive years lay ahead. During World War II, a heart attack was nearly fatal but meticulous care of his health thereafter enabled him to carry on with his usual efficiency and much the same vigor. Retirement from the University of California in 1946 at the age of seventy brought teaching offers from all parts of the country. First, however, in the spring of 1946 the Kroebers went to England where he received the Huxley Medal. After spending the next year in Berkeley, they visited Columbia University for summer school, then spent a year at Harvard in 1947–48. From 1948 to 1952 he was visiting professor at Columbia and in early summer, 1952, he organized the Wenner-Gren World Conference on anthropology held in New York. (This was published in *Anthropology Today*, 1953). In 1954 he was visiting professor at Brandeis University; in 1955–56, he was a Fellow of the Center for Advanced Studies in the Behavioral Sciences at Stanford, California, and in the fall of 1956 he gave the Messenger Lectures (on "Style and Civilization") at Cornell University. He visited the Center at Stanford again in the spring of 1957, was visiting professor at Yale University in 1958, and in the fall of 1959 had a major role in the Darwin Centennial symposium and conference at the University of Chicago. The Kroebers returned to Berkeley and then attended the summer conference in Austria in 1960. He had planned a seminar at Berkeley on the Indians of California for the fall of 1960.

The scholar and scientist

THEORETICAL VIEWS If one accepts Kroeber's date of 1860 for the beginning of "organized anthropology," his own professional activities covered six-tenths of the history of such anthropology. They expectably reflect trends of a half century ago; and yet Kroeber's interests were so deeply individual, so strongly marked by his bent for natural history, and so pervasively colored by his intuition and esthetic perceptivity that to attempt to describe a "Kroeber school of anthropology" or to explain his intellectual position as a systematic, scientific methodology would gravely misrepresent him. It is even now premature to assess his influence on anthropology.

Kroeber not only had an insatiable curiosity about phenomena of all kinds, but he insistently viewed them in contexts, matrices, or wholes. What was not part of a living or developing whole did not interest him; he even found it repugnant to dissect an animal in order to study its organs in isolation. His life-long endeavor or problem was to understand the nature of the contexts of phenomena. In cultural studies this meant a primary interest in total systems of human behavior and in how to conceptualize these systems. He described himself as primarily—"congenitally"—a humanist and a natural historian, or natural scientist, and he expressly repudiated any contention, or at least disavowed interest in the contention, that cultural analysis could employ the method of the physical sciences; that is, a method which isolates phenomena in order to discover particular causes and effects. Any studies he made of parts of culture always had the "adhering context" in mind.

Kroeber also disclaimed a social science orientation: "It is clear that I am not by temperament a social scientist." This statement, however, seems to reflect partly a disinclination to deal with problems of human welfare, which strongly oriented much social science (although he had a certain concern with human progress expressed in value terms and with liberation of thought), and partly his own strong intellectual roots in the humanistic and natural science components of anthropology which were put down during his youth when the social science component was still nebulous. Perhaps, most importantly, Kroeber's lack of social science orientation meant that his interest in structure and function and in the microscopic analyses involved therein seemed to him to have secondary importance or at least never to have primary importance, in the characterization of whole cultures.

Kroeber's early interest in languages, natural history, and contexts predisposed him to accept those precepts of Boas' teaching that have become basic in American anthropology. In Boas, he found advocacy of unrelenting empiricism, which repudiated the earlier deductive systematizers and theoreticians who had arranged cultural data in various *a priori* categories and developmental schemes. He found Boas' stress upon fact over theory, and therefore upon the primary importance of intensive firsthand ethnographic field work, congenial. Probably no anthropologist has spent as many years as Kroeber collecting and dealing with original cultural data or furthering field research programs.

Kroeber also followed Boas in the holistic and cultural relativistic view:

the concept that each cultural pattern or configuration is unique, different from all others, and comprehensible only in terms of itself. His dedication to this view involved him in a lifetime of inquiry about the "nature of culture"—about how to characterize cultures and diagnose their distinguishing stylistic features. This approach inevitably led to a taxonomy of cultural types which, especially in the absence of structural criteria, essentially precluded categories of cross-cultural recurrence. A classificatory scheme which has a special category for each culture does not, of course, lend itself to generalizations, to abstractions of form and function, or to deductions or inferences concerning causality, processes, or regularities.

Kroeber differed from Boas in several crucial respects. Deeply interested in history from childhood, he added time depth to the essentially synchronic ethnology of Boas and most of Boas' students, who were less opposed to, than uninterested in, utilizing historical data. Kroeber observed that Americans tended to view the past "not as a receding stereoscopic continuum but as a uniform non-present."

He was also uncompromising in his insistence that culture should be conceptualized in Herbert Spencer's terms as phenomena of a superorganic level: that culture derives from culture and that conceptualizations or explanations—"reductionism"—which introduce psychological, organic, or environmental factors are indefensible. Kroeber's history was superorganic and supra-individual; it was deterministic and had no place for the great man theory. Kroeber's conviction that culture is superorganic influenced his views on psychology and anthropology. As an anthropologist, he was no more interested in the effect of culture upon the individual (the culture and personality approach) than the individual upon culture (the great man theory of history). During the nineteen-thirties, the cultural and personality approach began to offer a means of placing the characterization of cultural contexts upon a psychological rather than stylistic basis. These studies, which at first were based strongly upon psychoanalysis, assumed that cultural personality types were formed during childhood, owing to specific socializing processes, and were later projected into cultural patterns of adult life. Kroeber had taken a graduate minor in psychology, he had read psychoanalysis during his early professional years, he had been psychoanalyzed for three months in 1920, he had maintained an office and practiced psychoanalysis successfully in San Francisco between 1921 and 1923, and he abandoned the practice only because of the pressure of university duties. But he remained uncompromisingly opposed to reductionism. Personality problems at a psychological level, which he regarded as directed toward "personality betterment," were a different matter than cultural problems at a superorganic or sociocultural level.

Kroeber's life-long position was clearly set forth in his doctoral dissertation on Arapaho art published in 1901. Just as any art simultaneously manifests tendencies of geometric forms to become symbols of realism, and realistic forms to become conventionalized or geometric designs, so any culture consists of many interrelated and often indistinguishable tendencies. These tendencies "are both eternally living and everlastingly changing. They flow into one another; they transform themselves; they are indistinguishably combined where they coexist."

Kroeber's approach to the nature of culture was two-fold. On the one hand, he characterized cultures by means of culture element lists, that is, in terms of the minutiae of their content. On the other hand, he sought major styles, philosophies, and values. The first concept is that a society or several societies have an agglomeration of culture elements which have no other necessary connection than the historical, or diffusional, fact of clustering territorially. Much of Kroeber's work dealt with element distributions, especially the University of California Element List Surveys during the nineteen-thirties. Areas defined by elements were given time depth by construing the distributions as historical adhesions, layered as in a cake. The most widely spread elements represented the oldest layer, which had been supplemented, or supplanted, by increments which introduced greater complexity and which modified patterns in more restricted areas, or more recent historical layers. This approach is especially well exemplified in *The Peoples of the Philippines* (1919) and *The Handbook of the Indians of California* (1925).

Intermediate between dealing with element content at one extreme and predominant styles at the other was attention to clusters or categories of elements, such as ceremonialism in central California, which disclosed cultural emphasis.

Kroeber's treatment of styles, however, presented certain difficulties because, like all relativistic approaches, it is essentially subjective and intuitive. Each scholar can devise his own terms and view culture according to his own interests. Boas had written of "style," of "fundamental psychic attitudes," and of the influence of cultural practices upon "man's mental life." This was less reductionism to a psychological level of characterization than concern with cultural attitudes manifest in the typical individual. All-pervasive attitudes are glimpsed in some of Boas' ethnographies, but they are far from explicit. [Ruth] Benedict, in *Patterns of Culture*, was more satisfyingly explicit in her use of analogies drawn from Greek mythology, such as Dionysian for the pervading frenzy alleged to have characterized Plains Indian behavior and Apollonian as descriptive of the serenity of the Pueblo, and her book continues to be a best seller. But such recourse was a matter of personal taste, and even mythical allusions might be exhausted before all of the world's cultures were diagnosed in this manner. More importantly, Benedict's characterizations did not depend upon the structural features of her societies.

Kroeber sympathized with Benedict's humanistic characterization of wholes, but denied that "pattern" so-conceived was a factor that integrated—was the binding force of—the whole culture. He not only conceived style as more than esthetic or literary characterizations, but eventually, if incidentally, he introduced some structural characteristics. In the higher civilizations, at least, he saw not one but many styles. In 1951 he described style as "a self-consistent way of behaving . . . selected out from among alternatively possible ways. . . . And it is selective with references to values"; that is, culture ascribes special value to particular themes or interests. He distinguished styles from "reality culture," that is ways of living, including technology, and from "social structure and relations" (see below). "The style successively forms, develops, matures, decays, and either dissolves or atrophies into a dead petrification," or it may disintegrate and reconstitute itself as a new style. Its history is irreversible. This approach to style is one of descriptive analysis. "*The causes of qualities and values are . . . difficult to find. We can do little more than describe the circumstances around which a style forms*" (italics mine). The styles—pattern values or directions—of the High Middle Ages of Europe after A.D. 900 included: total commitment to Christianity, a sense of nationalism, Romanesque-Gothic architecture, stained glass, sculpture, revival of learning, Scholastic philosophy. This was followed by the beginning of the Modern Western Civilization: wider geographic knowledge, trade, civilian architecture, painting, weakening of the Church, development of science, new kinds of philosophy, and printing.

Kroeber's conception of culture was thus inseparably part of his sense of history, and his erudition made him uniquely competent to take the grand view. He constantly saw changes in styles as flows and continua, pulses, culminations and diminutions, convergences and divergences, divisions, blends and cross-currents by which cultures develop and mutually influence one another. He dealt with culture history in all parts of the world and in all periods from the Paleolithic to the present day.

One of his greatest works, *Configurations of Culture Growth* (1944), deals with the superorganic nature of culture, especially with respect to individual geniuses who cluster at climaxes or culminations in human history. The book undertakes to show that individual achievements express but do not explain cultural climaxes. Inherent ability was given scope by high points of civilization, and obversely the scarcity of great men during periods of cultural decline or dark ages was the function of contexts that caused genius to remain latent. Like his studies of women's fashions, the intent was to show that culture changes according to its own tendencies. He was not concerned, as some have thought, with any inherent periodicity or regularity in rhythms of particular phenomena.

It is as a social scientist that Kroeber is most difficult to assess. In 1940, he explained that by "natural science," in contrast to social science, he meant an approach that was "empirical, inductive, and free of any motivation of applicability or social control." This was really a repudiation of interest in human welfare problems. He concluded that standard ethnography, archeology, and culture history in terms both of disparate traits or culture elements and of wholes follow the methodology of language studies, whereas, "in contrast, consciously functional anthropology, social anthropology, and sociology tend to be non-historical, reductionist, and interested in cause." Frequently he cited linguistic studies as the model of his holistic, superorganic, and historical view of culture. Parts of speech would lose meaning if isolated from the grammars or structures of language; language forms cannot be explained by psychological processes operating through particular individuals; they are significant essentially in their historicity.

This dichotomy between natural science and social science is more a declaration of Kroeber's personal interests than of inherent logic. A functional-historical approach is conceivable, and some of us have used it. Reductionism may be necessary if one is interested in breaking out of the culture-comes-from-culture formulation and in seeking causes or processes, such as the effects of demographic trends or ecological adaptations upon culture; but regularities may also be formulated in purely culturalogical terms. While I cannot agree that functionalism need be concerned with "timeless process," as Kroeber contends, it is true that process is normally an abstraction, whether of synchronic or diachronic relationships, that is derived from more than one culture and therefore partly removed from the reality of particulars. Kroeber, in short, was concerned more with style than with structure, more with the particulars of individual histories than with generalized processes, and more with wholes than with parts.

What this signifies, I believe, is that Kroeber's incredibly vast knowledge and fertile imagination led him to the macroscopic or grand view, and not that such a view requires a different conceptualization of culture than the microscopic view. Primary concern with wholes is inevitably macroscopic. Cultural relativism can deal with wholes in terms of unique styles, whereas, characterization of structures, which developed later in the history of anthropology, more fruitfully begins with particulars of individual cases and with detailed processes and gradually generalizes broader categories. The structuralists have, perhaps, been overly cautious in postulating types of society that have comparative and evolutionary significance; and the lack of a coherent taxonomy and of any consensus regarding taxonomic criteria became painfully evident during the last few years owing to participation of anthropologists in various Darwin centennials which dealt with cultural as well as with biological evolution. Kroeber, for example, noted in 1959 at the University of Chicago Darwin Centennial that anthropology is pre-Linnaean taxonomically. Earlier characterizations of culture, including Kroeber's, however, used ethos, styles, values, patterns, and other relativistic diagnostics, which were inherently ill-adapted for a comparative or developmental taxonomy that would disclose processes of change. Until the nineteen-thirties, folklore, religion, art, and other humanistic aspects of culture had, in fact, a far more central place than structure in cultural studies.

Kroeber's awareness of the confused status of cultural taxonomy and evolution, however, did not lead him to postulate abstract, cross-cultural categories based primarily upon structure. Characteristically, he approached problems of structures via cultural wholes, but he did suggest crucial hypotheses in several papers. These contributions have received far too little attention, partly because his repeated disavowals of interest in delimited problems and in causality obscured the implications of his work, partly because his positive formulations and hypotheses were usually stated as highly provisional and often submerged in the raw data of great substantive monographs, but mainly perhaps because he was disinclined to be argumentative and rarely indulged in sufficient forensic zeal and repetition of a thesis.

Kroeber was never indifferent to any trend in anthropology, however, and early in his career he dealt with the problem of structure as it was then phrased: the relationship between kinship terms, marriage rules, and descent groups. This problem was derived from the nineteenth-century theories, which postulated that kinship terms reflected marriage systems that had existed in the past if not in the present. None really dealt with whole societies, such as bands, hordes, communities, tribes or other total units of interpersonal relationships. In 1909, Kroeber's *Classificatory Systems of Relationship* had warned against regarding kinship terms as reflections of sociological systems—especially marriage systems—when several different relatives were designated by the same term and suggested that the terms had linguistic rather than sociological connotation and that they were psychological extensions of terms to several categories of people. In 1917, his *Zuñi Kin and Clan*, one of the first major field studies directed toward kinship problems, emphasized the error of supposing that a strong clan system necessarily precluded a nuclear family system or indicated that the matrilineal clan developed before the family. He also questioned the inference that a high correlation between certain kinds of exogamous organizations and classificatory systems proved a causal connection between these isolated phenomena. Skeptical that a single sociological factor could explain a particular phenomenon, he suggested that both exogamy and kinship terms more broadly express descent systems and tendencies of the total context. He made a similar point in an introductory course when he pointed out that beer-drinking, eating of sauerkraut, and love of certain kinds of music had a high correlation in Germany, but were related only within the historical context and not conceivably by direct causal effect of one upon another.

His *Basic and Secondary Patterns of Social Organization* (1938, republished in *Nature of Culture*, 1952) relates problems of kinship systems to the larger question of what is basic or primary and what is secondary in a total culture. It offers an hypothesis for cultural taxonomy that ascribes major importance to structural features and their transformations. Starting with Radcliffe-Brown's Australian data, he uses a distributional or age-area method to infer sequential change of marriage and kinship systems, and then postulates that, in the social organisation of primitive people generally, patterns of group residence and subsistence associations may be primary, or invariant, whereas clans, moieties, marriage classes, totems, and other elaborations may be secondary or "unstable embroideries on the primary patterns."

The central question of what is basic and stable, and what is secondary—what is the central core and what are the variable and peripheral features—ran through several other works which bear crucially on the problem of cultural taxonomy. Earlier, he had found that so emotion-laden a custom as the method of disposing of the dead changed with surprising ease. His several studies of changes in women's fashions also had the central theme of relative changeability. He finally postulated a general dichotomy: first, "relatively primary and stable patterns and constituents of cultures"; and, second, features which are "relatively secondary, unstable, within the field of innovation from internal cultural causes and perhaps more readily invested with conscious group emotions."

This states a problem of cultural change and offers a taxonomic generalization. The problem is amenable to scientific method rather than mere intuitive insights, but it is especially difficult because it involves whole cultures rather than social structures. "I submit that, in addition to unilateral descent reckoning, much of the formalized social organization of primitive peoples is in the nature of unconscious experiment and play of fashions rather than the core or substance of their culture. In certain cases, as in Australia, it may well represent the pinnacle of their achievement, just as experimentation and play with abstractions, words and plastic forms resulted in the pinnacles of Greek civilization, while science, technology, or exploitation of nature are those of our own. But the pinnacles are end products, not bases."

He came at the problem of differential stability again in *Reality Culture and Value Culture* (1951, republished in 1952), wherein he noted that at least four components of culture change in their own distinctive ways. He stated "there seems to be a certain importance in the conceptual distinction between . . . reality culture" and "value culture." The former includes science, technology, and on occasion other aspects of culture. The latter includes ethos, morality, art, and other expressions of value. Reality culture is "largely diffusional and accumulative"; value culture is "ever re-creative." "A third major segment, the societal, seems to be neither specifically accumulative nor specifically creative." Language is a fourth segment. In the 1959 Darwin Centennial he also suggested dissimilarity in the history of components of culture—e.g., technology which is cumulative, art which pulses, society which is somewhat indeterminant.

. . .

Kroeber always remained a relativist, if not a holist. In the final analysis he saw in each culture a unique emphasis upon one or several bands in the total spectrum of possible human behavior, wherein kinship systems, types of sculpture, science, and philosophy could be equally important diagnostic criteria. Since different components of culture, however, changed in their own ways and emphasis on style constantly shifted, his cultures could not flow through time as integrated wholes.

Substantive works

While Kroeber's substantive works are only partly separable from his theoretical contributions, the former are perhaps best known, though not necessarily of greatest importance. The distribution of his publications by subject and year is instructive.

In total number, the ethnology of California naturally ranks first with more than seventy papers. The peak was in the nineteen-twenties and 'thirties, but the interest continued throughout his life. Essays on languages, especially of California, are a close second, and eventually they exceeded ethnology. During his last decade he acquired a renewed interest in language. Articles and monographs essentially on theory, although always massively substantive, exceed the previous categories, and if general works are included, they number more than eighty. Interestingly, these show two peaks: one in the nineteen-tens, with the first probings; the other, between 1940 and 1960, began when Kroeber was sixty-four years old. Science is clearly indebted to his longevity, for most of the incisive delineations and elaborations of his views were written after an age when most persons have passed their productive years, and many were presented after his retirement. Writings on American Indian cultures were also interpretative and theoretical, and these acquired momentum after 1920. They reached a peak in the 1930s, except that Peru, one of his special fields, was the subject of some twenty-five articles between 1920 and 1960. Folklore constituted thirteen papers between 1898 and 1910, and thereafter was reduced to seven papers, and art, his Ph.D. dissertation subject, was the main theme of only four papers in his lifetime.

Kroeber was never a physical anthropologist, and, although he summarized basic information in his *Anthropology*, his publications on the subject were negligible. He also had no special predisposition to be a field archeologist, despite his interest in prehistory. Peruvian culture history is based on archeology, which he fully utilized, but his own field research in the area was restricted. His total archeological output, apart from Peru, is not over twenty papers.

This distribution of effort indicates first a substantive interest directed initially toward California cultures and languages, later toward the Western Hemisphere and Peru in particular, and eventually toward world culture history and major civilizations; and second, the unfolding of a point of view, which he might express in a discussion of arrow-release distributions, changes in burial customs, practices concerning dogs, salt, and tobacco in California, fashions in women's dress, the novel in Asia and Europe, or in terms of major historic trends, which dealt not only with world phenomena but with such interpreters as Spengler, Toynbee, and other historians. These bolder efforts came mainly within the last three decades of his life.

One of Kroeber's greatest works was the *Handbook of the Indians of California* published in 1925. This thousand-page volume, which has long been a collector's item, is not only a compendium of everything known about the Indians at that time but sets forth culture areas and subareas and their historic implications. Such ordering of data had been anticipated in a paper in 1907 on the religions and religious cults of California, by several other topical studies, and in 1923 by an essay on the history of California cultures. Whereas his contemporary, Clark Wissler, delineated native New World culture areas about this same time mainly in terms of technological adaptations to distinctive environments, Kroeber tended to emphasize religious organization and belief.

By the nineteen-thirties, Kroeber and his associates began to sense a defect in the element distribution method, which had utilized lists of traits to show variations and culminations within certain aspects of culture and to show similarities between tribes. Too often, particular elements had not been mentioned at all in ethnographies, so that neither their presence nor absence was certain. In 1934, the late Stanislaw Klimek came to California from Poland with a statistical formula, which, though devised for biometrics, purportedly expressed the similarity between any two societies as a coefficient of correlation based upon mutually present and absent traits. Klimek's formula underlined the inadequacy of comparable data for all tribes, and Kroeber obtained funds for an ambitious four-year field project of element list surveys which was carried out by thirteen field workers and included 254 tribes and tribal subdivisions west of the Rocky Mountains. The lists ranged from 3,000 to more than 6,000 elements, the presence and absence of which were recorded for each local group.

The territorial plotting of element distributions raised questions about the mechanism of diffusion of each element, which had usually been conceived as a fairly simple process through which one society transmitted cultural features to another merely because of contiguity. Kroeber modified this concept in his article *Stimulus Diffusion* (1940), by showing that cultural products may be imitated by peoples who had no direct contact with their originators. It is incredible that assessment of the many kinds, conditions, and contexts of diffusion have today gone little beyond Kroeber's formulations.

The California element surveys could only suggest cultural emphases, styles, or configurations, which interested Kroeber so much, and Kroeber made comparatively little use of the data. The lists could scarcely record social structures, for these had not been conceptualized or broken down into significant elements so as to be amenable to such recording. My own part in this survey dealt with the Paiute and Shoshone, whose element lists had to be published separately from structural and cultural ecological analyses.

About 1920, Kroeber had decided to broaden his own field of substantive research beyond California, the Plains, and Zuñi. He first visited Mexico, and in 1924 he visited Peru, following up interests arising from Max Uhle's collections. He returned to Peru in 1926, and on later occasions. He always kept abreast of all Americanist research, but Peru became his special interest. His esthetic perceptivity was especially important in sensing the stylistic relationships in Peruvian ceramics and other art manifestations that helped establish a stylistic chronology—a skeletal framework for determining time and place relationships of associated materials—upon which other understandings, e.g., social and political, depended.

Kroeber's enlarged interests in cultural areas and cultural continuities led to another of his major works, *Cultural and Natural Areas in Native North America* (1939). By this time, so much was known about American Indians that no one but Kroeber, now the leading Americanist, would presume to synthesize the knowledge in a single work. Moreover, when major cooperative works were written on special areas, such as Meso-America (e.g., *The Maya and Their Neighbors*), Kroeber was usually asked to write the summary, interpretative chapter. *Cultural and Natural Areas* not only delineated cultural areas (without statistical techniques) but related them to natural areas and, more importantly, introduced the concept of culture climax. Earlier element distribution studies had employed the concept of culture centers within areas, which were more complex and therefore presumed to be more inventive, and of margins, which were the simple, uninventive peripheral recipients of cultural achievements. Kroeber's concept of cultural climax avoided the implication that greatest complexity meant the locus of inventiveness and called attention instead to cultural intensification.

Kroeber expanded the culture area concept to even larger territories or "spheres of influence," such as "the Greater Southwest," and the "South Asia sphere." This reflected his predisposition to recognize historicity in territories of element distributions which were explainable by cultural diffusion. Continuing on the comparatively solid ground of describing areas or spheres in terms of element content and emphasis, rather than configuration, Kroeber enlarged his historical interpretations. He interpreted cultural development in the Western Hemisphere much as he had done in California. Later, in his Huxley lecture, "The Oikoumene" (1946), he delineated the cultural particulars, such as the arch, wheel, and alphabet, that distinguished the Old World from the New World. Underlying such global interpretations was vast knowledge of cultural history during all periods and a life-long tendency to organize the data in terms of diffusion and distributions. A similar method of organizing data was given his students, as when we made distributional studies of Indian games, and it underlay the element list surveys.

Finally, Kroeber's *Anthropology* (edition of 1948) is probably the most important single work ever written in anthropology. It was first published in 1923 as a modest introductory text because there had been no general summary since E. B. Tylor's *Anthropology* of 1881. For many years, it was the principal text for introductory courses in the United States. The new edition of 1948 became something else. This 850-page book gives a basic résumé of nearly all recent fields of anthropology, incisive appraisals of new trends, and statements of Kroeber's own views on subjects previously published elsewhere, together with many points not made before. Its notable omission is the social science and structural components of anthropology. While the 1948 edition offers freshmen and sophomores solid fodder, it is not now the principal introductory text. But, perhaps more importantly, it constitutes a basic survey of modern anthropology which well serves Ph.D. candidates and all others wishing a sophisticated view.

Concluding comments

It is impossible in a brief memorial article to do justice to a great scientist whose works are still a very living part of anthropology and related disciplines. Kroeber's place in history will be determined by the scholars who continue to be influenced by his writings in the future, rather than by those of us who now undertake so myopically to assess his achievements.

In histories of social science, appraisals of the great minds tend strongly to show the interests and preoccupations of the historians. The present article is a very humble attempt to suggest some of Kroeber's main achievements, but it cannot claim objectivity. The comments on Kroeber's achievements are made in the light of my own view that causes, explanations, or processes which are not peculiar to each relativistically unique culture can be identified. This is a fairly new approach, and whether the mounting body of causal hypotheses represent a new trend will be determined only by time.

In spite of my views, which differ in some ways from Kroeber's, I am deeply convinced that Kroeber's 500 odd publications are, and will be for many decades, an almost inexhaustible mine not only of information but of problems, concepts, and hypotheses which have not yet made sufficient impact upon the world of scholarship. I have tried to indicate that Kroeber frequently touched, with deep insights, many problems that searchers for causes might well heed. Some of his syntheses and interpretations could readily be classed as "hard science." For example his unpretentious summary of the parallel developments of the early Old World and New World civilization in *Anthropology* (1948), comes as near to a formulation of causality, or process that operated cross-culturally as can be made, even while disavowing such intent.

Foremost among the basic scientific problems raised by Kroeber is that of classifying whole cultures. Parts of culture, such as social systems or categories of religious concepts, are amenable to cross-cultural classification. A taxonomy of whole cultures has proved to be extremely difficult; perhaps it is impossible. While Kroeber was not especially interested in taxonomy for its own sake, his constant preoccupation with the nature of culture took him vastly farther than anyone else in attempting it.

LAURA BOHANNAN

Prince Hamlet in Africa

Laura Bohannan (under the pen name of Elizabeth Bowen) is the author of *Return to Laughter*, a description of her experiences while doing fieldwork in West Africa. She is also the author, with her husband Paul Bohannan, of numerous works on the Tiv, most recently, *Tiv Economy* (1968).

ust before I left Oxford for the Tiv in West Africa, conversation turned o the season at Stratford. "You Americans," said a friend, "often have lifficulty with Shakespeare. He was, after all, a very English poet, and ne can easily misinterpret the universal by misunderstanding the articular."

I protested that human nature is pretty much the same the whole world ver; at least the general plot and motivation of the greater tragedies vould always be clear—everywhere—although some details of custom night have to be explained and difficulties of translation might produce ther slight changes. To end an argument we could not conclude, my iend gave me a copy of *Hamlet* to study in the African bush: it would, e hoped, lift my mind above its primitive surroundings, and possibly I night, by prolonged meditation, achieve the grace of correct interpreta-on.

It was my second field trip to that African tribe, and I thought myself eady to live in one of its remote sections—an area difficult to cross even n foot. I eventually settled on the hillock of a very knowledgeable old nan, the head of a homestead of some hundred and forty people, all of hom were either his close relatives or their wives and children. Like the her elders of the vicinity, the old man spent most of his time perform-g ceremonies seldom seen these days in the more accessible parts of the ibe. I was delighted. Soon there would be three months of enforced olation and leisure, between the harvest that takes place just before the sing of the swamps and the clearing of new farms when the water goes

---

ura Bohannan, "Shakespeare in the Bush," *Natural History*, 75, 7 (August–ptember 1966), 28–33.

down. Then, I thought, they would have even more time to perform ceremonies and explain them to me.

I was quite mistaken. Most of the ceremonies demanded the presence of elders from several homesteads. As the swamps rose, the old men found it too difficult to walk from one homestead to the next, and the ceremonies gradually ceased. As the swamps rose even higher, all activities but one came to an end. The women brewed beer from maize and millet. Men, women, and children sat on their hillocks and drank it.

People began to drink at dawn. By midmorning the whole homestead was singing, dancing, and drumming. When it rained, people had to sit inside their huts: there they drank and sang or they drank and told stories. In any case, by noon or before, I either had to join the party or retire to my own hut and my books. "One does not discuss serious matters when there is beer. Come, drink with us." Since I lacked their capacity for the thick native beer, I spent more and more time with *Hamlet*. Before the end of the second month, grace descended on me. I was quite sure that *Hamlet* had only one possible interpretation, and that one universally obvious.

Early every morning, in the hope of having some serious talk before the beer party, I used to call on the old man at his reception hut—a circle of posts supporting a thatched roof above a low mud wall to keep out wind and rain. One day I crawled through the low doorway and found most of the men of the homestead sitting huddled in their ragged cloths on stools, low plank beds, and reclining chairs, warming themselves against the chill of the rain around a smoky fire. In the center were three pots of beer. The party had started.

The old man greeted me cordially. "Sit down and drink." I accepted a large calabash full of beer, poured some into a small drinking gourd, and tossed it down. Then I poured some more into the same gourd for the man second in seniority to my host before I handed my calabash over to a young man for further distribution. Important people shouldn't ladl beer themselves.

"It is better like this," the old man said, looking at me approvingly and plucking at the thatch that had caught in my hair. "You should sit and drink with us more often. Your servants tell me that when you are not with us, you sit inside your hut looking at a paper."

The old man was acquainted with four kinds of "papers": tax receipts bride price receipts, court fee receipts, and letters. The messenger wh brought him letters from the chief used them mainly as a badge of office for he always knew what was in them and told the old man. Personal letters for the few who had relatives in the government or missio stations were kept until someone went to a large market where there wa a letter writer and reader. Since my arrival, letters were brought to me t be read. A few men also brought me bride price receipts, privately, with requests to change the figures to a higher sum. I found moral arguments were of no avail, since in-laws are fair game, and the technical hazards of forgery difficult to explain to an illiterate people. I did not wish them to think me silly enough to look at any such papers for days on end, and I hastily explained that my "paper" was one of the "things of long ago" of my country.

"Ah," said the old man. "Tell us."

I protested that I was not a storyteller. Storytelling is a skilled art among them; their standards are high, and the audiences critical—and vocal in their criticism. I protested in vain. This morning they wanted to hear a story while they drank. They threatened to tell me no more stories until I told them one of mine. Finally, the old man promised that no one would criticize my style "for we know you are struggling with our language." "But," put in one of the elders, "you must explain what we do not understand, as we do when we tell you our stories." Realizing that here was my chance to prove *Hamlet* universally intelligible, I agreed.

The old man handed me some more beer to help me on with my storytelling. Men filled their long wooden pipes and knocked coals from the fire to place in the pipe bowls; then, puffing contentedly, they sat back to listen. I began in the proper style, "Not yesterday, not yesterday, but long ago, a thing occurred. One night three men were keeping watch outside the homestead of the great chief, when suddenly they saw the former chief approach them."

"Why was he no longer their chief?"

"He was dead," I explained. "That is why they were troubled and afraid when they saw him."

"Impossible," began one of the elders, handing his pipe on to his neighbor, who interrupted, "Of course it wasn't the dead chief. It was an omen sent by a witch. Go on."

Slightly shaken, I continued. "One of these three was a man who knew things"—the closest translation for scholar, but unfortunately it also meant witch. The second elder looked triumphantly at the first. "So he spoke to the dead chief saying, 'Tell us what we must do so you may rest in your grave,' but the dead chief did not answer. He vanished, and they could see him no more. Then the man who knew things—his name was Horatio—said this event was the affair of the dead chief's son, Hamlet."

There was a general shaking of heads round the circle. "Had the dead chief no living brothers? Or was his son the chief?"

"No," I replied. "That is, he had one living brother who became the chief when the elder brother died."

The old men muttered: such omens were matters for chiefs and elders, not for youngsters; no good could come of going behind a chief's back; clearly Horatio was not a man who knew things.

"Yes, he was," I insisted, shooing a chicken away from my beer. "In our country the son is next to the father. The dead chief's younger brother had become the great chief. He had also married his elder brother's widow only about a month after the funeral."

"He did well," the old man beamed and announced to the others, "I told you that if we knew more about Europeans, we would find they really were very like us. In our country also," he added to me, "the younger brother marries the elder brother's widow and becomes the father of his children. Now, if your uncle, who married your widowed mother, is your father's full brother, then he will be a real father to you. Did Hamlet's father and uncle have one mother?"

His question barely penetrated my mind; I was too upset and thrown too far off balance by having one of the most important elements of *Hamlet* knocked straight out of the picture. Rather uncertainly I said that I thought they had the same mother, but I wasn't sure—the story didn't say. The old man told me severely that these genealogical details made all the difference and that when I got home I must ask the elders about it. He shouted out the door to one of his younger wives to bring his goatskin bag.

Determined to save what I could of the mother motif, I took a deep breath and began again. "The son Hamlet was very sad because his mother had married again so quickly. There was no need for her to do so, and it is our custom for a widow not to go to her next husband until she has mourned for two years."

"Two years is too long," objected the wife, who had appeared with the old man's battered goatskin bag. "Who will hoe your farms for you while you have no husband?"

"Hamlet," I retorted without thinking, "was old enough to hoe his mother's farms himself. There was no need for her to remarry." No one looked convinced. I gave up. "His mother and the great chief told Hamlet not to be sad, for the great chief himself would be a father to Hamlet. Furthermore, Hamlet would be the next chief: therefore he must stay to learn the things of a chief. Hamlet agreed to remain, and all the rest went off to drink beer."

While I paused, perplexed at how to render Hamlet's disgusted soliloquy to an audience convinced that Claudius and Gertrude had behaved in the best possible manner, one of the younger men asked me who had married the other wives of the dead chief.

"He had no other wives," I told him.

"But a chief must have many wives! How else can he brew beer and prepare food for all his guests?"

I said firmly that in our country even chiefs had only one wife, that they had servants to do their work, and that they paid them from tax money.

It was better, they returned, for a chief to have many wives and sons who would help him hoe his farms and feed his people; then everyone loved the chief who gave much and took nothing—taxes were a bad thing.

I agreed with the last comment, but for the rest fell back on their favorite way of fobbing off my questions: "That is the way it is done, so that is how we do it."

I decided to skip the soliloquy. Even if Claudius was here thought quite right to marry his brother's widow, there remained the poison motif, and I knew they would disapprove of fratricide. More hopefully I resumed, "That night Hamlet kept watch with the three who had seen his dead father. The dead chief again appeared, and although the others were afraid, Hamlet followed his dead father off to one side. When they were alone, Hamlet's dead father spoke."

"Omens can't talk!" The old man was emphatic.

"Hamlet's dead father wasn't an omen. Seeing him might have been an omen, but he was not." My audience looked as confused as I sounded. "It *was* Hamlet's dead father. It was a thing we call a 'ghost.' " I had to use the English word, for unlike many of the neighboring tribes, these people didn't believe in the survival after death of any individuating part of the personality.

"What is a 'ghost?' An omen?"

"No, a 'ghost' is someone who is dead but who walks around and can talk, and people can hear him and see him but not touch him."

They objected. "One can touch zombis."

"No, no! It was not a dead body the witches had animated to sacrifice and eat. No one else made Hamlet's dead father walk. He did it himself."

"Dead men can't walk," protested my audience as one man.

I was quite willing to compromise. "A 'ghost' is the dead man's shadow."

But again they objected. "Dead men cast no shadows."

"They do in my country," I snapped.

The old man quelled the babble of disbelief that arose immediately and told me with that insincere, but courteous, agreement one extends to the fancies of the young, ignorant, and superstitious, "No doubt in your country the dead can also walk without being zombis." From the depths of his bag he produced a withered fragment of kola nut, bit off one end to show it wasn't poisoned, and handed me the rest as a peace offering.

"Anyhow," I resumed, "Hamlet's dead father said that his own brother, the one who became chief, had poisoned him. He wanted Hamlet to avenge him. Hamlet believed this in his heart, for he did not like his father's brother." I took another swallow of beer. "In the country of the great chief, living in the same homestead, for it was a very large one, was an important elder who was often with the chief to advise and help him. His name was Polonius. Hamlet was courting his daughter, but her father and her brother . . . [I cast hastily about for some tribal analogy] warned her not to let Hamlet visit her when she was alone on her farm, for he would be a great chief and so could not marry her."

"Why not?" asked the wife, who had settled down on the edge of the old man's chair. He frowned at her for asking stupid questions and growled, "They lived in the same homestead."

"That was not the reason," I informed them. "Polonius was a stranger who lived in the homestead because he helped the chief, not because he was a relative."

"Then why couldn't Hamlet marry her?"

"He could have," I explained, "but Polonius didn't think he would. After all, Hamlet was a man of great importance who ought to marry a chief's daughter, for in his country a man could have only one wife. Polonius was afraid that if Hamlet made love to his daughter, then no one else would give a high price for her."

"That might be true," remarked one of the shrewder elders, "but a chief's son would give his mistress's father enough presents and patronage to more than make up the difference. Polonius sounds like a fool to me."

"Many people think he was," I agreed. "Meanwhile Polonius sent his son Laertes off to Paris to learn the things of that country, for it was the homestead of a very great chief indeed. Because he was afraid that Laertes might waste a lot of money on beer and women and gambling, or get into trouble by fighting, he sent one of his servants to Paris secretly, to spy out what Laertes was doing. One day Hamlet came upon Polonius's daughter Ophelia. He behaved so oddly he frightened her. Indeed"—I was fumbling for words to express the dubious quality of Hamlet's madness—"the chief and many others had also noticed that when Hamlet talked one could understand the words but not what they meant. Many people thought that he had become mad." My audience suddenly became much more attentive. "The great chief wanted to know what was wrong with Hamlet, so he sent for two of Hamlet's age mates [school friends would have taken long explanation] to talk to Hamlet and find out what troubled his heart. Hamlet, seeing that they had been bribed by the chief to betray him, told them nothing. Polonius, however, insisted that Hamlet was mad because he had been forbidden to see Ophelia, whom he loved."

"Why," inquired a bewildered voice, "should anyone bewitch Hamlet on that account?"

"Bewitch him?"

"Yes, only witchcraft can make anyone mad, unless, of course, one sees the beings that lurk in the forest."

I stopped being a storyteller, took out my notebook and demanded to be told more about these two causes of madness. Even while they spoke and I jotted notes, I tried to calculate the effect of this new factor on the plot. Hamlet had not been exposed to the beings that lurk in the forests. Only his relatives in the male line could bewitch him. Barring relatives not mentioned by Shakespeare, it had to be Claudius who was attempting to harm him. And, of course, it was.

For the moment I staved off questions by saying that the great chief also refused to believe that Hamlet was mad for the love of Ophelia and nothing else. "He was sure that something much more important was troubling Hamlet's heart."

"Now Hamlet's age mates," I continued, "had brought with them a famous storyteller. Hamlet decided to have this man tell the chief and all his homestead a story about a man who had poisoned his brother because he desired his brother's wife and wished to be chief himself. Hamlet was sure the great chief could not hear the story without making a sign if he was indeed guilty, and then he would discover whether his dead father had told him the truth."

The old man interrupted, with deep cunning, "Why should a father lie to his son?" he asked.

I hedged: "Hamlet wasn't sure that it really was his dead father." It was impossible to say anything, in that language, about devil-inspired visions.

"You mean," he said, "it actually was an omen, and he knew witches sometimes send false ones. Hamlet was a fool not to go to one skilled in reading omens and divining the truth in the first place. A man-who-sees-the-truth could have told him how his father died, if he really had been poisoned, and if there was witchcraft in it; then Hamlet could have called the elders to settle the matter."

The shrewd elder ventured to disagree. "Because his father's brother was a great chief, one-who-sees-the-truth might therefore have been afraid to tell it. I think it was for that reason that a friend of Hamlet's father—a witch and an elder—sent an omen so his friend's son would know. Was the omen true?"

"Yes," I said, abandoning ghosts and the devil; a witch-sent omen it would have to be. "It was true, for when the storyteller was telling his tale before all the homestead, the great chief rose in fear. Afraid that Hamlet knew his secret he planned to have him killed."

The stage set of the next bit presented some difficulties of translation. I began cautiously. "The great chief told Hamlet's mother to find out from her son what he knew. But because a woman's children are always first in her heart, he had the important elder Polonius hide behind a cloth that hung against the wall of Hamlet's mother's sleeping hut. Hamlet started to scold his mother for what she had done."

There was a shocked murmur from everyone. A man should never scold his mother.

"She called out in fear, and Polonius moved behind the cloth. Shouting, 'A rat!' Hamlet took his machete and slashed through the cloth." I paused for dramatic effect. "He had killed Polonius!"

The old men looked at each other in supreme disgust. "That Polonius truly was a fool and a man who knew nothing! What child would not know enough to shout, 'It's me!' " With a pang, I remembered that these people are ardent hunters, always armed with bow, arrow, and machete; at the first rustle in the grass an arrow is aimed and ready, and the hunter shouts "Game!" If no human voice answers immediately, the arrow speeds on its way. Like a good hunter Hamlet had shouted, "A rat!"

I rushed in to save Polonius's reputation. "Polonius did speak. Hamlet heard him. But he thought it was the chief and wished to kill him to avenge his father. He had meant to kill him earlier that evening. . . ." I broke down, unable to describe to these pagans, who had no belief in individual afterlife, the difference between dying at one's prayers and dying "unhousell'd, disappointed, unaneled."

This time I had shocked my audience seriously. "For a man to raise his hand against his father's brother and the one who has become his father—that is a terrible thing. The elders ought to let such a man be bewitched."

I nibbled at my kola nut in some perplexity, then pointed out that after all the man had killed Hamlet's father.

"No," pronounced the old man, speaking less to me than to the young men sitting behind the elders. "If your father's brother has killed your father, you must appeal to your father's age mates; *they* may avenge him. No man may use violence against his senior relatives." Another thought struck him. "But if his father's brother had indeed been wicked enough to bewitch Hamlet and make him mad that would be a good story indeed, for it would be his fault that Hamlet, being mad, no longer had any sense and thus was ready to kill his father's brother."

There was a murmur of applause. *Hamlet* was again a good story to them, but it no longer seemed quite the same story to me. As I thought over the coming complications of plot and motive, I lost courage and decided to skim over dangerous ground quickly.

"The great chief," I went on, "was not sorry that Hamlet had killed Polonius. It gave him a reason to send Hamlet away, with his two treacherous age mates, with letters to a chief of a far country, saying that Hamlet should be killed. But Hamlet changed the writing on their papers, so that the chief killed his age mates instead." I encountered a reproachful glare from one of the men whom I had told undetectable forgery was not merely immoral but beyond human skill. I looked the other way.

"Before Hamlet could return, Laertes came back for his father's funeral. The great chief told him Hamlet had killed Polonius. Laertes swore to kill Hamlet because of this, and because his sister Ophelia, hearing her father had been killed by the man she loved, went mad and drowned in the river."

"Have you already forgotten what we told you?" The old man was reproachful. "One cannot take vengeance on a madman; Hamlet killed Polonius in his madness. As for the girl, she not only went mad, she was drowned. Only witches can make people drown. Water itself can't hurt anything. It is merely something one drinks and bathes in."

I began to get cross. "If you don't like the story, I'll stop."

The old man made soothing noises and himself poured me some more beer. "You tell the story well, and we are listening. But it is clear that the elders of your country have never told you what the story really means. No, don't interrupt! We believe you when you say your marriage customs are different, or your clothes and weapons. But people are the same everywhere; therefore, there are always witches and it is we, the elders, who know how witches work. We told you it was the great chief who wished to kill Hamlet, and now your own words have proved us right. Who were Ophelia's male relatives?"

"There were only her father and her brother." Hamlet was clearly out of my hands.

"There must have been many more; this also you must ask of your elders when you get back to your country. From what you tell us, since Polonius was dead, it must have been Laertes who killed Ophelia, although I do not see the reason for it."

We had emptied one pot of beer, and the old men argued the point with slightly tipsy interest. Finally one of them demanded of me, "What did the servant of Polonius say on his return?"

With difficulty I recollected Reynaldo and his mission. "I don't think he did return before Polonius was killed."

"Listen," said the elder, "and I will tell you how it was and how your story will go, then you may tell me if I am right. Polonius knew his son would get into trouble, and so he did. He had many fines to pay for fighting, and debts from gambling. But he had only two ways of getting money quickly. One was to marry off his sister at once, but it is difficult to find a man who will marry a woman desired by the son of a chief. For if the chief's heir commits adultery with your wife, what can you do? Only a fool calls a case against a man who will someday be his judge. Therefore Laertes had to take the second way: he killed his sister by witchcraft, drowning her so he could secretly sell her body to the witches."

I raised an objection. "They found her body and buried it. Indeed Laertes jumped into the grave to see his sister once more—so, you see, the body was truly there. Hamlet, who had just come back, jumped in after him."

"What did I tell you?" The elder appealed to the others. "Laertes was up to no good with his sister's body. Hamlet prevented him, because the chief's heir, like a chief, does not wish any other man to grow rich and powerful. Laertes would be angry, because he would have killed his sister without benefit to himself. In our country he would try to kill Hamlet for that reason. Is this not what happened?"

"More or less," I admitted. "When the great chief found Hamlet was still alive, he encouraged Laertes to try to kill Hamlet and arranged a fight with machetes between them. In the fight both the young men were wounded to death. Hamlet's mother drank the poisoned beer that the chief meant for Hamlet in case he won the fight. When he saw his mother die of poison, Hamlet, dying, managed to kill his father's brother with his machete."

"You see, I was right!" exclaimed the elder.

"That was a very good story," added the old man, "and you told it with very few mistakes. There was just one more error, at the very end. The poison Hamlet's mother drank was obviously meant for the survivor of the fight, whichever it was. If Laertes had won, the great chief would have poisoned him, for no one would know that he arranged Hamlet's death. Then, too, he need not fear Laertes' witchcraft; it takes a strong heart to kill one's only sister by witchcraft.

"Sometime," concluded the old man, gathering his ragged toga about him, "you must tell us some more stories of your country. We, who are elders, will instruct you in their true meaning, so that when you return to your own land your elders will see that you have not been sitting in the bush, but among those who know things and who have taught you wisdom."

PART FIVE

Ideology

The prevalent concept of reality rests not on the attempt to encounter reality, but on the reassuring sharing of viewpoints, labels, perspectives which makes superfluous the lonely and precarious struggle with the unknown.

ERNEST G. SCHACHTEL

INTRODUCTION

In this final section we shall present several essays that deal with the belief and value systems—the ideology—of various cultures. Each man constructs his own image of the world. But as we have seen, this image is strongly influenced by the existential and normative beliefs current in his society. For most people, culture defines a world whose temporal and spatial dimensions are related to social activity. Within this world, culture also teaches what kinds of entities exist and how men should relate to them. It provides standards of values by which men can judge one another and themselves.

Every society is bound together to some extent by its members' shared conceptions of what is real and what is good. This is not to deny that many groups have been torn apart by irreconcilable contradictions between ideology and social reality, or between competing ideologies. But some kind of common tradition is absolutely necessary for cooperative action, and even the most deviant and rebellious subgroups in our own society quickly develop their own jargon and standards of dress and behavior. To the extent that these standards are negations of the dominant culture, they too show its pervasive influence.

The first selection brings us back to the Kalahari Desert of South Africa to learn about leadership in the same Bushman band that was the subject of Elizabeth M. Thomas' selection in Part III. Here Miss Thomas introduces us to Toma, the leader, and his lovely wife, Tu. As we follow them in a series of ordinary activities, we begin to understand the equalitarian nature of this society and the subtle way authority is exercised in it.

Paul Radin recorded the autobiography of a Winnebago friend; in the section reprinted here, the speaker recalls his first experiences with peyote and his eventual conversion to the Indian peyote religion. The original version is extensively annotated by Radin to show how traditional Winnebago culture and unique life experiences affected this individual. Although the footnotes have been removed, the narrative is quite clear and should be of interest to readers from our drug-oriented society.

The selection by Robert Redfield presents an integrated account of the world view of a group of Mayan Indians. Their ideology has been strongly shaped by common participation in horticultural activities, but it also shows the influence of Spanish culture and especially that of the Roman Catholic Church.

A contrasting world view—that of the inhabitants of the Kingdom of Ruanda—is vividly summarized by J. J. Maquet in a selection that also describes some of the problems involved in studying the ideological system of culture. The author skillfully shows how the beliefs and the values of this African people reinforce one another. As among the Maya Indians, conceptions of ideal human relations and of "good actions" follow from the native system of beliefs about the nature of man and his relationship to the universe.

Layeh Bock's poem of welcome to a "stone-age people" about to be engulfed by civilization underlines many of the ironies of culture contact. It also calls attention to the different ways that various agents of change influence the native peoples they contact.

Finally, James Baldwin's essay on his experiences in a Swiss village is a fitting conclusion to the collection, bringing us back from a global tour to face the crucial social and ideological problems of our own society. If the experience of culture shock is indeed liberating, if facing and struggling with unfamiliar life ways can yield understanding, perhaps, then, we can learn to use our freedom from ethnocentrism and to apply our knowledge about culture to the crises of Western civilization. Livy wrote: "We fear things in proportion to our ignorance of them." Learning through culture shock is often a painful process. But it is surely worth the pain if, by diminishing our ignorance, it can give us freedom from fear.

ELIZABETH M. THOMAS

Leadership in a Bushman band

The following selection, like the selection in Part III on the Bushman food quest, is taken from Elizabeth M. Thomas' book *The Harmless People*; it is included here because of its relationship to problems of authority and leadership in a hunting and gathering society.

Toma the headman, sometimes known as Male Toma, an honorary name, sometimes known as Toma the Short, so-called because of his stocky build, was a famous person, and once had been a serf. He was born of serf parents at Gam, and as a boy had worked for the Chuanas, drawing their water and herding their cattle and goats.

When Toma was a boy, his father was murdered by a child, the result of a terrible accident which took place one day when Toma's father was arguing with the father of a boy named Gao. Gao, who couldn't have been more than ten years old, became upset and angry when he heard his father quarreling and, taking his father's weapons, shot Toma's father in the chest with a poisoned arrow. The old man was helped to the shade, the arrow was drawn out and the wound sucked, but as there is no antidote for arrow poison the old man lived only for the rest of the day and by night he was dead.

Oddly enough, the crime was connected with the old man and not with Gao, the young murderer, for ever after that day the old man was referred to as Tsamko Bone Arrow, while Gao in later years became known as Gao Wild Pig, after a pig he had killed which was in some way remarkable.

Toma flourished as a young man and became an excellent hunter with tireless legs, tireless eyes, and a deadly aim, and it was said of him that he never returned from a hunt without having killed at least a wildebeest, if not something larger. Hence, the people connected with him ate a great

---

Elizabeth M. Thomas, *The Harmless People* (New York: Alfred A. Knopf, Inc., 1958), pp. 182–187, 190–196, 199–203. Reprinted by permission of Alfred A. Knopf, Inc., and Marie Rodell.

deal of meat and his popularity grew. He once said of himself: "From the day I was born I was born for meat."

When Toma was in his late teens, some say, his powers in hunting attracted the attention of the headman of Gautscha Pan, who offered Toma the hand of his daughter, Tu, in marriage. Toma accepted, went to live with his wife's people, according to custom, and, when the old headman died, took over the leadership of the people in the area. He was not the true headman—his position would not be inherited by his son, for headmanship is passed only from father to son—but he was recognized as headman while he lived and it was a great honor to him that this was so.

Tu's brother was the rightful headman of Gautscha, but he had abdicated to live with his wife's people in the north. Her elder sister's husband, a man named Gao Big Feet, also had a right to the leadership in that his wife, Dikai, was older than Tu. But neither ever contested Toma's position as leader, for it was not a position which Toma held by force or pressure but simply by his wisdom and ability, and people prospered under him. No Bushman wants prominence, but Toma went further than most in avoiding prominence; he had almost no possessions and gave away everything that came into his hands. He was diplomatic, for in exchange for his self-imposed poverty he won the respect and following of all the people there. He enjoyed his position, and, being strangely free from the normal strains and jealousies of Bushmen, he saw justice clearly and hence he led his people well. At Gautscha his werf had been right beside the werf of his father's murderer, for Toma was friendly even with him.*

Toma had a short, stocky body and a shock of tangled hair. He was strong, too, and very co-ordinated, so that every motion he made was quick and controlled, and not a gesture of his was wasted. As a result of this enormous and unconscious control, accidents almost never happened to him. His face was broad, lined with many deep wrinkles at the corners of his eyes and mouth as though from smiling, though it was not from smiling that he got them but from years of squinting at the sun. His expression was usually dark and wondering, his forehead drawn intently into a frown, but sometimes he would abandon his gravity and laugh a high, reaching laugh that one could hear from far away, a laugh that came from his very soul, or, as Bushmen say, from his stomach. He listened diplomatically and intently whenever he was spoken to, staring at the ground, and had a habit of echoing, in a loud falsetto voice, the important phrases of every sentence he was told.

"We went to Keitsa Pan," someone might say to him.

A *werf* is the dwelling place of a Bushman household (see below). [Ed.]

"To Keitsa," Toma would reply.

"... and we slept there, but the blind flies were very bad..."

"Oh, bad, bad..."

"... but in the morning we saw two porcupines..."

"... yes, porcupines..."

"... and we killed them there. We made them cry..."

"... made them cry..."

"... made them cry."

Toma was considered to be very fortunate in his marriage. Of course it was through his wife, Tu, that he gained the leadership of the Gautscha people, his life free in the veld rather than in serfdom, and his two young sons, but besides all this his wife was beautiful, having a smooth face and great, clear eyes like a cat. Also, she was five feet tall, considered to be a very desirable height, and although no Bushman has ever been too fat, Tu was not too thin and her arms and legs were round. She had soft blue scars curving on her forehead which made her eyes seem to lift at the corners, and blue scars on her thighs that showed when she walked. Her chief virtues, in the eyes of Bushmen, were that she decorated herself with ornaments in her hair and kept her hands and face washed, thus demonstrating that she cared what she looked like, rather than letting herself go now that she was married. To show that she observed propriety, cared what people thought of her, she didn't leave her fire at night to go visiting, even to the scherm right next to hers. Rather, if she had something to say, she would shout it across the werf.

Her deference to appearances and public opinion seemed to make up for her faults, for she was considered to be almost a model personality in spite of her extremely jealous and vindictive moods which caused her to accuse others, quite unreasonably, of selfishness, greed, and other such things. Her husband and sons were not excepted, but this was something that Toma had learned to ignore. He would simply shrug his shoulders if she railed at him, pretend he didn't hear if she railed at others.

When she didn't assault her family with her tongue she sometimes harmed them actively. Very often she would lie sullen with narrowed eyes in front of her scherm watching the other women walk out to the veld in the morning on their way to dig veld food, and on these days her husband and sons would eat nothing unless, driven by hunger, they went to the veld themselves, the three of them together, to dig up a few roots and eat them raw. Tu herself did not experience hunger as a result of these moods, for she would have saved herself a morsel from the day before. It was her right to do this: among Bushmen every root is owned by its digger and is shared only at its owner's wish.

Toma might ask but would never command Tu to feed her family, for as he had learned to ignore her biting tongue he had learned to accept her moods. This was his way, appeasing her, and because Toma wanted peace perhaps as much as he wanted Tu, he pampered her.

This was not always so. One day gossiping people told us that early in their marriage Toma shot a fat kudu and Tu said: "Don't cook all the meat because my mother will be coming to visit us."

Toma remarked that the meat was there for any use, but Tu misunderstood him and, thinking that he denied meat to her and to her mother, she flew into a rage, attacked Toma, and gave him a nasty bite on his arm. Toma lost his temper entirely and pinched her cheeks together until his fingers met in her mouth. His anger had come now, the people said, and he threw her into the fire, saying: "She is a woman. Why does she make me so angry? Shall I take a stick?"

A small crowd had gathered, and, as usual, the family quarrel became a public affair. Several people helped Tu out of the fire, found her barely scorched, but her cousin seized Toma and began to shake him. This enraged Toma so much that he caught the cousin around the waist and threw him into the onlooking crowd. The people said: "We must stop Toma because if he is so angry he may kill someone," and with that they led the cousin out of Toma's sight.

Toma shouted after: "If you do that again, we will get our arrows and fight to the death. Stop here. I am very angry. Do not make me more angry."

One of the men who had helped Tu said to the cousin: "I took his wife from the fire. You, her cousin, almost got killed for the way you went at Toma. If you want to help people, don't get angry with them. Keep calm. Don't increase anger as you did with Toma." With these sage words the incident was over.

The people said: "After that everyone knew how angry Toma could be, so from that day on he never had another fight." Everyone honored and respected him, everyone except his wife.

But Tu had certain redeeming qualities. When she was in a good mood she was charming. She would smile at everyone, speak in a light voice instead of the low, menacing voice that she used when she was angry, a cat growling, and would be affectionate to Toma and her sons. Very often, when she was happy, she would dance a light, short dance to a song that she sang herself.

Tu had borne four children, four sons, to Toma, but the first two sons had died. One of these had died at birth, "had died in the veld without a name," said Toma. The oldest living children, born after the others were dead, were a boy of about eight years old and a boy of five. While we were there in 1953, Tu bore her first daughter, a strawberry of a baby who was named for two people—named first for Toma's sister, but also Norna for my mother; her name is Lorna, but Bushmen have trouble with the *l*. In order to fit us into their society, the Bushmen had given us names and niches in the kinship of Toma's family. My father was named for Toma's father, my mother was named for Toma's mother, my brother was named Toma for Toma, and I was called Dikai for Tu's sister. Toma therefore named his daughter for the person who was named for his mother—not at all unusual, as it often happens that a child may bear the names of two of its relations.

Now, hoping to find Toma once again, we started the truck motors, fired a rifle, called and called, in case he might be living far from the water, but no sound came from the great veld to answer us and we began to search in the bush around the pan for signs that might show us where he was.

. . .

It was very quiet and lonely there except for a few birds that flew high and far above us calling, and we called Toma's name again and again and our voices rang in the cold air, but we did not get an answer. Lazy Kwi, naked and barefoot in the frost, walked over the plain with his arms hugged against his chest for warmth and called more: "Toma . . . *Toma*," a little annoyed as he was tired, then waited, called again: "Toma . . . my brother . . . brother . . ." and as his voice died away no answer came; but a koorhan, a dark bird the size of a chicken, flew out of a clump of bushes far away and rose cackling up to the sky, where we saw it, black and clumsy, before it dropped to the earth again. The last pale light faded on the horizon and for a minute the sky looked like the cold sky over tundra or over an icy sea before the empty veld turned dark.

To clear the grass from our camping-site we lit a little grass fire, being too tired to pull up every blade of grass by hand, and the little flames seemed so cheerful and warm that we felt better right away. We made a cooking-fire and cooked our meat, then unrolled our blankets to lie upon, and we found that because the wind had died our cooking-fire shed so much heat that we were as warm as we would have been in a shelter.

We made coffee and talked all evening, and unnoticed our fire burned very low and we got colder, the night seemed darker and in the dark the koorhan began to call again, and when we looked far over the veld for the light of another fire but saw none it came to us that Toma might have been taken by the farmers after all. We talked for a while about that, but then Lazy Kwi said he believed that Toma was somewhere not very far away but was too clever to show himself. After our last expedition had left Nyae Nyae the last time, Lazy Kwi told us, Toma had waited months, whole seasons, for us to come back and when he had heard the trucks of the farmers he had gone to them, thinking it was us. "Now he is angry. Now he is too clever to make that mistake again," said Lazy Kwi.

That did seem possible, so we stood up and shouted Toma's name again; but even at night, when sound carries best, we heard only our echo, distant and diffuse, and at last we built up our fire and got ready to sleep. The night was perfectly quiet. No sound came from the wind or animals, only the sparks snapping from our fire, which burned for a while but soon died to embers and the smoke rose white and ghostly into the dark.

As we lay in our blankets, before we went to sleep, Lazy Kwi told us a story, told us something that had happened to him and to Toma while we had been away.

After Toma had mistaken the trucks of the farmers for our trucks, the rains had come. After the rains, when the veld was lush and tropical, when Gautscha Pan was full of water and succulent reeds, several herds of animals that do not ordinarily live in the desert had migrated south from the swamps and marshes of the Okovango River to eat the sweet grass of the pans. A herd of elephants had come and gone by, but some small herds of buffalo had come and these had stayed in the veld of Nyae Nyae, living among the pans.

One day the buffalo had come to Gautscha, and Toma, crouching on a limb of the baobab tree, had seen them wallowing in the pan and had taken his bow and arrow and, running fast and silently, had circled behind them, then had crept toward them, and from the reeds at the edge of the pan had shot a big male. The herd had bolted and Toma, after having inspected the tracks so that he would know his wounded bull when he saw its track again, had gone home. He had waited a day and a half, longer than usual because of the danger, and when the time had passed, returned with Lazy Kwi to the spot where the buffalo had been wounded. There he and Lazy Kwi had taken up the trail. The buffalo had separated from its herd and the two men had followed it silently, carefully, aware of the danger, avoiding the trail when it led through bushes. When, that night, they had not found the buffalo but knew from the freshness and pattern of the tracks that it was near and restless, they had waited in the veld, eating nothing themselves so that the buffalo would not eat and gain strength, remaining awake, moving around so that they would not get stiff but remaining silent so that the buffalo, not hearing them, would relax, lie down, and itself get stiff and sore. In the morning the two men had found where the buffalo had slept, also a damp spot of its urine with black flecks in it (which I believe were flecks of blood) and Toma had pushed a poison arrow into the spot of urine so that the buffalo would be unable to urinate again, unable to rid itself of more poison.

The men had followed the buffalo's track for three days, knowing from its footprints that it was getting weaker, staggering, and in the morning of the fourth day they had come over a rise of ground and had seen it far ahead of them, lying on its side as if dead. The two men wisely had not gone up to it, but had squatted where they were to watch it, remaining this way for most of the day, and when the buffalo had not even flicked its tail or heaved its sides in breathing, Toma had considered it safe enough to approach. He had done this cautiously, very carefully, balancing his long spear in his hand, but just as Toma had stood near the buffalo, spear poised for the stab that would kill it surely, the buffalo had lurched to its feet, had chased Toma, and had tossed him on its horns.

The great boss, the heavy mass of horn on the buffalo's forehead, had cracked Toma's ribs and one curved horn had hooked in Toma's side, passing through his body and out his back. Toma had lain unconscious and Lazy Kwi had carried him home; later, other hunters of Toma's band had found the buffalo truly dead, partly eaten by vultures, and had taken the meat; but nothing, no medicines or cures that the Bushmen had used, had helped Toma, and the people had expected him to die.

Gautscha was the country of Toma's wife, and when Toma had realized how sick he was he had wanted to return to his own people, the people of Gam. Lazy Kwi and another man had carried him there and it was there that the second group of farmers had found him, unable to escape or to resist, and they had taken him away. His wife was still waiting at Gautscha and Lazy Kwi had returned there to tell her that her husband had gone.

At the farm, though, Toma's luck had begun to turn. The farmer had gradually managed to heal his wounds with medicine and treatment, and by the start of the dry season Toma had felt quite well. One night, when the veld was quiet and dark, Toma had thanked the farmer in his heart, had gathered all the Bushmen on the farm together, and had led the people over the veld, all the way back to Nyae Nyae. It had been a long walk, a long way, but Toma had managed. Now, said Lazy Kwi, Toma's wound ached on cold days and sometimes his vision was blurry, but he was pleased with himself and pleased to be back in his own country.

Lazy Kwi was pleased with him too, and he smiled when he finished the story.

When the first light of morning came, the air was so cold that our breath made clouds. We got up, fed the fire, and cooked the remainder of last night's meat, then drove off in the jeep again, for in that early light we had seen the smoke of three veld fires on the horizon, one in the south, two in the west, perhaps kindled by Bushmen during the night, perhaps revived by the wind from old embers, and we planned to make a circle to investigate them all.

On the way we found a bee tree that had been raided for its honey and we believed that Toma had done it, although the break was old and the bees were gone away; but after looking at it a moment Lazy Kwi remembered that he had done it himself during the last rains. He remembered too that there had been very little honey and that he had got stung, and since that was all he remembered we went on again to the source of the first of the three fires.

It was there that we found Toma. He had been there all the time, only a few miles from where we had camped, and when he heard our jeep coming he watched us over the top of a bush before showing himself to see first who we were.

We saw him when he ran toward us. He was quite far off and we saw first his dark figure detach itself from the bush and run with long, swinging strides toward our jeep. He waved his arms and we knew at once that this, at last, was Toma. Before he reached us a second figure appeared from behind another bush and ran beside him, and we knew from the disjointed stride that this second man was Gao Big Feet, Toma's brother-in-law. We turned our jeep toward them and soon we met and the two men embraced us and laughed and said that they had known we would come back someday, and then they climbed in the jeep and took us to their werf, stopping first to get their spears and quivers, which they had left in the bushes, for no Bushman, no matter how excited, ever greets people with his weapons on his back because this might be taken as a sign that he was quarrelsome, looking for a fight.

Their werf was in a tiny thicket of thorn trees at the edge of the plain, screened in front by bushes, carefully concealed, but on a rise of ground where a man standing could easily scan the surrounding plain without being seen himself. There Toma and Gao Feet could observe the movements of the antelope that crossed the plains below them, waiting patient in the dappled shade of their trees' broad leaves as lions do. The two families stood in front of their bushes to meet us and they, too, embraced us and they all climbed in the jeep to do this, then climbed out again and stood back to see how we were.

We got out and sat with them in their werf to talk before deciding what we would do next. Looking around, we saw that only the two families lived here, for there were only two sleeping-places, set, for the sake of a little privacy, on the opposite sides of one of the scrawny trees. The women had not built huts, but had scooped little hollows for themselves and their husbands which they had lined with soft grass bedding, and had put up two arching sticks at each of these hollows to mark the place where the door would be if a scherm had been there, for the Kung as well as the Gikwe need a sense of place. In fact, the Kung need it even more, for without their grass and marking-sticks the Kung feel homeless. Their sleeping hollows were like the soft grass nests of pheasants, hidden in the leaves.

The Bushmen all lit pipes and passed them—each pipe reached everybody, everybody shared and smoked, and the pipes circled slowly for an hour or more until the tobacco was gone. There was a brass pipe made of an old cartridge, a bone one, a horn one, and last of all a copper one that tasted very bad.

. . .

We asked for other people, the other members of Toma's large band, and Toma told us that they were well, living far away in a mangetti forest. Naturally, Toma's family had not seen this group for some time because of the distance, but Toma said now that he would take us to see them someday soon because he believed that we would be able to help them; one man in their band, a man called Short Kwi, or sometimes Kwi the Hunter, had been bitten in the leg by a puff adder and was very badly hurt. We got the impression that he had been bitten recently and, hoping that we might draw the poison from the wound, we said that we would leave at once. But Toma said that it had happened during the last rainy season, so there was no use hurrying; other Bushmen had cut the wound and had sucked the poison, saving Short Kwi's life, but his leg was so badly hurt that he couldn't use it. It had turned black, said Toma, and black liquid ran out at the wound. We thought then that there would be nothing we could do to help; but perhaps rumor had exaggerated the misfortune, and so we told Toma that we would certainly go to do what we could.

Short Kwi came from a famous family; he was the younger brother of the man who murdered Toma's father, but Short Kwi was famous in his own right, famous as a hunter. He often killed more game in a year than many other men kill in their lives, a great hunter among a hunting people. The other Bushmen told stories about him—about the time he had killed four wildebeests in a herd of many, about the time he had killed an eland, a wildebeest, and a wild pig all in one day. It was his technique of hunting to be relentless in his pursuit; therefore, if he shot an animal and suspected others to be in the vicinity he would let the wounded animal run where it would while he hunted on and shot another, and another, and when all were as good as dead he would rest, then return to pick up the trail of the one that he felt would die the soonest. He almost never lost an animal, for his eyes were sharp and he could follow a cold trail over hard ground and even over stones; he could tell from fallen leaves whether the wind or passing feet had disarranged them; and the meat that resulted from his prolific hunting was never wasted, for he would bring other hunters to help him dry it, then carry it off to a werf somewhere to share with others.

He knew the habits of animals from the ways of the largest antelope all the way down to the smallest species of mice; in fact, he must have known animals very well, for he could always find them. He knew when he was in danger and when he was safe, and he was as brave as he was careful. Once, Short Kwi, John, and two other hunters were tracking a bull wildebeest that one of the hunters had shot. They came upon it lying down, surrounded by a very large pride of lions. There were twenty or thirty lions in all, having got there first and claiming the wildebeest as their own, for the bushes were full of lions walking back and forth, watching several other lions brave the fallen wildebeest, still able to protect itself with its horns. The braver lions were standing near the wildebeest, obviously steeling themselves for the attack, when the hunters arrived. The Bushmen had followed the wildebeest's trail through thorns and over the parching desert and were not to be deprived, and, speaking softly to the lions, they said: 'We know you are strong, Big Lions, we know you are brave, but this meat is ours and you must give it back to us."

Even after these words the lions did not give ground. Their round eyes watched the hunters and they began to growl, and the four men, quite unarmed except for their arrows and spear (to use a spear would have been folly), said respectfully: "Great Lions, Old Lions, this meat belongs to us," and then advanced on the lions, throwing little stones and clods of dirt. The lions in the bushes began to back away, while the braver lions stood their ground until a clod struck one of them, causing him to huff and run back a little. At this, the courage of the other lions broke and they all turned and scrambled for the safety of their companions, by now quite far away.

The hunters, victorious in this battle of nerves, had the bull wildebeest all to themselves, but now found that they could not approach it either. Having fended off the lions (it thought), it now tried to lunge to its feet to fend off the men. Short Kwi borrowed the spear from its owner and hurled it into the wildebeest's neck, where it stuck fast. Now they had no weapon at all. Their arrows would be useless. The sticks and stones they threw at the spear did not dislodge it and all their efforts to retrieve it by creeping up on the wildebeest from behind did not succeed, for as soon as one of them would edge near enough to touch the spear the wildebeest would toss its horns so quickly that the man would have to jump back, grazed. At last, while one of the men distracted the wildebeest from the front, Short Kwi backed off and rushed at it, jumped over it, and, as he passed over its back, jerked the spear free. The bull lunged and the curved horns hooked upward, but too late. Short Kwi was gone. Wanting a picture, John asked Short Kwi to do it again, but Short Kwi shook his head. "This time he will remember," Short Kwi said, and dispatched the bull by hurling the spear into its throat.

Sometimes, as on these occasions, Short Kwi hunted with others, but mostly he hunted alone. He knew every bush and stone in the area of thousands of square miles that he ranged over, and he lived for hunting. Caring more for this, his passion, than for society, he often hunted as he did when we had first heard of him, alone in the veld with only his wife—a young woman who was intelligent and gay and almost pretty, to whom Short Kwi was devoted—his baby daughter, and his mother-in-law.

We had met him for the first time at Gautscha. He had come in from the veld one night to visit his brother, and we had met him in the morning. Short Kwi was a young, small man, shorter than his wife and so slender that he looked almost like a child. With long, light feet that took him everywhere, with heavy thighs but light calves like the thin shanks of a greyhound, and with a narrow, deep chest and lungs that never winded, he was obviously built for hunting. In the rainy season when the veld was soft and muddy he often hunted with only a spear and ran the great antelopes down, for though their hooves sunk and split in the mud, causing them eventually to tire, Short Kwi never tired and his strong legs bore him after them relentlessly, sweeping him down the long plains like a wind of death.

His life in the veld seemed lonely, but I doubt that it was; he had his wife, who adored him, for company in the evenings, and although she may have missed companionship more than he did, they were both shy, both quiet, and it may be that they both enjoyed their life apart. Short Kwi hunted most of the time. He would hunt on and on and when word would reach the large band of his wife's family that he had killed, the band would go out to where the animal was, dry the meat, and eat it. When there was enough meat Short Kwi would rest, would relax in the sun, would talk with his wife or make himself a new skin bag or garment, and when word would reach him that all the meat was gone he would move again. The men of his wife's family hunted too, of course, but never as successfully as he, yet his great ability set him so far apart from ordinary mortals that for once the Bushmen forgot their jealousy and agreed that he was the best hunter the Kalahari had ever known.

PAUL RADIN

An Indian skeptic takes peyote

Paul Radin was an ethnologist who specialized in American Indian culture and the study of comparative religion. His major works include: *Social Anthropology*, *Primitive Religion*, *Method and Theory of Ethnology*, and *Primitive Man as Philosopher*, as well as many articles and monographs on the Winnebago and their neighbors.

The Indians were celebrating their midsummer ceremony. I went there and took part and I drank all the time. I considered myself a brave man and a medicine man and I also thought myself a holy man, a strong man and a favorite with women. I regarded myself as being in possession of many courting medicines. I am a great man, I thought, and also a fleet runner. I was a good singer of Brave Dance songs. I was a sport and I wanted whiskey every day.

My mother and father had gone to Missouri River (Winnebago reservation in Nebraska) and left me in charge of the two horses they possessed, as well as a vehicle which I was using at the time. Later on, in the fall, when the cranberry season started, I lived with three women. I never did any work, but simply went from one of these women to the other. After a while an annuity payment was made. I went around "chasing the payments" and I sold the horses at that time and spent the money.

Then my father and mother asked me to come to the Missouri River (Nebraska) but I had been told that my father and mother had eaten peyote and I did not like it. I had been told that these peyote eaters were doing wrong, and therefore I disliked them; I had heard that they were doing everything that was wicked. For these reasons we did not like them. About this time they sent me money for my ticket and since my brothers and sisters told me to go, I went. Just as I was about to start, my

---

Paul Radin, *The Autobiography of a Winnebago Indian*, UNIVERSITY OF CALIFORNIA PUBLICATIONS IN AMERICAN ARCHAEOLOGY AND ETHNOLOGY, 16, (Berkeley: University of California Press, 1920), 48–64.

youngest sister, the one to whom we always listened most attentively, said to me, "Older brother, do not you indulge in this medicine eating (peyote) of which so much is said." I promised. Then I started out.

As soon as I arrived (in Nebraska) I met some people who had not joined the peyote eaters and who said to me, "Your relatives are eating the peyote and they sent for you that you also might eat it. Your mother, your father, and your younger sister, they are all eating it." Thus they spoke to me. Then they told me of some of the bad things it was reported that these people had done. I felt ashamed and I wished I had not come in the first place. Then I said that I was going to eat the medicine.

After that I saw my father, mother, and sister. They were glad. Then we all went to where they were staying. My father and I walked (alone). Then he told me about the peyote eating. "It does not amount to anything, all this that they are doing, although they do stop drinking. It is also said that sick people get well. We were told about this and so we joined, and, sure enough, we are practically well, your mother as well as I. It is said that they offer prayers to Earthmaker (God)," he said. He kept on talking. "They are rather foolish. They cry when they feel very happy about anything. They throw away all of the medicines that they possess and know. They give up all the blessings they received while fasting and they give up all the spirits that blessed them in their fasts. They also stop smoking and chewing tobacco. They stop giving feasts, and they stop making offerings of tobacco. Indeed they burn up their holy things. They burn up their war-bundles. They are bad people. They give up the Medicine Dance. They burn up their medicine bags and even cut up their otter-skin bags. They say they are praying to Earthmaker (God) and they do so standing and crying. They claim that they hold nothing holy except Earthmaker (God). They claim that all the things that they are stopping are those of the bad spirit (the devil), and that the bad spirit (the devil) has deceived them; that there are no spirits who can bless; that there is no other spirit except Earthmaker (God)." Then I said, "Say, they certainly speak foolish." I felt very angry towards them. "You will hear them for they are going to have a meeting tonight. Their songs are very strange. They use a very small drum," said he. Then I felt a very strong desire to see them.

After a while we arrived. At night they had their ceremony. At first I sat outside and listened to them. I was rather fond of them. I stayed in that country and the young peyote eaters were exceedingly friendly to me. They would give me a little money now and then and they treated me with tender regard. They did everything that they thought would make me feel good, and in consequence I used to speak as though I liked their ceremony. However I was only deceiving them. I only said because they were so good to me. I thought they acted in this way because (the peyote) was deceiving them.

Soon after that my parents returned to Wisconsin, but when they left they said they would come back in a little while. So I was left there with my relatives who were all peyote followers. For that reason they left me there. Whenever I went among the non-peyote people I used to say all sorts of things about the peyote people and when I returned to the peyote people, I used to say all sorts of things about the others.

I had a friend who was a peyote man and he said to me, "My friend, I wish very much that you should eat the peyote." Thus he spoke and I answered him, "My friend I will do it, but not until I get accustomed to the people of this country. Then I will do it. The only thing that worries me is the fact that they are making fun of you. And in addition, I am not quite used to them." I spoke dishonestly.

I was staying at the place where my sister lived. She had gone to Oklahoma; she was a peyote follower. After a while she returned. I was then living with a number of women. This was the second time (there) and from them I obtained some money. Once I got drunk there and was locked up for six days. After my sister returned she and the others paid more attention than ever to me. Especially was this true of my brother-in-law. They gave me horses and a vehicle. They really treated me very tenderly. I knew that they did all this because they wished me to eat the peyote. I, in my turn, was very kind to them. I thought that I was fooling them and they thought that they were converting me. I told them that I believed in the peyote because they were treating me so nicely.

After a while we moved to a certain place where they were to have a large peyote meeting. I knew they were doing this in order to get me to join. Then I said to my younger sister, "I would be quite willing to eat this peyote (ordinarily), but I don't like the woman with whom I am living just now and I think I will leave her. That is why I do not want to join now, for I understand that when married people eat medicine (peyote) they will always have to stay together. Therefore I will join when I am married to some woman permanently." Then my brother-in-law came and she told him what I had said, and he said to me, "You are right in what you say. The woman with whom you are staying is a married woman and you can not continue living with her. It is null and void (this marriage) and we know it. You had better join now. It will be the same as if you were single. We will pray for you as though you were single. After you have joined this ceremony, then you can marry any woman whom you have a right to marry (legally). So, do join tonight. It is best. For some time we have been desirous of your joining but we have not said anything to you. It is Earthmaker's (God's) blessing to you that you have been thinking of this," said he.

I eat peyote

Therefore I sat inside the meeting-place with them. One man acted as leader. We were to do whatever he ordered. The regalia were placed before him. I wanted to sit in some place on the side, because I thought I might get to crying like the others. I felt ashamed of myself.

Then the leader arose and talked. He said that this was an affair of Earthmaker's (God's), and that he (the leader) could do nothing on his own initiative; that Earthmaker (God) was going to conduct the ceremony. Then he said that the medicine (peyote) was holy and that he would turn us all over to it; that he had turned himself over to it and wished now to turn all of us over to it. He said further, "I am a very pitiable (figure) in this ceremony, so when you pray to Earthmaker, pray also for me. Now let us all rise and pray to Earthmaker (God)." We all rose. Then he prayed. He prayed for the sick, and he prayed for those who did not yet know Earthmaker. He said that they were to be pitied. When he had finished we sat down. Then the peyote was passed around. They gave me five. My brother-in-law said to me, "If you speak to this medicine (peyote), it will give you whatever you ask of it. Then you must pray to Earthmaker, and then you must eat the medicine." However I ate them (the peyote) immediately for I did not know what to ask for and I did not know what to say in a prayer to Earthmaker (God). So I ate the peyote just as they were. They were very bitter and had a taste difficult to describe. I wondered what would happen to me. After a while I was given five more and I also ate them. They tasted rather bitter. Now I was very quiet. The peyote rather weakened me. Then I listened very attentively to the singing. I liked it very much. I felt as though I were partly asleep. I felt different from (my normal self), but when I (looked around) and examined myself, I saw nothing wrong about myself. However I felt different from (my normal self). Before this I used to dislike the songs. Now I liked the leader's singing very much. I liked to listen to him.

They were all sitting very quietly. They were doing nothing except singing. Each man sang four songs and then passed the regalia to the next one. (Each one) held a stick and an eagle's tail feather in one hand and a small gourd rattle, which they used to shake while singing, in the other. One of (those) present used to do the drumming. Thus objects would pass around until they came back to the leader, who would then sing four songs. When these were finished, he would place the various (things) on the ground, rise, and pray to Earthmaker (God). Then he called upon one or two to speak. They said that Earthmaker (God) was good and that the peyote was good, and that whosoever ate this medicine (peyote) would be able to free himself from the bad spirit (the devil); for they said that Earthmaker forbids us to commit sins. When this was over they sang again.

After midnight, every once in a while, (I heard) someone cry. In some cases they would go up to the leader and talk with him. He would stand up and pray with them. They told me what they were saying. They said that they were asking (people) to pray for them, as they were sorry for their sins and that they might be prevented from committing them again. That is what they were saying. They cried very loudly. I was rather frightened. (I noticed also) that when I closed my eyes and sat still, I began to see strange things. I did not get sleepy in the least. Thus the light (of morning) came upon me. In the morning, as the sun rose, they stopped. They all got up and prayed to Earthmaker (God) and then they stopped.

During the daytime, I did not get sleepy in the least. My actions were a little different (from my usual ones). Then they said, "Tonight they are going to have another meeting. Let us go over. They say that is the best (thing) to do and thus you can learn it (the ceremony) right away. It is said that their spirits wander over all the earth and the heavens also. All this you will learn and see," they said. "At times they die and remain dead all night and all day. When in this condition they sometimes see Earthmaker (God), it is said." One would also be able to see where the bad spirit lived, it was said.

So we went there again. I doubted all this. I thought that what they were saying was untrue. However I went along anyhow. When we got there I had already eaten some peyote, for I had taken three during the day. Now near the peyote meeting an (Indian) feast was being given and I went there instead. When I reached the place, I saw a long lodge. The noise was terrific. They were beating an enormous drum. The sound almost raised me in the air, so (pleasurably) loud did it sound to me. Not so (pleasurable) had things appeared at those affairs (peyote meetings) that I had lately been attending. There I danced all night and I flirted with the women. About day I left and when I got back the peyote meeting was still going on. When I got back they told me to sit down at a certain place. They treated me very kindly. There I again ate peyote. I heard that they were going to have another meeting nearby on the evening of the same day. We continued eating peyote the whole day at the place where we were staying. We were staying at the house of one of my relatives. Some of the boys there taught me a few songs. "Say, when you learn how to sing, you will be the best singer, for you are a good singer as it is. You have a good voice," they said to me. I thought so myself.

That night we went to the place where the peyote meeting was to take place. They gave me a place to sit and treated me very kindly. "Well, he has come," they even said when I got there, "make a place for him." I thought they regarded me as a great man. John Rave, the leader, was to conduct the (ceremony). I ate five peyote. Then my brother-in-law and my sister came and gave themselves up. They asked me to stand there with them. I did not like it, but I did it nevertheless. "Why should I give myself up? I am not in earnest, and I intend to stop this as soon as I get back to Wisconsin. I am only doing this because they have given me presents," I thought. "I might just as well get up, since it doesn't mean anything to me." So I stood up. The leader began to talk and I (suddenly) began to feel sick. It got worse and worse and finally I lost consciousness entirely. When I recovered I was lying flat on my back. Those with whom I had been standing, were still standing there. I had (as a matter of fact) regained consciousness as soon as I fell down. I felt like leaving the place that night, but I did not do it. I was quite tired out. "Why have I done this?" I said to myself. "I promised (my sister) that I would not do it." So I thought and then I tried to leave, but I could not. I suffered intensely. At last daylight came upon me. Now I thought that they regarded me as one who had had a trance and found out something.

Then we went home and they showed me a passage in the Bible where it said that it was a shame for any man to wear long hair. That is what it said, they told me. I looked at the passage. I was not a man learned in books, but I wanted to give the impression that I knew how to read, so I told them to cut my hair, for I wore it long at that time. After my hair was cut I took out a lot of medicine that I happened to have in my pockets. These were courting medicines. There were many small bundles of them. All these, together with my hair, I gave to my brother-in-law. Then I cried and my brother-in-law also cried. Then he thanked me. He told me that I understood and that I had done well. He told me that Earthmaker (God) alone was holy; that all the things (blessings and medicines) that I possessed, were false; that I had been fooled by the bad spirit (devil). He told me that I had now freed myself from much of this (bad influence). My relatives expressed their thanks fervently.

On the fourth night they had another meeting and I went to it again. There I again ate (peyote). I enjoyed it and I sang along with them. I wanted to be able to sing immediately. Some young men were singing and I enjoyed it, so I prayed to Earthmaker asking him to let me learn to sing right away. That was all I asked for. My brother-in-law was with me all the time. At that meeting all the things I had given my brother-in-law were burned up.

The fact that he (my brother-in-law) told me that I understood, pleased me, and I felt good when daylight came. (As a matter of fact) I had not received any knowledge. However I thought it was the proper way to act, so I did it.

After that I would attend meetings every once in a while and I looked around for a woman whom I might marry permanently. Before long that was the only thing I thought of when I attended the meetings.

I am converted

On one occasion we were to have a meeting of men and I went to the meeting with a woman, with whom I thought of going around the next day. That was (the only) reason I went with her. When we arrived, the one who was to lead asked me to sit near him. There he placed me. He urged me to eat a lot of peyote, so I did. The leaders (of the ceremony) always place the regalia in front of themselves; they also had a peyote placed there. The one this leader placed in front of himself this time was a very small one. "Why does he have a very small one there?" I thought to myself. I did not think much about it.

It was now late at night and I had eaten a lot of peyote and felt rather tired. I suffered considerably. After a while I looked at the peyote and there stood an eagle with outspread wings. It was as beautiful a sight as one could behold. Each of the feathers seemed to have a mark. The eagle stood looking at me. I looked around thinking that perhaps there was something the matter with my sight. Then I looked again and it was really there. I then looked in a different direction and it disappeared. Only the small peyote remained. I looked around at the other people but they all had their heads bowed and were singing. I was very much surprised.

Some time after this (I saw) a lion lying in the same place (where I had seen the eagle). I watched it very closely. It was alive and looking at me. I looked at it very closely and when I turned my eyes away just the least little bit, it disappeared. "I suppose they all know this and I am just beginning to know of it," I thought. Then I saw a small person (at the same place). He wore blue clothes and a shining brimmed cap. He had on a soldier's uniform. He was sitting on the arm of the person who was drumming, and he looked at every one. He was a little man, perfect (in all proportions). Finally I lost sight of him. I was very much surprised indeed. I sat very quietly. "This is what it is," I thought, "this is what they all probably see and I am just beginning to find out."

Then I prayed to Earthmaker (God): "*This, your ceremony, let me hereafter perform.*"

As I looked again, I saw a flag. I looked more carefully and (I saw) the house full of flags. They had the most beautiful marks on them. In the middle (of the room) there was a very large flag and it was a live one; it was moving. In the doorway there was another one not entirely visible. I had never seen anything so beautiful in all my life before.

Then again I prayed to Earthmaker (God). I bowed my head and closed my eyes and began (to speak). I said many things that I would ordinarily never have spoken about. As I prayed, I was aware of something above me and there he was; Earthmaker (God) to whom I was praying, he it was. That which is called the soul, that is it, that is what one calls Earthmaker (God). Now this is what I felt and saw. The one called Earthmaker (God) is a spirit and that is what I felt and saw. All of us sitting there, we had all together one spirit or soul; at least that is what I learned. I instantly became the spirit and I was their spirit or soul. Whatever they thought of, I (immediately) knew it. I did not have to speak to them and get an answer to know what their thoughts had been. Then I thought of a certain place, far away, and immediately I was there; I was my thought.

I looked around and noticed how everything seemed about me, and when I opened my eyes I was myself in the body again. From this time on, I thought, thus I shall be. This is the way they are, and I am only just beginning to be that way. "All those that heed Earthmaker (God) must be thus," I thought. "I would not need any more food," I thought, "for was I not my spirit? Nor would I have any more use of my body," I felt. "My corporeal affairs are over," I felt.

Then they stopped and left for it was just dawning. Then someone spoke to me. I did not answer for I thought they were just fooling and that they were all like myself, and that (therefore) it was unnecessary for me to talk to them. So when they spoke to me I only answered with a smile. "They are just saying this to me because (they realize) that I have just found out," I thought. That was why I did not answer. I did not speak to anyone until noon. Then I had to leave the house to perform one of nature's duties and someone followed me. It was my friend. He said, "My friend, what troubles you that makes you act as you do?" "Well, there's no need of your saying anything for you know it beforehand," I said.

Then I immediately got over my trance and again got into my (normal) condition so that he would have to speak to me before I knew his thoughts. I became like my former self. It became necessary for me to speak to him.

Then I spoke to him and said, "My friend, let us hitch up these horses and then I will go wherever you like, for you wish to speak to me and I also want to go around and talk to you." Thus I spoke to him. "If I were to tell you all that I have learned, I would never be able to stop at all, so much have I learned," I said to him. "However, I would enjoy telling some of it." "Good," said he. He liked it (what I told him) very much. "That is what I am anxious to hear," said he. Then we went after the horses. We caught one of them, but we could not get the other. He got away from us and we could not find him. We hunted everywhere for the horse but could not discover where he had run to. Long afterwards we found it among the whites.

Now since that time (of my conversion) no matter where I am I always think of this religion. I still remember it and I think I will remember it as long as I live. It is the only holy thing that I have been aware of in all my life.

After that whenever I heard of a peyote meeting, I went to it. However my thoughts were always fixed on women. "If I were married (legally) perhaps these thoughts will leave me," I thought. Whenever I went to a meeting now I tried to eat as many peyote as possible, for I was told that it was good to eat them. For that reason I ate them. As I sat there I would always pray to Earthmaker (God). Now these were my thoughts. If I were married, I thought as I sat there, I could then put all my thoughts on this ceremony. I sat with my eyes closed and was very quiet.

Suddenly I saw something. This was tied up. The rope with which this object was tied up was long. The object itself was running around and around (in a circle). There was a pathway there in which it ought to go, but it was tied up and unable to get there. The road was an excellent one. Along its edge blue grass grew and on each side there grew many varieties of pretty flowers. Sweet-smelling flowers sprang up all along this road. Far off in the distance appeared a bright light. There a city was visible of a beauty indescribable by tongue. A cross was in full sight. The object that was tied up would always fall just short of reaching the road. It seemed to lack sufficient strength to break loose (of what was holding it). (Near it) lay something which would have given it sufficient strength to break its fastenings, if it were only able to get hold of it.

I looked at what was so inextricably tied up and I saw that it was myself. I was forever thinking of women. "This it is with which I was tied," I thought. "Were I married, I would have strength enough to break my fastening and be able to travel in the good road," I thought. Then daylight came upon us and we stopped.

Then I thought of a man I used to know who was an old peyote-man. He always spoke to me very kindly. I went over to see him. I thought I would tell him what had happened to me. When I arrived there he was quite delighted. It was about noon and he fed my horses and asked me to eat with him. Then when we were through eating, I told him what had happened to me. He was very glad and told me that I was speaking of a very good thing. Then (finally) he said, "Now I shall tell you what I think is a good thing (for you to do). You know that if an old horse is balky, you can not break him of (this habit); even if you had bought him and tried to break him (of this habit), you would not succeed. If, indeed, you succeeded, it would only be after very hard work. However if you had a young horse, you could train it in any way you wished. So it is in everything. If you marry a woman who has been in the habit of getting married frequently, it would be difficult for her to break herself of a habit she loves. You are not the one she loves. If you marry her you will lead a hard life. If you wish to get married, take your time. There are plenty of good women. Many of them are at (government) schools and have never been married. I think you would do best if you waited for some of these before marrying. They will return in the middle of summer. So, don't think of any of these women you see around here, but wait until then and pray to Earthmaker patiently. That would be the best, I think." I liked what he told me and thanked him. I decided to accept his advice, and I did not look around for women after that. I was to wait about three months and (during that time) I paid strict attention to the peyote ceremony.

On one occasion while at a meeting, I suffered (great pain). My eyes were sore and I was thinking of many things. "Now I do nothing but pay attention to this ceremony, for it is good." Then I called the leader over to me and said to him, "My elder brother, hereafter only Earthmaker (God) shall I regard as holy. I will make no more offerings of tobacco. I will not use any more tobacco. I will not smoke and I will not chew tobacco. I have no further interest in these. Earthmaker (God) alone do I desire (to serve). I will not take part in the Medicine Dance again. I give myself up (to you). I intend to give myself up to Earthmaker's (God's) cause." Thus I spoke to him. "It is good, younger brother," he said to me. Then he had me stand up and he prayed to Earthmaker (God). He asked Earthmaker (God) to forgive me my sins.

The next morning I was taken home. My eyes were sore and I could not see. They took me back to a house and there they put a solution of the peyote into my eyes and I got well in a week.

One night, when I was asleep, I dreamt that the world had come to an end. Some people Earthmaker (God) took, while some belonged to the bad spirit (devil). I belonged to the bad spirit (the devil). Although I had given myself up (become a peyote-man) I had not as yet been baptized. That was why Earthmaker (God) did not take me. All those who belonged to Earthmaker (God) were marked, but I was not. I felt very bad about it when I woke up, even although I had only dreamt about it. I felt very bad indeed. I wanted them to hurry and have another peyote meeting soon anywhere. I could hardly wait until I reached the place where the next meeting was to take place. I immediately told the leader (what I wanted) and asked him to baptize me and he baptized me in the morning. After that morning I felt better.

Then I went to work and I worked with a railroad work-gang. I was still working when the time for the midsummer celebration approached. I always went to the peyote meeting on Saturday nights.

The old man was right in what he had told me. The girl students returned in the summer. Shortly (after they returned) a man, a friend of mine who had gone around with me, asked me if I wanted to get married. "Yes, I do," I answered. Then he said, "Listen, I have been thinking of something. What kind of a woman do you wish to marry?" I told him what I had in mind. Then he said, "Come home with me. I have a younger sister. I want her to marry a good man; I would like to have her marry you," he said. Then I went home with him. When we got there (and discussed the matter) the girl gave her consent. The parents also consented.

So there I got married and what I expected has taken place and I have lived with her ever since. On one occasion, after she was used to me, she told me this. (Before she had married, she had determined that) if she ever got married, she would not care to marry a very young man. "I wanted a man who ate peyote and who paid attention to the ceremony." Such a man she desired and such a person was I, she said. She loved me, she said, and she was glad that she had married me. That is what she had asked Earthmaker (God) in prayer. "And, indeed, it has happened as I wished," she said. She believed it was the will of Earthmaker (God) that we had done this, she said. She was therefore glad (that she had married me). Together we gave ourselves up (to the peyote) at a peyote meeting. From that time on we have remained members of the peyote (ceremony).

ROBERT REDFIELD

The world view of the Yucatecan Maya

Robert Redfield was Distinguished Service Professor of Anthropology at the University of Chicago. An outstanding teacher, he did research in Middle America and India. In addition to *The Folk Culture of Yucatan* his publications include: *Tepoztlan* and *Chan Kom* (some of the first ethnological studies of Mexican peasant villages), *The Little Community, The Primitive World and Its Transformations*, and *Peasant Society and Culture.*

In this [selection] an attempt is made to indicate some of the outlines of the design for living which is to be recognized in the thought and action of the native of Chan Kom. Most of the facts to be involved have appeared in the Chan Kom monograph; they are here stated with different connections and emphases. In order to make clear the qualities of organization and internal consistency with which this [selection] deals, the materials used are those drawn from the older people, and particularly from those older people who appeared to have the most thoughtful and penetrating view of the world around them. The attempt is, therefore, to present part of the conception of the world and of life held by the more reflective members of the older generation in Chan Kom at the time just before the recent period of expansion, increasing mobility, and education—in, let us say, 1928. . . .

As the view of life of the older native is a whole, there is no single appropriate point of beginning. Adopting the figure of a network for the organized conceptions and practices, one may say that one may lay a finger upon the fabric at any point and find an entrance. Any one thread leads to other threads, and some threads wind their way through most of the texture. Such a thread, in the network of ideas governing the native of Chan Kom, is the milpa. An account of village life must recur often to the milpa; the connections of the milpa with other elements in the design are manifold.

Four chief terms define the terrestrial world within which man moves: the bush, the cenote, the village, and the milpa. The first two are of

---

nature, that is to say, of the gods, while the village and the milpa are what man has made out of nature with the permission and protection of the gods. The bush covers almost everything; it is the background within which lie all other special features of earth's surface. It is never reduced permanently to man's use; the milpas are but temporary claims made by men upon the good will of the deities who animate and inhabit the bush; after a few years each planted field returns to its wild state and becomes again an undifferentiated part of the forest. Therefore, each new invasion of the tall bush must be accomplished with prudent and respectful attention to the gods of the bush, the *kuilob-kaaxob*. For the same reason —that it is only when the gods grant to man the use of a piece of bush that is then wild, that is theirs—a man makes the ceremony of recompense ("dinner of the milpa") and makes the offering of first fruits only in respect to the first crop grown on land he has cleared.

The milpero marks off only so much bush for felling as will correspond with the future milpa. Thus an understanding is reached between the kuilob-kaaxob and the milpero: the milpero respects the bush, making use of only so much as he needs and wasting none; in return the gods of the bush will refrain from deflecting the swung ax against the milpero's foot. All relations with the gods have this character of a contract or, rather, of mutual expressions of good faith. The ceremonies that attend the fields and the beehives are essentially renewed pledges of pious respect and temporary discharges of a persisting obligation that is reciprocal between gods and men. Whenever a man takes from the fields or from the hives their yield, it is felt that he owes an appropriate return to the deities for what they have granted him. The first-fruit ceremonies and the rituals called "dinner of the milpa" and "dinner of the hives" formally return to the gods what they have granted. If the return is not at once made, the agriculturalist recognizes the existence of a debt that must be discharged. For each yield a certain return is due. Thus a large fowl and a small one should be offered for each springtime yield of honey. But the return need not be made at once; the debt may accumulate. But, when at last the appropriate ceremony is performed, the fowls sacrificed equal in number and kind the amount of the total obligation. So man keeps an account with the gods. Yet it is not simply a matter of arithmetical accounting. Good will must be present too. A man who scrimps against the deities is "haggling"; his health will suffer and his crops will fail. So one does not too long accumulate a debt to the deities. As another year passes without the performance of the proper ceremony, as the harmonious adjustment between man and the gods is by that much more disturbed, so increases the danger of sickness and crop failure, misfortunes by means of which the gods punish.

The obligation not to fell more bush than one needs is a part of the more general obligation never to take from the gods all the yield that is available. When the honey is taken from the hives, a little is left. When the ripe corn is taken from the field, some ears must be offered to the gods before man eats of them. When a deer is slain, certain parts must first be given to the spiritual protectors of the deer before the hunter eats his venison. For all the yield of bush and field is the gods', because the bush and the animals therein belong to the gods. These offerings return in part and in symbol what is essentially the property of the gods and which is by them ceded to men of pious conduct.

The bush is, then, the principal lodging-place of the supernatural beings. All aspects of nature have their spiritual aspect; each tree or knoll or cave may hold an invisible being and should therefore be approached with circumspection and without irreverence; and some natural features are more particularly associated with supernatural beings. The silk-cotton tree is the haunt of the x-tabai, the being in woman's form who may entice men to their death. The mounds of red earth made by the leaf-cutter ant are the abiding-place of the devil and are therefore likewise to be avoided. And throughout the bush and especially along the roads may pass the balamob, the invisible protectors of the cornfield and of the village. In certain places the bush is taller; there grow wine palms, and there the milpero finds mounds built by the ancients. Here especially lurk the *aluxob*, little mischievous beings, who are not the owners of wood or field, as are the gods, but who must on some occasions be propitiated. The bush teems with unseen inhabitants. Especially at night does the native hear a multitude of rustlings, murmurings, and whistlings that make known the presence of the many beings who people the bush. And each of these is disposed, well or ill, toward man, and of them man must take account.

Of all natural features, that attended by the most important considerations is the cenote—the natural well perforated by erosion through the limestone upon which grows the bush. The bush, even in the rainy season, is tough and thorny and after months without rainfall is a sere and dusty tangle of brittle branches and vines. But the cenote, a shaft down to the distant water, is ringed with fresh verdure. From its mouth emerges air, moist and cool; swallows twitter about its sides. The plants about the cenote are green and soft and luxuriant; they are, therefore, the plants used in the ceremonies to the rain-gods. Similarly the frogs, toads, and tortoises that are found near the cenotes are the animals of the rain-gods. The cenotes are the places of the rain-gods, the chaacs. These, residing behind a doorway in the eastern sky, come to earth and are also thought of as dwellers in these natural wells. The land is known largely by the cenotes; they are the points by which are located other features of the bush. In the prayers uttered by the shaman-priest in the agricultural ceremonies all the cenotes in the region in which the native moves and makes his milpas are mentioned by name; thus the priest calls, one by one, upon the chaacs associated with the cenotes. For the chaacs have within their power the granting or the withholding of the rain upon which the maize and, therefore, the life of the people depends. Of all the gods of nature, the chaacs come first in importance.

The chaacob, the balamob, and the kuilob-kaaxob are guardians, respectively, of the rain, the village and the milpa, and the bush. Lesser features of nature have also their protectors. The deer are watched over by spiritual beings called "zip," who have the form of deer; and the cattle have their guardian who is himself in form a great steer. Certain birds who frequent the milpa but appear not to eat the grain are the *alakob* of the balamob, as the frogs are the alakob of the rain-gods. The principal wild animals are the domestic animals of their protectors; they are yielded to man only under appropriate conditions, as crops are yielded and the honey which the bees make. The bees, too, are under the tutelage of special deities. All these wild animals are, therefore, referred to in prayers as alakob, "domestic animals"; and, when man makes an offering to the gods, he offers his own alakob, hens or turkeys.

All these supernatural beings are not of the substance of which this world is made. They are, the native says, "of wind." The wind that blows suggests these beings and may, in fact, be them. The wind that blows from the cenotes, or from dry caves, comes from the sea to which all winds return. The winds, as they blow to refresh the land or to fan the flames at burning time, are beneficent; but there abound innumerable winds, often not felt at all—winds only in the sense of incorporeal spirits—that are evil, actually or potentially. These winds may go about of themselves, but also they attend all supernatural beings and all critical, dangerous, or morally wrong situations and human beings involved in such situations. Together the gods of bush, milpa, rain, and village are "the Lords," the yuntzilob. Wherever the yuntzilob go, the winds go too. So the gods are a source of danger to men; their sacred quality involves a peril. Also the Lords may send the evil winds to punish the impious or those careless of their obligations to the deities. So the ceremonies, besides propitiating the deities, ward off the evil winds or, in certain cases, clear from the bodies of the afflicted the evil winds that have attacked them.

The cenotes are particularly the sources of the winds. As the water makes its cycle, carried by the rain-gods from the cenotes up into the sky to fall as fertilizing rain upon the milpa, so the winds have their sources in the sea and pass up through the cenotes. Therefore, in certain ceremonies offerings are thrown into the cenotes to propitiate the winds.

The cenotes are also the openings to the underworld; the suicide, worst of sinners, hurls himself into the cenote to pass directly into hell.

Except for rainfall, the cenotes are the only source of water. They determine the position of human settlements. Each cluster of milpas that has any permanency of settlement, each established village, centers about a cenote. The cenotes in the uninhabited bush retain more of their sacred quality; some, indeed, may not be approached by women and are visited by men only when water of that high degree of sacredness is to be fetched for use in the most important ceremony. But the cenote of the village becomes a part of the mundane and human life. To it the women and girls come for water; there they exchange gossip and talk, and there the cattle are driven to water.

The village, like the world itself, is a square with its corners in the four cardinal directions. The cenote is its center. So five crosses should be set up in each village: one at each corner and one at the cenote. Each village has its five (some say four) protecting balamob. Four hover above the four entrances to pounce upon noxious beast or evil wind that might attempt to enter. The fifth stations himself above the center point. The milpa also is square, and similarly oriented, and provided with its five balamob. Five rain-gods occupy, respectively, the cardinal points of the sky and the center of the heavens. In all these sets of five the smallest of the five occupies the position either at the east or at the center. Though he is the smallest, he is the most powerful. The word for him (*thup*) suggests to the native the smallest and the most powerful of a series; by the same adjective is known the kind of corn that produces small ears early in the season; for this corn, because of its special virtue in ripening before other corn, a special ceremony must be made.

Of the four cardinal directions, the east is dominant. From the east blow the principal winds, out of the east arise sun, moon, and planets; and from the east, in springtime, the first clouds and rains, carried by the chaacs, emerge. In the dense forests to the east dwell the bee-gods and a number of lesser supernatural beings; and inconceivably far, somewhere to the east, lies Jerusalem, where Jesus Christ lived. When a man prays, therefore, he faces east; and every altar, from the little table of poles set up by a milpero in his field, when he makes an offering at the time of sowing, to the altar elaborately laid out by the shaman-priest for the rain ceremony, is oriented to the points of the compass and so arranged that the worshiper kneels before it to face the east. At the rain ceremony the rain-gods of the cardinal directions are impersonated by men placed at the four corners of the altar, and four boys, impersonating frogs, alakob of the rain-gods, sit at the four supports of the altar.

The milpa, also, is thought of as square, and its four corners are protected by four balamob; a fifth, the thup, is sometimes conceived as occupying the central point. When the agriculturalist makes an offering in the milpa, he sets one bowl of cornmeal-in-water in each corner of the milpa and may add a fifth in the center. In the center of the field he builds his granary, and here he leaves his corn for months, it may be, coming there after the harvest only from time to time to supply the needs of his household. There the maize is safe, for who would take it from under the eyes of the unseen gods who have set a watch upon it? The milpa is, indeed, not only a work place but a place of worship. It is a place that must not be sullied. One works, eats, talks, and prays in a milpa. But one should not act boisterously in a milpa. Though one may take one's wife to a milpa, one should not have sexual intercourse under the sky out in a milpa but only within a house or shelter.

That the milpa, like the cenote and the bush, is set aside from the ordinary life of the village is indicated when the native says that the milpa is *zuhuy*. Everything that is protected from or is not exposed to the contamination of the ordinary, the earthly, the profane, is zuhuy. What is held from contaminating experiences is zuhuy: a girl who does not go about with other people, especially with men; a fowl penned by itself to make it ready for offering to the gods; a tablecloth that has never been used; water in a cenote to which women have not had access. What is appropriate to or associated with the gods is zuhuy: balche, the bark beer offered to the gods at the rain ceremony; the piece of ground upon which the ceremony has just been held; a milpa. The maize is zuhuy, especially as long as it is growing in the milpa. One does not rudely grasp a growing maize plant; one does not wantonly throw kernels of maize on the ground or crack them between the teeth. The Virgin herself is one of the guardians of the maize; by such a term she is addressed in the prayers used in agricultural ceremonies. So long as the maize is in the milpa it is not referred to by the word used for maize as it is prepared for eating or as it is sold in the market (*ixim*) but by the same word (*gracia*) used to denote the spiritual essence of offerings made to the gods.

Not only have the gods their special functions and their special positions in the quadrilaterals of village, milpa, earth, and sky but they have also their positions in a hierarchy of power and authority. When the offerings are laid out on the altar of the agricultural ceremonies, this relative order of power and importance is expressed in the placing of the offerings: the largest breads are committed to the highest beings and are closest to the candle that marks the central point of the eastern side of the table altar, while the smaller breads, for the lesser gods, are placed farther away from the candle. There are, the native recognizes, two hierarchies, but the two interlock, and there is one supreme head to them both. This is the *Hahal Dios*, the Great God, who sits in a place, called Glory, very remote, beyond the sky. Nothing happens but that he has it so; yet he is too remote to deal directly with men. The great saints sit high, but below him, and below them are the lesser saints and the souls of the virtuous and baptized dead. Some of the saints are protectors of the animals of the forest and are to be propitiated along with the windlike supernatural deer who watch their corporeal kinds. The saints have their embodiment in their effigies, but these are also saints, with personalities and powers in their own right, especially those of miraculous origin. Each family may have a saint of this sort, but every village must have one. This saint is the protector of the entire community and the intermediary between the people and the Hahal Dios, as the balamob of the village protect it from terrestrial invasion by evil winds and marauding animals. One of the great saints, St. Michael, is chief of the chaacs. Through him the Hahal Dios controls the rain. Captain of the chaacs when they ride across the sky is the *Kunku-Chaac*, the great rain-god. Under orders from St. Michael, he leads the other rain-gods, who are subordinated to him down to the least chaac, the thup, who, being the least, has special powers to produce rain in torrents.

As it is with the gods, so it is the proper condition of men that they respect their proper order of duty and responsibility. One must be chief and father, expecting and receiving respect and obedience, while he gives protection and dispenses justice. So it is with the family, where the father is the head; so with the village where the comisario (chosen by the people more frequently than was the old batab who held his office for life) leads his people, composes their disputes, and determines punishments; and so it is with the state, where the governor has this role. Under each such leader come others who are next in authority. Everyone in a post of authority has supporters—his *noox*. When one stick is set up to support another, it is a noox. So the comisario has his *suplente*, and so the *cargador*, who is in principal charge of the annual festival of the patron saint, has his *nakulob* to help him. The municipal officers are a hierarchy, and so are the men composing the organization that maintains the festival of the patron; in each case there is one head and a distribution of authority and responsibility downward. In the case of the organization maintaining the festival this hierarchy is expressed in the ritual wherein certain festal foods are solemnly and publicly transferred from the outgoing cargador to his successor and are then distributed among the supporters of the new cargador, first to the three next responsible, and then among the lesser followers and votaries.

In the natural order of authority men are above women, and the old above the young. So, when a married couple leave the church, the bride walks ahead of her husband to show that he is to command; and so they walk afterward on the trail. A woman's activities center around the hearth; her usual path is from the house to the cenote. The path of men leads to the milpa and to the town; men and not women are concerned with public affairs. At all gatherings for the discussion of affairs outside the large family only men are present, or, if women are present, they do not take part. When the ceremony of *hetzmek* is performed to assure that an infant will develop as it should, the objects placed in its hand to symbolize its future capacities include a needle if it be a girl, an ax if a boy.

Among one's kinsmen one occupies, at every age, a well understood position in an order of respect, authority, and responsibility. To one's father one owes the greatest obedience and also respect; while he cares for you, his commands are to be obeyed. To one's father's or mother's brothers, but especially to the former, respect and obedience, but less, are due. One's older brother is distinguished from one younger than one's self by a different term which implies the obedience due him. If the father dies, the oldest brother will take his place at the head of the family. To an older brother (*zucuun*) one may go for help and advice as one would to a father or an uncle. But these kinsmen by blood are not the only members of this constellation of duty and obligation. By baptism and by hetzmek ceremony the parents provide *padrinos* for the child, older persons who stand ready to aid, to advise, and, if necessary, to chide their godchild. To these persons one shows the greatest respect, and this respect is expressed, throughout life, in gestures of greeting and in the making of gifts. Upon marriage one's parents-in-law become still another pair of these older persons to whom respect is due. So the younger person is inclosed, so to speak, within pairs of older persons. And the older persons, linked with one another through the sponsorship involved in baptism or hetzmek, and in the marrying of their respective offspring, are linked with one another in bonds of mutual respect and trust. After one marries and has children, one arranges, for each, the padrinos of the baptism and of the hetzmek and later sees to it that one's son finds a wife. And each of these undertakings to complete the social position of that child for whom one is responsible creates a new tie between oneself and one's wife and the person or the couple chosen to sponsor one's child or with the parents of the child's spouse. Or, at the least, it solemnizes and sanctifies a relation of intimacy and trust that has already come into existence through kinship or friendship.

Each of these relationships is created in ritual and sanctioned by tradition; some are renewed or later recognized in other rituals. When parents come to ask a couple to sponsor their child at baptism, they express their solemn petition through formal speech expressed through an intermediary, and the unbreakable relation established is signalized by the offering and acceptance of certain traditional foods and by eating and drinking together. The petitioner kisses the hand of the man he seeks as compadre, for, though the respect is to be mutual, the gratitude moves from the child's parents to the godparents. This gratitude later receives formal recognition in a special ceremony when the parents kneel before their compadres and wash their hands and in which the tie between the child and his godparents is expressed by placing the child in the godparents' arms. The responsibility assumed by the godparents of the baptism is paralleled by that assumed by the person who "makes hetzmek" with the child, first placing it astride the hip, where it will therefore be carried until it learns to walk; and a short domestic ceremony expresses this relationship and the assurance which performance of the ritual gives of the future sound development of the child. The relationships established by marriage are likewise signalized in procedures that are formal, solemn, traditional, and appropriate. Marriage is not only an arrangement for the adult condition of two young people; it is also the forging of a new relationship between two groups of kindred. As men take the leadership, so the parents of the boy come to the parents of the girl to ask for the girl's hand. As formal matters should be expressed through third persons, it is well to engage one specializing in the negotiation of marriages to express the petition and prosecute the negotiations. As every petitioner brings a gift, those coming with the petition bring rum, chocolate, cigarettes, and bread. And as the matter under consideration is important and concerns relatives on both sides, as well as the boy and girl, four visits are made and negotiations are extended. In the determination of the amount and nature of the gift to be made to the girl by the boy's parents and in the settlement of the details of the marriage arrangements, grandparents and perhaps godparents have an appropriate place, as well, it may be, as have uncles on both sides or elder brothers. If the old-style marriage is followed, a ceremony will be held in which the boy's parents are hosts. In this, by an order of kneeling and of offering rum, by the formal speeches made by the sponsor of the marriage, and finally by the offering of cooked turkeys by the boy's father to the girl's father and by the boy's father to the sponsor of the marriage, all the new relationships of obligation and respect are expressed and appropriately sealed.

So each new tie in the web of social relationships is fastened with rituals meaningful of the character and importance of the relationships. As ties are broken by death, new ones are formed. The new ties bring in new individuals, but they merely repeat the old patterns so that the design in the texture is always the same.

Death does not quite break the old ties. After the soul has been released from the body it does not go directly to its destination (whether *metnal* in the underworld, Purgatory, or Glory above). The behavior of the living, after a death, is such as to conduce the soul, by appropriate stages, to its ultimate destination in the other-world, where it will no longer trouble the living. If dying is difficult, chants will be sung to loosen the soul from the body. An opening must be left in the roof for the soul to pass through. The soul will return once to visit its home before it sets off on the road to the other-world. To make sure that it will not lose the way, in the event that the death takes place away from home at some settlement in the bush, corn may be scattered along the path to the village that the soul may not go astray in the woods. The soul may be addressed in speech and charged to come to the place of burial. Of the nine days of prayer which follow a death, that held on the third day tells the soul that it has left the body and must take the road away from earth; on this day the soul returns to its home to collect its sins, which it must carry to judgment. Therefore, the house must not then be swept; nothing must be done to make it difficult for the soul to collect the sins. The prayers on the seventh day commend the soul to God and start it on its journey. The living should not cry; this might wet the road of the dead and delay its passage.

Thereafter the souls of the baptized will no longer remain near their old homes. At certain times after the death, and at last on the anniversary of the death, prayers must be held for the repose of the souls of the recently dead. But only on All Souls' Day do the dead return; on this day food is to be set out for them, their names are to be called, and prayers are to be said for them. This the souls ask, and, if it is denied, they will visit the living with sickness and misfortune. Cases are known, and stories are told, of people who have neglected these obligations and who have been punished accordingly. To make sure that no soul is overlooked, a special offering is set out on All Souls' Day for "the nameless souls." The relation between the presence of the souls of the dead and danger to the living is apparent in the fact that, when, two or three years after interment, the bones of the dead are removed from the cemetery to make room for other interments, the people feel free to express their sorrow and mourning. To have done so earlier when the soul was about would have been to induce the soul to remain.

The proper course of man is set by piety and a prudent application of practical knowledge. The first need of man is to plant maize that one may eat. So, beginning as a small boy, one learns how this may best be done. In choosing the place in which to make milpa, one learns to seek the wine palm and the *uaxin* tree and to avoid the aloe. In felling the bush, one learns to leave certain trees and how to cut the others. In burning the felled trees, one comes to judge the signs of coming rain and to make use of the weather prognostications of the h-men. So each activity by which a livelihood is gained or by which life and health are kept involves much knowledge as to how to act if certain results are to follow. A fruit tree had best be planted just after a full moon; one should drive two cross-shaped sticks through a papaya tree to cause it to bear; the proper part of the plastron of a tortoise, tied around a child's neck, will protect it from whooping-cough. But many of these courses of action, felt to be in themselves direct and practical, lie within a context of piety. There are many things one should do if one is wise; there are more important things one must do because it is virtuous. Yet virtue and prudence are so closely intertwined in thought and action that they can hardly be separated. The good man is the fortunate man. The man whose soul is at peace can expect his body to be in good health. The maize must be cared for, and the gods of the maize must be attended. To fail in the latter is to sin; one's fellows will condemn one, and, furthermore, misfortune will visit one. The milpa is a working-place; it is also a place in which approach is made to the powerful unseen beings. To make milpa is also to participate in those acts by which one establishes good relations with the gods. Not to make milpa is to put oneself outside that round of action, partly individual, partly communal, by which, in prayer and offering, the good will of the yuntzilob and of the saints is kept. A man who has enough maize to last him for a year or more will make at least a little milpa so as to maintain his part in these acts of virtue and of responsibility to the gods. A man personally incapacitated to make milpa will make milpa by employing the labor of others, even at economic loss. To give up making milpa entirely is to take a step serious for the soul as well as for its practical consequences.

Health of body and peace of soul depend upon the maintenance of conditions of balance. Extremes, and the meeting of extremes, are to be avoided. The relationships with the saints and with the yuntzilob rest, as already stated, upon preservation of a balance expressed in offering and ritual performance, on the one hand, and in protection and favor, on the other. To let the account go too long unpaid is to court misfortune. One's body, too, is best off if equable conditions are maintained. Excessive exercise or the excitement attendant upon association with the other sex, as at dances, carries with it the danger of sickness. "The evil winds come at such times." A menstruating woman, or even a person with a wound, carries the danger to others of the contagion inherent in such abnormal conditions. The shaman-priest who leads a ceremony in which are invoked the yuntzilob exposes himself to the winds the nearness of deity involves; he must be appropriately purified. When the men come back from lassoing the bulls at a festal bullfight, their lassos are loaded with these winds, and a ceremony is performed to cleanse them. To sick persons, especially to newborn infants, these dangers of attack from winds are greatest; and from such persons everyone who has been exposed to winds, even the man who has walked in the bush where a balamob may have passed, will prudently keep away.

Good health involves also the maintenance of that median condition which the native expresses in terms of heat and cold. Some persons are naturally hot, others cold. Two persons representing the extremes of such natural conditions should not marry; the outcome will not be fortunate. Nor should a man whose blood is "hot" attempt to raise kinds of domestic animals known to be characteristically "cold." The foods one eats and the beverages one drinks are known to have their characters in terms of these opposites. Something that is a little too "hot," as beef, may be made safer for consumption by adding a little lime juice, which is "cold." But it is dangerous to bring the greatest extremes together: honey is very "hot," and it should not be followed by water, which is "cold." If a man has a fever, he is hot, and he may be treated with moderate amounts of herbs or foods which are cold. On the other hand, a person who is weak is "cold" and should be given "hot" things to eat and drink. The plants that are "cold" are, in some cases, the plants that grow near the cenote and that are used in the rain ceremony. For drought is the fever of the milpa. As man's fever may be treated with cold plants, so it is appropriate to use "cold" plants in seeking an end to drought.

The word "taman" expresses for the conservative native those appreciated qualities which may be roughly identified with our "piety." A man who is taman maintains faithfully the ceremonies of the field and of the hive. He is respectful of the maize, and in his milpa his behavior is decent and circumspect. Such a man takes his part when the offerings are made to the patron saint. He does not forget his dead and makes for them occasional novenas and sets out for them the dinner of the souls on All Souls' Day. When his harvest has been good, when his beans are ripe, or when the new ears of maize are ready to eat, he sees to it that cooked beans or new ears are hung in his yard for the yuntzilob to partake of. He participates in the new-corn ceremony over which the shaman-priest presides; and, if his harvest is good, he makes a novena in his house for the patron saint and the Hahal Dios. When he takes the honey from his hives, he is careful not to injure any bee, and, if he moves his hives, he secures permission of the bee-gods by making the proper ceremony. A man who is taman does not throw maize grains on the ground or throw water onto a dog. He does not quarrel or raise his voice against children.

The kind of valued behavior implied by the word "taman" represents an ideal which few attain but with which everyone feels his own conduct should in some degree correspond. Some of the norms of virtue are more compelling than others. Industry, for example, and obedience to authority, whether that of the comisario or of one's father, are expected of everyone, and a serious failure in these respects is not compatible with continued residence in the community. A man may be slow to set out the offerings for the yuntzilob, but he will certainly work in his milpa, and he will certainly not omit entirely his ritual obligations. Nor is the virtue implied by "taman" inclusive of all conduct which the society applauds. One may seek to lead his fellows in public office, provided always one works for the good of the entire community. One may seek recognition at festivals, as a leader of the dancing, or by providing fierce bulls for the festal bullfights. Certainly it is good to acquire corn and cattle, provided one is generous. If one is so inclined, a man may learn to play a cornet, and a woman may distinguish herself at embroidery. But none of these achievements will be attended with the approval of one's fellows if it involves significant departure from the normal ways of life. The success of the bullfighter or the wealth of the fortunate agriculturalist must be regarded as attained through piety and right conduct, and indeed too much success in any line of endeavor is likely to arouse the suspicion that the conduct of the successful one has not always been right.

The pattern of meanings and standards that has here been sketched is a background, a mold of conduct, within which individual interests and enterprise must work themselves out. The conceptions here presented as the view of life of the villager are not, of course, present in the form here offered with any degree of entirety at most times, or even, probably, at any time. Men and women go about as they do elsewhere, attending to immediate concerns. They solve the present difficulty. They do the day's work; they plan to sow or to harvest; they laugh at something that amuses them, or they worry over illness or misfortune. Yet the scheme of ideas is there, nevertheless. It is forever implicit in their conduct. It provides the goals of their action. It gives a reason, a moral worth, to the choices they make. It says: "Yes, this is right" and "This is why." With such a charter they may be unhappy because unfortunate, but they cannot feel themselves lost.

JACQUES MAQUET

An African world view

Jacques Maquet is a professor of anthropology at Case Western Reserve University in Cleveland, Ohio. His specialties are political anthropology and the anthropology of aesthetics. He spent two years in Ruanda as a social anthropologist with the Institute for Scientific Research in Central Africa (1950–1951).

The world-view of a people refers to a kind of reality which is not directly observable. We can observe things and behaviour, but not ideas or mental attitudes. These have to be inferred. Furthermore, although the concepts and propositions which make up the world-view of the Banyarwanda* are all arrived at by induction, they do not possess the same logical status. They are located, so to speak, on different levels of abstraction. Some are arrived at by immediate inference from observation, as when we say, for instance, that for Banyarwanda "the invisible world is a fearful reality." This statement may be immediately inferred from the behaviour of the Ruanda people: their words, when they tell us their beliefs about the action of the spirits of the dead, and their behaviour if they are threatened by them. On the other hand, a statement such as "strictly contractual relationships are inconceivable for a Munyarwanda" is much more abstract because it is reached by successive stages from an analysis of the political organization of Ruanda. The validity of the two kinds of statement is not necessarily affected by their degree of abstraction. Even a proposition which seems very far removed from its factual foundation may be checked by the observation of other relevant facts.

Ideas concerning the place of man in the world, his destiny, his main values, his attitudes in relation to his fellow men, the rules of his

---

Jacques Maquet, "The Kingdom of Ruanda," from Daryll Forde (ed.), *African Worlds* (London: Oxford University Press and the International African Institute, 1954), pp. 164–189. Reprinted by permission of the author.

* The inhabitants of Ruanda. Ba– is the plural and Mu– is the singular prefix in this Bantu language. [Ed.]

behaviour, and the meaning of the invisible world, may find expression in many kinds of social phenomena. However, as might be expected, some of these phenomena are particularly significant, as, for instance, folk-tales concerning the creation of the world and the arrival of the Batutsi in the country, proverbs, and forms of cult. To these special attention has been given.

The validity of an unstated cultural premise will, of course, be established with more certainty if it is found implied in several and very different cultural phenomena. For instance, an analysis of the political structure may lead to the discovery of the principle of the fundamental inequality of the three castes of ancient Ruanda. The same principle is also implied in tales explaining the origin of the three groups and the sources of their social roles.

This study refers to the period when the Ruanda cult had not yet been subjected to the impact of Western culture. This is not very far back in time, for it seems that the first white man to be seen in Ruanda was Count von Götzen, who travelled through the country with a German scientific-military expedition in 1894. The first permanent occupation of the country was not more than fifty years ago, and important changes in the culture have been brought only during the past thirty years. The present Ruanda culture has lost the coherence that existed in pre-European days. Those who have become more closely associated with alien activity, and have therefore felt its influence more constantly, now share a culture made up in part of their ancestral way of life and in part of their interpretation of the Belgian variety of Western culture as it operates in a colonial situation. Even those who have not been brought into direct contact with whites feel that their old patterns of life are losing their validity. But that more or less hidden part of the old culture, consisting of basic assumptions on the relationships of man with the world and with other men, has suffered the least change. To be sure, the legends of the descent of the first Batutsi meet with more scepticism than in the past, but the fundamental beliefs that this story reflects are still profoundly embedded in the Ruanda ethos. Even when new institutions, based on assumptions conflicting with the earlier ones, are imposed under external pressure and adopted, the principles shaping the older institutions will subsist and, if participation in the new institutions is unchecked, these will be completely reinterpreted in accordance with the former premises. Some manifestations of the continuing existence of the ancient assumptions in the contemporary context will be considered here, but we shall be mainly concerned with the Ruanda world-view as it was at the beginning of this century.

Ruanda is a highland country in East Africa lying in the region delimited by lakes Kivu, Victoria, and Tanganyika. Its area is 24,500 square kilometres; its population amounts to almost two million inhabitants, the highest density in Africa south of the Sahara. Three socio-"racial" castes are to be distinguished among its peoples: pastoralist Batutsi (about 10 per cent of the population), agriculturalist Bahutu (about 85 per cent), and Batwa, hunters and potters (about 5 per cent).

Man and the material world

The world in which men are placed and which they know through their senses was created *ex nihilo* by *Imana*. The Ruanda word *kurema* means to produce, to make. It is here rendered "to create" because our informants say that there was nothing before *Imana* made the world. This belief concerning the origin of the material world is universal and clear. To any question on this point, the answer is ready.

The Banyarwanda assert that we do not see the whole of the material world which was created at that time. The world of our experience is flat; its limits are far away and made of fences like the ones we see around kraals.* On these fences there is a big rock which is the sky we see. Beyond the rock there is another world (*ijuru*) similar to our own, with hills, trees, and rivers. This world may be said to be heavenly only in the sense that it is above the sky: it is not a paradise but rather a richer duplicate of our world. Under the soil on which we tread there is yet another world (*ikuzimu*) also conceived as similar to our own. There is nothing infernal about it. The material universe is thus a kind of three-storied construction. It is not impossible to go from one floor to another: some people and animals came from the world above to the intermediate world and, according to some legends, one man at least went to the lower world.

In our world the moon and the stars (which are kinds of glow-worms) stay high up in the sky. The sun rises in the morning and in the evening reaches the end of the world where a powerful man kills it and cuts it into pieces. Then he throws the main bone across the vault of heaven to the East where it grows up and the following morning the same process begins again.

In essentials our world was created as we see it now, but there have been some changes in the course of its history. Some hills were raised up by the kings of Ruanda; the formation of Kivu Lake is accounted for in different folk-tales. Cattle, which rank so high in the Ruanda scale of values, also made a special appearance on the intermediate world. The stories give more than one version of their origin but they agree on their

* Native village communities. The word "kraal" also designates an enclosure for domestic animals. [Ed.]

arrival in a world already constituted and inhabited by men. According to some tales, creatures did not originally have the same bodily form as they have now. It is said, for instance, that horns were given to animals after they had been created.

This, and a belief that the world is now slowly degenerating, getting old (people's stature is decreasing, cows give less milk), suggest that the Ruanda conception of the universe is not a wholly static one. The world does not remain the same, it is in process of evolution. However, when direct questions are asked, it appears that this conception of the life of the universe has not been the subject of speculation and is not of great importance to the Banyarwanda.

Without *Imana* the world would not continue to exist and his action is necessary to maintain life. *Imana's* action, however, is not manifested in particular interventions; it is conceived rather as an underlying force which sustains the whole universe but does not interfere in the development of the life of nature. Seeds are put into the ground and after some time plants come up, the banana-trees produce their yields, the cows breed. All this is the normal course of things and we may expect the recurrence of these events at the proper times. This universal order, indeed, is not independent of *Imana*. He made plants grow and animals multiply, but he does not have to act to give fertility in each case. The scholastic distinction between prime cause and secondary causes can very well be applied to Ruanda conceptions. *Imana* acts as the prime cause of the universe and therefore any event may be imputed to him. On the other hand, nature itself includes the secondary causes which account for the regular unfolding of its course.

But this natural order is not unalterable. *Imana* remains master of the rules he has established. There are numerous stories of miracles worked by *Imana* (a stick becomes a cow, teeth are granted to a girl who had none, etc.). Other beings besides *Imana* may act on nature: the spirits of the dead and even some men, the sorcerers. They may prevent somebody's beans from growing, they may have a man or a cow struck down by lightning. In particular, rain, so important in this country where rainfall is very irregular, has been regarded as under man's control. There were rain-makers (*bavubyi*) who had the dangerous responsibility of regulating rainfall.

Natural forces—rain, wind, hail, storms—are not considered as persons having desires and intentions that could be influenced by prayers or offerings. It seems that only thunder is personalized, and is regarded as a king (*Mwami*). When a person has been struck by lightning, it is said that the Thunder-King has honoured his subjects with a visit and has taken one of them with him. Lightning receives the same salute as the king of Ruanda.

Banyarwanda implicitly distinguish between the regular course of nature and more or less unexpected events. Towards the former they assume a rational attitude. They do not look to the invisible world to account for the alternation of the phases of the moon, the growth of plants, the breeding of cattle. These phenomena are explicable on the level of secondary causes. Neither *Imana* nor the occult powers interfere in the normal course of material nature. It would be misleading to conceive of the Ruanda people as "primitives" living in an irrational world where every phenomenon is an enchantment demanding explanation in terms of an intervention of the invisible world. They look at the world in its regular course in the same way as does a product of Western culture.

Of course, a Munyarwanda could not explain the interplay and the exact action of secondary causes as a Western scientist would do. But neither could the great majority of people in our culture. They believe that some specialists know exactly how natural phenomena work, and they have an idea of the type of explanation the specialists use. Banyarwanda have fundamentally the same attitude.

In relation to natural phenomena which do not appear with such regularity that they may be expected at about this or that time, the ideas of the Banyarwanda are quite different. Because of their unexpectedness, these events resemble the consequences of human intention. As a man suddenly becomes angry and hits somebody, so thunder strikes. If an occurrence is clearly an exception to natural laws, as Banyarwanda know them, they are confused. If I have taken ordinary care of my banana-grove and it does not produce so many or such good fruits as the trees of my neighbours on the same hill, there must be some reason to be sought outside the normal order of the world. Moreover, these unexpected events may often be dangerous and detrimental. Since any Munyarwanda has, as we shall see later, many powerful enemies in the invisible world, he is easily led to suspect them. Consequently, when confronted with happenings in the material world which do not fit into their conception of the normal order of things, the Banyarwanda explain these events as due to a special intervention of supernatural forces. *Imana* himself may be responsible, but when the event is regarded as harmful, ghosts or sorcerers bear the blame.

In this interpretation of unusual events, the Banyarwanda differ significantly from the people of the West. First, it should be emphasized that for us, events which seem to be exceptions to the laws of nature are much rarer. Those who scientifically know a certain field of spatio-temporal reality can show that events unforeseen by laymen, such as a storm, are in fact completely in accordance with the order of nature. When the event seems inexplicable to the specialist, the uninitiated person is generally unaware of the fact and indeed often displays a greater belief in physical science than do scientists themselves. A basic assumption of our culture is that science (of the physico-chemical type) can explain any material phenomenon. Thus any event in that sphere of reality will be interpreted in accordance with that belief. The event may, however, be of such a type that a "scientific" explanation does not seem possible. For instance, the unpredictable event (a storm, a famine) may happen several times in the same place and no reason can be found for that repetition. The Western mind will then usually have recourse to the concept of chance, by which is meant that the numerous conditions which must be realized in order to produce the event may happen accidentally to coincide more than once. There is no inevitability in the repetition of that constellation of conditions, it may just happen. The concept of chance, by which we avoid recourse to the supernatural in such cases, is not used by Banyarwanda. For them a phenomenon of the material world is either a part of the normal course of nature and is explicable in itself, or it is extraordinary and must be understood as a supernatural interference.

Man and the non-material world

IMANA, THE CREATOR *Imana*, the creator, is a person. He is conceived as an intelligence, a will, an emotivity. He is extremely powerful: "the plant protected by *Imana* is never hurt by wind," "*Imana* has very long arms," "*Imana* goes above any shield." He is non-material. His action influences the whole world; but Ruanda is his home where he comes to spend the night. He is always invoked as "God of Ruanda" (*Imana y'i Ruanda*).

Imana is essentially good: "your enemy is digging a pitfall for you, *Imana* prepares your exit," "*Imana* gives, he does not sell." This is why he takes care of men and why there is no cult in his honour. He is so good, I have been told, that he does not require any offering.

There is a special creative act of *Imana* at the beginning of each person's life. Impregnation in itself would not be sufficient to produce a new human being. This is why the young wife, at evening, leaves a few drops of water in a jar. *Imana*, as a potter, needs some water to shape the clay into a child in her womb. Then, after birth, *Imana* decides what life is to be for that individual: happy or unhappy. If, later on, a man is miserable, poverty-stricken, in bad health, it is said that he was created by *Ruremakwaci*. This way of speaking has led some observers to understand that besides *Imana*, there was another creator, perhaps subordinate, perhaps an evil spirit. As a matter of fact, *Ruremakwaci* is the name given to *Imana* when he does not create very successfully, when "he is tired," or, for some inscrutable reason, decides that a certain destiny will be unhappy. This is consistent with the Ruanda linguistic habit of assigning different names to one cause according to its different effects.

Imana's influence is thought to be always beneficial for human beings. It happens very often that obstacles are placed in the way of his action by malevolent agencies of the invisible world, but from him only good things come. This is not completely consistent with the belief in an unfortunate predestination by *Imana*. It should be noted, first, that the theory of predestination has not a very deep impact on the attitude of Banyarwanda. A person who thinks himself unhappy, and might thus suspect that he has been predestined to a miserable life, does not seem to be submerged by a feeling of doom. Unless he is brought to despair by a situation from which there is no escape, he will go on living and trying to improve his condition. Secondly, this inconsistency will be better understood if we consider the attitude of Banyarwanda towards the king (the *Mwami*) in similar circumstances. The *Mwami*, the supreme authority, is good, yet he may be harmful and cruel to some of his subjects. As his power is absolute, as he is magically identified with Ruanda itself, he may never be criticized. Thus the victims of some arbitrary royal decision, and their friends, go on saying that the king is good but that his favourite counsellor is very bad and is responsible for what they suffer. As might be expected, in Ruanda God is conceived according to the image of the *Mwami*, and thus when some misfortune occurs, the blame is put on another name of God or on the ghosts or sorcerers.

The beneficent action of *Imana* is general and remote. *Imana* is the source of all gifts, but he does not interfere very much in individual lives unless he is invoked. He is not the vigilant deity whom no single detail of the lives of his creatures can escape and who, when he acts, takes into account all the antecedents of the situation. There is a story of a man who borrowed beans from different people. When repayment of the loans was demanded, he was always able by his wits to avoid fulfilling his obligations. One creditor—Death—insists on being paid and pursues him. The debtor, when fleeing, calls upon *Imana* who saves him.

Imana—as is illustrated by this tale—is not the guardian of ethics and social order. He is not offended when somebody is robbed, but only if the offence is directed against himself, as when somebody disobeys a particular order of his or abuses his name. Then he punishes the offender by sending him misfortunes during his earthly life.

THE SPIRITS OF THE DEAD The spirits of the dead (*bazimu*), with whom *Imana* has no closer relationships than he has with living people, constitute the second category of non-material beings. They continue the individuality of living persons and have the same names. It is usual to say: "when he will be a *muzimu*. . . ." Though non-material, they are localized by their activity, in contrast to *Imana* who, having a much wider range of action, cannot be so precisely localized. They live in the lower world whose ruler is *Nyamuzinda* ("the one with whom one is forgotten"). Banyarwanda have not elaborated a very detailed picture of post-mortem existence. Although, according to some informants, the deceased kings of Ruanda constitute a kind of governing body in the underworld, there are no social distinctions. Life is neither pleasant nor unhappy. The *bazimu* do not drink, eat, or mate but their existence in other respects is similar to that in the world of the living. The *bazimu* sometimes come back to this world, returning to the places where they used to live. An ancestor and some other spirits may stay permanently in the hut where their descendants live or in the small huts made for them in the enclosure around the dwelling.

Whatever their temper when they were in this world, the *bazimu* are bad. Direct ancestors in both lines (although the system of descent is patrilineal) are believed to protect their living descendants, if they showed them proper filial behaviour when they were in this world, if they observe prohibitions and avoidances and if they do not forget to make offerings. But all other *bazimu* belonging to one's patrilineage (*mulyango*) are always harmful. The *bazimu* of other families are less detrimental except where there are feuds between the families. Ghosts are thus essentially malevolent towards the living. At best they are not actively injurious.

In order not to irritate the dead various observances and interdicts must be complied with. The "cult" of the *bazimu* is accordingly aimed at appeasing them. They are frequently offered a few drops of milk or hydromel.* Sometimes they require the immolation of a goat or even a bull. A girl spends some time in the small hut dedicated to a *muzimu* in order that he may enjoy having a woman. Other practices are, however, more difficult to interpret. Water may be given to the *muzimu* while at the same time he is told very loudly that it is milk. The explanation given by most informants is that *bazimu* are rather stupid and that these mock offerings are not given to the direct ancestors, who are respected, but only to collaterals who, as *bazimu*, are hated. However, it is not very clear how one can at the same time fear the powerful *bazimu* and deceive them so grossly.

Among the *bazimu*, a small group, *Ryangombe* and his *imandwa*, is particularly powerful and important. *Ryangombe* is said to have been the chief of a small band of friends and clients. He was accidentally killed by a buffalo during a hunting party. In order not to leave *Ryangombe*, his friends threw themselves on the bull's horns. *Imana* gave them a special

---

Hydromel is a drink made of honey mixed with water. [Ed.]

place, the Karisimbi, a former volcano, where they have a notably more agreeable life than the other *bazimu*. To have the privilege of joining them there, Banyarwanda have to be initiated into the sect (*kubandwa*). The members of the sect believe that non-initiates go after death into an active volcano, the Nyiragongo, where they suffer torments of fire. We have here an interesting instance of conflicting ideologies in a non-literate society: the common belief that all *bazimu* reside in the under-world and the belief of initiates, who are extremely numerous, in a mildly paradisal life for themselves and a hell for other people. During their earthly sojourn the initiates have other advantages, for the powerful *imandwa* do not harm them and indeed protect them from the injurious activities of other spirits.

The relations between *Ryangombe* and *Imana* seem to be conceived as those between a client (*mugaragu*) and his patron (*shebuja*), persons who are linked by that typical Ruanda institution called *buhake*, in which a man in an inferior situation in the scale of wealth and social power asks another to grant him his protection and the possession of some cows; in return the client becomes his patron's man and owes him various services. *Ryangombe* is believed to be protected by *Imana* and to act more or less as his intermediary with regard to the initiates. But *Imana* is not present in *Ryangombe's* paradise. The cult of *Ryangombe* has importance as a force of social cohesion. Batutsi, Bahutu, and Batwa may all be initiated. This function is quite overtly stressed: *Ryangombe* has said himself that he should be called upon by everybody.

DIVINERS AND SORCERERS Two categories of men have special relations with the invisible world: diviners (*bapfumu*) and sorcerers (*barozi*). The former are interpreters of *Imana's* will, which they can discern in the figures made by knuckle-bones, in the viscera of chickens, rams, and bulls, or even by intuition without the aid of any instrument. Some of them use a medium, usually female, possessed by *Biheko* (one of the *imandwa*) or are possessed themselves. Thanks to them it is possible to oppose a certain defence against the *bazimu*. They can identify the spirit who causes illness or sterility or is killing the cattle: they can tell what will appease him. Batutsi and Bahutu practise as *bapfumu*. It was formerly a very respectable calling; the techniques and methods of interpretation are often transmitted from father to son. Sorcerers (*barozi*), on the contrary, are criminals obliged to conceal their activities. If found they could be immediately killed. Some of them are believed to use poisons; for instance, a powder made from the lungs of a person who has died from tuberculosis is mixed in food. Others act by magical means: sending a *muzimu* to strangle somebody, acting through lightning or an animal, using spells. Besides a certain training in th formulae, they have to acquire a magical force handed on by another sorcerer.

Such, very sketchily drawn, is the non-material world of Banyarwanda. This world is dominated by *Imana*, essentially powerful and good. The century-old problem of evil in the world, particularly acute when there is a belief in the existence of a being who is omnipotent and infinitely good, has been solved by putting the responsibility for all evil and all suffering on agents other than *Imana*. These agents are mostly human, for *bazimu* are indeed human personalities and sorcerers are men. *Imana* himself does not cause any evil but he allows the causes of evil to act. As God's beneficent action is remote, we may say that the invisible world is on the whole malevolent. Under the serene reign of the prime cause, ill-willed secondary causes have a large freedom of action which they use to torture men. Compared with the earthly world, the invisible one is rather disquieting, our informants told us. When daily life is painful, when personal security is threatened by external dangers, the thought of the invisible world present in this one has not the psychological function of relieving anxieties.

But to what extent is the invisible world a permanent presence in the lives of Ruanda people? Not to a very great extent, it seems. Their existence is not permanently dominated by the fear of *bazimu* and sorcerers. As in the material world and its regular changes, Banyarwanda consider that there are "natural" events in the human sphere, i.e. in the domain of human existence and the part of the world that man changes by his action (agriculture, cattle-rearing, hut-building, etc.). By "natural" we mean that these events are understood without reference to the action of the supernatural world. Some antecedent events or acts are regarded as natural causes of others. To get a cold at the beginning of the dry or the rainy season is considered to be due to the change of weather. It is known that yaws can be got by contagion. Even death is very often accepted without seeking any magical explanation. It is expected, for instance, that people will die because of old age. If beans had been planted on poor soil, a bad crop would not mean that the field had been bewitched. Thus when recurrences have been observed or when "causes" have been discovered in the sphere of human phenomena, events happening according to these recurrences or following these causes are considered as intelligible without any reference to the supernatural world. But when events cannot be explained by reference to natural antecedents or causes, or are surrounded by peculiar circumstances, the intervention of ghosts or sorcerers is suspected and a diviner is consulted. If somebody has tuberculosis (*igitundu*) and none of his forebears or the people with whom he lives has suffered from that disease, it is thought that sorcery is the cause. If somebody dies from an illness usually considered "natural," but the death occurs a few days after a theft of which he is the supposed culprit, he is said to have been magically stricken at the request of the robbed person.

This attitude is in fact quite coherent. When the natural cause is known, the event is attributed to it; when it is not known, or appears extraordinary on account of the circumstances, the explanation is given in terms of beliefs concerning the non-material world. Why do Westerners not use a magical frame of reference on similar occasions? First, their wider knowledge of natural sequences of antecedents and consequents makes the residuum of naturally inexplicable facts more restricted. For instance, a sudden death appears to them quite understandable for purely medical reasons. To Banyarwanda, on the contrary, a sudden death is an event of which the physical causes are completely unknown. Second, even for residual facts not scientifically explained, there is in Western culture a faith that, given time and effort, a scientific explanation will be found. The Munyarwanda has no such belief in positive science. Third, for the disconcerting circumstances which may be coincidental with illness or death, the concept of chance, which does not appear frequently in Ruanda culture, is resorted to. However, Western believers in a provident God see in these exceptional circumstances, not an accidental constellation, but a sign of the meaning God intends to give to the illness or death.

A threat permanently dominating the mind of the Bahutu was that of being accused of sorcery. This danger was connected with the invisible world but was objective enough, for such an accusation could result in being killed and, of course, merely to refrain from anti-social magic did not ensure immunity from being called a *murozi*.

The nature and situation of man

Kazikamuntu (which may mean Root-of-Men) is the common ancestor of all mankind. Created by *Imana*, he had, among other children, Gatutsi, Gahutu, and Gatwa who, as their names indicate, are the ancestors of the three Ruanda social and "racial" groups. Gatwa killed one of his brothers and for that reason was cursed by his father. Gahutu, who had been chosen by his father as heir and successor, had been commissioned by him to accomplish an important mission. As a result of overeating, Gahutu fell asleep and could not collect the information his father wanted. Gatutsi, on the other hand, got it by his sobriety and cleverness. Kazikamuntu then chose Gatutsi to be the chief of the brothers. There are numerous versions of this tale. Moreover, the stories concerning man's creation are often inextricably mixed with the legends about the arrival of the Batutsi in Ruanda. The same names appear sometimes in the creation, sometimes in the conquest stories. In general the latter are better known. The summary given above is thus only one of the various accounts of the origin of mankind.

According to a widely known folk-tale, Death, personalized as a sort of animal, was hunted by *Imana*. He told all men to stay at home in order that Death should not find a hiding-place. An old woman, however, went out to work in her banana-grove. Death, pursued by *Imana*, asked her protection. Moved by pity, she let the animal hide under her skirt. *Imana*, in order to punish her, decided then that death should stay with men. This story might perhaps suggest a belief that there was a time when men did not die. But we could not find other elements to corroborate that interpretation.

On the ontological character of man two points are certain. First, an adult human being is considered to be different from an animal by virtue of his faculty of speech (*kivuga*), his intelligence (*ubwenge*), and his will (*ugushaka*); but the difference, if any, between a small child and an animal is not quite clear. Second, no one of these attributes is equated with the surviving spirit (*muzimu*). There is something in the human being which, after his death, becomes *muzimu*, but there is no agreement as to what it is. According to a fairly common opinion, the *muzimu* is the metamorphosis of the *igucucu*, the shadow cast by the body in sunshine. But according to some informants, this shadow is only an image of the spiritual shadow which is the essence of the post-mortem spirit. In conformity with that opinion, the living man is said to be made of three components: the body (*mubili*) which, after death, becomes a corpse (*murambo*); life (*buzima*), which disappears; and the shadow (*igucucu*) from which the surviving spirit (*muzimu*) results.

The heart is believed to be the seat of intelligence and affectivity. It is conceived as a single organ although some ways of speaking suggest that it is double. For instance, it is frequently said: "One heart told me this, one heart told me that." This is another application of the habit of attributing opposed effects of the same cause to several causes, but this is only a verbal habit which does not deceive anybody.

These uncertainties regarding the nature of man indicate that Banyarwanda do not make any clear-cut distinction between the concepts of body and mind. Although they recognize parts in man, they prefer to consider the unit rather than its components.

Whatever the culture, human experience is made up of a sequence of events and activities, such as working, eating, sleeping, maturing, suffering, mating, getting old, and dying. What is the Ruanda attitude in face of these universals of human life? In many societies these happenings are considered not in their naked reality but in terms of the beliefs held as true in the particular culture. For instance, in a society with a Christian ideology, to suffer is not only to be hurt but also to expiate one's sins, to purify one's soul, and to identify oneself with Christ. For serious Christians, suffering cannot be stripped of its religious meaning without being completely distorted. Banyarwanda, on the contrary, seem to take a very "secular" view of the human condition. Their belief in the supernatural world does not greatly influence their attitude to the unavoidable hardships and pleasures of life. All our informants agree that to die means above all to quit life. They believe that they will become *bazimu* but that leaves them rather indifferent. Even initiates do not show any enthusiasm for the idea of joining *Ryangombe* and his *imandwa* at their feasts. To abandon his children, his herds, his friends, is a sad thing for a Mututsi. But it is accepted, without dramatizing it, as one of those facts which belong to the normal order of things.

If quitting this life is so unfortunate, is human existence such a cheerful experience for Banyarwanda? Enjoyments and the pleasant things of life are very unevenly distributed in Ruanda. The superior caste, the Batutsi, form about 10 per cent of the population. But, by various means, principally by the institutionalized exchange of cattle for services and dues, Batutsi have been able to gather a much higher proportion of consumers' goods. They do no manual work and have leisure to cultivate eloquence, poetry, refined manners, and the subtle art of being witty when talking and drinking hydromel with friends. Bahutu, perhaps 85 per cent of the population, do not enjoy such gracious living. They have to produce for themselves and for Batutsi. On a very poor soil, with technologically primitive implements, it is necessary to work hard to secure the surplus production required by the Batutsi. Moreover, the great social influence of Batutsi has given opportunities for the arbitrary exercise of power, so that there are many insecurities in a Muhutu's life. But exploitation has been kept within limits set by the wisdom and the interests of the Batutsi, and a system of protection has assured a minimum of security to the Bahutu. As to the Batwa, they are so low in the social hierarchy, and are considered so irresponsible that they have had a greater independence of action. Formerly they lived on the margin of Ruanda society. They had a reputation for grossly enjoying any opportunities for eating, drinking, making music, and dancing. It should be added that Banyarwanda, according to our standards, have been rather defenceless against disease, that starvation was a real threat for the majority when the rains failed, that ritual observances and interdicts were numerous, and that when somebody happened to be involved in a charge of sorcery he had good reason for great fear. Thus it seems that, for an ordinary Munyarwanda, life is objectively hard, often dangerous but bearable. This partly explains the Ruanda outlook upon the totality of life. It might be described as a mild optimism. As many of our informants put it: "Existence for Banyarwanda was not easy, it was even often very painful, but on the whole, life was rather a good thing."

As everywhere, some individuals were at some time of their lives plunged into circumstances which offered apparently no way out. A Mututsi who had incurred the king's displeasure and was for that reason left without protectors, friends, or cattle was in a desperate situation; only with difficulty could he gain a bare subsistence. A Muhutu against whom an accusation of sorcery was repeated; an unmarried girl of a noble family whose pregnancy became publicly known; all these, if they failed to escape from their predicament by skill and rational behaviour (such as obtaining the king's mercy, denying the charge of sorcery and looking for the protection of a powerful man, using abortifacients or denying the pregnancy), would have recourse to the *bapfumu*, seeking to know what spirit or sorcerer was responsible for their misfortune and how to appease the malevolent being. If all the practices and offerings recommended by the diviner had no effect, then they called upon *Imana*, and if their prayers were unanswered, only drastic solutions remained, such as exile in a foreign country or suicide. But these tragic destinies were not numerous and they did not shake the belief of the majority in the moderate happiness of living.

There is a further reason for their generally cheerful acceptance of the conditions of their existence. Banyarwanda are not inclined to speculate about the inaccessible. Westerners are given to imagining how beautiful and good life might be if humanity and the universe were different from what they are. This trend of thinking is quite alien to Banyarwanda and, when it is suggested, appears futile to them. The usual, the normal (in the sense of what we are accustomed to, and what we have reason to expect) is often self-explanatory. When a particular event fits into the normal scheme of things, there are no questions to be asked. If everybody has to relinquish this existence and die, death is no scandal or absurdity. It is the way *Imana* has arranged things. There is no further problem.

Cultural values

Human action is determined partly by cultural values, partly by the socially recognized means of attaining them. By cultural values we mean the final or intermediate aims that are considered the proper purposes of human activity in a particular society.

In a stratified society, such as that of Ruanda, each layer is likely to have its own set of values, although some of those originating in one group may extend to others. Let us begin with the Batutsi. When a

Mututsi informant is asked what the people of his group wish for above all, the answer comes immediately: "children and cattle." A further question, "why?," discloses that these are not ultimate values sought for themselves, but intermediate ones, means to reach more abstract ends. The latter are power (*amaboko*) and reputation (*ugukomera*).

Power is understood here in connexion with persons (power over somebody) rather than with things (power to do something). It is, to paraphrase Lasswell's definition, the ability that a person, engaged in a human relationship with another, has to oblige the latter to do or not to do something (on pain of suffering severe privation). Power is essentially the capacity to exert a significant pressure on somebody. In Ruanda, to be powerful is to be able to exact from others tribute in labour or in kind, or support for one's claims to some advantage to be obtained from the king. In the latter case pressure may remain undefined and indirect: for instance, a threat to withhold backing which may later be necessary to the person who is now asked to support a request. We desire to have cattle, say our informants, because by giving one or two beasts to a Muhutu, he becomes our client (*mugaragu*) and then has to do, to a large extent, what we ask of him. We also like to have cattle in order to get as vassal another Mututsi who lacks them. The services expected from a vassal are not manual, but he will increase the influence of his lord by his family connexions and will be useful through his diplomatic shrewdness in dealing with his lord's intrigues. Finally, we desire to become ourselves the vassals of great chiefs, or even of the king, because we are then under the protection of somebody very important, we get more cows and that allows us to have more clients.

In order to become powerful it is important, almost indispensable, to have many children. Girls, by their marriages, extend one's family connexions and bring their fathers a few cows as bridewealth. Boys at an early age begin their military training which gives them a complete education in the skills, knowledge, and virtues pertaining to their noble condition. This training is given them as *intore* (chosen ones) at the royal court or at the court of an important chief. For a father to have a son at court would reinforce his influence: through his son he knows what is going on, and the king or the chief is constantly reminded of the father by the son's presence—an important security for the father. The boy could also increase the influence of his family by becoming the client of a powerful Mututsi, and thereby getting protection and cows for himself and his parents' family (*mulyango*). Finally, the marriages of his sons could create new links between the father and the families of his daughters-in-law.

In complex societies like our own the roads to power are many. In Ruanda it does not appear that power could be readily attained except through the possession of children and cows. As we shall see, warlike valour could confer very high prestige, but not necessarily power. Great warriors were often granted herds of cattle by the king as rewards for their prowess, and could then gain power by their cattle, but not directly.

If we press our analysis farther, we may say that from the point of view of power, the significance of children is to provide cattle or connexions. On the other hand, cattle give direct power (over the Bahutu clients) or ensure connexions. In relation to Bahutu labourers, cattle have many of the social functions of money in our culture. They enable the man who owns them to exert pressure on those who have few or none of their own and who try to acquire them in exchange for services. In order to facilitate comparison with other ways of life, we may use the term wealth (as a medium of exchange) instead of cattle. As for connexions, what is meant here is that type of relationship in which one party may require something from the other under the threat of some sanction. In Ruanda, of course, it would be considered very improper to give orders or to utter a threat, but beneath the polite phrasing, the true meaning of the relationship is clear. Consequently we may say that in Ruanda, the only means to power are wealth and relationships in which sanctions are implied.

The other ultimate value of Banyarwanda, reputation, is also closely connected with children and cattle. First, because powerful men are greatly respected and everybody knows the significance of daughters, sons, and cattle as means to power. Second, because cattle have also a high prestige-value in themselves. Indeed to entertain friends properly and to maintain the superior style of living of the nobles, one must have plenty of milk. Milk is the beverage of the high caste. They also drink hydromel and banana-beer, but milk is more characteristic of the Mututsi way of life. It was considered a complete food, and true Batutsi were said to live on milk alone. As each cow did not produce much milk, it was necessary to have an important herd to provide for the needs of a well-to-do Mututsi family. Moreover, cattle had an important aesthetic value in Ruanda. To be expert in cattle-breeding was required of the nobility. A whole category of poetry was devoted to the praises of famous cows, individually identified. Very beautiful cows (called *inyambo*) were regarded as belonging to the king even if they had been produced in somebody else's herd. In many festivities cattle were presented to the king or to great chiefs. All this indicates that cattle were objects of keen interest and aroused feelings of pride similar to those associated in some Western sub-cultures with the ownership of hunters or luxury cars. Cattle were the privileged possession of the superior caste, just as in Europe, in the Middle Ages, a noble had to have some landed property. Without losing status, he could not exchange his real estate for gold or goods even if they were worth much more. Such being the feelings and emotions attached to the possession of cattle in Ruanda, their high prestige-value is readily understandable.

The antiquity of a family is highly valued in Ruanda. Almost any Mututsi is able to give the names of his ancestors for six or eight generations. A family has property which is handed on from one generation to another, common ancestors to be honoured, a set of traditions and legends. It is a living reality in which one is proud to participate. Against that background one may appreciate how children, and particularly sons, give prestige to the parents. To have many children ensures that family traditions will be maintained, that the importance of the family will increase, that its property will be kept and even enlarged, that the ancestors will be honoured. This not only makes the parents happy, but is recognized by other people and their esteem for the father is enhanced.

Besides recognition of their power, admiration for their cattle, and the respect paid to them on account of their having many children, the Batutsi seek more specific reputations. They like to be recognized as courageous. They came to Ruanda by conquest and, till the European occupation, their main social function as a caste was to make war, more often offensive than defensive. Consequently military courage (*ubutwari*) was highly praised. There are numerous and interminable poems made by official bards, telling stories of battle and commemorating military prowess. The young Batutsi, during their training, were taught to compose such poems and even to invent imaginary doughty deeds. Special signs, or badges of honour, were granted to those who had killed seven or fourteen enemies during an expedition; there was a special ceremony to honour warriors who had killed twenty-one persons in a campaign. Some informants were still able to give the names of warriors who had received these marks of honour.

It is worthwhile to note, however, that even in a society so focused on military values, great warriors could gain an extreme popularity but not, at least directly, social power. Martial valour as such was not even considered a special qualification for becoming commander of the army (*mutware w' ingabo*). During battles, indeed, the chief of the army had to stay motionless in his headquarters. He was magically identified with his army: he could not move backwards without endangering the advance of the army. This type of command did not require much courage. An army commander was, on the other hand, very high in the power scale. Members of the army had to give him cattle on certain occasions (when he was taking up his duties, when he was reviewing the herds of the army members); the king granted him cattle in some circumstances, for instance, after a battle had been won, or he entrusted to the army the care of some herds. By these means the army chief had control of many beasts: he could then increase his clientship, and thus his social power, by gifts of cattle.

A Mututsi also greatly desires to be regarded as having *ubugabo*. This means the quality of being a man (*mugabo*); it includes trustworthiness in keeping promises, generosity in treating one's friends well, liberality towards the poor, moral courage in accepting one's responsibilities. In a society where relations of inferiority and superiority are predominantly personal, in the sense that authority is rarely abstract (a law, a principle) but generally identified with a person (chief, king, lord, etc.), emphasis is laid on fidelity in any personal relationship.

Another quality that the Batutsi are extremely proud to have is *itonde*. This may be translated as "self-mastery." To lose one's temper, to manifest violent emotion by crying is really shameful. Anger, in particular, should not be violently expressed. The demeanour of a Mututsi should always be dignified, polite, amiable, if a little supercilious. Batutsi manners have often been called hypocritical. This would be true if such behaviour were displayed in an extrovert culture where it is considered unethical not to express to a person exactly what one thinks about him. But in Ruanda it is taken for granted that only vulgar persons reveal all their attitudes and emotions. This is understandable in a strongly hierarchical society, where the authority of a superior is not restricted to certain specific domains of the life of his inferior, and where to express any disagreement with the superior is thought inappropriate. This is the point of view alike of the inferior (and everyone in Ruanda, except the king, has a superior) and of the superior (and any Mututsi is the superior of a certain number of people). Bahutu are not, and are not expected to be, very self-controlled; they are correspondingly impressed by the external dignity of the Batutsi. An aristocratic caste usually emphasizes those differences which constantly remind others how far removed they are from the noble set.

When inquiries were made as to the kind of reputation the Batutsi specially wanted to avoid, the answers given did not generally indicate qualities opposed to those thought desirable, but referred to reputations in which an external danger is involved. Above all, a Mututsi fears to be considered an enemy of the king. This is partly because he feels a genuine respect for the king, but mainly because to be reputed the king's enemy was formerly extremely dangerous. It could mean dispossession of all property, severance of all social relations, exile, or death. A Mututsi also fears to be considered a traitor to his chief. This is less dangerous but it involves sanctions: if a Mututsi has been disloyal to his lord (*shebuja*), the latter may take back from him all he gave him previously and eventually all his cattle.

All this relates to the good or bad reputations people desire or fear while living, but the Batutsi are equally concerned with their posthumous fame. To be remembered as a great warrior or a powerful cattle-owner was the normal ambition of any Mututsi. Some deaths were particularly glorious: for example, to be killed in battle or to lose one's life rather than surrender one's cattle, because this is to be deprived of the only means of living in a manner appropriate to one's rank.

The longing for fame after death seems to be deeper and commoner than in our culture. It is not unlike the Ciceronian concept of *gloria*. It is a desire to go on living in men's memory quite apart from a belief in a supernatural immortality and, like *gloria*, has nothing to do with mythological conceptions of the beyond. Banyarwanda do not think that the spirits of the dead will take pleasure from the great reputations they have on earth, or so at least our informants told us. "If *bazimu* know perhaps the fame that the people from whom they come enjoy among the living, it is definitely not for that reason that we hope to be famous after our death." It is possible, however, that it may be connected with the belief that the living will make more offerings to the *muzimu* of somebody who is widely remembered, though we did not find evidence of any belief that the spirits would suffer a kind of second death, and disappear completely if and when they were forgotten by the living.

To sum up, the ultimate values for the aristocracy are power and reputation. Children and cattle are their main intermediate values in the sense that they are the almost indispensable means for achieving these ends. The originality of Ruanda culture does not lie in its high valuation of power and fame. These are recognized ends in many cultures. What is distinctive is the paucity and the indispensability of the means provided in that society for effecting these purposes.

An ordinary Muhutu could never hope to achieve a position of power over other men comparable to that which a Mututsi could attain without difficulty. A well-to-do Muhutu could acquire a few servants either by ensuring the subsistence of other Bahutu poorer than himself or, like a Mututsi, by the gift of cattle. But this was not common. Ambition for power is proper to people who do not have to worry about fundamental human needs such as food, shelter, etc. The ultimate value for Bahutu is security, for this means protection from the things our informants say they fear above all: accusations of witchcraft, starvation, and the arbitrary actions of the powerful. There are no direct methods of protecting oneself against the first of these threats. All that can be done preventively is to be a good neighbour, not to be envied by anybody, not to have enemies.... But there are ways of reducing the other two dangers and these are the intermediate values which the Bahutu earnestly seek: work, children, and patronage.

Bahutu till the soil from which they have to get subsistence, the tribute demanded by the chief, and perhaps a surplus. This surplus is extremely important because it will enable them to acquire some goats, sheep, even a cow, to have the time to work for their lord, to store enough food to get a few servants who will then increase production. Surpluses may be obtained only by work. That is why, among Bahutu, the man or the woman who works hard and competently is highly considered. Work enables Bahutu to achieve some security against starvation and even to attain moderate wealth.

There is a Ruanda proverb that the dog is not feared because of his fangs but because of his master. This is the main reason why a Muhutu wants to have a patron. A peasant rich enough to own a couple of cows needs the protection of somebody more powerful than himself in order to avoid the arbitrary exactions of some member of the dominant class. Patronage was institutionalized by the *buhake* agreement mentioned above. Like the lord in medieval Europe, the patron was bound to protect his client in most of the dangerous situations of life. A second reason for seeking a patron lay in the material and moral advantages accruing from the possession of cattle.

If we wish to state Bahutu values in more abstract terms, we may say that they seek security through the production of agricultural goods and the protection of a powerful patron.

Although he is not indifferent to his reputation, the Muhutu does not seem to stress its importance as much as does the Mututsi. The reputation he desires reflects the values of his caste. He likes to be considered a *mugabo* (a rich man) and a *mukungu*—a very rich man possessing a few cows, many fields, goats, and bee-hives. He enjoys the recognition of his fidelity to his master and his qualities as a labourer.

The Batwa never had the stability of peasants. They were hunters, potters, dancers, buffoons, and were regarded by their neighbours as being on the margin of society. They did not possess anything that others could envy. Consequently security from exactions was not such an important value for them. As people who lived a hazardous and unsettled existence, they greatly appreciated momentary and immediate satisfactions, and among these, food, especially during periods of scarcity, was the object of their activity. Their principal means of securing food varied according to their particular occupations. Hunters depended on their ability and their courage, of which they were very proud. Dancers, musicians, and buffoons relied on their talents and on the favour of their masters, their loyalty to whom was widely recognized. Indeed it is said that one could rely upon a Mutwa much more than on anybody else.

The social and economic situation of the Batwa explains and to some extent determines the value they attach to gratifying the basic need for food. Ability in their specialized occupations and a blind faithfulness to their masters were the best means to achieve that satisfaction, but skills and loyalty were also valued for themselves.

Rules of human action

These values, ultimate and intermediate, were eagerly sought by Banyarwanda but, as in any society, some means for realizing them were prohibited under certain circumstances. Stealing is rarely, if ever, culturally accepted as an ordinary practice for getting rich. Socially defined values are to be reached by socially approved means. We do not suggest that, in a particular society, the rules of action appear as merely social imperatives, or that the only basis for these rules is social. We would point out that some rules of action, whatever their origin and their philosophical foundation, are part of the collective heritage in any society. In Ruanda, as elsewhere, there are such rules of action. Murdering somebody who is not an enemy of one's family is prohibited. Women are forbidden to commit adultery and, among Batutsi and Bahutu, unmarried girls may not have sexual intercourse. When an order is issued by somebody in authority it has to be obeyed.

Does submission to the rules appear only as the rational behaviour of one who wishes to avoid an external punishment or is it moral conduct? Does a prospective offender refrain from wrong-doing simply in order to avoid very probable and unpleasant consequences, or is it his conscience which tells him that he should not follow his desire?

Of course this is not an either-or problem, but the question of degree or relative stress is important. Even in cultures which lay most stress on the moral motivation to action, external social sanctions are useful deterrents from prohibited behaviour. In Ruanda these external sanctions exist. Those who steal cattle, or set fire to huts, or commit adultery are punished by the political or family authorities. Social sanctions are not only physically enforced penalties, such as corporal punishment and compensations, but also the unorganized reactions of the people who know the delinquent: kin, neighbours, clients, and lord. For the Batutsi, for whom reputation stands high in the scale of values, this is extremely important. According to our informants, the fear of being considered a man without loyalty or without dignity, the dread of being despised by one's family, prevent many breaches of rules. To use Kluckhohn's terminology, we may say that Ruanda's is a shame-culture. But it is also a guilt-culture. When a Munyarwanda has transgressed some rule so secretly that there is not the slightest chance of his being found out and incurring punishment and shame, he nevertheless feels guilty and knows, our informants told us, that his action is bad. When a child has disobeyed his father without the latter's knowledge, he thinks not only of the unpleasant consequences that the discovery of his misbehaviour might produce but also (and some informants say "mainly") of the wickedness of the act itself. The Ruanda word for conscience, *kamera*, means something that is internally felt. It is situated in the heart.

That the Banyarwanda have a "conscience" will not be rated as a great discovery by some. But since some recent studies, such as Kluckhohn's on the Navaho, have stressed the fact that, in some cultures, submission to rules seems to be realized almost entirely through a rational concern to avoid punishment or shame, it does not seem superfluous to consider how far observance of rules is, or is not, linked to ethical principles and feelings of guilt.

Let us now attempt to indicate more precisely how moral wrong is conceived in the Ruanda culture. As has been already mentioned, *Imana* is not the guardian of the moral order. Sometimes he seems to be regarded as its author in the sense that he might have decided that men should not steal; but it is clear that when a man steals another man's cows, *Imana* is not personally offended. Those who are offended are those who have been wronged by the action, or those who had issued an order which has been disobeyed. When *Imana* has not been directly injured (as by blasphemies), or when the injury done to another has not been specifically forbidden by him, he is not thought to be offended. The victim could, however, ask *Imana* to punish the wrongdoer and if he then became ill, it would be said that *Imana* had punished him.

The other agencies of the supernatural world have even slighter relations with ethical values. The *bazimu* are naturally malevolent and punish only those actions which they take to be directed against themselves. A way to honour the spirit of somebody who had been a thief during his life was to simulate a robbery. *Ryangombe* and his fellows were not models of morality during their earthly existence and they did not care about the ethics of their followers. Nor was there any punishment after death. For those who believe that there are two kinds of life after death—happy or unhappy—the qualification for the happy one is not to live a blameless life on earth, but to undergo initiation into the *Ryangombe* cult.

Thus the ethics of the Banyarwanda are not integrated on a religious basis such as the will of God. What is the principle of integration, or rather, we should first ask, are their ethical conceptions integrated? On the surface they consist, like any moral code, of a multiplicity of prohibitions, orders, and exhortations. Have they achieved a synthesis of these separate elements by reducing the multiplicity to one or a few principles? Or, what amounts to the same thing, could they give a definition of good and evil?

In Ruanda a great number of particular rules are subsumed under general principles such as: do not do what is harmful to people of your group or of your country; do what people related to you would like; submit to your superiors. Principles such as these are already on a higher level of abstraction than the particular rules. When informants are asked to account for a given rule or principle they give as the final justification: "It has always been done that way in Ruanda." We may perhaps express the Ruanda definition of good and evil in these terms: That is good (or evil) which tradition has defined as good (or evil).

Tradition is indeed a powerful force in cultures which, as in Ruanda, have been isolated for centuries from world currents. Each generation is more conscious of the importance of what it has received from the preceding one than is possible when much of what constitutes its way of life comes not from its ancestors but from some other social tradition. Moreover, their relations with their neighbours whom they frequently subjugated have persuaded Banyarwanda of the excellence of the ways of life transmitted by their forefathers. In such a situation the traditional character of a rule appears to be sufficient justification. If the ancestors, who were so wise, behaved in that way it would be preposterous to question it.

But it would be misleading to picture the Banyarwanda as following blindly the moral rules framed in a remote past without having any idea of their purpose. Some old men have a clear understanding of the social significance of certain rules. They explained, for example, that the duality of the rules concerning adultery committed by the husband or by the wife was accounted for by the importance of the wife's function in procreation. She has thus a greater responsibility than the husband for maintaining the integrity of the family.

Does this kind of thinking extend so far as independence of tradition? Some informants told us that, apart from the authority of custom, some actions were thought of as dishonourable in themselves. But these informants were Christians and, apparently, very much influenced by their religion. Moreover, they could not quote a clear case of conflict between tradition and ethics.

No moral code can achieve an absolute character in all its precepts. Prohibitions and commands frequently relate only to certain categories of persons and situations. Even the Christian Western ethic, which realizes to a very considerable extent universality and absoluteness, qualifies some of its commands. The degree of absoluteness and universality of the Ruanda rules of conduct is much lower. We might say that most of its precepts are qualified in relation to persons and circumstances. To steal cattle was forbidden, but a Mututsi could take the cattle of a Muhutu who had no lord. For a Muhutu to rob a foreigner was not forbidden. A wife might not commit adultery, but she was allowed to have sexual relations with people when ordered by her husband to do so and, even without her husband's permission, a woman could have intercourse with her husband's brothers and parallel cousins. Killing a man was prohibited, but not if he was an enemy of Ruanda or of the family, and if the feud had not been barred by the king. Banyarwanda certainly had no idea of rules of behaviour applicable to all men in virtue of their common humanity. This is perfectly consistent with the Ruanda conception of mankind and the very significant inequalities which Banyarwanda observe between themselves and neighbouring peoples and, among themselves, between the different castes.

To conclude, the rules of human action which prohibit or enjoin the use of certain means in order to achieve the culturally recognized values of Ruanda are sanctioned, not only by organized and unorganized social reactions but also by individual conscience or guilt feelings. The foundation of this moral code is not religious or supernatural but traditional; its content is a multiplicity of rules synthesized under a few moral principles. Particular precepts do not have a universal application but are relative to persons and groups.

Human relations

Two principles dominate the field of human relations in Ruanda: inequality of men and indefinite reciprocity.

For the Banyarwanda all men have indeed a common nature; they are ultimately the descendants of the same ancestor. But this notion does not seem to be very significant, for Banyarwanda are much more impressed by the differences displayed by the various castes. The characteristics of these castes are stereotyped and repeated in many folk-tales. Batutsi are intelligent (in the sense of astute in political intrigues), apt to command, refined, courageous, and cruel. Bahutu are hard-working, not very clever, extrovert, irascible, unmannerly, obedient, physically strong. Batwa are gluttonous, loyal to their Batutsi masters, lazy, courageous when hunting, lacking in restraint. These characteristics, with differences in stress and shading, are generally recognized by all Banyarwanda. As they reflect the Mututsi point of view, it appears that the superior caste has been able to make other people see themselves in important respects as Batutsi see them. Moreover, those qualities are considered to be innate, not acquired. A Mututsi is born clever and a Muhutu impulsive. Some tales, more widely known than those concerning the creation of man, relate how the first Batutsi came to Ruanda from the heavenly world. According to some versions of this tale, they came with their servant, Mutwa, who mated with a forest ape. From that union all Batwa are descended. Such tales clearly reveal the fundamental differences which the Banyarwanda see among their castes.

When such a picture of "natural" differences, so significant from the point of view of power, is accepted, the inevitable consequence is that some men are born chiefs and others labourers. Inferiority and superiority are due not to personal qualities but to membership of certain groups. By belonging to different castes, people have fundamentally unequal rights. If an ordinary Mututsi kills a Muhutu, one kinsman of the murderer could eventually be killed in retaliation if the king authorized it. If the murderer was a Muhutu and the victim a Mututsi, two lives were taken.

The principle of the fundamental inequality between social groups thus established in Ruanda has spread from the original inter-caste relations to intra-caste situations. A man superior to another member of his class because of his functions or his wealth, or even his ability, tends to assume towards his inferior an attitude similar to that of a Mututsi *vis-à-vis* a Muhutu. Of course the conception of inequality between superiors and inferiors of the same class is not so rigid as that between the castes, but it permeates all hierarchical situations in Ruanda.

The theme of inequality was embodied in the indigenous political organization, so that political relations clearly express the attitudes socially expected from superiors and inferiors. They are quite understandable if one bears in mind that they originate from an inter-caste situation. Authority as such is all-embracing. According to Western conceptions, any authority is defined not only as regards the people who are subject to it, but also in respect of the matters falling within its competence. A man who gives orders to another because they are on different levels in a hierarchical scale may be considered his equal in other relations. In Ruanda, there is almost no sphere of life in which an inferior is free from the interference of his superior. Because Batutsi are considered fundamentally superior to the Bahutu, there is no field in which they can feel equal. This attitude has been transferred to any hierarchical situation. The complementary attitude of dependence is, of course, expected from the inferior. Inferiority is the relative situation of a person who has to submit to another in a clearly defined field; dependence is inferiority in the totality of life. The dependent person has to submit to his master in any question. There is no domain where he is free even to express a contrary opinion. As the dependent has always to acquiesce even when orders are quite impracticable, he has to conceal his opinions and find excuses for not doing what has been ordered. Double-dealing, politeness, or a utilitarian conception of language, are the only defences of the dependent. Some time ago, a Ruanda deliberative assembly of people of standing was asked its opinion on a contemplated reform. When the most important person had given his views, everybody voted for his proposition. But after the assembly, many expressed disagreement. At the time of the vote, they had considered it improper and impolite not to agree with their superior.

On the other hand, no superior enjoys a purely arbitrary power. There are norms which are informally enforced by social pressure; and this is particularly important for people so concerned about their reputations. Since, moreover, there are several chiefs of equal rank belonging to different political structures, it is not difficult for the subject of one superior to secure support in opposing him from another. Finally, there is the possibility of appeal to a higher authority empowered to control subordinate chiefs. All this limits, in fact, the authority of chiefs, but nevertheless the authority of a superior cannot be questioned by his subjects. They may escape, intrigue, or look for another protector, but they cannot offer direct opposition. The Western conception of contract, derived from Roman law, with well-defined obligations on both parties who are equal before and during the contract, is accordingly not understood or acted upon even by Banyarwanda who have long been familiar with our culture.

Any superior is a protector, and his protection is of the same character as his authority: all-embracing and limited only by his own convenience. In any difficulty, the inferior may ask the help of his master, and, if help is refused, it will not be on the grounds that the superior is not concerned with that aspect of the life of the subordinate. On the other hand, the superior himself will be the only judge of the limits of his intervention, for the dependent has no right to require anything from his superior.

Everywhere men in authority enjoy advantages denied to those whom they command, but it is often felt that justification is needed for these privileges. In Ruanda such rationalizations do not seem to be required. It is taken for granted by everybody, the subjects included, that superiors as such should derive profits from their position. The very high standard of living of Europeans is accepted without any criticism by "traditional" Banyarwanda not yet imbued with egalitarian principles.

The conception of authority as all-embracing, unlimited, protective, profitable, and of inferiority as dependent, devoid of rights, fundamentally weak, and generally exploited, is exactly suited to a structure of castes composed of human beings who are thought to be fundamentally different and unequal. On these inter-caste relations all hierarchical relations have been modelled. This means that the conceptions and attitudes which have just been sketched pervade most human relations in Ruanda. Indeed, very many human interactions involve persons who, in Ruanda, are placed on a hierarchical scale: man and woman, husband and wife, mother and child, father and son, old and young, craftsman and apprentice, etc., and when there is also a superiority-inferiority situation, even though confined to one aspect of the relation, the whole of that relation is impregnated with inequality.

Another basic principle governing the field of human relations in Ruanda is that of indefinite reciprocity. Whenever somebody receives a service, whenever goods are given to someone, a return is expected. This return is not the exact counterpart of what has been provided and is not due immediately or at a precisely determined time. By the granting of a favour, an almost permanent relationship is established between two persons, extending eventually to their immediate relatives. Undoubtedly some obligations are more formalized, such as those resulting from some kinds of exchange (*kuguza*), loan (*gutiza*), etc. But many relations which, in Western culture, would result in strictly defined obligations, do not have the same consequence in Ruanda. The man who receives a service or a gift is not expected to return its equivalent immediately. Such behaviour would even be frowned upon. He should wait till he is asked to return other services or goods. This is indeed the intention of the man who grants the favour: to put somebody under an undefined obligation.

There are several reasons for these relations of reciprocity. First, in an economy in which there is no standard value in relation to which everything may be assessed, it is not easy to determine a precise equivalent for goods. Second, where there is no standard medium of exchange, such as money, which can be accumulated without deteriorating, it is usually difficult to have the required equivalent to hand. Third, in a material culture in which the technological development does not allow of specialization, one has to rely on many people. It is thus very useful to have permanent debtors. Finally, and this is very important, the principle of reciprocity is much more consistent with other parts of the Ruanda culture than are alternative methods. In that culture people are not regarded as independent and equal. Consequently any relation will be so interpreted as to magnify the elements of dependence and inequality implicit in it. Moreover, to have power over somebody is an ultimate value for the Batutsi. They will thus prefer to keep a debtor under the vague obligation to do something, some day, rather than receive immediate compensation.

LAYEH A. BOCK

Greetings to the Ghom

Layeh Bock's poem was inspired by a news broadcast. Her writings have been published in *Thunderbird*, *Café Solo*, *Anubis*, and elsewhere. The changes predicted for Ghom culture are analogous to those which have taken place in many societies under the impact of Western civilization.

"*It was announced in Port Moresby, New Guinea, today that a group of people—whose existence was previously unknown—has been discovered in a remote area of Australian New Guinea. A spokesman for the Australian administration said the newly found group—known as the Ghom People—included about one hundred natives who live in a secluded area between two mountain ranges. They still use stone axes and lead a generally nomadic existence, hunting and fishing for a livelihood.*"

(CBS RADIO NEWS, March 13, 1963, 5:00 P.M.)

Halfway around geography, you're found:
Event broadcast as scattered waves of sound;
Already you have served a modern use—
You've filled some seconds of the time for news.
Foundations shift their weight of paperwork,
Allowing for the unexpected quirk
Of extra applications for first-hand
Investigation of a virgin land.
("Thirty-two. Unmarried. Published papers on
The kinship systems of West Iran.")
At the Seminary, guts are churned
By the very thought of souls unburned.
(Harris, a senior, becomes enthralled:
"I've had my doubts, but now I know—I'm Called!")
The research man at *Life* attacks Bob's ear
With tips as he packs photographic gear:

"To the Ghom on Their Discovery," from an unpublished M.A. thesis.

"The climate's lousy—swampy, humid, hot;
Be sure to tape the tins or your film will rot;
Cut down on provisions: if you need more,
By now the Ghom must have a trading store."

They'll come: ambitious, unburdened by doubts,
Trader, priest, scholar, newsman, all the touts
Of higher living standards, true beliefs.
As once your neighbors' rulers gave them chiefs
By being sure their absence must be feigned
(Satraps strut now where pleasant chaos reigned),
Your guests will bring unwitting gifts:
The too
Objective interest in all you do
Of scientists will introduce the sense
(Here history begins) of your . . . difference.

The missionary's kit will hold the Fruit,
Tucked into the folds of his decent suit.
The trader, paying most for your best notions,
Will turn your hands to unfamiliar motions.
Pictures will be published—privacy ends;
Today's celebrities can't choose their friends.
Each piece of baggage spills the adman's lure:
Before, you had few comforts. Now you're poor.

They share a motive secret from themselves.
And no surprise in that—for what man delves
Beneath the high ideals that guard his ways?
Revenge *is* sweet—and sweetest is to gaze
On dying, when the dead man's had too long
That which we desire, but call "wrong."

You dared to live your life apart, so far,
In ignorance of us and all we are.

JAMES BALDWIN

Black man in the Alps

James Baldwin is an outstanding American novelist, playwright, and essayist. His works include the novels *Go Tell It on the Mountain*, *Giovanni's Room*, and *Another Country*, and two collections of essays—*Nobody Knows My Name* and *The Fire Next Time*. In this essay, Baldwin describes and reflects upon his own experiences in Switzerland and America.

From all available evidence no black man had ever set foot in this tiny Swiss village before I came. I was told before arriving that I would probably be a "sight" for the village; I took this to mean that people of my complexion were rarely seen in Switzerland, and also that city people are always something of a "sight" outside of the city. It did not occur to me—possibly because I am an American—that there could be people anywhere who had never seen a Negro.

It is a fact that cannot be explained on the basis of the inaccessibility of the village. The village is very high, but it is only four hours from Milan and three hours from Lausanne. It is true that it is virtually unknown. Few people making plans for a holiday would elect to come here. On the other hand, the villagers are able, presumably, to come and go as they please—which they do: to another town at the foot of the mountain, with a population of approximately five thousand, the nearest place to see a movie or go to the bank. In the village there is no movie house, no bank, no library, no theater; very few radios, one jeep, one station wagon; and, at the moment, one typewriter, mine, an invention which the woman next door to me here had never seen. There are about six hundred people living here, all Catholic—I conclude this from the fact that the Catholic church is open all year round, wheras the Protestant chapel, set off on a hill a little removed from the village, is open only in the summertime when the tourists arrive. There are four or five hotels, all closed now, and four or five *bistros*, of which, however, only two do any business during the winter. These two do not do a great deal, for life in the village seems

---

James Baldwin, "Stranger in the Village," *Notes of a Native Son*, pp. 159–175. Reprinted by permission of the Beacon Press and Michael Joseph,

to end around nine or ten o'clock. There are a few stores, butcher, baker, *épicerie*, a hardware store, and a money-changer—who cannot change travelers' checks, but must send them down to the bank, an operation which takes two or three days. There is something called the *Ballet Haus*, closed in the winter and used for God knows what, certainly not ballet, during the summer. There seems to be only one schoolhouse in the village, and this for the quite young children; I suppose this to mean that their older brothers and sisters at some point descend from these mountains in order to complete their education—possibly, again, to the town just below. The landscape is absolutely forbidding, mountains towering on all four sides, ice and snow as far as the eye can reach. In this white wilderness, men and women and children move all day, carrying washing, wood, buckets of milk or water, sometimes skiing on Sunday afternoons. All week long boys and young men are to be seen shoveling snow off the rooftops, or dragging wood down from the forest in sleds.

The village's only real attraction, which explains the tourist season, is the hot spring water. A disquietingly high proportion of these tourists are cripples, or semicripples, who come year after year—from other parts of Switzerland, usually—to take the waters. This lends the village, at the height of the season, a rather terrifying air of sanctity, as though it were a lesser Lourdes. There is often something beautiful, there is always something awful, in the spectacle of a person who has lost one of his faculties, a faculty he never questioned until it was gone, and who struggles to recover it. Yet people remain people, on crutches or indeed on deathbeds; and wherever I passed, the first summer I was here, among the native villagers or among the lame, a wind passed with me—of astonishment, curiosity, amusement, and outrage. That first summer I stayed two weeks and never intended to return. But I did return in the winter, to work; the village offers, obviously, no distractions whatever and has the further advantage of being extremely cheap. Now it is winter again, a year later, and I am here again. Everyone in the village knows my name, though they scarcely ever use it, knows that I come from America—though, this, apparently, they will never really believe: black men come from Africa—and everyone knows that I am the friend of the son of a woman who was born here, and that I am staying in their chalet. But I remain as much a stranger today as I was the first day I arrived, and the children shout *Neger! Neger!* as I walk along the streets.

It must be admitted that in the beginning I was far too shocked to have any real reaction. In so far as I reacted at all, I reacted by trying to be pleasant—it being a great part of the American Negro's education (long before he goes to school) that he must make people "like" him. This smile-and-the-world-smiles-with-you routine worked about as well in this situation as it had in the situation for which it was designed, which is to say that it did not work at all. No one, after all, can be liked whose human weight and complexity cannot be, or has not been, admitted. My smile was simply another unheard-of phenomenon which allowed them to see my teeth—they did not, really, see my smile and I began to think that, should I take to snarling, no one would notice any difference. All of the physical characteristics of the Negro which had caused me, in America, a very different and almost forgotten pain were nothing less than miraculous—or infernal—in the eyes of the village people. Some thought my hair was the color of tar, that it had the texture of wire, or the texture of cotton. It was jocularly suggested that I might let it all grow long and make myself a winter coat. If I sat in the sun for more than five minutes some daring creature was certain to come along and gingerly put his fingers on my hair, as though he were afraid of an electric shock, or put his hand on my hand, astonished that the color did not rub off. In all of this, in which it must be conceded there was the charm of genuine wonder and in which there was certainly no element of intentional unkindness, there was yet no suggestion that I was human: I was simply a living wonder.

I knew that they did not mean to be unkind, and I know it now; it is necessary, nevertheless, for me to repeat this to myself each time that I walk out of the chalet. The children who shout *Neger!* have no way of knowing the echoes this sound raises in me. They are brimming with good humor and the more daring swell with pride when I stop to speak with them. Just the same, there are days when I cannot pause and smile, when I have no heart to play with them; when, indeed, I mutter sourly to myself, exactly as I muttered on the streets of a city these children have never seen, when I was no bigger than these children are now: *Your* mother *was a nigger*. Joyce is right about history being a nightmare—but it may be the nightmare from which no one *can* awaken. People are trapped in history and history is trapped in them.

There is a custom in the village—I am told it is repeated in many villages—of "buying" African natives for the purpose of converting them to Christianity. There stands in the church all year round a small box with a slot for money, decorated with a black figurine, and into this box the villagers drop their francs. During the *carnaval* which precedes Lent, two village children have their faces blackened—out of which bloodless darkness their blue eyes shine like ice—and fantastic horsehair wigs are placed on their blond heads; thus disguised, they solicit among the villagers for money for the missionaries in Africa. Between the box in the church and the blackened children, the village "bought" last year six or eight African natives. This was reported to me with pride by the wife of one of the *bistro* owners and I was careful to express astonishment and pleasure at the solicitude shown by the village for the souls of black folk.

The *bistro* owner's wife beamed with a pleasure far more genuine than my own and seemed to feel that I might now breathe more easily concerning the souls of at least six of my kinsmen.

I tried not to think of these so lately baptized kinsmen, of the price paid for them, or the peculiar price they themselves would pay, and said nothing about my father, who having taken his own conversion too literally never, at bottom, forgave the white world (which he described as heathen) for having saddled him with a Christ in whom, to judge at least from their treatment of him, they themselves no longer believed. I thought of white men arriving for the first time in an African village, strangers there, as I am a stranger here, and tried to imagine the astounded populace touching their hair and marveling at the color of their skin. But there is a great difference between being the first white man to be seen by Africans and being the first black man to be seen by whites. The white man takes the astonishment as tribute, for he arrives to conquer and to convert the natives, whose inferiority in relation to himself is not even to be questioned; whereas I, without a thought of conquest, find myself among a people whose culture controls me, has even, in a sense, created me, people who have cost me more in anguish and rage than they will ever know, who yet do not even know of my existence. The astonishment with which I might have greeted them, should they have stumbled into my African village a few hundred years ago, might have rejoiced their hearts. But the astonishment with which they greet me today can only poison mine.

And this is so despite everything I may do to feel differently, despite my friendly conversations with the *bistro* owner's wife, despite their three-year-old son who has at last become my friend, despite the *saluts* and *bonsoirs* which I exchange with people as I walk, despite the fact that I know that no individual can be taken to task for what history is doing, or has done. I say that the culture of these people controls me—but they can scarcely be held responsible for European culture. America comes out of Europe, but these people have never seen America, nor have most of them seen more of Europe than the hamlet at the foot of their mountain. Yet they move with an authority which I shall never have; and they regard me, quite rightly, not only as a stranger in their village but as a suspect latecomer, bearing no credentials, to everything they have—however unconsciously—inherited.

For this village, even were it incomparably more remote and incredibly more primitive, is the West, the West onto which I have been so strangely grafted. These people cannot be, from the point of view of power, strangers anywhere in the world; they have made the modern world, in effect, even if they do not know it. The most illiterate among them is related, in a way that I am not, to Dante, Shakespeare, Michelangelo,

Aeschylus, Da Vinci, Rembrandt, and Racine; the cathedral at Chartres says something to them which it cannot say to me, as indeed would New York's Empire State Building, should anyone here ever see it. Out of their hymns and dances come Beethoven and Bach. Go back a few centuries and they are in their full glory—but I am in Africa, watching the conquerors arrive.

The rage of the disesteemed is personally fruitless, but it is also absolutely inevitable; this rage, so generally discounted, so little understood even among the people whose daily bread it is, is one of the things that makes history. Rage can only with difficulty, and never entirely, be brought under the domination of the intelligence and is therefore not susceptible to any arguments whatever. This is a fact which ordinary representatives of the *Herrenvolk*, having never felt this rage and being unable to imagine it, quite fail to understand. Also, rage cannot be hidden, it can only be dissembled. This dissembling deludes the thoughtless, and strengthens rage and adds, to rage, contempt. There are, no doubt, as many ways of coping with the resulting complex of tensions as there are black men in the world, but no black man can hope ever to be entirely liberated from this internal warfare—rage, dissembling, and contempt having inevitably accompanied his first realization of the power of white men. What is crucial here is that, since white men represent in the black man's world so heavy a weight, white men have for black men a reality which is far from being reciprocal; and hence all black men have toward all white men an attitude which is designed, really, either to rob the white man of the jewel of his naïveté, or else to make it cost him dear.

The black man insists, by whatever means he finds at his disposal, that the white man cease to regard him as an exotic rarity and recognize him as a human being. This is a very charged and difficult moment, for there is a great deal of will power involved in the white man's naïveté. Most people are not naturally reflective any more than they are naturally malicious, and the white man prefers to keep the black man at a certain human remove because it is easier for him thus to preserve his simplicity and avoid being called to account for crimes committed by his forefathers, or his neighbors. He is inescapably aware, nevertheless, that he is in a better position in the world than black men are, nor can he quite put to death the suspicion that he is hated by black men therefore. He does not wish to be hated, neither does he wish to change places, and at this point in his uneasiness he can scarcely avoid having recourse to those legends which white men have created about black men, the most usual effect of which is that the white man finds himself enmeshed, so to speak, in his own language which describes hell, as well as the attributes which lead one to hell, as being as black as night.

Every legend, moreover, contains its residuum of truth, and the root function of language is to control the universe by describing it. It is of quite considerable significance that black men remain, in the imagination, and in overwhelming numbers in fact, beyond the disciplines of salvation; and this despite the fact that the West has been "buying" African natives for centuries. There is, I should hazard, an instantaneous necessity to be divorced from this so visibly unsaved stranger, in whose heart, moreover, one cannot guess what dreams of vengeance are being nourished; and, at the same time, there are few things on earth more attractive than the idea of the unspeakable liberty which is allowed the unredeemed. When, beneath the black mask, a human being begins to make himself felt one cannot escape a certain awful wonder as to what kind of human being it is. What one's imagination makes of other people is dictated, of course, by the laws of one's own personality and it is one of the ironies of black-white relations that, by means of what the white man imagines the black man to be, the black man is enabled to know who the white man is.

I have said, for example, that I am as much a stranger in this village today as I was the first summer I arrived, but this is not quite true. The villagers wonder less about the texture of my hair than they did then, and wonder rather more about me. And the fact that their wonder now exists on another level is reflected in their attitudes and in their eyes. There are the children who make those delightful, hilarious, sometimes astonishingly grave overtures of friendship in the unpredictable fashion of children; other children, having been taught that the devil is a black man, scream in genuine anguish as I approach. Some of the older women never pass without a friendly greeting, never pass, indeed, if it seems that they will be able to engage me in conversation; other women look down or look away or rather contemptuously smirk. Some of the men drink with me and suggest that I learn how to ski—partly, I gather, because they cannot imagine what I would look like on skis—and want to know if I am married, and ask questions about my *métier*. But some of the men have accused *le sale nègre*—behind my back—of stealing wood and there is already in the eyes of some of them that peculiar, intent, paranoiac malevolence which one sometimes surprises in the eyes of American white men when, out walking with their Sunday girl, they see a Negro male approach.

There is a dreadful abyss between the streets of this village and the streets of the city in which I was born, between the children who shout *Neger!* today and those who shouted *Nigger!* yesterday—the abyss is experience, the American experience. The syllable hurled behind me today expresses, above all, wonder: I am a stranger here. But I am not a stranger in America and the same syllable riding on the American air expresses the war my presence has occasioned in the American soul.

For this village brings home to me this fact: that there was a day, and not really a very distant day, when Americans were scarcely Americans at all but discontented Europeans, facing a great unconquered continent and strolling, say, into a marketplace and seeing black men for the first time. The shock this spectacle afforded is suggested, surely, by the promptness with which they decided that these black men were not really men but cattle. It is true that the necessity on the part of the settlers of the New World of reconciling their moral assumptions with the fact—and the necessity—of slavery enhanced immensely the charm of this idea, and it is also true that this idea expresses, with a truly American bluntness, the attitude which to varying extents all masters have had toward all slaves.

But between all former slaves and slave-owners and the drama which begins for Americans over three hundred years ago at Jamestown, there are at least two differences to be observed. The American Negro slave could not suppose, for one thing, as slaves in past epochs had supposed and often done, that he would ever be able to wrest the power from his master's hands. This was a supposition which the modern era, which was to bring about such vast changes in the aims and dimensions of power, put to death; it only begins, in unprecedented fashion, and with dreadful implications, to be resurrected today. But even had this supposition persisted with undiminished force, the American Negro slave could not have used it to lend his condition dignity, for the reason that this supposition rests on another: that the slave in exile yet remains related to his past, has some means—if only in memory—of revering and sustaining the forms of his former life, is able, in short, to maintain his identity.

This was not the case with the American Negro slave. He is unique among the black men of the world in that his past was taken from him, almost literally, at one blow. One wonders what on earth the first slave found to say to the first dark child he bore. I am told that there are Haitians able to trace their ancestry back to African kings, but any American Negro wishing to go back so far will find his journey through time abruptly arrested by the signature on the bill of sale which served as the entrance paper for his ancestor. At the time—to say nothing of the circumstances—of the enslavement of the captive black man who was to become the American Negro, there was not the remotest possibility that he would ever take power from his master's hands. There was no reason to suppose that his situation would ever change, nor was there, shortly, anything to indicate that his situation had ever been different. It was his necessity, in the words of E. Franklin Frazier, to find a "motive for living under American culture or die." The identity of the American Negro comes out of this extreme situation, and the evolution of this identity was a source of the most intolerable anxiety in the minds and the lives of his masters.

For the history of the American Negro is unique also in this: that the question of his humanity, and of his rights therefore as a human being, became a burning one for several generations of Americans, so burning a question that it ultimately became one of those used to divide the nation. It is out of this argument that the venom of the epithet *Nigger!* is derived. It is an argument which Europe has never had, and hence Europe quite sincerely fails to understand how or why the argument arose in the first place, why its effects are so frequently disastrous and always so unpredictable, why it refuses until today to be entirely settled. Europe's black possessions remained—and do remain—in Europe's colonies, at which remove they represented no threat whatever to European identity. If they posed any problem at all for the European conscience, it was a problem which remained comfortingly abstract: in effect, the black man, *as a man*, did not exist for Europe. But in America, even as a slave, he was an inescapable part of the general social fabric and no American could escape having an attitude toward him. Americans attempt until today to make an abstraction of the Negro, but the very nature of these abstractions reveals the tremendous effects the presence of the Negro has had on the American character.

When one considers the history of the Negro in America it is of the greatest importance to recognize that the moral beliefs of a person, or a people, are never really as tenuous as life—which is not moral—very often causes them to appear; these create for them a frame of reference and a necessary hope, the hope being that when life has done its worst they will be enabled to rise above themselves and to triumph over life. Life would scarcely be bearable if this hope did not exist. Again, even when the worst has been said, to betray a belief is not by any means to have put oneself beyond its power; the betrayal of a belief is not the same thing as ceasing to believe. If this were not so there would be no moral standards in the world at all. Yet one must also recognize that morality is based on ideas and that all ideas are dangerous—dangerous because ideas can only lead to action and where the action leads no man can say. And dangerous in this respect: that confronted with the impossibility of remaining faithful to one's beliefs, and the equal impossibility of becoming free of them, one can be driven to the most inhuman excesses. The ideas on which American beliefs are based are not, though Americans often seem to think so, ideas which originated in America. They came out of Europe. And the establishment of democracy on the American continent was scarcely as radical a break with the past as was the necessity, which Americans faced, of broadening this concept to include black men.

This was, literally, a hard necessity. It was impossible, for one thing, for Americans to abandon their beliefs, not only because these beliefs alone seemed able to justify the sacrifices they had endured and the blood that they had spilled, but also because these beliefs afforded them their only bulwark against a moral chaos as absolute as the physical chaos of the continent it was their destiny to conquer. But in the situation in which Americans found themselves, these beliefs threatened an idea which, whether or not one likes to think so, is the very warp and woof of the heritage of the West, the idea of white supremacy.

Americans have made themselves notorious by the shrillness and the brutality with which they have insisted on this idea, but they did not invent it; and it has escaped the world's notice that those very excesses of which Americans have been guilty imply a certain, unprecedented uneasiness over the idea's life and power, if not, indeed, the idea's validity. The idea of white supremacy rests simply on the fact that white men are the creators of civilization (the present civilization, which is the only one that matters; all previous civilizations are simply "contributions" to our own) and are therefore civilization's guardians and defenders. Thus it was impossible for Americans to accept the black man as one of themselves, for to do so was to jeopardize their status as white men. But not so to accept him was to deny his human reality, his human weight and complexity, and the strain of denying the overwhelmingly undeniable forced Americans into rationalizations so fantastic that they approached the pathological.

At the root of the American Negro problem is the necessity of the American white man to find a way of living with the Negro in order to be able to live with himself. And the history of this problem can be reduced to the means used by Americans—lynch law and law, segregation and legal acceptance, terrorization and concession—either to come to terms with this necessity, or to find a way around it, or (most usually) to find a way of doing both these things at once. The resulting spectacle, at once foolish and dreadful, led someone to make the quite accurate observation that "the Negro-in-America is a form of insanity which overtakes white men."

In this long battle, a battle by no means finished, the unforeseeable effects of which will be felt by many future generations, the white man's motive was the protection of his identity; the black man was motivated by the need to establish an identity. And despite the terrorization which the Negro in America endured and endures sporadically until today, despite the cruel and totally inescapable ambivalence of his status in his country, the battle for his identity has long ago been won. He is not a visitor to the West, but a citizen there, an American; as American as the Americans who despise him, the Americans who fear him, the Americans who love him—the Americans who became less than themselves, or rose to be greater than themselves by virtue of the fact that the challenge he represented was inescapable. He is perhaps the only black man in the world whose relationship to white men is more terrible, more subtle, and more meaningful than the relationship of bitter possessed to uncertain possessor. His survival depended, and his development depends, on his ability to turn his peculiar status in the Western world to his own advantage and, it may be, to the very great advantage of that world. It remains for him to fashion out of his experience that which will give him sustenance, and a voice.

The cathedral at Chartres, I have said, says something to the people of this village which it cannot say to me; but it is important to understand that this cathedral says something to me which it cannot say to them. Perhaps they are struck by the power of the spires, the glory of the windows; but they have known God, after all, longer than I have known him, and in a different way, and I am terrified by the slippery bottomless well to be found in the crypt, down which heretics were hurled to death, and by the obscene, inescapable gargoyles jutting out of the stone and seeming to say that God and the devil can never be divorced. I doubt that the villagers think of the devil when they face a cathedral because they have never been identified with the devil. But I must accept the status which myth, if nothing else, gives me in the West before I can hope to change the myth.

Yet, if the American Negro has arrived at his identity by virtue of the absoluteness of his estrangement from his past, American white men still nourish the illusion that there is some means of recovering the European innocence, of returning to a state in which black men do not exist. This is one of the greatest errors Americans can make. The identity they fought so hard to protect has, by virtue of that battle, undergone a change: Americans are as unlike any other white people in the world as it is possible to be. I do not think, for example, that it is too much to suggest that the American vision of the world—which allows so little reality, generally speaking, for any of the darker forces in human life, which tends until today to paint moral issues in glaring black and white—owes a great deal to the battle waged by Americans to maintain between themselves and black men a human separation which could not be bridged. It is only now beginning to be borne in on us—very faintly, it must be admitted, very slowly, and very much against our will—that this vision of the world is dangerously inaccurate, and perfectly useless. For it protects our moral high-mindedness at the terrible expense of weakening our grasp of reality. People who shut their eyes to reality simply invite their own destruction, and anyone who insists on remaining in a state of innocence long after that innocence is dead turns himself into a monster.

The time has come to realize that the interracial drama acted out on the American continent has not only created a new black man, it has created a new white man, too. No road whatever will lead Americans back to the simplicity of this European village where white men still have the luxury of looking on me as a stranger. I am not, really, a stranger any longer for any American alive. One of the things that distinguishes Americans from other people is that no other people has ever been so deeply involved in the lives of black men, and vice versa. This fact faced, with all its implications, it can be seen that the history of the American Negro problem is not merely shameful, it is also something of an achievement. For even when the worst has been said, it must also be added that the perpetual challenge posed by this problem was always, somehow, perpetually met. It is precisely this black-white experience which may prove of indispensable value to us in the world we face today. This world is white no longer, and it will never be white again.

a note on the type

The text of this book was set in Monotype Imprint 101, a face designed by Edward Johnston and J. H. Mason after an old face of the late 18th century.

The cutting of Imprint in 1912 was of great typographical importance for it was the first original book type to be designed specially for mechanical composition. Its success proved that mechanically-set type could rival in appearance the best examples of hand composition.

Composed by Spottiswoode-Ballantyne Ltd,
Printed and bound by Colonial Press, Inc. Clinton, Mass.

Typography by Anne Hertz